Understanding
NATIONAL ACCOUNTS

François Lequiller   Derek Blades

OECD

ORGANISATION FOR ECONOMIC CO-OPERATION AND DEVELOPMENT

ORGANISATION FOR ECONOMIC CO-OPERATION AND DEVELOPMENT

The OECD is a unique forum where the governments of 30 democracies work together to address the economic, social and environmental challenges of globalisation. The OECD is also at the forefront of efforts to understand and to help governments respond to new developments and concerns, such as corporate governance, the information economy and the challenges of an ageing population. The Organisation provides a setting where governments can compare policy experiences, seek answers to common problems, identify good practice and work to co-ordinate domestic and international policies.

The OECD member countries are: Australia, Austria, Belgium, Canada, the Czech Republic, Denmark, Finland, France, Germany, Greece, Hungary, Iceland, Ireland, Italy, Japan, Korea, Luxembourg, Mexico, the Netherlands, New Zealand, Norway, Poland, Portugal, the Slovak Republic, Spain, Sweden, Switzerland, Turkey, the United Kingdom and the United States. The Commission of the European Communities takes part in the work of the OECD.

OECD Publishing disseminates widely the results of the Organisation's statistics gathering and research on economic, social and environmental issues, as well as the conventions, guidelines and standards agreed by its members.

This work is published on the responsibility of the Secretary-General of the OECD. The opinions expressed and arguments employed herein do not necessarily reflect the official views of the Organisation or of the governments of its member countries.

Adapted and translated from *Manuel de comptabilité nationale*
published by Economica, France
49 rue Héricart, 75015 Paris – *http://www.economica.fr/*
Reprinted 2007

Preface

In today's "information society", statistics are thriving. Media pay more attention to economic indicators than ever and analysts spend more time in running their statistical and econometric models, trying to interpret and forecast economic trends. In this context, statistical offices have dramatically increased the amount of data and metadata they publish to satisfy growing demand. New monthly indicators have been produced on important phenomena (activity of the service sector, services prices, vacancies, etc.). There is ongoing competition among OECD countries and regions to produce the most accurate and timely indicators.

Though short-term and structural economic indicators are proliferating, media, analysts and policy makers still pay great attention to the evolution of the gross domestic product (GDP) and to the other variables (investment, consumption, etc.) produced in the framework of the national accounts. In addition to annual national accounts figures, quarterly and even monthly data are available in several countries. The borders of national accounts have also been extended to include new areas, namely social and environmental variables. The integration between economic and financial accounts has been enhanced, coherently with the growing importance of capital markets and the financial dimension of today's economy.

To make a long story short, today's national accounts are at the core of a modern system of economic statistics, and they provide the conceptual and actual tool to bring to coherence hundreds of statistical sources available in developed countries. The question, however, is whether users are fully aware of the data richness national accounts can provide. Do they fully exploit the analytical and statistical potential of national accounts? More conceptually, can we assume that users are aware of the changes introduced in national accounts over the last two decades – which are quite important for drawing meaningful analytical conclusions from them? Are we sure that when analysts use productivity data to make inflation forecasts or to assess the long-term economic growth capabilities of a country, they are aware of the limitations that data can have? And what about the international comparability of data?

For example, are we sure that the differential in economic growth observed over the last ten years between the United States and the European Union is real and not just a statistical artefact? What are the implications for the evaluation of the future of the world economy of a 17% upward revision of the Chinese GDP published at the end of 2005? Is GDP a good measure of wellbeing or should we look at other measures, reorienting policies towards other targets? Can we trust national accounts figures concerning public deficit, or are these figures manipulated for political reasons – for example including or excluding public institutions from the perimeter of the public administration just to reduce the deficit? These are fundamental questions for those who want to understand what is going on in the economy, especially as policy decisions that influence the life of millions of citizens are taken every day on the basis of these figures.

The authors of this book have made a special effort to answer these questions and many more, keeping the necessary conceptual and statistical rigour, but using, as much as possible, language that will allow non-specialists to understand the "religion of national accounts". Because of the complexity of the topic, national accountants have been sometimes considered as an esoteric group of "statistical priests". Well, this book demonstrates that at least some of them are able to explain the key concepts (and even some secrets) of national accounts in an attractive and interesting way. The authors have made interesting choices to achieve this goal: for example, each chapter begins with an introduction discussing some economic statements or policy recommendations of the OECD, and then the chapter explains the definition of the variables used in these economic analyses and, also, their limitations. The book also contains a notable number of concrete examples, illustrated by data from different OECD countries. The book also has Statlinks to the OECD national accounts databases, which allow users to go beyond the figures presented in the book and to learn how to make use of the widest sources of national accounts data worldwide.

Another smart choice made by the authors is to conclude each chapter with a summary of "what should be remembered" and several exercises, whose answers will be made available on the web pages devoted to the manual. Last, but not least, the book includes a chapter on international comparisons and three special chapters on the United States, China and India. These chapters are particularly important for those who want to understand how the world economy works and will work in future. While the US case is especially important for the completeness of its national accounts data, this book offers, for the first time, a well structured description of Chinese and Indian data, extremely useful even for specialists of national accounts.

Let me conclude by thanking Derek Blades and François Lequiller, who have successfully completed a difficult task, putting their unique skills in national accounts to the service of a wide audience of non-specialists. Too often statistics are seen as a necessary, but very dry, subject. I always try to advocate the importance of statistics to non-specialists remembering that the origin of the word "statistics" is "science of the State". I use this argument not only to convince people that they should be interested in the subject as individual citizens, but also to underline the ethical spirit that animate statisticians in doing their work. In this context, I would like to pay tribute to Derek and François, who have contributed so much to the theory and the implementation of national accounts. Their past and current work in the OECD has been very important to support the analytical and policy activity of the Organisation, and, on behalf of the latter, I would like to thank them for this additional effort.

Enrico Giovannini
Chief Statistician and Director, Statistics Directorate, OECD

Table of contents

Note to the Reader

This manual contains a large quantity of data, essentially extracted from OECD sources. *StatLinks* are used to provide access to the data underlying most of the tables and graphs in the book. However, the reader must remember that national accounts are constantly revised. Differences can thus be found between two values of the same variable in two different tables or electronic files as well as between the variables used in the manual and those provided by the latest publications of national accounts by various statistical offices. This is not due to errors, but simply to the fact that the various parts of the manual have been updated at different dates over a period of two years (mid 2004-mid 2006).

Acknowledgements

The authors would like to thank Robert Parker, former Chief Statistician and Associate Director for National Economic Accounts at the Bureau of Economic Analysis, for providing the special chapter on US national accounts.

Special thanks for a thorough review of the manuscript to: J.P. Berthier, A. Friez, V. Koen, C. La Rosa, P. Schreyer, F. Koechlin, B. Cournède, P. Catte, C. Aspden, M. Chavoix-Mannato, I. Joumard, F. Wolff, M. Harary, X. Xu, R. Kolli, Y.G. Cho.

M. Viriat assisted in preparing the manuscript for typesetting. Z. Yang created the *StatLinks* and the glossary.

The excellent translation from the French original version is due to F. Wells, and the editing of the manuscript to S.J. Stefanopoulos.

Chapter **1**

THE ESSENTIAL
MACROECONOMIC AGGREGATES

In this first chapter, our aim is to give an initial definition of the essential macroeconomic variables, listed in the table below, and taken from the *OECD Economic Outlook* for December 2004.[1] We have chosen to illustrate this chapter using the example of Germany, but we might as well have chosen any other OECD country, since the structure of the country chapters in the *OECD Economic Outlook* is the same for all countries. ▶ I.

I. Each chapter of this book uses an example from a different country.

Table 1. **Main macroeconomic variables**

Germany,[a] 1995 euros, annual changes in percentage

	2002	2003	2004	2005	2006
Private consumption	−0.7	0.0	−0.7	0.8	1.9
Gross capital formation	−6.3	−2.2	−2.0	0.6	3.4
GDP	0.1	−0.1	1.2	1.4	2.3
Imports	−1.6	3.9	6.4	4.9	7.5
Exports	4.1	1.8	8.1	5.7	8.1
Household saving ratio[1]	10.5	10.7	11.1	11.1	10.8
GDP deflator	1.5	1.1	0.9	0.8	0.9
General government financial balance[2]	−3.7	−3.8	3.9	−3.5	−2.7

1. Net saving as % of net disposable income.
2. % of GDP.
a) The report dates from December 2004. At that time, the data for 2004, 2005 and 2006 were forecasts by the OECD economists. The data for 2002 and 2003 were actual observations by the Statistiches Bundesamt, the FRG's statistical office.

Source: OECD (2004), *OECD Economic Outlook*, December No. 76, Volume 2004, Issue 2, OECD, Paris.

StatLink: *http://dx.doi.org/10.1787/563276026371*

Comments on Germany made by OECD economists in December 2004 included the following:

"Based on strong export growth, the German economy is recovering from three years of stagnation. Weak domestic demand is still weighing on activity although there are signs that investment is strengthening. Private consumption declined as consumers' confidence remained subdued and rising unemployment, tighter social security benefits, and accelerating consumer prices reduced disposable income growth. The general government deficit is likely to remain between 3½ and 4 per cent of GDP this year and next, not falling below 3 per cent before 2006."

According to the OECD economists, who were making their comments at the end of 2004, Germany was, at last, expected to experience an acceleration of growth in its gross domestic product ▶ II. (commonly known as GDP) in 2006. The table shows the stagnation of GDP in 2002 (+0.1%) and in 2003 (−0.1%), followed by an expected slight recovery in 2004 (+1.2%) and then by a slightly stronger one in 2005 (+1.4%). The two tenths of a percentage point difference between 1.2% and 1.4% may seem very small, but it must never be forgotten that national accounts variables are very often measured in billions. ▶ III. In the case of Germany, 1% of GDP amounts to roughly 22 billion euros, so that 0.1% is equivalent to 2.2 billion euros, corresponding to the total annual net earnings in 2003 of roughly 67 000 workers, a substantial number.

II. Definitions of terms appearing in bold are available in the glossary of this book.
III. In practice, most OECD countries technically compile their national accounts in millions, and thus many tables published appear in millions. But this is far from meaning that the data are accurate at the level of millions. It is wise to round these data to billions.

In this chapter, we begin by defining GDP, before turning to the other principal indicators used by the OECD economists: private consumption, gross fixed capital formation, GDP deflator, household saving ratio, and financial balance of general government. For all the national accounts data discussed in this chapter, we refer the reader to the OECD website for this book, or to the general OECD website under the heading "quarterly national accounts" or "annual national accounts". The quarterly national accounts are more pertinent for those who wish to have the most recent figures.

1. Defining GDP

GDP, gross domestic product, is the most frequently used indicator in the national accounts. It lies at the heart of the entire system of national accounts, and its definition is now internationally agreed upon (see Box 1 on "The reference manuals"). GDP combines in a single figure, and with no double counting, all the *output* (or *production*) carried out *by all the firms, non-profit institutions, government bodies and households* in a given country during a given period, regardless of the type of goods and services produced, provided that the production takes place within the country's economic territory. In most cases, it is calculated quarterly or annually, but it can also be calculated monthly.

However, measuring a country's total output is not a simple matter (see Section "Accuracy" and "Limitations and pitfalls" at the end of this chapter), and national accountants have therefore had to devise innovative methods of calculation.

The output of a single firm can be measured fairly easily. In the case of a firm making pasta, for example, it can be measured as tonnes of pasta made during the year, or, if we multiply the number of tonnes by the price of the pasta, by the amount of output valued in dollars (or in euros in the case of Germany, since this is the national currency). But we shall see that it makes little sense to add together the output measured in dollars from all firms to

---

Box 1. **The reference manuals**

The standards governing national accounts are enshrined in two international reference manuals: the "System of National Accounts 1993" (SNA 93), which is recognised globally, and the European version of this called the "European System of Accounts 1995" (ESA 95). The global manual (SNA 93) is co-signed by the five major international economic organisations: the United Nations, the International Monetary Fund, the OECD, the World Bank and the European Commission. The European manual is totally compatible with the global manual and includes additional useful details. It also has a more legally binding character because, according to European regulations, EU member countries are obligated to implement it. These manuals have contributed substantially to improving the international comparability of data, although further progress still has to be made in this endeavor (see Chapter 3). The current complete version of SNA 93 is available online: *http://unstats.un.org/unsd/sna1993/toctop.asp*. A new version is now being prepared and due to be published in 2008.

---

arrive at a macroeconomic figure. That is because the result of this calculation depends heavily on the way the firms are organised.

Take again the example of the pasta manufacturer and compare two different production scenarios in a given region. Suppose that in the first year there is only one firm, firm A, that makes both the pasta and the flour used to make the pasta. Its output amounts to 100 000 dollars, corresponding to 100 tonnes of pasta, with each tonne valued at 1 000 dollars. Now suppose that the following year, firm A is split into two, with firm A1 specialising in making flour and selling 30 000 dollars' worth to firm A2, which carries out the final production of pasta. Firm A2 makes the same quantity of pasta as in the first year, *i.e.* 100 tonnes, and at the same price, *i.e.* 1 000 dollars per ton.

Pasta industry

	Year 1	
	Firm A	
Output	$ 100 000	
	Year 2	
	Firm A1	Firm A2
Output	$ 30 000	$ 100 000

In the first year, the output in this region will be worth 100 000 dollars; in the second year, the value of total output could be the sum produced by firm A1, *i.e.* 30 000 dollars, and that of firm A2, *i.e.* 100 000 dollars, resulting in a total of 130 000 dollars. But it would clearly be absurd to use this total as our macroeconomic indicator of activity in the region. It shows an increase of 30% (130 000/100 000 = 1.30, often written as + 30%, or more simply 30%), when in fact no change at all took place at the strictly macroeconomic level.

The same quantity of pasta was produced at the same price. All that changed was the legal and commercial organisation of the firms.

The above discrepancy generated the national accountants' innovative idea of calculating the contribution of each firm not as its output, but as its **value added**. This expression is profound since it consists of measuring *the value* that the firm *adds* to that of the firms that supply its inputs. Let us consider the pasta example again. Compared with the situation in the first year, when there was only firm A, the value added by firm A2 is not equal to 100 000 dollars. That is because firm A2 buys 30 000 dollars' worth of flour, whereas previously it had made this flour itself and did not count this as output. Therefore, the national accounts system proposes calculating the value added of firm A2 as 100 000 – 30 000 dollars. In other words, the value of the firm's output minus the value of the products used to carry out its production during the period.

The products consumed in the production process during the period are known as **intermediate consumption**. By deducting their value from that of output, one eliminates the *double counting* that occurred earlier when summing of the output of firms A1 and A2. In the second year, the output of flour was in fact counted twice: once in the value of the output of firm A1 (30 000 dollars) and a second time in the value of the output of firm A2 (whose 100 000 dollars in output in fact includes the value of the flour bought and used in the production process).

If one applies this same reasoning to all firms, calculating for each its value added, it is then possible to add together the value added of each firm, *without double counting*. The result will be an indicator that is independent of the way firms are organised. This is illustrated in the following table, which includes the farm that produced the wheat from which the flour was made. For the sake of simplicity, let us assume the farmer uses no intermediate consumption; he obtains his wheat solely from his labour and machinery, without buying seeds or fertilisers. As can be seen from the following diagram, the total of the output of each unit changes, but the *sum of the value added of each unit* remains equal to 100 000 dollars, regardless of the pattern of organisation.

This is why GDP is defined as being equal to the sum of the value added of each firm, government institution and producing household in a given country: **GDP = Σ value added.** ▶ **IV.** Because each value added is itself equal to output minus intermediate consumption, the end result is: **GDP = Σ outputs – Σ intermediate consumptions.**

IV. To be more precise, one should say "GDP = Σ gross values added, plus taxes minus subsidies on products". See Table 5.

The composite formula for GDP (known as an "**aggregate**") constitutes a macroeconomic indicator of output that is independent of the pattern of organisation and avoids double counting. It provides a good illustration of the three essential rules followed by national accountants when they move from the microeconomy to the macroeconomy:

● avoid double counting;

Year 1		
	Farmer	Firm A
Input	Labour + machinery	Labour + machinery + wheat
Output	Wheat	Pasta
Output	$ 10 000	$ 100 000
Intermediate consumption	0	$ 10 000
Value added	$ 10 000	$ 90 000

Year 2			
	Farmer	Firm A1	Firm A2
Input	Labour + machinery	Labour + machinery + wheat	Labour + machinery + flour
Output	Wheat	Flour	Pasta
Output	$ 10 000	$ 30 000	$ 100 000
Intermediate consumption	0	$ 10 000	$ 30 000
Value added	$ 10 000	$ 20 000	$ 70 000s

- devise aggregates that are economically significant (*i.e.* whose value is independent of non-economic factors); and
- create indicators that are measurable in practice.

GDP *vs.* other aggregates

Why the bizarre title "gross domestic product," or GDP? It should be clear by now that "product" describes what one is trying to measure, *i.e.* the result of production. "Domestic" indicates that the output measured is produced within the economic territory of the country, or the group of countries, concerned. (It is in fact entirely possible to calculate GDP for a group of countries, such as that of the euro area.) "Gross" means the consumption of fixed capital is not deducted (see below).

"Domestic" is also in opposition to "national", as in GNI or gross national income, which is the current title of what was referred to as GNP, or gross national product, in previous systems of national accounts ("GNP" is still widely used out of habit). GDP measures the total *production* occurring within the territory, while GNI measures the total *income* (excluding capital gains and losses) of all economic agents residing within the territory (households, firms and government institutions).

To convert GDP into GNI, it is necessary to add the income received by resident units from abroad and deduct the income created by production in the country but transferred to units residing abroad. For example, the earnings of workers living in Germany but working in neighbouring parts of Switzerland or Luxembourg have to be added to the German GDP to obtain its GNI. Conversely, the earnings of the seasonal or regular workers living in France or Poland and working across the border in Germany have to be deducted from the German GDP to obtain the German GNI.

For large countries like Germany, the difference between GDP and GNI is small (0.4%, as seen in the following table). But it is larger for a small country like Luxembourg, which pays out a substantial percentage of its GDP as workers' earnings and other so-called "primary income" to the "rest of the world" (which is the term used by national accounts to signify "all countries other than Luxembourg", in this case). Primary income includes interest paid on money invested in Luxembourg. Luxembourg also receives substantial primary income from abroad, including interest. In the final analysis, the difference between GDP and GNI is around −11.5% for Luxembourg. Ireland is in a comparable situation to Luxembourg, since it pays out substantial dividends to the parent companies of the American multinational firms that have set up there, partly, but not entirely, for tax reasons. The result is that Ireland's GNI is 16.2% lower than its GDP. While for these three countries GNI is lower than GDP, the opposite also happens – Switzerland is a case in point.

Table 2. **Reconciliation of GDP and GNI for Germany, Luxembourg and Ireland**
Millions of euros

Year 2003	Germany	Luxembourg	Ireland
Gross domestic product	2 128 200	23 956	134 786
+ primary income (including earnings) received from the rest of the world	+104 610	+52 972	+30 296
− primary income (including earnings) paid to the rest of the world	−118 630	−55 722	−52 139
= Gross national income	2 114 180	21 206	112 943
Difference between GDP and GNI (%)	−0.7	−11.5	−16.2

Source: OECD (2006), National Accounts of OECD Countries: Volume I, Main Aggregates, 1993-2004, 2006 Edition, OECD, Paris.

StatLink: http://dx.doi.org/10.1787/783541142830

A distinction is also made between GDP and net domestic product (NDP). In order to produce goods and services ("the output") at least three factors are required: labour (the "labour force"), goods and services (intermediate consumption) and capital (machinery). These various factors represent the "inputs" in the production process.

In order to arrive at a genuine measurement of the *new wealth created during the period*, a deduction has to be made for the cost of using up capital (such as the "wear and

1 THE ESSENTIAL MACROECONOMIC AGGREGATES
2. The first fundamental equation:
deriving GDP in volume

tear" on machinery). This is known as **consumption of fixed capital**. When this consumption is deducted, the result is **net value added**, and NDP is the sum of these net values added: NDP = Σ Net Values Added. Although less widely used than GDP, NDP is, in theory, a better measure of the wealth produced since it deducts the cost of wearing out the machinery and other capital assets used in production. For similar reasons, in theory, Net National Income is a better measure than GNI of the income created because Net National Income deducts the cost of using up capital assets. However, OECD economists tend to prefer GDP or GNI (over NDP and NNI) for two reasons. First, methods for calculating consumption of fixed capital are complex and tend to differ between countries, thus creating doubts about the comparability of results. Second, when ranking countries or analysing growth, the differences between GDP and NDP are small and do not change the conclusions.

2. The first fundamental equation: deriving GDP in volume

V. Economists and journalists have acquired the unfortunate habit of using the general term "growth" instead of specifying "growth in real GDP". A typical sentence is: "growth is 2%" instead of "growth in real GDP is 2%". This lack of precision sometimes results in bizarre terminology, such as "negative growth", which is an oxymoron; it would be better to say "a decrease of GDP in volume". Incidentally, national accountants prefer the term "GDP in volume" to "real GDP" because inflation is just as real as growth.

Let us go back to Table 1: "Main macroenomic variables", shown at the very beginning of the chapter. Comments from OECD economists (shown below the table) indicate that they are not interested in GDP growth as such, but in the growth of "real" GDP. ▶ **V.** What does this expression mean?

The A-B-C of macroeconomics consists of distinguishing what part of the change in national accounts aggregates at current prices stems from a change in the quantities produced and what part stems from a change in prices. Let us suppose, for example, that the output of pasta is worth 100 000 dollars in the first year and 110 000 dollars in the second. The macroeconomist will immediately want to know if this 10% growth (which may be described as "nominal" or "in value" or, better still, "at current prices") is due to an increase in the quantity of pasta or to an increase in its price. An increase in quantity is good news, while an increase in prices ("inflation") tends to be bad news. Keeping in mind the aim of separating the good growth (the quantities) from the bad growth (inflation), national accountants have developed sophisticated methods for separating out movements in GDP "at current prices" into two components: 1) an indicator of the change in quantity (the "real GDP" or, preferably, "**GDP in volume**"); and 2) an indicator of the change in prices, called the "**GDP deflator**". These methods are described in detail in Chapter 2.

Recall that the 100 000 dollars' worth of pasta production mentioned earlier equals 100 tonnes of pasta (the quantity) multiplied by 1 000 dollars (the price per tonne). In almost the same way, the index of the growth rate of GDP at current prices is exactly

THE ESSENTIAL MACROECONOMIC AGGREGATES
2. The first fundamental equation:
    deriving GDP in volume

1

equal to the index of the growth rate of GDP in volume multiplied by the index of the growth rate of the GDP deflator:

Fundamental equation (1)

[1 + the growth rate (divided by 100) of GDP at current prices] =
    [1 + the growth rate (divided by 100) of GDP in volume] x
    [1 + the growth rate (divided by 100) of the GDP deflator]

This is a fundamental equation in the national accounts, and the term "deflator" stems directly from it. This is because one can derive from this fundamental equation the following equation (with "/" standing for "divided by"):

[1 + (Growth rate of GDP in volume/100)] =
[1 + (Growth of GDP at current prices/100)] / [1+ (Growth of the GDP deflator/100)]

In this way, starting with GDP growth at current prices, one "deflates" (*i.e.* divides) this by the price indicator (the GDP deflator) to obtain the volume indicator (GDP volume). Conversely, in the previous version of the equation, GDP growth in volume was "inflated" by the price indicator in order to obtain GDP growth at current prices. Note that these equations showing the breakdown into volume and price movements apply not only to GDP but also to some of the other key variables in the national accounts, notably investment and consumption. Note also that this equation also applies to absolute levels. Thus, GDP in volume at absolute levels (*i.e.* in millions of dollars of the "base" year) is equal to GDP at current prices at absolute levels (*i.e.* in millions of dollars) divided by the implicit deflator, expressed as a price index divided by 100. When this operation is done, the base year for GDP in volume corresponds to the year for which the price index is conventionally equal to 100.

Macroeconomists pay very little attention to the evolution of GDP at current prices. It does not even appear in the main OECD table for Germany (see Table 1). In contrast, its two main components – real GDP and the GDP deflator – feature prominently in the table, one of them being used to measure growth and the other to measure inflation. GDP at current prices is, however, used as the denominator to standardise many important aggregates, such as the public deficit, the balance of exports and imports, national savings, etc. Ratios calculated as percentages of GDP, with both numerator and denominator usually expressed in current prices, are used to make international comparisons of variables that would otherwise depend on the size of the country.

Figure 1 illustrates for Germany the relationship between GDP at current prices, GDP in volume and the GDP deflator. Unlike the earlier OECD table, which shows growth rates, this chart contains "absolute amounts". In other words, the two aggregates – GDP at current prices and GDP in volume – are expressed in billions of euros.

It can be seen that German GDP at current prices was roughly 2 200 billion euros in 2004, while the German GDP in volume (*i.e.* at constant prices, shown in the chart as "GDP at prices of 2000") was around 2 100 billion euros for the same year. The GDP

1 THE ESSENTIAL MACROECONOMIC AGGREGATES
2. The first fundamental equation:
deriving GDP in volume

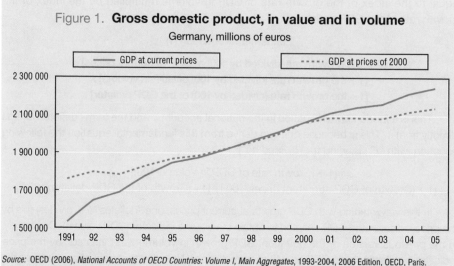

Figure 1. **Gross domestic product, in value and in volume**
Germany, millions of euros

Source: OECD (2006), *National Accounts of OECD Countries: Volume I, Main Aggregates*, 1993-2004, 2006 Edition, OECD, Paris.
StatLink: *http://dx.doi.org/10.1787/142154615437*

deflator (inflation) cannot be calculated in billions of euros and therefore does not appear as a separate line on the chart.[2] However, the GDP deflator can be inferred as the gap between GDP in volume and GDP at current prices. The widening of this gap after the year 2000 indicates, in principle, the existence of inflation.[3] This is indeed the case, as can be seen from the fact that after 2000, GDP at current prices (the dark line) increases much faster than GDP in volume (the dotted line).

Notice that the two lines coincide in the year 2000. That is because in this chart, GDP in volume for all the years has been calculated using the prices prevalent in the year 2000. It is for this reason that the legend for the dotted line refers to GDP "at 2000 prices". By definition, the two aggregates – GDP at current prices and GDP in volume – have to be equal for this particular year (known as the "base year" or the "reference year"). It is interesting to note that in Table 1, economists had used aggregates in volume expressed at "1995 prices", while in the Figure 1, we have an aggregate at "2000 prices". The explanation is that national accountants regularly update the base year. When Table 1 was published, Germany was still using 1995 as its base year. When Figure 1 was produced, the base year had changed to 2000. We shall come back to these questions in Chapter 2, but what one should infer from this example is that, while it is very important whether the aggregate is in volume or not, the choice of the base year is less important, especially when applied to growth rates, which is what economists focus on.

Table 3 shows the variations in Germany's GDP deflator. It can be seen that the years 2000 to 2003 were characterised by fairly low inflation, which remained below 2%.

For comparison, the table also shows the annual variation in the consumer price index (CPI).[4] This index is another indicator of inflation that is better known and more frequently used than the GDP deflator, mainly because it is available monthly and relates to the aggregate that is of most interest to people, namely consumption. The GDP deflator, also called "the implicit GDP price index" or, simply "implicit GDP deflator", is on the one hand more general in scope than the CPI, since it also covers capital goods. But on the other hand, it is less general because it measures only domestic inflation, with increases in import prices not directly taken into account. Moreover, except for the very few countries that compile their national accounts each month, the GDP deflator is available only quarterly.

Table 3. **GDP deflator and consumer price index**

Germany, annual growth rates in percentage

	2002	2003	2004	2005	2006
GDP deflator	1.5	1.1	0.9	0.8	0.9
Consumer Price Index (HICP)	1.3	1.0	1.7	1.3	0.6

Source: OECD (2004), *OECD Economic Outlook*, December No. 76, Volume 2004, Issue 2, OECD, Paris.

StatLink: *http://dx.doi.org/10.1787/454532272722*

3. Defining demand: the role of investment and consumption

Let us return to Table 1 at the beginning of this chapter. The OECD economists had noted that the stagnation of GDP between 2002 and 2004 was due to weak domestic demand. Private consumption had declined but *"there [were] signs that investment [was] strengthening"*.

The upturn in investment by firms and households can be seen in Table 1 by looking at the variable "gross capital formation", which had declined 6.3% in 2002, 2.2% in 2003 and 2.0% in 2004, but was expected to rebound by 0.6% in 2005, followed by a 3.4% increase in 2006. Like real GDP, this variable is shown in Table 1 "at 1995 prices", in other words, "in volume". For a macroeconomic aggregate, growth of more than 3% in volume is a good performance, even if China or Eastern European countries show even better performance. However, at the time of writing, this was still only a forecast waiting to be confirmed.

In the national accounts, investment, *i.e.* the purchase of machinery (including software) and buildings (offices, infrastructure, dwellings) and the constitution of stocks (inventories) is known as gross capital formation (GCF). When stock-building (or "changes in inventories") is excluded, leaving only the purchases of buildings and machinery, the result is known as gross fixed capital formation (GFCF). This variable measures total expenditures on products intended to be used for future production. These types of products are

1

THE ESSENTIAL MACROECONOMIC AGGREGATES
4. Second fundamental equation: reconciling
   global output and demand

collectively known as "fixed" capital.[5] Why not simply call them investment, as economists in fact often do? Because the word "investment" in everyday use applies as much to financial investment ("I invest in shares of the stock market") as it does to investment in machinery and buildings. So to make a clear distinction between the two applications, the national accountants use this somewhat peculiar terminology. Finally, the word "gross" indicates that the expenditure is measured without deducting the consumption of fixed capital (the wear and tear).

VI. Private consumption includes household consumption expenditure and also expenditure by "non-profit institutions serving households" (NPISHs). For the definition of "households" and "NPISHs", see Chapters 5 and 6.

The OECD economists were counting to some extent on "private consumption" to underpin demand in 2005 and 2006 in Germany. "Private consumption" is essentially what the national accountants call household final consumption expenditure. ▶ **VI.** This variable covers all purchases made by consumers: food, clothing, housing services (rents), energy, durable goods (notably cars), spending on health, on leisure and on miscellaneous services. Consumption expenditure does not, however, include households' purchases of dwellings, which are counted as household GFCF. The "consumption" variable is in contrast to "GFCF", with consumption intended to designate purchases that are consumed (in the sense of "used up" or "destroyed") during the period, while GFCF refers to purchases intended to be used for future production. However, this distinction is somewhat arbitrary, since purchases of cars by households (goods that are certainly intended to last) are classified as consumption (see Section "Limitations and pitfalls"). Why "final" consumption? It is in contrast to intermediate consumption, referred to earlier.

After GDP, household final consumption is undoubtedly the most important variable in the national accounts, representing in general around 60% of GDP. Indeed, the economic model providing the underlying framework for the national accounts is aimed at maximising this consumption, although today there is increasing concern that consumption should be sustainable in the longer term ("sustainable development").

4. Second fundamental equation: reconciling global output and demand

Final consumption and investment are two of the main components of "final" macroeconomic demand. The great attraction of the national accounts is that they constitute a "reconciled" model of the economy, balancing supply and demand. In fact, the second fundamental equation of the national accounts can be written as follows:

Fundamental equation (2)

GDP = Sum of final demand aggregates

THE ESSENTIAL MACROECONOMIC AGGREGATES
4. Second fundamental equation: reconciling
   global output and demand

1

In order to grasp the origin of this essential accounting equation, let us return to the example of the pasta industry.

	Year 2		
Input	labour + machinery	Labour + machinery + wheat	Labour + machinery + flour
Output	Wheat	Flour	Pasta
Output	$ 10 000	$ 30 000	$ 100 000
Intermediate consumption	0	$ 10 000	$ 30 000
Value added	**$ 10 000**	**$ 20 000**	**$ 70 000**

Recall that GDP is equal to total value added or, equivalently, to total output minus total intermediate consumption. If one adds up the output, this means adding together the 10 000 dollars' worth of wheat, the 30 000 dollars' worth of flour and the 100 000 dollars' worth of pasta, resulting in a total of 140 000 dollars. If one now deducts the intermediate consumption, this means removing the 10 000 dollars' worth of wheat and the 30 000 dollars' worth of flour, leaving the 100 000 dollars' worth of pasta. If one simplifies matters by ignoring possible inventory accumulation in the factory and in the distribution circuit, the 100 000 dollars corresponds exactly to the purchases by households, in other words to household final consumption expenditure. This example shows that GDP, the sum of all values added, is equal, *by definition*, to final demand which, in this case, consists only of household demand for pasta.

Only a small amount of elaboration is needed to bring this example much closer to reality. If one introduces a firm that makes the machinery used to manufacture pasta, it can be verified that GDP equals exactly the consumption of pasta plus the purchase of the machinery used to make it, *i.e.* household consumption plus GCF. This opens the system up to GCF in addition to household consumption. In addition, if we assume that the economy is open to imports and that there is external demand reflected in exports, the equation is now supplemented with these additional flows:

GDP + Imports = Household consumption + GCF + Exports

The left-hand side of the equation consists of supply at the macroeconomic level, made up of domestic production (GDP) and external supply (imports). The right-hand side consists of final demand, broken down into domestic demand (household consumption and GCF) and external demand (exports). Macroeconomists often use this equation in another, mathematically equivalent form:

GDP = Household consumption + GCF + Net Exports

The left-hand side now consists solely of GDP, the principal indicator of economic activity. The right-hand side consists of the "final uses" that are the major components of domestic demand together with "net exports", which is simply the difference between

1 THE ESSENTIAL MACROECONOMIC AGGREGATES
4. Second fundamental equation: reconciling
   global output and demand

exports and imports. This accounting equation is fundamental in analyzing the economic condition. It provides a perfect illustration of the impact of demand on supply, according to Keynesian reasoning. It is no accident, in fact, that national accounting was developed during the 1940s, just after Keynes' major discoveries.

To be fully precise, the above equation has to be made slightly more complex, as shown in Table 4. The second fundamental equation in the national accounts can easily be verified by looking at this table. The addition of the rows in bold type (total final consumption, gross capital formation, external balance of goods and services) is equal to GDP, to the nearest million euros. This table introduces the concept of *final consumption of NPISHs* ("non-profit institutions serving households"), which accounts for only a tiny proportion of GDP (2.1%),[6] so that economists often add it to household consumption, thus creating the "private consumption" aggregate.

Table 4. **GDP: expenditure approach**
Germany, 2004[a]

Codes		Million euros	% of GDP
GDP	Gross domestic product	2 177 000	
P3	**Total final consumption**	**1 677 450**	
	of which:		
P31-S14	Household final consumption expenditure	1 225 870	56.3
P31-S15	Final consumption of NPISHs	44 900	2.1
P31-S13	General government final consumption expenditure	406 680	18.7
P5	**Gross capital formation**	**385 480**	
	of which:		
P51	Gross fixed capital formation	378 550	17.4
P52	Changes in inventories	6 930	
B11	**External balance of goods and services**	**114 070**	
	of which:		
P6	Exports	834 820	38.3
P7	Imports	720 750	33.1

a) This table shows the official SNA codes, which the reader can find on the website accompanying this book. These codes facilitate the understanding and manipulation of the data.

Source: OECD (2006), *National Accounts of OECD Countries: Volume I, Main Aggregates*, 1993-2004, 2006 Edition, OECD, Paris.

StatLink: *http://dx.doi.org/10.1787/502048533886*

THE ESSENTIAL MACROECONOMIC AGGREGATES
5. Third fundamental equation: reconciling global
   output and income

1

A much more important introduction is that of *general government consumption* (18.7% of GDP), which exceeds GFCF (17.4%) but is substantially smaller than household consumption (56.3%). We shall return to the significance of this "general government consumption" variable in Chapter 5. The table also shows stock-building ("changes in inventories"). Although usually small in absolute terms, stock-building nevertheless plays an important role in the short term. In fact, inventories come into play as a "shock absorber" between production and final demand from households and firms. Note that unlike other variables, changes in inventories are not shown in macroeconomic tables as a percentage of GDP or as a growth rate, but as contributions to GDP growth (see Box 2 "Contributions to growth").

Short-term macroeconomic analysis relies heavily on the fundamental equation (2) but expressed in volume. The equation provides a mathematical explanation of GDP growth in terms of its various components. The value of national accounts is that the general macroeconomic concept of the influence of demand on supply in this way takes concrete form as an accounting equation.[7] This was the same equation underpinning the OECD economists' remark: *"Based on strong export growth, the German economy is recovering from three years of stagnation... [but] weak domestic demand is still weighing on activity..."* .

5. Third fundamental equation: reconciling global output and income

The previous section dealt with the first macroeconomic reconciliation, between global output (measured by the sum of the values added) and final demand. There is a second reconciliation, this time between global output and the income of economic agents. Any production activity generates income that is shared between the three "factors of production": labour, capital and intermediate consumption. Since value added is equal to output minus intermediate consumption, this second macroeconomic reconciliation can be written more simply by eliminating intermediate consumption and using value added as the global indicator of output. This means that there are now just two factors creating value added, namely labour and capital, which are compensated respectively by salaries and by the profits generated through production. It is these types of income that subsequently enable economic agents – households and firms – to consume and invest. For example, the 100 000 dollars of GDP of our now-familiar pasta industry are divided between the profits of the farmer, the two firms A1 and A2, and the salaries of the staff at firms A1 and A2.

In the end, our two macroeconomic reconciliations can be summarised in the following double fundamental equation:

Fundamental equation (3)

1

THE ESSENTIAL MACROECONOMIC AGGREGATES
5. Third fundamental equation: reconciling global
   output and income

Box 2. **Contributions to growth**

In this box, the sign Δ will be used to express the difference between two years (or two quarters), so that ΔGDP_t signifies $GDP_t - GDP_{t-1}$, in other words the difference between GDP in year (quarter) t and GDP in year (quarter) t–1. Using this notation, $\Delta GDP_t/GDP_{t-1}$ will be equal to the GDP growth rate for year (or quarter) t compared with year (or quarter) t–1.

The starting point is a simplified volume equation: $GDP_t = C_t + I_t + X_t$ (where GDP = Final consumption + GFCF + Exports). For this simplified equation, we assume that there are no imports and no inventories. Mathematically, this results in the "difference" equation: $\Delta GDP_t = \Delta C_t + \Delta I_t + \Delta X_t$. Dividing both sides by GDP_{t-1} then results in equation (a): $\Delta GDP_t/GDP_{t-1} = \Delta C_t/GDP_{t-1} + \Delta I_t/GDP_{t-1} + \Delta X_t/GDP_{t-1}$.

Dividing and multiplying each term on the right-hand side by its value in t–1 and reorganising, one obtains equation (b): $\Delta GDP_t/GDP_{t-1} = (C_{t-1}/GDP_{t-1})(\Delta C_t/C_{t-1}) + (I_{t-1}/GDP_{t-1})(\Delta I_t/I_{t-1}) + (X_{t-1}/GDP_{t-1})(\Delta X_t/X_{t-1})$.

The verbal translation of this second equation is as follows: GDP growth breaks down exactly into the contribution of consumption plus the contribution of investment plus the contribution of exports. Each contribution is equal to the weight of the variable multiplied by the growth rate of the same variable in the current period. The weight of the variable is equal to its value in the previous period divided by the GDP of the previous period.

This breakdown of growth is widely used by macroeconomists. As can be seen, it is based on the second fundamental equation. Exercise 4, at the end of this chapter, will enable you to carry out a practical application. It involves the calculation of the contribution of changes in inventories and net exports. Since these variables can be positive or negative, it is necessary to use version (a) of the above equation to calculate their contributions to growth, and not version (b). In macroeconomic tables expressed in growth rates, changes in inventories and net exports are never shown in terms of percentage growth rates but solely as contributions to growth.

It is important to note that the calculation of contributions to growth basically relies on the accounting identity between GDP and final demand. Unfortunately, this mathematical link is no longer fully valid when using chain-linked volume measures because the results are not additive. Chapter 2 explains chain-linked volume accounts, their advantages and disadvantages, and shows how to compile contributions to growth in this new context.

Output (sum of the values added) =
Income (employees' salaries + company profits) =
Final demand (Consumption + GCF + Net exports)

We shall be evaluating the way in which the national accounts record income in the chapters dealing with the accounts of households, enterprises and government sectors. For the moment, let us note simply the following fundamental result: GDP is also equal to total income. This is the third fundamental equation. Note also that in the national accounts one talks of "**compensation of employees**" rather than salaries, because the cost of labour

THE ESSENTIAL MACROECONOMIC AGGREGATES
5. Third fundamental equation: reconciling global
   output and income

1

includes social contributions paid by the employers, and that profits are known as **operating surplus** or, in some cases, as **mixed income**.[8] The operating surplus is described as "gross" when no deduction is made for the cost of the depreciation of capital, known as "consumption of fixed capital" in the national accounts. It is in fact preferable to analyse this surplus in "net" terms, in other words, after deducting consumption of fixed capital, as we shall see in Chapter 7.

Three ways to measure GDP

To summarise, there are three "approaches" to GDP: 1) the output approach (the sum of gross values added); 2) the final demand approach (consumption + investment + net exports); and 3) the income approach (compensation of employees + gross operating surplus + gross mixed income).[9]

Table 5 illustrates the equality of the three approaches for 1991 and 2004. The presentation is slightly more complicated than the double equation set out above, notably because of the introduction of **taxes net of subsidies**. For the time being, however, we will ignore this difficulty. The reader can verify that the "three" GDPs are exactly equal, at 1 502.2 billion euros in 1991 and 2 177.0 billion euros in 2004.[10] Comparison between the two years illustrates certain fundamental changes that have taken place in Germany since reunification. For example, the share of employee compensation in GDP fell slightly from 56.2% in 1991 to 52.0% in 2004. As Figure 2 shows, this reduction was fairly continuous.

Saving ratio and the general government financial balance

The principal macroeconomic indicators used by the OECD in Table 1 include two aggregates to which no reference has yet been made: the *household saving ratio* and the *general government financial balance*. They are shown again below.

Summary of recent results and forecasts
Germany

	2002	2003	2004	2005	2006
Household saving ratio[1]	10.5	10.7	11.1	11.1	10.8
General government financial balance[2]	−3.7	−3.8	−3.9	−3.5	−2.7

1. Net saving as % of net disposable income.

2. % of GDP.

Source: OECD (2004), *OECD Economic Outlook,* December No. 76, Volume 2004, Issue 2, OECD, Paris.

The **household saving ratio** is equal to **saving** by households expressed as a percentage of their **disposable income**,[11] both these variables being expressed at current prices, and represents the portion of household income that is not consumed. In 2004, the German household saving ratio was 11.1%. In other words, out of every

1 THE ESSENTIAL MACROECONOMIC AGGREGATES
5. Third fundamental equation: reconciling global
output and income

Table 5. **The three approaches to GDP**

Germany, billion euros

Codes[1]		1991	2004
GDP	Gross domestic product (output approach)	1 502.2	2 177.0
B1B	Value added at base-year prices	1 359.5	1 965.1
D21	+ taxes net of subsidies on the products	142.7	211.9
GDP	Gross domestic product (demand approach)	1 502.2	2 177.0
P3	Final consumption expenditure	1 140.9	1 677.5
P5	+ Gross capital formation	364.9	385.5
P6	+ Exports of goods and services	395.2	834.8
P7	− Imports of goods and services	398.7	720.8
GDP	Gross domestic product (income approach)	1 502.2	2 177.0
D1	Compensation of employees	844.0	1 133.1
B2 + B3	+ Gross operating surplus and gross mixed income	515.1	811.9
D2	+ Taxes net of subsidies on production and imports	143.1	232.1

1. These are the official SNA codes

Source: OECD (2006), *National Accounts of OECD Countries: Volume I, Main Aggregates,* 1993-2004, 2006 Edition, OECD, Paris.

StatLink: *http://dx.doi.org/10.1787/400886162203*

Figure 2. **Employee compensation**

As a percentage of GDP, Germany

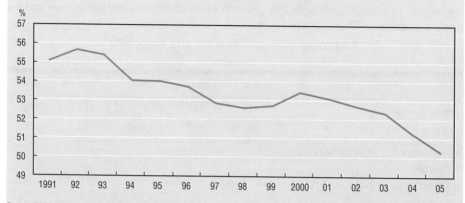

Source: OECD (2006), *National Accounts of OECD Countries: Volume I, Main Aggregates,* 1993-2004, 2006 Edition, OECD, Paris.

StatLink: *http://dx.doi.org/10.1787/706731537741*

UNDERSTANDING NATIONAL ACCOUNTS – ISBN 92-64-02566-9 – © OECD 2006

THE ESSENTIAL MACROECONOMIC AGGREGATES
5. Third fundamental equation: reconciling global
   output and income

1

thousand euros of household income (after tax), 111 euros were saved – for investment in housing, kept as cash or used to purchase financial products such as shares, bonds or life insurance. This variable is of great importance in macroeconomics, as its evolution determines the relationship between income and consumption. As can be seen from the table, the household saving ratio rose in 2002 and 2003, probably reflecting an increase in precautionary saving in response to the economic slowdown and the rising unemployment. This rise in the saving ratio contributed to a slowdown in consumption in Germany.

The *general government financial balance* corresponds to what is commonly referred to as the public surplus or deficit. ▶ **VII.** In the national accounts, it has the more complicated but fairly eloquent title "net lending/net borrowing of general government". This variable is equal to the difference between the sum of all general government revenues and the sum of general government expenditures, whether they be "current" (civil service salaries, interest on the public debt) or "capital" (investment). A negative difference shows that government has a borrowing requirement. That is because when revenue falls short of expenditure it will be necessary to find financing for the difference, mainly through borrowing and hence increasing the public debt. A positive difference shows the existence of a financing capacity. Since the 1991 unification, this has occurred only once (in 2000) in Germany.

VII. "General government" includes the central government, local authorities, social security and the various organisations depending on them. However, it does not cover enterprises such as railways, telephone companies or electricity firms, which are state-owned in some countries. We shall be returning to these classifications in Chapters 7 and 9.

It has become customary, especially for European countries since the signing of the Maastricht Treaty, to express "net lending/net borrowing of general government" as a percentage of GDP at current prices. This is one of the cases in which GDP at current prices is used in absolute terms as the denominator of a magnitude. This approach makes it possible to compare deficits between countries while automatically adjusting for the different size of their economies, and it underlies the "Maastricht criterion" stipulating that the public deficit must not exceed 3% of GDP. During the recent past, the financing requirement of the German government has been estimated by the OECD and the EU Commission to be systematically in excess of the critical 3% threshold. However, thanks to the support of France, which had also exceeded the 3% threshold, Germany avoided the threat of sanctions imposed by the European Commission, and this subsequently led to reform of the Stability and Growth Pact in 2005.

This completes our presentation of all the variables that appear in Table 1 "Main macroeconomic variables". Let us review the main points.

1 THE ESSENTIAL MACROECONOMIC AGGREGATES
5. Third fundamental equation: reconciling global
output and income

Notes

1. The "OECD Economic Outlook" contains the biannual macroeconomic forecasts for each OECD country and the OECD area as a whole. Each edition is numbered, with the edition for December 2004 being the 76th in the series.

2. When not shown as a growth rate, the GDP deflator is shown, like all price indices, as a series of dimensionless numbers whose change represents changes in prices, with the value in a given base year equal to 100.

3. Strictly speaking, one should use a logarithmic scale for the vertical axis.

4. In fact, what we have here is the European version of this index, known as the "Harmonised index of consumer prices" for Germany.

5. In contrast to "variable" capital, consisting of changes in inventories. These expressions go back to Karl Marx, who provided the far-distant inspiration for some of the ideas behind the national accounts.

6. Non-profit institutions may account for an appreciable part of GDP but most of them are recorded in a different sector in the national accounts. For example, mutual insurance institutions are included in the insurance sector. The NPISH sector covers only a small portion of all non-profit institutions, specifically those that are both financed and controlled by households.

7. Unfortunately, modern calculating methods mean that fundamental equation 2 no longer holds exactly in volume. We shall be returning to this problem of non-additivity in Chapter 2. For the time being, it is possible to ignore this difficulty.

8. "Mixed income" is the term applied to the gross operating surplus of "non-incorporated enterprises". Further light will be thrown on this point in Chapter 6.

9. One could also calculate the three approaches in terms of Net Domestic Product: the output approach (the sum of net values added); the final demand approach (consumption + net investment plus net exports); and the income approach (compensation of employees + net operating surplus + net mixed income).

10. This equation is not strictly verifiable for all countries, because of statistical discrepancies – notably in the case of the United States. See Chapters 10 and 12. Moreover, and this is a remark valid for the rest of the book (including exercices), the numbers shown in the tables are often rounded, so that totals do not match exactly the sum of their components. It may happen that there is a mistake, but more often it is simply that the sum of rounded numbers is not exactly equal to the rounding of the sum. This is the case in Table 5 with the value of 1 502.2 for the GDP (demand approach) for 1991. If one compiles P3 + P5 + P6 − P7, one obtains 1 502.3, and not 1 502.2. There is no mistake here. It is simply that the equality holds exactly when numbers are expressed in millions of euros, but does not when they are rounded into billions.

11. In this case, the saving and the disposable income are both net, meaning that consumption of fixed capital on dwellings and other capital goods owned by households is deducted from both aggregates. It is also possible to calculate the saving ratio on a gross basis.

Key points

▶ GDP is the sum of output within the country's territory minus the sum of intermediate consumption (increased by taxes net of subsidies on products).

▶ GDP is equal to the sum of the gross value added of each firm, non-profit institution, government body and household producing on the territory (increased by taxes net of subsidies on products).

▶ The change in GDP expressed in volume is the principal indicator of the change in macroeconomic activity.

▶ First fundamental equation: the index of the variation in GDP (or any other variable) at current prices breaks down precisely into the product of the index's variation in volume and the index's variation in prices, the latter being known as the "deflator" or the "implicit price index". The deflator can be used as a measure of inflation but differs from the consumer price index.

▶ Second fundamental equation: GDP is equal to the sum of the final demand aggregates.

▶ Third fundamental equation: GDP is equal to the sum of incomes (compensation of employees, gross operating surplus and gross mixed income of firms) increased by taxes net of subsidies on production.

▶ There are therefore three equivalent approaches to GDP: the output approach (sum of gross values added); the final demand approach (the sum of final consumption, GFCF, changes in inventories and net exports); and the income approach (sum of employee compensation, gross operating surplus and mixed income).

Going Further

How are these figures obtained?

This is probably the most difficult question to answer in a short textbook on national accounts, but we shall attempt to do so. The illustrations will be taken from the French case, the one the authors know best. However, it will not be possible to give the reader precise answers, since many different methods are used, as is only natural in drawing up accounts covering all economic agents, including in the French case some 25 million households.

Despite their name, the national accounts bear only a partial similarity to the accounts of a company. The general frameworks are similar but the data sources are entirely different. The company accountant has at his disposal a ledger showing to the last cent all the transactions carried out by the firm during the period. The national accountant obviously has nothing similar for all agents, especially for households. For this reason, it is not unreasonable to speak of "national accounts statistics". The addition of the word "statistics" implies acceptance of the notions of approximation, estimation and revision, things in which the national accountants excel but which are anathema to company accountants.

In France, the principal methods for calculating the figures in the national accounts are based on the exploitation of the extremely comprehensive administrative sources available. These consist, on the one hand, of the database built up by Insee (the French public statistics office) on the basis of companies' tax declarations and, on the other, on the centralised information gathered by the public accounting system regarding government institutions. The tax source provides Insee with regular and virtually exhaustive information on more than 2 million French firms. Because these firms are obliged to submit fairly complete accounts drawn up according to precise rules (the "plan comptable general" or general accounting framework), it is possible to use these accounts to calculate the value added of each individual firm (in the case of the large firms) or for groups of firms (in the case of the small ones) and then to add them up. This covers the private sector (referred to as the "market" sector in the national accounts). As regards the "non-market" sector (central government, local authorities and tens of thousands of government institutions) the centralisation of their accounts is carried out by the "Direction de la Comptabilité Publique" (Public Accounts Directorate) in the Finance Ministry, making it possible to calculate fairly precisely the value added for the non-market sector.

UNDERSTANDING NATIONAL ACCOUNTS – ISBN 92-64-02566-9 – © OECD 2006

There is no such direct source in the case of households, whose consumption represents 60% of GDP. The national households' account is often calculated indirectly by using statistics from other sources. For example, the compensation of employees received by households is calculated by adding up compensation of employees paid out by firms, non-profit institutions and public units. Another common method is to obtain estimates of household aggregates "by difference". Take dividends for example. The dividends paid out by firms are known and the receipts of these dividends by firms and public bodies are also known. The balance of payments provides estimates of the dividends paid to, and received from, the rest of the world, from which one can compile the net dividends received from abroad (dividends received from abroad less dividends paid to other countries). There is a macroeconomic "accounting identity" which states that: "Dividends paid by firms = Dividends received by general government and firms + Net dividends from abroad + Dividends received by households". Turning this equation around gives: "Dividends received by households = Dividends paid by firms – Dividends received by firms and by general government – Net dividends received from abroad". Dividends received by households can therefore be calculated in this way as a "balance", *i.e.* what is left over. National accountants readily admit that it would be better to have direct sources concerning households, since calculation as a balance has the drawback of concentrating all measurement errors on the single household item. However, it is out of the question to ask households to draw up accounts, and it is therefore necessary to make the best of what is available.

As for the measurement of changes, the sources differ between quarterly accounts (these being the first to be published) or annual accounts. Quarterly accounts use monthly indicators to extrapolate the value of the national accounts variables. These indicators may not correspond perfectly to the definition used in the national accounts but are rapidly available. For example, use is made of the monthly turnover statistics that Insee obtains using Value-Added Tax (VAT) declarations in order to extrapolate, as a growth rate, the "output at current prices" variable. The figure for turnover is admittedly not exactly equal to output, since there may have been changes in inventories between the two periods concerned, but it is the only reasonably similar variable readily available. These "provisional" figures are subsequently revised when Insee has at its disposal (one year later) first-hand information regarding companies' accounts, the result being the so-called "semi-definitive" and, (two years later) the "definitive" accounts based on quasi exhaustive companies' accounts. This term is in fact an overstatement, because these "definitive" accounts can themselves later be revised when a new "base" year is introduced. We shall be returning to these issues in Chapter 10.

Accuracy of national accounts

National accounts could more appropriatly be called "national accounts statistics", so that users do not think they are as reliable as the business accounts of a company.

This is not true. In particular, while GDP for technical reasons is often expressed in millions of units of the national currency, users should be aware that they are very, very far from being accurate at the level of millions. National accounts' quality is highly dependent on the quality of the statistical system that exists in a given country. And in all countries, at varying degrees, this system does not cover all units, leaving a significant number of adjustments to be made. National accounts data are therefore approximations. It is not even possible to give a summary figure of the accuracy of the GDP. Indeed, national accounts, and in particular GDP, are not the result of a single big survey for which one might compile a confidence interval. They are the result of combining a complex mix of data from many sources, many of which require adjustment to put them into a national accounts database and which are further adjusted to improve coherence, often using non-scientific methods.

It is useful to know that GDP levels can be revised by 1 to 3 percentage points when new benchmark data are introduced (excluding conceptual changes). It can even happen, although rarely, that some countries modify their estimate of GDP by more than 15% (Italy in 1987, China in 2005). In international comparisons, it is important to note that the quality of national accounts is not the same in all countries (see Chapter 3 on international comparisons). Overall, the OECD Statistics Directorate believes it may be misleading to establish a strict order of ranking countries based on GDP per capita at purchasing power parity in cases when countries are clustered around a narrow range of outcomes of less than 5 percentage points.

Limitations and pitfalls to be avoided

The results provided by the national accounts are now such a familiar part of everyday economic information that there is a tendency to forget how extremely ambitious the original project was and still is. It is no accident that the two major creators of modern national accounts (Simon Kuznets of the United States and Richard Stone of the United Kingdom) were both awarded Nobel prizes for economics (Kuznets in 1971 and Stone in 1984). However, it must be realized that, in order to achieve the aim of summarising a country's entire economic activity in a set of internally consistent tables, national accounts have to accept significant approximations and adopt conventions that are sometimes arbitrary. It is necessary to be well aware of these conventions in order to avoid certain pitfalls. The following are a few of them.

Households' internal production (cooking, cleaning, running errands) is not covered in the national accounts. The principal reason is that inclusion would involve making very bold estimates of market value. This leads to the familiar criticism of GDP that if a man marries his cook the result is a reduction in GDP – perfectly true, but the problem is nevertheless marginal.

On the other hand, the national accounts include an estimate of the production of services in the form of the accommodation house owners provide for themselves. This is called "imputed rents" and is fairly difficult to estimate, since there is no observable transaction involved. However, if one were not to make this estimate, the change in GDP could be affected by a change in the proportion of households owning their own dwelling.

GDP includes the value added of general government. However, part of the production of general government ought in fact to be counted as the intermediate consumption of other branches. The national accounts assume that the services of general government are final uses. But in reality, firms also use the services of the police and other collective services provided by government. However, since there is no means of measuring this intermediate consumption, it is ignored, and GDP can therefore be said to be correspondingly overestimated.

The underground economy is badly measured in the national accounts. While, in principle, illicit activities should be included in GDP, this is impossible in practice. However, statistical offices make adjustments to take into account "underground" employment or tax fraud. In the case of France, for example, these adjustments increase GDP by around 4%.

Expenditure on research and development (R&D) is considered by some economists as investment. But in the national accounts, R&D is treated as current expenditure, in other words intermediate consumption, and therefore it is not included in GDP. However, it will probably be included in the future, when the new SNA 2008 is to be implemented.

On the other hand, the current version of the international system of national accounts (SNA 93) contains a recommendation that software be counted as GFCF (investment) and not as intermediate consumption (current expenditure), with the result that GDPs have been revised upwards, by between 1% and 4% depending on the country. This is because GFCF forms part of final demand and hence GDP, whereas intermediate consumption does not. Unfortunately, the practical application of this recommendation poses problems because most firms do not record their spending on software as investment, but as current expenditure.

Expenditure for the purchase of a house is recorded as GFCF, but expenditure by households on durable goods, cars in particular, is classified as consumption. And yet the services rendered by a car generally last a fairly long time, although obviously not as long as those of a house. However, it was necessary to draw a line somewhere between consumption and investment.

It may seem strange that GDP rises if there are more road accidents. This is partly because of greater activity by emergency services. On the contrary, one would intuitively like to see GDP diminishing in such circumstances. But this would be to confuse a measure of output (GDP) with a measure of welfare, which GDP is not. At most, GDP is a measure of the contribution of production to welfare. There are a great number of other dimensions to welfare that GDP does not claim to measure.

We shall be returning to these conventions throughout this book. They may be open to criticism, but it must not be overlooked that they have been the subject of lengthy discussions by national accountants and were often chosen for sound practical reasons. For example, we shall see in Chapter 10 that indirect taxes can be said to be counted twice over in GDP, but this was the only solution that met other criteria.

While the national accounts system has the above major limitations, it should not be criticised out of misunderstanding about its objectives and definitions. For example, many people fail to understand why GDP does not fall following major natural catastrophes (or terrorist attacks). This is because they misunderstand the definition of GDP, which, as we have seen, measures output during a given period. People tend to confuse GDP with the country's economic wealth. Undoubtedly, major calamities destroy part of the economic wealth (buildings, houses, roads and infrastructure*), but they do not, *per se*, constitute negative production and so do not directly contribute to a decline in GDP. Destruction can indirectly affect production in a negative or positive way. When a factory is destroyed it ceases production, but it also has to be rebuilt and this constitutes production. For this reason, paradoxically, it is possible for a natural catastrophe to have a positive impact (in the purely mathematical sense of the word "positive") on GDP.

The above remarks should also make it clear to the reader that GDP does not represent "the national wealth", as is sometimes said. National wealth is the stock of the nation's assets, while GDP is a flow of output. At the very most, GDP might be considered a measure of the change in national wealth. But even this is incorrect, since GDP does not contain the whole of this change because it excludes capital gains and losses. It is therefore preferable to speak of GDP as total output during a specific period.

Shortcuts

The national accounts are complicated and at the same time have important implications. For example, a major part of the EU member countries' contributions to the budget of the European Commission depends directly on their relative levels of GDP (GNI to be more precise). When methods are modified or figures are revised, it is useful for national accountants to know rapidly whether these modifications have "an impact on GDP", in their jargon. In order to find a quick answer to this question, the national accounts experts use certain "shortcuts". For example, they use this rule based on final demand: GDP is modified only if an element of final demand is modified.

---

* Only a very few economic accounting systems, and not the national accounts, include an evaluation of human capital. This is why human losses do not appear in this list.

Consider the following example. In 2004, the accounts for the year 2002 are recalculated using the database consisting of comprehensive company accounts. It then turns out, on the basis of these more reliable statistics, that the output of temporary employment services (in other words, the hiring of manpower) was substantially underestimated in the initial estimates. This leads to an appreciable increase in total output. Does this have an impact on GDP? The immediate answer is, no! The hiring of manpower is not part of household consumption; it is not investment; it does not enter foreign trade (or only to a very small extent). It therefore does not enter into final demand and is instead intermediate consumption. As a consequence, GDP is unaffected. This does not mean, however, that no modification has taken place. For one thing, the distribution of value added between the various branches has changed, with that of services increasing and that of manufacturing decreasing because of the increase in its intermediate consumption. However, the modification in total output is neutralised by an increase in intermediate consumption. See Exercise 7 for a practical application of this point.

This final demand rule works well in numerous cases. Take two other examples, software and VAT (Value Added Tax, a type of sales tax). The new system of national accounts SNA 93 introduced new rules for the treatment of software. Instead of being recorded as intermediate consumption, purchases of software were to be regarded as GFCF. Does this modification have an impact on GDP? The answer is, yes, because GFCF forms part of final demand, which is modified accordingly. Suppose the government decides to finance its expenditure by reducing income tax (which is unpopular) by 5 billion euros and by correspondingly increasing VAT (a less painful tax). This modification appears to be neutral at the macroeconomic level, since the deficit is unchanged. But that is not actually the case. Because final demand includes household consumption, which is measured at market prices and includes VAT, GDP will be increased by 5 billion euros (everything else remaining equal). It can therefore be shown that the precise origin of government financing (direct or indirect taxes) can affect the Maastricht public deficit criterion without any change in the deficit itself. This is because the denominator of the ratio on which the criterion is based is GDP. The ratio can therefore change even if the numerator, in this case the deficit, is unchanged. The national accounts are full of surprises.

On the other hand, GDP does not change if two elements of final demand are adjusted in opposite directions. For example, if the estimate for exports is reduced, and if this reduction is offset by an increase in final consumption, GDP remains unchanged.

Exercises   *Answers at www.SourceOECD.org/understandingnationalaccounts*

Exercise 1: Observations and forecasts

Go to the OECD website (*www.oecd.org*), find the most recent issue of the "Economic Outlook" and update Table 1 at the beginning of this chapter using the most recent figures. Comment on the differences between the new figures and the old. What has happened to bring about the change in the figures? In which direction did the OECD forecasters err?

Exercise 2: A simple calculation of GDP

Consider four firms: firm A, a mining enterprise, extracts iron ore; firm B, a steelmaker, uses iron to make steel sheets and ingots; firm C, a carmaker, makes automobiles using steel; firm D, a manufacturer of machinery and robots, also uses steel. Calculate the production, intermediate consumption and values added in millions of euros based on the following assumptions.

Firm A extracts 50 000 tonnes of ore, at 200 euros per tonne, its purchases during the period are limited to the purchase of one machine made by firm D, costing 10 million euros. Firm B produces 15 000 tonnes of steel sheet at 3 000 euros per tonne, having bought and used all the ore produced by firm A. Firm C has manufactured 5 000 vehicles and sold them all to households for 15 000 euros each, having purchased 20 million euros' worth of steel sheet from firm B, but using only 18 million euros' worth in the manufacture of its cars. In addition, Firm C imported 5 000 engines from a foreign subsidiary, each being valued at 4 000 euros, and purchased domestically 2 robots made by firm D. Firm D sold one machine for 10 million euros and two robots, each worth 5 million euros, having used 10 million euros' worth of steel sheet from firm B.

Calculate the GDP of this economy. Calculate also the final demand of this economy, assuming that it has no exports. Verify that GDP is equal to final demand. (Remember that purchases of machinery are not intermediate consumption, but GFCF).

Exercise 3: Relationship between current prices, volume and deflator

The table below shows the series for GDP growth at current prices and the GDP deflator growth rate in the case of France. GDP at current prices in 1995 was equal to 1 181 849 million euros. Calculate the series for GDP first in current prices and then in volume in millions of "1995 euros". Show how to calculate the growth of GDP in volume directly from the initial growth rates, without using absolute amounts and without using division.

	1995	1996	1997	1998
Gross domestic product at current prices (% growth rate)	3.37	2.57	3.22	4.37
(2) GDP deflator (% growth rate)	1.67	1.45	1.29	0.94
(3) GDP at current prices (Meuros)	1 181 849			

Exercise 4: Calculation of contributions to growth

The following table shows the French quarterly national accounts for Q3 2002, in volume, in millions of 1 995 euros. Using the box earlier in the text, calculate to two decimal places the breakdown of growth in Q3 2002 for the contributions to GDP of domestic demand excluding inventories, changes in inventories and net exports. Comment.

Quarterly national accounts, at 1995 prices

Million euros

	Q2 2002	Q3 2002
Gross domestic product	347 951	348 697
Imports	94 327	94 562
Domestic demand excluding inventories	343 796	344 638
Changes in inventories (including acquisitions of valuables)	−2 817	−3 885
Exports	101 299	102 505

Exercise 5: The public deficit and the Maastricht criterion

On the basis of the following table, determine whether France met the public deficit criterion (not more than 3% of GDP) during the period in question.

Billion euros	1996	1997	1998	1999	2000
Total expenditure	672.5	687.7	703.2	723.9	747.7
Total revenue	623.1	649.7	668.4	701.9	728.7
Gross domestic product	1 212.2	1 251.2	1 305.9	1 355.1	1 416.9

Exercise 6: Synonyms

There are a number of terms that are used in national accounts, but economists use a wide range of synonyms for them. Choose from the list in italics below all the correct synonyms for: (A) GDP at current prices; (B) GDP in volume; (C) GDP deflator; (D) public deficit. Beware that not all of them are synonyms for any of the above.

1. GNP 2. GNI at current prices 3. Nominal GDP 4. Sum of output in euros 5. GDP in quantities 6. GDP in value 7. GDP at constant prices 8. Sum of gross values added in volume 9. Deflated Net Domestic Product 10. Real GDP 11. GDP price index 12. Consumer price index 13. GDP at 1995 prices 14. Sum of deflated incomes 15. "Growth" 16. Financing capacity of public enterprises 17. General government net borrowing.

Exercise 7: Impact of modifications to GDP

(Follow-up to Exercise 2 and application of the "Shortcuts" Section.) In Exercise 2, you calculated the GDP of this economy. Let us now suppose that we omitted to mention that firm C, the car maker, hired manpower from firm E, the temporary employment agency, for the sum of 15 million euros. Has the GDP of the economy been modified by this fresh information? Confirm your reply by reconstituting the table for the different industries, with comments.

Exercise 8: Deflators and growth

There has recently been controversy regarding the comparability of growth as measured in Europe and in the United States. More particularly, this concerns the deflator for firms' investment in computers, now a very large item of expenditure. The statistical methods used in the United States mean that the relevant deflator falls faster than in Europe (see box in section 3 of Chapter 2). First, show why for the same growth in purchases of computers at current prices, this difference in statistical method leads to a difference in GDP growth in volume. Go on to explain why this difference in GDP diminishes (to a vanishing point) if European countries produce few computers (or none).

Chapter 2

DISTINGUISHING BETWEEN VOLUME AND PRICE INCREASES

Everyone wants the maximum possible growth, although today that the preference is for "durable" or "sustainable" growth. The generic term "growth" indicates the overall change in the quantity of goods and services produced and made available to consumers and investors. The prime task of national accounts is to separate out, within the change in the observed monetary aggregates, the part of growth that stems from a change in quantities from the part that is due to a change in prices. An increase in quantities or, as the national accountants would say, in "volumes" is generally a good thing. A rise in prices, known as inflation, is not generally good news. A change in a monetary aggregate has accordingly very limited interest in the national accounts. However, it takes on economic significance when, to use the national accountants' jargon, one carries out its "volume/price breakdown". This is why this highly technical chapter comes first, even before those on output and final uses.

1. A word of caution: compare volumes

The following table, taken from the OECD national accounts database, compares GDP growth for the Netherlands, Mexico and Turkey between 1980 and 2003. Looking at this table, one might get the impression that Mexico and Turkey posted formidable growth compared with the Netherlands. Indeed, while the Netherlands is reported to have annual average growth of 4.6%, Mexico was bounding along at 37.1% and was itself outstripped by Turkey, with 62.3%. This conclusion, however, contains a huge trap. It only takes a glance at the second line of the table's title to see the words "current prices", meaning that the table is comparing amounts calculated at the average prices of each year. Consequently, these amounts reflect the full impact of the rise in prices, or the inflation occurring between 1980 and 2003. As it happens, Mexico and Turkey are two countries that continued to suffer from galloping inflation during this period, whereas the Netherlands experienced significantly lower inflation starting at the end of the 1980s.

Average annual % GDP growth, 1980-2003

Current prices

Netherlands	+4.6
Mexico	+37.1
Turkey	+62.3

The above international comparison is therefore not meaningful. It is necessary to separate the wheat (the growth, understood as being "in volume") from the chaff (the inflation, or the change in prices). Table 1 shows the figures in volume, accompanied by those for the changes in prices. The performance of the Netherlands then turns out to be much better: its volume growth is only slightly lower than those of the other two countries, while its inflation is dramatically lower. ▶ I. The aim of this chapter is to explain in detail how statisticians set about distinguishing changes in volume from changes in prices, in other words arriving at what is known as the *volume/price breakdown*.

I. If, in addition, the volume growth is adjusted for population growth, the Netherlands performance comes out even better, with volume growth per head of 1.7% a year over the same period, compared with 0.5% for Mexico and 1.7% for Turkey.

But even if this second international comparison is correct, it still lacks something, since it provides information only on the changes and says nothing about the comparative *level of* each country's GDP. Filling this gap seems like a simple matter. One takes GDP at current prices and then makes two modifications. First, divide by the number of inhabitants to obtain GDP per head, so as to avoid comparing things that are not strictly comparable. Second, use the same currency. OECD practice is to express all amounts in United States dollars, but one could just as well have used the euro or the Mexican peso; the essential thing is to use one single unit of account. Table 2 shows the level of GDP per head for these three countries, expressed in US dollars. What does it tell us? That the inhabitants of the Netherlands have an annual average income well above those of the other two countries: if the figure for the Netherlands is conventionally equal to 100, that of Turkey is 10.7 and that of Mexico is 19.3. But are we comparing things that are genuinely comparable?

Table 1. GDP, volume and price indices
Average annual growth in percentage, 1980-2003

	Volume	Prices
Netherlands	+2.3	+2.3
Mexico	+2.4	+33.9
Turkey	+4.1	+60.0

Source: OECD (2006), *National Accounts of OECD Countries, Volume I, Main Aggregates, 1993-2004, 2006 Edition*, OECD, Paris.
StatLink: *http://dx.doi.org/10.1787/508232480000*

Table 2. GDP per capita
2003

	In US dollars	Netherlands = 100
Netherlands	31 602	100.0
Mexico	6 091	19.3
Turkey	3 385	10.7

Source: OECD(2006), *National Accounts of OECD Countries: Volume I, Main Aggregates, 1993-2004, 2006 Edition*, OECD, Paris.
StatLink: *http://dx.doi.org/10.1787/731223078504*

2 DISTINGUISHING BETWEEN VOLUME
AND PRICE INCREASES
2. The volume/price breakdown applied to
changes over time

The answer is not really, since even when the figures are expressed in a common unit of account, they fail to obey our watchword of only comparing volumes. Prices of certain goods and services can be very different from one country to another. For example, the price of renting a 100 m^2 apartment may be 2 000 euros in Amsterdam (the Netherlands), while for the same money one can rent a 300 m^2 apartment in Istanbul (Turkey) or Mexico City. One therefore has to go further and eliminate differences in price levels so as to be able to compare solely the *volumes* producedin each country and not figures that are affected by differences in price levels. The OECD makes this adjustment by using "purchasing power parity". Table 3, based on this adjustment, provides the proper comparison for volume among the three countries. While it confirms that the standard of living in the Netherlands is much higher, it raises the levels of GDP per head for Turkey and Mexico. This international comparison of absolute levels in the national accounts uses what the statisticians describe as the *spatial volume/price breakdown*. This technique will be described in more detail in Chapter 3. The present chapter will focus on *temporal volume/price breakdown*.

Table 3. **GDP per capita using purchasing power parities**
2003

	In US dollars, adjusted for purchasing power parity	Netherlands = 100
Netherlands	30 317	100.0
Mexico	9 543	31.5
Turkey	6 937	22.9

Source: OECD(2006), *National Accounts of OECD Countries: Volume I, Main Aggregates, 1993-2004, 2006 Edition*, OECD, Paris.
StatLink: *http://dx.doi.org/10.1787/853524217471*

2. The volume/price breakdown applied to changes over time

To respect the watchword "compare volumes", it is necessary to calculate national accounts aggregates in volume. To do this, the first step is to take detailed statistics, product by product, each one expressed in volume. Then, in a second step, aggregate them, or calculate their total.

Generally speaking, the detailed statistics typically available to national accountants are of three types: *a)* statistics expressed in quantities, such as the number of tonnes of steel produced; *b)* statistics expressed in current prices (also called "in value"), such as figures taken from company accounts; and *c)* price indices, such as the numerous components of the household consumer price index (CPI). Statistics of type *a)* are used directly by national accountants to calculate the change in volume within the detailed classifications. The variation in the output volume of a specific type of steel, as measured in the national accounts, will then equal the variation in the tonnage produced of this steel.

If statistics expressed in quantities are not available, national accountants combine statistics of types *b)* and *c)* to obtain an indicator of volume. As we saw in the first fundamental equation in Chapter 1, if one divides the change in magnitude expressed in current prices (or "in value") by the change in the price of the corresponding products, one obtains a measure of the change in volume. This is what national accountants call "deflation". Exercise 1, at the end of this chapter, illustrates a very simple case of "deflation".

To calculate macroeconomic growth, national accountants use hundreds of statistical series that are either directly expressed in quantity or derived via this process of deflation. In the case of France – and the figures are probably similar in other countries – almost 85% (in terms of value added) of the detailed series of output in volume in the national accounts are derived from the deflation of a series at current prices by an appropriate price index. In order for the deflation approach to work well, it is necessary to have good figures for sales or corresponding monetary flows (at current prices) and suitable price indices. National statistical offices in the OECD countries construct indicators of this kind, the best-known being the indices of turnover, of consumer prices and producer prices. These indicators are essential for the national accounts, but to enumerate them would go beyond the scope of this textbook. In the remainder of this chapter, we shall deal only with the problem – quite difficult in itself – of how to combine (*i.e.* aggregate) these detailed statistics in volume.

3. The difficulties of aggregation

If we had a very simple economy that produced and consumed just one product, there would be no difficulty in measuring the macroeconomic growth in volume. One would simply have to calculate the number of tonnes (or, more generally, any physical units) of this single product. However, the economy is made up of a multitude of products, goods and services, very different from each other. How can one add these together in order to obtain a macroeconomic indicator? First, we need a common unit of measurement. One could, for example, add the physical units expressed in tonnes. But how meaningful would it be to add tonnes of apples to tonnes of clothes and to tonnes of battle tanks? The result might possibly be useful for the logistic management of an army on the move, but it obviously has little macroeconomic meaning. Is it even legitimate to add, one by one, all the cars produced in a country in order to create a macroeconomic indicator? Not really, since adding a small cheap car to a luxury car would give a false picture of the total output: a large car "counts" for more in economic terms than a small one. Therefore, we have a problem of "aggregation" that is fundamental to macroeconomic measurement.

The answer to this problem is fairly obvious to economists. It consists of relying on the price structure. Once products are expressed in monetary units, it becomes legitimate to add them together. Therefore, adding the number of small cars multiplied by their price to the number of luxury cars multiplied by their price will equal the total turnover of the carmakers, and it will also equal the total value of cars bought by households. These aggregate figures, in which units are "weighted" by their prices, are additive and have a macroeconomic meaning. The relative price of products provides a good economic weighting system for physical quantities because it represents the relative cost of manufacturing the products and/or the relative utilities attributed to them by consumers. Clearly, prices are not always set by the relative costs or the relative utilities, and they might be influenced by monopolistic behaviour or by distortions due to taxation. Even so, broadly speaking, the structure of relative prices provides a valid weighting system.

To calculate volumes, national accountants therefore rely on the summation of physical units weighted by the prices of these units. This still leaves one problem, however. Since the aim is to measure the change in volume, one wants to compare several different periods. Unfortunately, prices vary at the same time as the physical quantities. It will therefore be necessary to "freeze" the variation in prices. To calculate the evolution in volume between two periods, national accountants compare the sum of the physical units in the first period, weighted by a given price structure, with the sum of the physical units in the second period, weighted by the *same* price structure. An example will make this easier to grasp.

Let us suppose that there are two types of cars, small cars, which we shall call "s" and large cars, which we shall call "l". We shall denote the number of units of the small cars by Q_s and the number of units of the large cars by Q_l. We shall add to these variables a subscript t to signify that this is the value of the variable in period t. For example, $Q_{s,t}$ signifies the number of units of small cars produced (or purchased) in period t. P_s denotes the price of the small car and P_l that of the large. In order to calculate the evolution in volume between period t and period t', national accountants compare the amount $(Q_{s,t} \cdot P_s) + (Q_{l,t} \cdot P_l)$, which is the volume in period t, with the amount $(Q_{s,t'} \cdot P_s) + (Q_{l,t'} \cdot P_l)$, which is the volume in period t'. It can be seen that prices remain constant in this comparison, with P_s and P_l used for both periods. It is in fact possible to choose different price pairs: those of period t, those of period t', or a combination of the two. However, regardless of the choice, the pairing will be the same for the two periods. Hence the terminology used to describe this system of calculating volumes, namely *constant-price accounting*. Exercise 2, at the end of this chapter, provides an example of constant-price accounting.

The manipulation of volumes can produce certain surprises for those unfamiliar with the system. Let us suppose that the price of the large cars is twice that of the small ones. Let us also suppose that the carmaker produces exactly the same total number of cars (say, 100) in both years but that the proportion of the large cars rises from 50% to 80%. Let us calculate the variation in volume using the previous formula. This equals $(80 \times 2) + (20 \times 1)$, which is the volume of cars produced in the second year, divided by $(50 \times 2) + (50 \times 1)$, which is the volume of cars produced in the first. The result of this calculation is 1.2, signifying an increase of 20%. ▶ II. This means that, despite the fact that the total number of cars expressed in units has

II. This example shows that to measure the change in volume there is no need to know the absolute price of the small or large cars. All that matters is their relative pricing.

remained unchanged, the national accounts record a growth of 20%. Is this really a surprise? No, because the volume in the national accounts measures not the increase in the number of cars, but the utility derived by the consumers. This utility has indeed increased by 20% when measured using the yardstick of relative prices. This is not surprising, since the utility of a luxury car is greater than that of a small car. It is essential to fully understand the difference between an increase in quantities and an increase in volume in order to grasp the measurement of growth as recorded in the national accounts.

In particular, volume takes into account all kinds of differences in quality. For example, the national accounts do not add together tonnes of top-grade petrol and tonnes of second-grade petrol, since the two products are not entirely substitutes for each other, despite their similarity. The national accountants also consider the type of sales outlet involved (small local store or supermarket), since this is one of the characteristics of the product, and in principle will not add together two identical products distributed through different retailing circuits. The impact of taking into account these differences in quality is most striking in the case of computers (see Box 1). This case illustrates another essential difficulty of measuring volume and prices when new products are introduced into the market. In this case, constant-price accounting is an inadequate instrument, because it presupposes that all products existed in the first period of comparison, which, by definition, cannot be true for entirely new products (mobile telephones, for example, in the middle 1990s).

4. Volume indices and price indices

At this point, it is necessary to take a fairly long mathematical digression to explain the notions of volume index and price index so that the reader can fully understand how volume is measured in the national accounts. A **volume index** is a weighted average of the changes between two periods in the quantities of a given set of goods or services. Traditionally, these indices are given a standard value of 100 for a given period, although in this text the indices are implicitly standardised as 1, and not 100. This is of little importance, however, since both volume and price indices are numbers that can be interpreted only in terms of change. By convention, the time period used as the starting point will be denoted as being period 0 and the period being compared with it as period t. The two time periods can be consecutive or non-consecutive.

The ratios of the quantity or the price of a given product in period t to the quantity or the price of the same product in period 0, *i.e.* q_t/q_0 or p_t/p_0, are known as the quantity ratio and the price ratio, respectively. The quantity and price ratios are independent of the units in which the quantities and prices are measured. Most of the indices can be expressed in the form of weighted averages of these price or quantity ratios, or can be derived from them. The various formulae differ mainly in the weighting attached to the individual price or quantity ratios and in the particular type of mean used – arithmetic, geometric, harmonic, etc.

Box 1. Measured in the national accounts, the volume of computers rises very sharply

Let us suppose that in year A, 1 000 computers of type X were sold, having a power of P_x and a clock speed of V_x. Let us now suppose that in year A + 1, 1 000 computers were again sold, this time of type Y, having a power of P_y and a clock speed of V_y, for the same unit price. The spectacular advance in microprocessor technology means that P_y and V_y are considerably greater than P_x and V_x.

The national accounts are not going to say that the volume of computers is equal to the number of computers. Account will be taken of the quality of each computer and these qualities will be weighted by their prices. In most cases, however, the computer of type Y did not even exist in the previous period A so that no price is available to provide the weighting. The statisticians then carry out econometric (also known as "hedonic") studies of the relationship between the prices of computers and their key characteristics, such as their power and their speed, the purpose being to determine what value purchasers of computers put on improvements to each of these characteristics. Using these relationships, they estimate what the computer type Y would have cost in year A, had it existed. Let us suppose, for example, that the price of the new computer type Y is estimated to be 20% higher than that of the computer of type X in year A. This means that the price of Y has decreased by 20% since year A. It is a realistic hypothesis, as it is well known that PC prices fall very rapidly even when their power is increasing. The volume of computers in the national accounts for year A + 1 will therefore be calculated "at year A prices", *i.e.* at prices that are 20% higher than those of year A. The volume of computers as measured in the national accounts therefore rises much faster than the number of computers bought. It is indeed this phenomenon that explains why the national accounts now make use of chained accounts rather than constant-price accounts (see following boxes).

The same phenomenon would be observed in cars if the prices of Mercedes fell to become closer to those of Fiats. The public would buy Mercedes instead of Fiats, and the national accounts would record a sharp increase in volume, even though the number of cars sold remained unchanged. Unfortunately, this phenomenon does not occur in cars.

The two most commonly used indices are those of Laspeyres and Paasche, named after two 19th-century statisticians. Most national accounts systems (and in particular the European systems) use Laspeyres indices to calculate volumes and Paasche indices to calculate changes in prices. Both the Laspeyres and Paasche indices can be defined as weighted averages of price or quantity ratios, the weights being the values at current prices of goods or services in one or other of the two periods being compared.

Let $v_{ij} = p_{ij} \, q_{ij}$ be the value at current prices of product i in period j. The Laspeyres volume index (L_q) is a weighted average of the quantity ratios:

$$L_q = \sum_i \frac{v_{i0} \cdot \dfrac{q_{it}}{q_{i0}}}{\sum_i v_{i0}} \tag{1}$$

The period providing the weights for the index is known as the "base" period. It typically (but not always) coincides with the "reference" period for which the index has a standardised value of 100. Since the summation always involves the same set of goods and services, it is possible to dispense with the subscript i in expressions of type (1). And since by definition v_i is equal to $p_i q_i$, it is also possible to replace it in (1) to obtain (2):

$$L_q = \frac{\sum p_0 q_t}{\sum p_0 q_0} \tag{2}$$

Algebraically, expressions (1) and (2) are identical. This means that the change in volume at constant prices can be calculated in two ways with the same result: either as the average of the *changes* in quantity of the various products weighted by the values at current prices in the base year; or, as the amount of quantities in period t multiplied by the prices in the base year divided by the value at current prices in the base year. Exercise 3, at the end of this chapter, illustrates this result using the example given earlier of the small and large cars.

The Paasche price index can be defined in reciprocal fashion to the Laspeyres index, applying the values at current prices in period t as weights and using a harmonic mean of the price and ratio quantities instead of an arithmetic mean.

The Paasche price index P_p is defined as follows:

$$P_p = \frac{\sum v_t}{\sum v_t \cdot \frac{p_0}{p_t}} = \frac{\sum p_t q_t}{\sum p_0 q_t} \tag{3}$$

It will be seen from this formula that what we have is indeed a price index, since in this case it is the prices that vary and the quantities that remain fixed, in contrast to the volume indices we saw earlier. The Paasche index can be interpreted as the reciprocal of a Laspeyres index "turned backwards", in other words the inverse of a Laspeyres index for period 0, with period t as the base period. The reciprocity between the Laspeyres and Paasche indices leads to numerous symmetries that can be exploited in calculations.

In particular, the product of a Laspeyres *volume* index and the corresponding Paasche *price* index is equal to the change in the value, at current prices, of the goods or services between period 0 and t, *i.e.*:

$$L_q . P_p = \frac{\sum p_0 q_t}{\sum p_0 q_0} \cdot \frac{\sum p_t q_t}{\sum p_0 q_t} = \frac{\sum v_t}{\sum v_0} \tag{4}$$

Relationship (4) is fundamental in national accounts. Reading it from right to left, it shows that the variation of an aggregate at current prices is equal to the product of the volume index and the price index. It expresses mathematically what we called the "first fundamental equation" in Chapter 1. This equation is constantly exploited in national accounts. For example, it is used to obtain indirectly the volume index by dividing the relative variation in values by the Paasche price index, in a method discussed earlier and known as "deflation":

$$L_q = \frac{\dfrac{\sum v_t}{\sum v_0}}{P_p} \tag{5}$$

Because it is generally easier, and less costly, to calculate price indices than volume indices, it is the usual practice in economic statistics to calculate volumes using deflation. This practice is constantly applied in national accounts (see Exercise 4).

5. Constant prices

Let us now consider a chronological series of Laspeyres volume indices, *i.e.*:

$$\frac{\sum p_0 q_0}{\sum p_0 q_0}, \frac{\sum p_0 q_1}{\sum p_0 q_0} \dots \frac{\sum p_0 q_t}{\sum p_0 q_0} \tag{6}$$

If one multiplies all the items in the series by the common denominator $\Sigma p_0 q_0$, one obtains the so-called "constant-price" series, which we saw an example of earlier, in the case of the small and large cars:

$$\sum p_0 q_0, \sum p_0 q_1 \dots \sum p_0 q_t \tag{7}$$

The relative movements of this series, from one period to another, are identical to those of the corresponding Laspeyres indices given by (6), since the two series differ only by a scalar equal to the first term of the second series. The term "constant prices" is justified by the fact that these aggregates use the price structure of a fixed period, in this case period 0.

This system of accounts at constant prices was widely used by national accountants since it has one very useful property, namely that the aggregates obtained are additive; in other words, it is legitimate to add or subtract "bits" of these accounts. For example, the volume of output for cars plus trucks is exactly equal to the volume of output of the two together. It will be seen later that this property of additivity is lost when this system is abandoned in favour of the more complicated volume indicators recommended in the current version of the international manual SNA 1993, and applied by nearly all OECD countries.

The units in which these accounts at constant prices are expressed nevertheless remain artificial. Given that what is involved is the multiplication of a dimensionless series (the series of indices in (6)) by a value in the current prices of the base year ($\Sigma p_0 q_0$), one might conclude that the result is a series expressed in the current monetary unit (billions of euros, example). However, since the prices are those of a past year and not current prices, the terminology "accounts in [base year] [monetary units]" is used – for example "in 1995 euros" for the euro area.* Although this terminology is widely used, it does have an inherent weakness: there are as many values of the "1995 euro" as there are transactions in the national accounts. The series for household consumption in volume uses a value of the "1995 euro" equal to that deflated by the household consumer price indicator, whereas the series for GFCF uses a value deflated by the price index for GFCF, and so on.

When the national accounts are calculated at constant prices and the base period is 2000, one speaks of aggregates "at 2000 prices". But, increasingly, national accounts in volume are not strictly calculated at constant prices, but are obtained through a chaining process of constant prices for the previous year. It is this complication that we are now going to tackle below.

6. "Chained" accounts and the loss of additivity

Without going into the detailed problems of volume indices, it is relatively easy to explain why constant prices are not fully satisfactory for economic analysis. The choice of a fixed year means that one is using price structures that become more and more remote from the current structure, the further one moves away from the base year. Take the French case, for example. Prior to recent reforms of the French national accounts, the pattern of relative prices used in France for calculating changes in volume in the current year dated as far back as 18 years, because the French national accounts continued using the old "base 1980" until 1998. The increasing remoteness from the base period can clearly lead to measurement distortions. For example, the "quantities" of computers bought towards the end of the 1990s were rising steeply from year to year. It was hardly reasonable to weight these increases using the price structure of the year 1980, when the relative prices of computers were very high. On the contrary, it was precisely because the relative prices of computers fell sharply that the market for computers boomed. Weighting this increase using the old price structures led to changes in volume being overstated and the decrease in prices being understated in the more recent periods, thus distorting the historical picture (see Box 2).

It is for this reason that the national accounts use what is now called the "chain-linking method". The most widely used method involves three stages. In the first stage, the accounts are calculated at the prices of the previous period. The price structure of the previous period is valid for weighting the changes in quantity in the current period. In this way, one obtains the change in the aggregates between the preceding and the current period, referred to in the case of annual accounts, as "accounts at previous year's prices". Next, these changes are chained (*i.e.* multiplied each one with the subsequent one),

---

* It may seem somewhat absurd to talk of "1995 euros" when the euro was not yet in existence in that year. But this is a presentation commonly used in all time series in European national accounts. All series denominated in euros are expressed in euros even for periods before 1999, the year the euro was launched. Prior to 1999, pricing corresponds to the series in national currencies (the franc, for example, for France) divided by the exchange rate between the national currency and the euro on 1 January 1999 (6.55957/1 in the case of the franc).

Box 2. **An example of distortion due to the use of constant prices**

The use of constant prices taken from a distant base year leads to distortions in the evolution of volume, which become all the more significant when there are substantial variations in relative prices. The best-known example is that of computers. Using the case of France, let us calculate the volume of equipment GFCF, including traditional types of machinery as well as computers (excluding transport). Between 1980 and 2000, the price index for computers, with 1980 = 100, plummeted to 8.7. In the same period, the price index for other types of equipment rose, reaching 136.1 at the end of the period. Now let us compare the volume of the aggregate formed by computers plus the other types of equipment (see Figure 1). When one uses the constant prices of the year 1980, this combination shows a rise of 316% between the two dates. When one uses the constant prices of the previous year and then chains them, the figure is only 143%, and this is the correct figure. The first figure, based on the structure of relative prices in 1980 overstates the recent increases in investment in computers, increases that are explained in large part precisely because the relative prices of computers have fallen.

---

aggregate by aggregate. In this way, one obtains a series of growth rates each of which uses the price structure of the previous period. Finally, in order to provide volume series in levels, this series is multiplied by the value of the accounts at the current prices of the reference year, currently, for many countries, the year 2000 (but this changes every five years).

The advantage of the chain-linking method is that the previous period's price structure is more relevant than the price structure of a fixed period from further into the past. It can be shown, however, that in theory an even better measure of volume changes is obtained when the average price structure of the previous and current period is used. Chained volumes using the previous year's structure are usually described as "Laspeyres chains"; indices that use the average of the previous and the current period are described as "Fisher chains". For practical reasons, most countries use Laspeyres chains, although both Canada and the United States are now using Fisher chains (see Box 3). The differences between the two are generally very small. Fisher chains are well-suited to the method used to produce national accounts in the United States. But Fischer chains are considered too complicated by other countries in particular because they are entirely non additive. These countries indeed use production processes for their national accounts that require the use of accounting identities, thus necessitating at least additive accounts in prices of the previous year.

Presentation of the accounts based on Laspeyres chained volumes should be called "accounts at previous year's prices, chained, reference 2000". However, in practice, countries and economists continue to use the term "constant prices" or even describe the series as "in 2000 euros". (Exercise 5, at the end of this chapter, shows a chained-volume presentation in three stages.) The advantage of chained accounts compared with accounts at constant prices is that they avoid distortions arising from changes in the price structure over time and the overstatement discussed earlier. The United States, whose statistical office was the first to introduce chained accounts, has calculated that the use of a

DISTINGUISHING BETWEEN VOLUME
AND PRICE INCREASES
7. Unpleasant practical consequences
  of chain linking

2

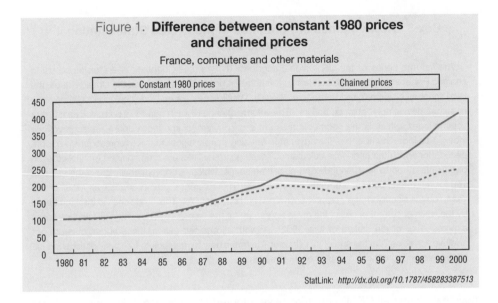

Figure 1. **Difference between constant 1980 prices and chained prices**

France, computers and other materials

StatLink: *http://dx.doi.org/10.1787/458283387513*

US GDP between 2001 and 2003: instead of being 2.7% annually, US GDP growth would have been 4.3%, which seems unrealistic. The bulk of the difference comes, once more, from computers, whose large quantity increases in 2001-2003 would have been overestimated had the pricing of 1996 been used.

The great disadvantage of the chain-linking method is that additivity of the chain-linked volume levels is no longer possible. In particular, and this is of fundamental importance, it is no longer possible to derive one aggregate in volume by taking a combination (sum of or difference between) other aggregates also expressed in volume. For example, an item in a less detailed classification is not exactly equal to the sum of the corresponding items in a more detailed one. Exercise 6, at the end of this chapter, shows how it is possible to calculate with all due rigour an aggregate that is not supplied by a statistical institute. Box 5, "Contributions and additivity", shows that this problem also affects the calculation of contributions to growth.

7. Unpleasant practical consequences of chain linking

Chain linking has now been adopted by nearly all OECD countries, both for annual and quarterly accounts. As explained above, it has a substantial advantage compared to the use of pricing in a fixed year because it gives more accurate aggregate volume *growth rates*. It has, however, a major practical drawback because given the loss in additivity in chain-linked levels, users cannot easily make simple calculations based on accounting identities, a situation that makes the life of macroeconomists quite miserable. For example,

2 DISTINGUISHING BETWEEN VOLUME
AND PRICE INCREASES
7. Unpleasant practical consequences
of chain linking

Box 3. **How volumes are obtained in the United States national accounts**

The volume series of the US national accounts (NIPAs, see Chapter 12) are obtained using chained Fisher volume indices that are currently "referenced" to year 2002 (in the United States, the term "reference" is preferred to the term "base"). These series are entitled "chained (2002) dollars", or sometimes, simply "chained dollars". The volume change of each quarter is compiled as a Fisher volume index, which is the geometric mean of a Laspeyres volume index and a Paasche volume index. This index number has the advantage of using price weights that are representative of both periods for which the change is calculated. These quarterly links are then chained (multiplied each one to the other) to form an index number time series, which is conventionally given the value of 100 for the reference year, currently the year 2002. This reference year changes every four or five years, on the occasion of a comprehensive revision of the NIPAs. This time series is then multiplied by the value at current prices of the given aggregate for the year 2002. Thus users obtain time series expressed in "billion dollars of year 2002". As with all chained series, these aggregates are not additive. Exercise 7, at the end of this chapter, illustrates how to manipulate forecasts of the US data, taking into account these complex chained series.

now that almost all OECD countries have adopted chain linking, it is not possible for a scrupulous economist to derive a simple total, such as the volume time series of total final demand based on the sum of internal plus external final demand. More generally, the second fundamental equation of Chapter 1, GDP = C + GCF + X − M, does not hold mathematically for volume time series expressed in chain-linked levels because there is an additional residual term between the two elements of this equality. This residual term has no economic interpretation.

In practice, economists regularly use totals, sub-totals or differences to make their economic models function. The less scrupulous (or those in a hurry) simply ignore the problem of non-additivity and continue to use these identities as if they were still valid. As the residual term is often small, this remains acceptable in many cases. However, it becomes imprudent when manipulating aggregates containing time series with significant differences in relative pricing over time, such as the pricing of computers compared to other machinery.

In the OECD, the main forecasting model of the Economics Department ("Interlink") functions, like others, with sums and differences. However, because the OECD wants to obtain exactly what OECD countries publish, it is obligated to be as scrupulous as possible. Thus, all totals, sub-totals or differences are obtained through a two-steps process that replicates almost exactly the chain-linking calculation made by the national accounts of each country. For example, total final demand, as in our example above, is not compiled directly but in two steps. First, one calculates separately internal demand and external demand in volume terms expressed *in prices of the preceding period.* This is obtained via the application of the growth rate of each of these variables to the current price level of the preceding year. Second, the sum of the two amounts will be calculated, and the corresponding correct growth rate can be derived from it. This is a valid process because volumes expressed in *prices of the preceding year* are additive, at least for countries that use chained Laspeyres indices (most OECD countries). It is a very good approximation for the few countries that use Fisher indices (USA, Canada).

An interesting feature of this scrupulous approach is that it does not use any of the volume levels expressed in chain-linked terms. Only *growth rates and levels at current prices* are used. The question is therefore raised: why do statistical offices continue to publish volume time series in chained-linked levels? The answer seems to be that it is by force of habit, since volume time series in chain-linked levels are of no real use; they cannot be used in accounting identities, and they cannot be used to compile shares. They can only be used to derive growth rates. But then why not simply publish growth rates? This is typically why the US Bureau of Economic Analysis (BEA) recently stopped publishing some volume series expressed as chained-linked levels (*i.e.* "in 2002 dollars"), since these results were likely to be misinterpreted by users.

Last, but not least, we should consider the treatment of two variables that, by definition, have no meaning when expressed in terms of growth rates: the volume of changes in inventories and the volume of changes in net exports. These two variables appear in the main aggregate table for each OECD country in the *OECD Economic Outlook*. They are not expressed in terms of growth rates (as all other variables) but in terms of *contributions to GDP growth*. This is because growth rates have no meaning for these variables since they can be negative in one period and positive in the next, or conversely. These variables are therefore shown in terms of their contributions to GDP growth. If it is deemed essential to present them in terms of chain-linked *levels*, one simple solution is to calculate these levels so that they correspond to the level which would generate the exact contribution to growth as if the data were additive. ▶ III. This may seem complicated, but it is in fact simple and is illustrated in Exercise 7. See also the box "Going a step further: chain-linked levels of changes in inventories and other similar variables", at the end of this chapter.

Overall, the rationale of this subsection has been to show that because of the loss of additivity due to chain linking, volume series of national accounts expressed as chain-linked levels should be replaced by growth rates and/or contributions to growth. In particular, tables of contributions to growth are the only tables in volume that remain additive (when they are compiled correctly using additive accounts), regardless of whether Laspeyres or Fisher indices are used. Thus, it is more than probable that econometric models will increasingly use contributions to growth, and statistical offices should give these a high priority.

III. At present, many OECD countries calculate the level of chained net exports simply as the difference between chain-linked imports and chain-linked exports. But this approach does not result in an exact amount for the contribution of net exports to GDP.

8. The special cases

Since the national accounts cover the entire economy, they include certain products for which the notion of quantity is not always clear. The first case is that of unique products. For example, it is very difficult to calculate the change in volume for the output of shipyards because it is practically never the same ship that is built in successive years. Each ship is a unique product made up of a multitude of variable elements. In that case, how is one to make a comparison between the two years?

A second example is that of services provided between firms, such as software maintenance, or the services of business-law firms. How is the quantity of these services to be defined? One possibility is to rely on ancillary indicators like the number of hours worked. For example, the quantity of software maintenance could be regarded as equal to the number of hours worked by the computer experts. A very similar result could be obtained by using a volume indicator derived by deflating the turnover of the maintenance firms by an hourly wage index. This is what the national accountants often do in practice. However, the result is open to dispute. For one thing, this indicator implicitly assumes that there is no productivity gain affecting these software experts, which is not a realistic hypothesis. Fortunately, the measurement of the volume of these services does not affect GDP because they are intermediate consumption, and only elements contributing to final demand affect GDP (see the box "Shortcuts" in Chapter 1). How such services are measured nevertheless affects the allocation of GDP among sectors.

This difficulty crops up especially when measuring the volume of output for public services, which account for a very substantial part of GDP, since they include education and public health care, defence, law and order and general administration, all of which are elements of final demand. In these cases, there is simply no price available, since by definition this output is not offered for sale. In principle, therefore, one cannot even use deflation. Nevertheless, these services have a cost, consisting mainly of the pay received by the public employees, plus various types of intermediate consumption (for example, electricity, telecommunications, stationery and other office supplies) and also of consumption of fixed capital (wear and tear, for example, on school and hospital buildings). In order to calculate the volume of output, these costs will have to be deflated and then added together. For example, salaries can be deflated by a salary index for teachers, public hospital staff, military personnel and other government workers. As with the example of the software-service providers, this method implies constant productivity for these categories of personnel, which is disputable to say the least.

For this reason, many statistical offices are considering introducing direct indicators of volume, known as "output indicators". For example, in the case of education, the direct indicator might be the number of pupils successfully completing their schooling, although this indicator has the defect of considering all pupils as identical and assuming that the standard of examinations remains constant. In the case of public hospital services, the indicator could be the number of patients weighted by the cost of treatment, with a careful distinction being made between the different types of treatment. This is a highly promising indicator.

Unfortunately, it is not easy to find suitable indicators for the output of other services rendered by general government. For example, how is one to assess the output of tax inspectors, firemen or members of the armed forces? For these branches of general government, one is reduced to deflating the costs – and in particular, deflating wages paid by an index of salaries. The usual practice is to deflate wages paid by the increase in basic wage rates agreed upon by the government and employee representatives. However, the government's wage bill will change not only because of these agreed upon changes to the basic wage but also because of changes in the composition of the labour force: if there are more staff in higher grades this year compared to last year, then the government wage bill will rise. In addition, in most countries the wage scales for government employees provide for regular increases based on years of service. Note that a deflation process that depends only on agreed upon changes to the basic wage will mean that increases in the government wage bill that arise either because more staff are being hired in senior grades or because the government labour force is ageing (and presumably becoming more productive) will count as increases in the volume of output. There is, however, not much empirical evidence to show that the output of government increases either because more high-grade civil servants are employed or because the average length of service is increasing. It may or may not be true, but this is the best that national accountants can do at the present time.

The volume/price breakdown is even more difficult in the case of industries such as banking and insurance. We shall see in Chapter 4 that national accountants measure the output of these activities "by difference": the difference between interest receipts and payments in the case of the banks, and the difference between insurance premiums received and insurance indemnities paid out in the case of insurance. This way of measuring current price output provides no clear indication of how to allocate output between volume and price. The definition of volume in the case of these services therefore remains somewhat vague, and countries use different methods.

Other special cases relate to trade and transport margins and to taxes on products. Many countries estimate their national accounts using what is known as a supply and use balance (see Chapter 10) using the following equation:

Production
+ Imports
+ Trade and transport margins
+ Taxes on products
– Subsidies on products
= Intermediate consumption
+ Final uses

In order to establish this equilibrium in volume, "taxes and subsidies in volume" and "margins in volume" must be estimated. These are strange concepts, to say the least, since they relate to prices and comprise no element of quantity.

The convention adopted is as follows: the volumes are seen as equal to the tax (or marginal tax rate) of the base year (which is the previous year when using chain-linked Laspeyres) applied to the tax base of the current year, itself valued in volume terms. For example, the Value Added Tax (VAT) at 2000 prices on the consumption of cars in year 2001 would equal the VAT rate for the year 2000 applied to the the consumption of cars in the year 2001, at 2000 prices. In the case of a basic product, the VAT in volume will therefore move exactly in line with the tax base in volume. Exactly the same will be true of the subsidies and margins in volume at the basic level (see box below for an exception). National accountants attempt to present taxes and margins in volume, and – stranger still – create price indices for taxes and margins, only because they want to provide the same presentation for accounts in volume as for accounts at current prices.

Box 4. **The case of margins on computers**

As explained above, the volume trade margin on sales of computers evolves, by definition, in line with the volume of computer purchases. However, in many countries national accountants measure the volume of computer purchases not by the number of computers sold, but, to simplify, by their calculating power, and this power evolves much more rapidly than the number of computers sold. Is it then reasonable to think that the trade margin in volume on computers evolves in line with computer purchases in volume? This is tantamount to saying that the volume of the commercial service produced by a seller of computers in a retail outlet (or on the Internet) is proportional to the power of the computer – not a very convincing assumption. In fact, the volume of the commercial service is the same for a powerful computer as for a not-so-powerful one. To this extent, it would seem that the national accounts overstate the volume of output of the commercial service in the case of computers. Fortunately, the amounts involved are small and do not affect GDP, only the distribution of value added between industry and trade.

---

9. And what about the price indices?

So far, not much has been said about price indices because we preferred to concentrate on the estimation of volumes. In practice, however, once one has defined the method for calculating volumes, the method for calculating price indices is also entirely determined, because of the first fundamental equation set out in Chapter 1: *the variation in a variable at current prices breaks down exactly into its variation in volume and its variation in price.* This principle has been confirmed by formula (4) in the present chapter. Since the variation in current prices is a simple and self-evident notion, and since we have defined above the variations in volume, there is nothing to add on price indices apart from saying that the variation in prices is obtained by dividing an index at current prices by a volume index. Remember that when volume is expressed via a Laspeyres index, the result of this division is – by definition – a Paasche index (chained, in the case of chained accounts), and not a Laspeyres index.

In fact, macroeconomists make less use of price indices in the national accounts (which they often refer to as "implicit price indices" or "implicit deflators") than they do of volumes. In order to monitor inflation, they often prefer to use the Consumer Price Index (CPI) rather than the deflator of household consumption. For one thing, the CPI is available monthly and the household-consumption deflator quarterly at best. In the United States, however, macroeconomists are increasingly using the deflator of household consumption (called "Personal Consumption Expenditure (PCE) Implicit Price Index" – see Chapter 12). In the national accounts, the price index of household consumption is also widely used to calculate the purchasing power of household gross disposable income (see Chapter 6).

Box 5. Contributions and additivity

The problem of non-additivity in chained accounts also affects the calculation of contributions to growth. Let us recall first the method used for calculating a contribution. Using a simplified example, let us assume there are only two aggregates in GDP: household consumption, denoted by C_t, and exports, denoted by X_t. GDP_t will denote GDP in year t. Δ will be used to indicate the variation in an aggregate, so that ΔGDP will signify the variation of GDP between t and t+1. Using this notation, the GDP growth rate can be written as $\Delta GDP/GDP_t$.

Taking as starting point the equation $GDP_t = C_t + X_t$, it is possible to write $GDP_{t+1} - GDP_t = C_{t+1} - C_t + X_{t+1} - X_t$, which in turn gives, using our notations, $\Delta GDP = \Delta C + \Delta X$, or, dividing through by GDP_t: $\Delta GDP/GDP_t = \Delta C/GDP_t + \Delta X/GDP_t$. This last equation can also be rewritten if we multiply and divide both terms on the right-hand side by the same term (either C or X), as follows:

$$\Delta GDP/GDP_t = (C_t/GDP_t) . (\Delta C/C_t) + (X_t/GDP_t) . (\Delta X/X_t)$$

We therefore have the following result: the GDP growth rate is equal to the growth rate for consumption, weighted by the share of consumption in the previous year's GDP, plus the growth rate for exports weighted by the share of exports in the previous year's GDP. The two terms on the right-hand side of the equation are known as "contributions to the GDP growth rate" from consumption and exports, respectively. The sum of the two together is equal to the GDP growth rate.

As can be seen, the above result stems from the equation $GDPt = Ct + Xt$. With chain-linked data, however, this equation no longer strictly holds, since chain-linked accounts are not additive. Therefore, in order to calculate the precise contributions it is necessary to revert to additive accounts (see Exercise 6 at the end of this chapter), and then make the calculations. It is only by using additive accounts that contributions to growth can be correctly calculated. It is indeed this method that is used by statistical offices when they publish tables of contributions to growth. And it is important to note that the tables on contributions to growth published by statistical offices have not been calculated from the chained volume levels disseminated in traditional tables, but from additive accounts that are not easily available to users. One advantage of using the correct tables for contributions to growth is that because they are derived from additive accounts, they are themselves additive. Economists can therefore use these tables to calculate sums and differences in various types of contributions, including changes in inventories and net exports, as illustrated in Exercise 7.

Key Points

▶ To compare growth rates, use only the volume series and not the current price series.

▶ Detailed volume indices in the national accounts are commonly derived by deflating figures at current prices using the appropriate price indices.

▶ For aggregating quantities, national accountants use a fixed price structure. The volumes obtained in this way are known as constant-price accounts. The year corresponding to the fixed price structure is known as the base year.

▶ A change in volume is not the same thing as a change in quantity, since volume takes into account differences in quality and in the price levels of products.

▶ The Laspeyres volume index is the most widely used formula for calculating aggregated volume indices for national accounts.

▶ A Laspeyres volume index is a weighted average of changes in quantities, weighted by the values at current prices in the base year.

▶ The Paasche price index is the most widely used formula for calculating aggregated price indices in the national accounts.

▶ The product of the Laspeyres volume index and the Paasche price index is equal to the index of current prices.

▶ In most OECD countries, the national accounts in volume are calculated at the prices of the previous year, and then chained. The chained accounts use as weights the prices of the previous year and are therefore suitable for measuring changes in volume. Their drawback is their non-additivity.

▶ In North America, national accounts in volume also use the chaining principle, but they are based on Fisher volume and price indices. Their levels are not additive either.

▶ It is recommended that growth, and contributions to growth, figures be used to represent volume growth. Contributions to growth are additive when calculated from additive accounts.

 UNDERSTANDING NATIONAL ACCOUNTS – ISBN 92-64-02566-9 – © OECD 2006

Going further

Chain-linked levels of changes in inventories and other similar variables

The compilation of chain-linked changes in inventories is a problem. Let us use CI(Y) for the changes in inventories of year Y. In principle, if one applies the general formula for chain-linked volumes expressed at previous year prices, then CI(Y) chained linked = CI(Y − 1) chained linked x [CI(Y) in previous year's price/CI(Y − 1) at current prices].

But experience shows that the above multiplication formula in not applicable. Indeed, it results in extreme values for chain-linked changes in inventories (for reasons discussed at the end of this box). These extreme values cannot be used to calculate contributions to GDP growth, although, as explained in the main text, economists report volume changes in inventories exclusively as "contributions to growth of GDP". What is to be done? As discussed in the main text, one solution is to avoid presenting these series in terms of chain-linked levels. However, many statisticians still want to present these series in such a format. One proposal is interesting: it is based on the fact that the above multiplication formula is mathematically equivalent to the following additive formula:
CI(Y) chain-linked = CI(Y − 1) chained linked + [CI(Y) in previous year prices − CI(Y − 1) at current price]/Chained linked price index of CI(Y − 1).
However, this formula remains unusable because the chain-linked price index of CI(Y − 1) can also take extreme values.

A possibility is to substitute in the above additive formula a reasonable chain-linked price index instead the one liable to take extreme values. One could use the producer price index for the goods for which the changes in inventories are compiled, or, at the level of total changes in inventories, the chain-linked price index of GDP. It can be shown that if one uses the chain-linked price index for GDP, the formula ensures that the contribution to GDP obtained using the chain-linked CI(Y) is the correct one. Let us prove that.
The starting formula, which we shall call F, is:
CI(Y) chained linked = CI(Y − 1) chained linked + [CI(Y) in previous year prices − CI(Y − 1) at current price]/Price index of GDP(Y − 1).
This is equivalent to:
CI(Y) chained linked = CI(Y-1) chained linked + [CI(Y) in previous year prices − CI(Y-1) at current price]/[GDP(Y − 1) at current price/GDP(Y − 1) chained linked].
From this, one can derive:
[CI(Y) chained linked − CI(Y − 1) chained linked]/ GDP(Y − 1) chained linked
= [CI(Y) in previous year prices − CI(Y − 1) at current price]/[GDP(Y − 1) at current price.

The second term of the above equation is precisely the correct formula for calculating the contribution to GDP growth of CI(Y), because accounts in previous year prices are additive. Thus, formula F (applied as if the volume series were additive) ensures that the chain-linked series CI(Y) can be used to derive easily the correct contribution to growth. It is interesting to note that formula F shows that chain-linked changes in inventories can be compiled as the accumulation of change in inventory changes expressed in previous year prices, with each link being deflated by the chain-linked price index of GDP. This presentation of the chain-linked series of changes in inventories is intellectually satisfying because it presents a sensible relation between the change in the volume of changes in inventories expressed at previous year's prices and the change in inventory changes expressed in chain-linked volume level.

Formula F can be used as an alternative to the one illustrated in Exercise 7. In fact, the two are exactly equivalent and both give a time series from which one can derive the correct contribution to growth. Two final points before we close this box. First, formula F can be used for variables other than changes in inventories, for example net exports. Second, there are reasons why the first formula in this box gives extreme results. Mathematically, the reason is that because changes in inventories can be positive or negative and also very close to zero, the second term of the first equation can be massively positive or negative and extremely sensitive to minuscule revisions. Statistically, the reason is that chain linking is not suitable for measuring changes in inventories in volume terms. Indeed, it can be proven that chain linking should only be used when the price structure is changing regularly among the different goods or services being aggregated. A good example of this is the regular price decreases in computer prices relative to the pricing of other machinery. However, because inventories can comprise extremely heterogeneous goods from one period to another, they are not suitable for chain linking.

Exercises Answers at www.SourceOECD.org/understandingnationalaccounts

Exercise 1. Using deflation to derive volume

Deflation is a fairly easy concept to apply. Let us suppose that a seller of lollipops has a turnover of € 1 200 in October. He raises the prices of his lollipops by 12% on 1 November. His turnover in November is € 1 680. Calculate via deflation the increase in lollipop sales volume. Check your result using quantities, given that the price of a lollipop before the increase was € 1.25. Now suppose that instead of increasing his price by 12% he in fact reduced it by 12%, while maintaining the same turnover. What will the increase in volume be now?

Exercise 2. Calculation of volume at various price levels

Let us take three products, A, B and C, with the following series of quantities and prices in each of three periods:

	Period 1		Period 2		Period 3	
	Quantity	Price	Quantity	Price	Quantity	Price
A	20	5	40	3	60	2
B	150	0.2	145	0.25	160	0.25
C	12	25	6	40	5	35

Calculate, for each period, the amount at current prices, the volume at constant period 1 prices, the volume at constant period 2 prices and the growth rates 2/1 and 3/2 of the aggregate constituted by the totality of the three products. Comment on the results.

Exercise 3. Calculation of a Laspeyres index and equivalence of calculation methods

The aim of this exercise is to show the equivalence between the two Laspeyres formulas presented in section 4 of this chapter. Formula (1) corresponds to the calculation of a weighted index; formula (2) corresponds to the calculation of growth rates for accounts at constant prices.

Take the case of two types of car, small and large, and the respective quantities sold in two periods at various prices, as shown in the following table. First, use Formula (2) to calculate the volume growth rate for all the cars at constant prices, and then use Formula (1), to calculate a weighted quantity index. Check against the theoretical result.

	Period 1		Period 2	
	Quantity	Price	Quantity	Price
Small cars	1 000	10.0	600	10.5
Large cars	200	20.0	600	21.0

Exercise 4. Calculation of Laspeyres indices, Paasche indices and deflation

Let us again consider the table used in Exercise 3. Calculate the index for the change in current prices. Calculate the Paasche price index. Obtain the Laspeyres volume index by deflation. Verify that the result is the same as that given by Exercise 3.

Exercise 5. Calculation of " chained accounts " (chained Laspeyres indices)

The following table gives a sequence of prices and quantities for three products A, B and C. The aim of this exercise is to calculate the volume for the aggregate consisting of the set A + B + C adopting the method used in the French national accounts known as "accounts at previous year's prices, chained, base 2000". For this purpose, use the structure of the table. First, calculate the account for A + B + C at current prices for all four years. Then calculate the volumes of the last three years at the previous years' prices. After that, calculate the growth rates of these volumes (watch out for the trap). Finally, chain these growth rates using the year 2000 as base. The result is the accounts at previous year's prices, chained, base 2000. Is there a difference between the growth rates in this series and the growth rates in volume at previous year's prices?

	1999		2000		2001		2002	
	Quantity	Price	Quantity	Price	Quantity	Price	Quantity	Price
A	20.00	5.00	40.00	4.00	60.00	2.00	90.00	1.00
B	150.00	0.20	145.00	0.25	160.00	0.25	175.00	0.30
C	12.00	25.00	6.00	40.00	5.00	40.00	7.00	36.00
Aggregate A +B +C	1999		2000		2001		2002	
Accounts at current prices								
Accounts at previous year's prices								
Growth rates								
Accounts at previous year's prices, chained, base 2000								
Accounts at 2000 prices								
Growth rates								

Next, compare these results with those obtained by using constant prices (*i.e.* "accounts at 2000 prices") to derive absolute levels and growth rates.

Exercise 6. Chained accounts and the loss of additivity

The table below is an old official one taken from the French national accounts, listing annual GDP in volume (at previous year's prices, chained, base 1995), imports and the sum of the two, known as total resources. Since this table was drawn up, the French national accounts have changed to base year 2000, but this makes no difference in this exercise, which could just as well use a 2000 base with figures for years 2004, 2005, 2006 and 2007.

For each of the aggregates below, the year-to-year changes are also shown, with a high degree of precision (three decimal places). Make your own calculation of total resources by summing GDP and imports and comparing the result with the total given by INSEE, the French statistical office. Do you conclude that INSEE is no longer capable of simple addition? If not, where does the problem lie? Try to reconstitute the INSEE growth rate for between 2002 and 2001, using the accounts at the previous year's prices and knowing that for 2001, at current prices, GDP = 1 475 584 and imports = 388 709. What are your conclusions?

(million 1995 euros)	1999	2000	2001	2002
Gross domestic product	1299 510	1348 801	1377 067	1393 687
Evolution (%)		3.793	2.096	1.207
Imports	321 320	368 220	372 984	375 228
Evolution (%)		14.596	1.294	0.602
Total resources	1620 958	1715 964	1748 974	1767 876
Evolution (%)		5.861	1.924	1.081

Source: INSEE, National Accounts.

Exercise 7. Volume changes in inventories: levels or contributions to GDP?

Let us suppose GDP is broken down as final demand minus changes in inventories (FDLI) and changes in inventories (I). Here are the accounts, expressed in prices of year 1:

At prices of year 1	Year 1	Year 2
FDLI	1 430	1 468
I	−43	69
GDP	1 387	1 537

Is it correct to say that the accounts of year 1 are in current prices? Is it correct to say that the accounts for year 2 are in volume terms? Why are these accounts additive (*e.g.* GDP = FDLI + I)? Calculate growth rates for year 2. Why is it not possible to calculate a growth rate for I? Calculate contributions to change in GDP for both FDLI and I.

Below are the volume accounts for year 3, expressed in prices of year 2. Calculate growth rates and contributions to GDP growth.

At prices of year 2	Year 2	Year 3
FDLI	1 490	1 363
I	123	148
GDP	1 613	1 511

How would the OECD economics department present a table including the three years? Explain why it is not possible, because of changes in inventories, to easily present the same table but with all variables expressed in chain-linked levels (*i.e.* where year 1 is the reference year). Propose a solution whereby the levels of changes in inventories correspond exactly to those from which one can derive exact contributions to change of GDP.

Exercise 8. The US approach: forecasting using chained accounts

As explained in this chapter, the disadvantage of using chain-linked volume accounts is their lack of additivity, a feature that makes the life of forecasters quite uncomfortable. This exercise, largely inspired from a paper by the US Bureau of Economic Analysis (BEA), proposes a simple way to derive a very good approximation of BEA's results, which are based on sophisticated chained Fisher indices. The simplified approach uses additive accounts at prices of the "previous quarter".

The table below shows the situation in the beginning of 2002. The first two columns are data published by the BEA at that time. The first column contains data at current prices ("current dollar level"). The second column contains data in "chained-dollar levels". The third column shows a set of forecasts by an unknown forecaster for the second quarter of 2002 (2002Q2). These forecasts are expressed as growth rates (of course in volume terms). *Important notice:* in US accounts, quarterly growth is traditionally expressed at "annual rates". This means that quarter-to-quarter growth is raised by an exponent of 4. For example, 2.0 is the forecast growth rate for durable goods in the second quarter. In fact, this means the quarter-to-quarter growth is equal to $(1-(1 + 0.02)^{1/4}) = +0.496\%$. Only these quarter-to-quarter growth rates should be applied to previous quarter's levels.

Using the data of the first three columns, calculate GDP growth for 2002Q2 at an annual rate in two ways. First, using the correct approach, apply quarter-to-quarter growth to each component of GDP in 2002Q1 *at current dollar levels* to obtain the fourth column, which will therefore be in billions of dollars at prices of 2002Q1, or "2002Q1 dollar levels". You can now sum up these numbers to obtain GDP, from which the annual growth rate can be compiled. Indeed, because they represent accounts at prices of the preceding period, they are additive. The result should be a forecasted GDP growth of 1.3% at an annual rate. Second, using an incorrect solution, apply quarter-to-quarter growth to each component of GDP in 2002Q1 at *chained-dollar levels*. Obtain

UNDERSTANDING NATIONAL ACCOUNTS – ISBN 92-64-02566-9 – © OECD 2006

GDP growth using these data. Comment on the difference between the two ways to measure GDP. How can we then create a forecast for 2002Q3?

	2002Q1			Correct solution 2002Q2	Wrong solution
	Current dollar level	Chained dollar levels	Forecasted growth at annual rate	"2002Q1 dollars" levels	Chained dollars levels
Personal consumption expenditures					
Durable goods	859	976	2.0	?	?
Nondurable goods	2 085	1 921	−0.1	?	?
Services	4 230	3 642	2.7	?	?
Gross private domestic investment	1 559	1 551	7.9	?	?
Fixed investment					
Non residential					
Structures	288	243	−17.6	?	?
Equipment and software	838	954	3.3	?	?
Residential	463	384	2.7	?	?
Change in private inventories		−29		?	?
Net export of goods and services					
Exports					
Goods	680	738	15.9	?	?
Services	298	292	10.7	?	?
Imports					
Goods	1 102	1 250	27.9	?	?
Services	235	226	−2.1	?	?
Government consumption and investment					
Federal	672	598	7.5	?	?
State and local	1 267	1 099	−1.7	?	?
Gross domestic product before residual		9 343			?
Residual		20			?
Gross domestic product	10 313	9 363		?	?
Forecasted growth				??	??

In Chapter 2, we examined the comparability of data over time for the national accounts *of a given country*. We saw how to separate changes in volume from changes in prices. In this chapter, we shall examine the comparison of data *among several countries*. Inter-country comparisons are more difficult for at least three reasons: 1) despite the efforts to achieve international synchronization, the statistical methods for estimating national accounts variables can vary from one country to another; 2) individual countries' institutions can be different; and (3) countries do not have the same currency and the same price levels.

Despite these difficulties, it is part of the OECD's mission to make international comparisons in order to be able to recommend economic policies that have been successful. These international comparisons take place at three levels. The first and simplest consists of comparing the growth rates of certain variables, such as GDP in volume. In this case, the fact that countries have different currencies or institutions is not of great concern. On the other hand, differences in the statistical methods used can have a negative effect on comparability, although the extent of this is limited, as we shall see in the first section of this chapter. The second level, to be examined in the second section, consists of the inter-country comparison of ratios, for example the household saving ratio. In this case, differences in statistical methods as well as in institutions can have a negative effect on comparisons, but the existence of different currencies still has no effect. The third level consists of comparing the absolute levels of certain national variables among several countries, such as the level of GDP per head or the level of household consumption per head. This final type of comparison is the most problematic. That is because on top of the two factors already mentioned, there is the added problem of currency conversion, which has to be solved by using "purchasing power parities". These allow for a *spatial* volume/price breakdown (*i.e.* a volume/price breakdown among countries for a given point in time rather than a breakdown between different time periods for a given country).

1. Comparison of growth rates

The *OECD Economic Outlook*, a bi-annual survey of OECD countries, opens with the following Table 1 comparing GDP growth rates in volume for three major countries or areas.

This table shows what appears to be a quasi-structural difference in growth for these three major areas. Between 1992 and 2001, average annual growth in the United States was 2.2 percentage points higher than Japanese annual average growth and 1.4 points higher than that of the euro area. A difference of as little as 1 point, if it were to persist

Table 1. **GDP annual volume growth rate in percentage**

	1992-2001 average	2002	2003	2004	2005	2006
USA	3.4	1.9	3.0	4.4	3.3	3.6
Japan	1.2	−0.3	2.5	4.0	2.1	2.3
Euro area*	2.0	0.9	0.6	1.8	1.9	2.5

* The euro area comprises the 12 European countries that have adopted the euro as their common currency.
Source: OECD (2004), *OECD Economic Outlook: December No. 76, Volume 2004, Issue 2*, OECD, Paris. The figures for 2004, 2005 and 2006 are forecasts.

StatLink: *http://dx.doi.org/10.1787/507518331806*

systematically in the future would result in the relative economic power of the United States rapidly becoming even more substantial than it already is. In the space of 10 years, the United States would outstrip the others by 1.0110, *i.e.* +10.5 points! This is an enormous difference and should be cause for serious reflection by the other countries.

The above international comparison is not completely convincing, however. There is in fact a fundamental difference between the United States, Europe and Japan that is often overlooked: the population of the United States is structurally more dynamic, rising by 1.2% a year, compared with only around 0.3% growth for the euro area and Japan. This means that it is better to compare growth in *GDP per inhabitant* rather than in GDP itself, if valid long-term conclusions are to be drawn. Using this adjusted yardstick, the difference between the growth rates per head was only 1.3 points in the case of Japan (instead of 2.2), and 0.4 points for the euro area (instead of 1.4 points).

The differences remain appreciable, nevertheless, especially for Japan. For the euro area, the difference appears to be smaller, but this masks more substantial disparities within the area itself, with dynamic countries like Spain, Finland and the Netherlands compensating for weaker growth in less dynamic countries like France, Italy and Germany. The OECD's principal concern at the present time is therefore to use these results to

Table 2. **Growth in real GDP and in real GDP per inhabitant**

1992-2001, average annual growth rate in percentage

	Real GDP	Difference *vis-à-vis* the USA	Real GDP per inhabitant	Difference *vis-à-vis* the USA
USA	3.4		2.2	
Japan	1.2	−2.2	0.9	−1.3
Euro Zone	2.0	−1.4	1.8	−0.4

Source: OECD (2005), *Annual National Accounts, Main aggregates, Volume I, 1992-2005, 2005 Edition*, OECD, Paris.
StatLink: *http://dx.doi.org/10.1787/878022557032*

persuade the less dynamic countries to carry out structural reform in order to re-stimulate their growth and reduce their unemployment rates.

But is this comparison of GDP growth rates statistically valid? It is to the extent that through the adoption of international manuals for statistics and national accounts, the international community of statisticians uses definitions and conventions common to all countries. In the case of national accounts, the basic reference manual is the 1993 version of the System of National Accounts (SNA 93). Its European counterpart, the 1995 version of the European System of Accounts (ESA 95) has the weight of European law that EU members are obligated to apply. ▶ I. This is therefore reassuring for users. As a first approximation, there is indeed a high degree of comparability between OECD countries in regard to definitions and conventions. This is what enables the OECD to compile an international database of national accounts that constitutes the best source for making inter-country comparisons (see Box 1, "The OECD's International Database").

I. See Box 1 "The reference manuals" in Chapter 1 and also Chapter 15.

Box 1. **The OECD's International Database**

The OECD collects from each of its member countries several thousand series relating to annual and quarterly national accounts. The annual series are more detailed. Access to this unique database takes two forms: hard-copy publications and electronic access. The hard-copy publications are as follows:

● Every quarter: Quarterly National Accounts

● Once a year (January): National Accounts: Volume I, Main Aggregates

● Once a year (July): National Accounts: Volumes IIa and IIb, Detailed Tables

● Once a year (November): National Accounts: Volume IIIa, Financial accounts – Flows; Volume IIIb: Financial Accounts – Stocks; Volume IV: General Government Accounts.

Access to the corresponding electronic data is through SourceOECD: *www.SourceOECD.org*. This online library is available free of charge to students at subscribing institutions.

The OECD also provides access to extracts from the national accounts database: *www.oecd.org/ statistics/national-accounts*.

Extracts from the OECD's forecasting database are disseminated under the name of *OECD Economic Outlook Statistical Annex Tables*, published at the same time as the *OECD Economic Outlook, i.e.* twice a year (May and November for the text; July and January for the statistical tables): *www.oecd.org/eco/economic_outlook*.

Even so, is it possible to say that the comparability of national accounts data among countries is perfect? The answer is No. Although all countries refer to SNA 93, in practice they may not observe all the recommendations in the manual, they may use different statistical methods and the quality of their statistical systems varies. Moreover, the United

States constitutes a special case because even though its statistical system is of high quality and adheres to the substance of the recommendations in SNA 93, its presentation of the national accounts tables is different from that of other countries. This explains why this book contains a special chapter on the United States (Chapter 12).

It would be pretentious to claim to know all the sources of non-comparability between countries, despite the numerous contacts between statisticians at the international level. However, a recent OECD study has listed several significant factors liable to affect the international comparability of GDP growth in volume between Europe, Japan and the United States. Some of these are set to disappear, but four have still not yet been completely resolved.

First, there is the treatment of spending on weapons systems (tanks, fighter-bombers, warships), which is recorded as investment in the United States but as current expenditure in the other countries. The result is to raise "statistically" the level of United States GDP by around 0.6%. That is because investment generates consumption of fixed capital, which is included in the estimation of the value added of government, and thus in GDP. However, the study showed that the impact of this difference on the GDP growth rate was minimal (0.03% per year). ▶ II.

II. This difference should disappear in the 2010s, since the new SNA (planned for 2008) has opted for the method applied in the United States.

Second, the study pointed out that spending on software is treated as investment expenditure in the national accounts, whereas in company accounts it is normally treated as current expenditure. This situation has led the US national accountants to make estimates that are independent of software spending as recorded in company accounts, resulting in high recorded levels of investment in software. The other countries, by contrast, have been recording much lower levels of investment spending, in line with the figures in company accounts. Since investment spending is included in GDP and current expenditure is excluded, the level of United States GDP is accordingly "statistically" higher by around 1% to 2%. Here again, however, the impact on the growth rate remained limited, at around 0.1% per year.

Third, the study noted differences in the deflator used for purchases of computers. The United States uses the so-called "hedonic" method (see Chapter 2) to estimate the evolution in the price of computers. In the US national accounts, this has led to a sharp decline in the estimated price index for computers, amounting to roughly 10% per year. Most other countries had not yet adopted the same method. The result of using a steeply falling price index as the deflator is a strongly rising volume index. Many people have therefore concluded that United States growth is overstated in relation to European or Japanese growth. However, the OECD study showed that the impact of this difference in statistical methodology on GDP growth in volume is not as great as one might think, since only computers produced in the national territory are affected, and European countries are importers of computers rather than producers. All in all, the impact on GDP growth of this difference in statistical methodology is also estimated to be around 0.1% per year and should gradually disappear with the introduction of hedonic indices in all countries.

Fourth, the study raised the difficult question of the measurement of services, especially non-market services like education and healthcare. In addition to the OECD study, a recent United Kingdom study has drawn attention to the difference results obtained depending on whether the volume of output of education or healthcare is derived from "inputs" or "outputs" (see Box 2, "The Atkinson Report"). In the case of the United Kingdom, the difference could have an impact of 0.25% on annual GDP growth, given the importance of these sectors. In fact, some countries use the "input" method and others the "output" method. This difference is therefore capable of generating a substantial degree of international non-comparability, but it is not possible at the present time to evaluate the impact of this difference in the method of calculating output in volume between the United States, Europe and Japan.

Box 2. **The Atkinson Report**

Amid vivid political debate, the Atkinson report was commissioned by the UK National Statistician in December 2003 to review the changes introduced by the UK Office of National Statistics (ONS) to measure the output of government. The revised estimates showed falling productivity trends in government within the current UK national accounts. The ONS had progressively abandoned "input" methods (described in Chapter 2) and developed direct measures of output (more than most other OECD countries). The output methods were accused of underestimating growth. This independent report confirmed that the approach taken by the ONS was correct but made 54 recommendations on how to improve the measurement of public services, which in the UK, like in other OECD countries, account for about one fifth of total GDP.

The report showed that the method used to measure the volume of government output can make a considerable difference to the recorded growth rate of the economy. The UK growth rate 1995-2003 would have been about one-quarter per cent a year higher if the old input method had been used, and this would have halved the gap between the UK and the USA, which does not use output measures. Here are the two key points of the report:

The traditional Output = Input convention, which the ONS has rightly abandoned in recent years, does not capture the complex workings of the public sector, and the UK should not return to using this convention.

Direct measures of output should be used. For the sake of public accountability, an intrinsic case can be made for seeking to measure what is achieved by spending on public services. One cannot simply assume that outputs equal inputs in such a major part of the economy. Failing to measure the output would be to miss the essential connection between public services and private economic growth. Measurement of government output, should, as far as is possible, follow methodology parallel to that appropriate for the private sector.

The full report is available on the website of the ONS.

INTERNATIONAL COMPARISONS
2. Comparison of ratios: the example of
the saving ratio

3

Taking as a starting point what is known and approximately measurable, the OECD concluded that the impact of measurement differences on growth rates of GDP in volume was most probably less than 0.3% per year during the period under review. Therefore, if the United States annual growth rate exceeds those of other countries by less than 0.3 point, the difference is not considered significant. On the other hand, if the difference is greater than 0.3 points, solid conclusions can be drawn. As we have seen, United States growth, at least in the 1990s, was significantly higher than that of other countries. There are therefore good reasons for the other countries to ask themselves probing questions regarding their growth gap *vis-à-vis* the United States.

2. Comparison of ratios: the example of the saving ratio

The household saving ratio is one of the key variables in the national accounts (see Chapter 1). It equals saving divided by disposable income (and multiplied by 100 ▶ III.), and it represents the allocation of income between consumption and saving, an essential item of information in economic analysis. It turns out that the saving ratio is very significantly lower in the United States and in other countries like Australia (where it is even negative), than in Germany or Italy. Japan is estimated to be somewhere between the two extremes.

III. In calculating the saving ratio, the "net adjustment to the equity of pension schemes (D8)" should be added to the disposable income in the denominator of the ratio (see Chapter 6).

Table 3. **Household saving ratio in percentage**
Net saving, unless otherwise indicated

	2000	2001	2002	2003
Australia	2.9	0.8	−2.9	−3.2
Finland	0.2	−0.2	0.3	0.9
Germany	9.7	10.2	10.5	10.7
Italy	9.1	10.1	10.4	10.6
Japan	9.5	6.5	6.3	
United Kingdom*	5.0	6.5	5.3	5.8
United States	2.4	1.8	2.1	1.4

* For the United Kingdom, the gross saving ratio.
Source: National Accounts of OECD Countries, Volume I, Main Aggregates, 1993-2004, 2006 Edition.
StatLink: *http://dx.doi.org/10.1787/734511327772*

Table 3 shows that US households, on average, hardly save at all, allocating almost their entire incomes to consumption. Only 1.4% of net disposable income was saved in 2003. This demonstrates, on the one hand, the strong confidence in the future shown by

3

INTERNATIONAL COMPARISONS
2. Comparison of ratios: the example of
the saving ratio

US households and, on the other, their lack of concern regarding the financing of their country's investment. In fact, it is not US households that finance this investment but foreign investors who, having confidence in the US economy, continue to buy large amounts of US Treasury bonds. Some people worry about the dramatic impact on the world economy that could result from erosion of foreign investor confidence, while others think that this imbalance will gradually be reabsorbed without producing a crisis. One should note that the dramatic fall of the saving ratio in the US masks the fact that the potential wealth of households has been increasing given the impressive price increase of dwellings in the recent period. This automatic "saving" is not captured by the saving ratio, which excludes holding gains. Note that this self-confidence is not confined to North America, but is shared also by countries such as Australia or Finland, both of which have posted firm economic growth in recent years.

In contrast, it is striking to note the very different behaviour of German and Italian households, who save more than 10% of their net incomes. Many economists, in the OECD and elsewhere, are trying to find explanations for such wide differences among countries that are basically quite similar. Some economists believe households in Germany and Italy lack confidence in the ability of their economy to guarantee them a job and a good pension. But other possible explanations have also been put forward, and one of these is based purely on statistics. It is in fact possible to wonder whether differences in statistical methodology or purely institutional differences might explain these wide differences in the saving ratio. On this point, too, the OECD has carried out several studies, including one published quite recently that lists several sources of non-comparability.

The first source of non-comparability relates to the calculation of the saving ratio, which can be calculated in two different ways: 1) the "net" approach deducts households' consumption of fixed capital (CFC) from both the numerator (saving, denoted as S) and also from the denominator (disposable income, denoted as DI); or 2) the "gross" approach, in which the consumption of fixed capital is not deducted from neither the numerator nor the denominator. The first approach gives a "net" saving ratio equal to: $(S - CFC)/(DI - CFC)$; the second gives a "gross" ratio: S/DI. The first result is mathematically lower than the second. Table 3 above shows "net" ratios except for the United Kingdom.

While many countries publish "net" ratios, which are preferred by the OECD, the United Kingdom and some others have opted for the "gross" saving ratio. There are reasons for preferring a gross ratio. First, it corresponds more closely to the observed financial flows, whereas the net ratio is artificial in that it incorporates an imputed flow, *i.e.* the consumption of fixed capital. Second, it is probable that net ratios are less comparable between countries than gross ratios because of the differing methods used to calculate the consumption of fixed capital. In all cases, however, one must avoid improper comparison of a gross ratio with a net ratio. This is nevertheless the error that might be made by looking at Table 3, since in that table (as indicated in the footnote), the ratio for the United Kingdom is gross while for the other countries it is net.

INTERNATIONAL COMPARISONS
2. Comparison of ratios: the example of
the saving ratio

3

Table 4 below rectifies this error by showing net ratios for all countries, including the United Kingdom. As can be seen from this corrected table, saving behaviour in the United Kingdom turns out in to be comparable to that of the United States, and not, as Table 3 incorrectly indicated, somewhere between that of the United States and Germany. The lesson here is that when presented with international comparisons it is necessary to look closely at all the footnotes in order to avoid errors.

Table 4. **Household net saving ratios in percentage**

	2000	2001	2002	2003
Australia	2.9	0.8	−2.9	−3.2
Finland	0.2	−0.2	0.3	0.9
Germany	9.7	10.2	10.5	10.7
Italy	9.1	10.1	10.4	10.6
Japan	9.5	6.5	6.3	
United Kingdom	0.5	2.0	0.4	1.1
United States	2.4	1.8	2.1	1.4

Source: National Accounts of OECD Countries, Volume I, Main Aggregates, 1993-2004, 2006 Edition.

StatLink: http://dx.doi.org/10.1787/337551341040

A strictly comparable definition of the saving ratio is clearly a necessary condition for grasping differences between countries, but it is not a sufficient one. Relatively minor institutional differences can result in significantly different measures of saving. One example is the financing of retirement pensions. For the sake of simplicity, let us consider two cases: financing retirement pensions on a pay-as-you-go basis and on a capitalisation basis. In pay-as-you-go, the contributions of today's workers pay for the pensions of today's retirees. In the capitalization approach, the contributions by today's workers go into a fund that belongs to them and out of which their pensions will be paid in the future. In the first case, the national accounts record the contributions as deductions from the income of working households and pension benefits as additions to the income of retired households. In the second case, the contributions are saving (by today's workers), and the pensions paid are "dis-saving" (or "negative" saving) by pensioners.

For historical and cultural reasons, certain countries (continental Europe, Japan) prefer the pay-as-you-go systems, whereas in others capitalisation systems predominate. The saving ratio calculated by national accountants will therefore differ depending on the institutional approach used to account for pension financing. It is therefore interesting to see to what extent this explains the observed differences in saving ratios. The OECD has made such a calculation for the euro area and the United States. In this alternative calculation, it is assumed that all systems are pay-as-you-go. The following chart shows the result of this calculation. The continuous line shows the difference between the saving ratio

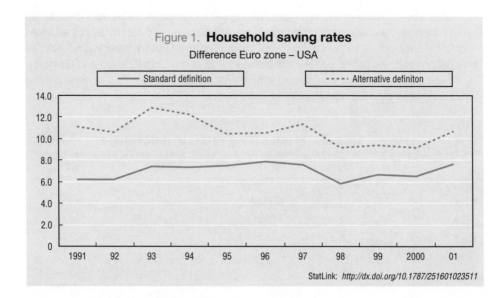

Figure 1. **Household saving rates**

Difference Euro zone – USA

StatLink: *http://dx.doi.org/10.1787/251601023511*

in the euro area and in the United States according to the "standard" definition in the national accounts. The result is a European saving ratio that is systematically greater, by around seven percentage points, than that of the United States. The dotted line shows the results using an alternative definition of the saving ratio in which the capitalisation systems (used in the United States) are treated as being pay-as-you-go systems. It can be seen that the difference *vis-à-vis* the United States is even larger than with the standard definition, amounting to almost 12 points near the beginning of the period to 10 at the end.

The conclusion to be drawn from the chart is that saving behaviour is even more different between the countries of the euro area and the United States than previously thought. The OECD has carried out other calculations of the same type to explain this wide difference in saving behaviour. For example, studies were carried out to see whether differences in the definition of consumption, in the respective shares of direct and indirect taxes or in the degrees of possession of durable goods could be explanations. So far, all these calculations have tended to confirm that there is indeed a fundamental difference in behaviour and not a statistical aberration. This is a reassuring conclusion in a way, but it illustrates the fact that in making international comparisons it is necessary to examine all possibilities of statistical non-comparability before drawing conclusions.

3. Comparison of levels of variables: GDP per head in volume

The Figure 2 below is very simple but telling. It shows the evolution in the volume levels of GDP per head for Japan, the euro area and the United Kingdom relative to the United

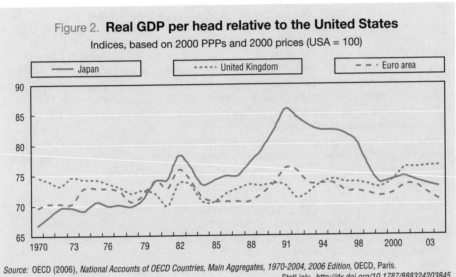

Figure 2. **Real GDP per head relative to the United States**

Indices, based on 2000 PPPs and 2000 prices (USA = 100)

Source: OECD (2006), *National Accounts of OECD Countries, Main Aggregates, 1970-2004, 2006 Edition*, OECD, Paris.

StatLink: *http://dx.doi.org/10.1787/888324203845*

States, which has been set to equal 100. The chart shows that GDP per capita in Japan and the euro area, as well as the UK, is between 70% to 80% of GDP per capita in the USA. It also reveals that around 1980 the relative levels of GDP per head for Japan, the euro area and the UK were roughly equal at 72.5% of the United States level. What happened in the 25 following years?

Between 1980 and 1994, Japan's economic growth was much faster than that of the United States, and, as a consequence, its GDP per head tended to approach that of the United States. However, its relative level peaked in 1991, at roughly 85%. From then on, Japan suffered a period of severe "deflation" (economic stagnation and falling prices) and lost in 10 years what it had gained *vis-à-vis* the United States in the previous 10. Therefore, between 1980 and 2003 Japan gained only 2.5 percentage points in relation to the United States.

Prior to 1980, the euro area had also shown some relative growth compared with the United States, and this had raised hopes of convergence at some point. But the euro area also started to stagnate by comparison between 1980 and 1994 and then to show a relative decline. In relation to the United States, the euro area's level of GDP per head for 2003 was 2.5 percentage points below what it had been in 1980. This was caused mainly by the large continental countries (Germany, France, and Italy) and not the smaller ones. Results for the United Kingdom, which is not part of the euro area, shows that this dismal picture is not true of all European countries. On the contrary, the United Kingdom, which had shown a relative decline in the 1970s, rebounded strongly in the early 1980s and has gained 2.5 percentage points in relative terms over the past 25 years.

Box 3. **GDP and the measurement of welfare**[*]

Criticisms are often voiced concerning the shortcomings of GDP per head as a measure of welfare, as more or less implied by international comparisons of GDP per head. In a way, these criticisms are justified. GDP per head is not a measure of economic and social "welfare". It is not even a measure of wealth. It is merely an overall measure of the production of goods and services. However, it should not be forgotten that this production is itself an important dimension of welfare. We are all consumers of goods and services, and we are all glad to have more of both. Strong GDP growth also goes along with a decline in unemployment. However, it is indisputable that there are dimensions of welfare that are not reflected in GDP, such as choice of leisure activities, social inequality, security of goods and persons, and quality of the environment. It is therefore reasonable to raise probing questions as to how best to guide economic development so that it serves human development and welfare.

How can these alternative factors be considered? Official statisticians (in national statistical offices) are inclined to tell users that instead of trying to say everything via a single indicator, such as GDP, they might consider using a set of indicators that enable them to make inter-country comparisons for some or all these factors, with GDP merely one of the indicators. This is in fact what the OECD does.

However, some economists (mainly in universities) advocate the construction of a single indicator, a sort of super-GDP, covering not only the production of goods and services but also social and environmental factors. This indicator, for example, would show a decline given deterioration in the environment, an increase in violence or a widening of socio-economic inequalities. It would then be a simple matter to rank countries according to their success at all these levels. Some organisations have created an index of this type, an example being the United Nations' "human development index", which has three components: standard of living, level of education and health standard. Many economists have also proposed indicators of this kind.

But the problem with a "super-GDP" indicator is that it is not clear how to combine social and environmental dimensions with the production of goods and services. In other words, what "prices" can be used to weight the environment or social inequalities, in relation to the production of milk or machinery? The weights being proposed remain fairly arbitrary, and this diminishes the credibility of such indices. In fact, it can be shown that varying the weights for the hard-to-quantify factors leads to a substantial change in country rankings. Therefore, until a genuine consensus is reached regarding the method of calculation, there is little chance that a super-GDP index will be calculated by official statisticians.

[*] Readers interested in alternative measures of well-being should read the recent OECD Economics Department Working Paper: *Alternative Measures of Well-Being, http://dx.doi.org/10.1787/832614168015.*

The above chart gives a striking picture of the evolution in the relative economic situations of the euro area, Japan and the UK. The OECD has concluded that the convergence of GDP per head between the United States and other OECD countries, which had been a feature of the postwar period, has come to a halt. It has therefore been sounding the alarm that large-scale structural reforms are needed in the leading European countries

INTERNATIONAL COMPARISONS
4. The spatial volume/price breakdown:
   purchasing power parities

3

and in Japan in order to prevent further widening of the gulf between a thriving United States economy and lagging economies elsewhere in the OECD. This conclusion may be open to discussion (see Box 3, "GDP and the measurement of welfare"), but it is based on data that cannot be ignored.

In purely statistical terms, Figure 2 is an ingenious comparison of absolute levels of GDP per head in certain countries with that of the United States, as well as a comparison of growth rates in GDP per head over time. It is important to understand that what is being compared here is *volumes* of GDP per head, and not monetary values of GDP per head. To compare GDP in volume for countries with different currencies – and different purchasing power for those currencies – it is necessary to calculate a spatial volume/price breakdown using a method known as "purchasing power parities" (PPP).

4. The spatial volume/price breakdown: purchasing power parities

The objective here is to compare absolute levels of GDP per head (or other variables such as consumption) among different countries or regions *in volume*, for a given period (usually one year). Why in volume? Because the aim is to compare the quantities of goods and services produced in each country and not the monetary value of this output. The monetary value will in fact be affected by the differences among price levels. How can this spatial (*i.e.* among countries, regions or zones) comparison in volume be done?*

Recall that when analysing growth over time for a given country, GDP in volume is calculated by dividing GDP at current prices by a price index that is equal to 100 for a set base period. Exactly the same approach is used for spatial comparisons. A figure for GDP in volume is obtained by dividing GDP at current prices by a "purchasing power parity" index, set to equal 100 for a given country. Thus, as in the case of a temporal price index, there is a "base" used as reference (and for which the index value is 100), but in the case of a spatial index the base is a country or a region, and not a time period. For the base in spatial comparisons, the OECD usually uses either the average level of prices for OECD countries, or more simply, the level of prices in the United States. For this reason, "purchasing power parities" presented by the OECD have USA = 1 (or 100).

For a simplified illustration of the purchasing power parities (PPP) method, let us consider first the case of countries with the same currency, thus avoiding having to manipulate exchange rates. Also for simplicity, there is only a single product – the hamburger. Let us suppose that the GDPs are expressed at current prices in the same currency (for example the euro) and equal to 1000 for country A and 1200 for country B during the

---

* For a complete presentation, readers should refer to: OECD (2005), *Purchasing Power Parities and Real Expenditures: 2002 Benchmark Year, 2004 Edition,* OECD, Paris.

3 INTERNATIONAL COMPARISONS
4. The spatial volume/price breakdown:
purchasing power parities

specified period. This can be written as $GDP_a = 1\ 000$, $GDP_b = 1\ 200$. Furthermore, since there is only one product, the hamburger, the respective GDPs can be written as $P_a \times H_a$ and $P_b \times H_b$, where P_a is the price in euros of a hamburger in country A, and H_a is the number of hamburgers produced in country A (similarly for country B).

Our objective is to compare the volumes, *i.e.* the quantities H_a and H_b. To do this, we shall calculate the price ratio PPP, called "the purchasing power parity of B with respect to A", as: $PPP = P_b/P_a$. By deflating the GDP of B by this PPP, in other words dividing GDP_b by PPP, we obtain $P_a \times H_b$. This results in the GDP in volume of country B expressed "in country A prices". By then dividing this volume by GDP_a, we obtain H_b/H_a, which is exactly the relative valuation in volume that we are after. It can be seen that: (1) PPP is a ratio of the price levels of identical products in the two countries; (2) the volume obtained by deflating a country's GDP by its PPP is a valuation of its GDP *at the base country's prices*, thus eliminating the difference between *price levels* in the two countries; and (3) the value of this GDP in volume in relation to the GDP at current prices of the base country gives a comparison *in volume*, which is our aim.

Now suppose the two countries do not have the same currency. Country A (the United States, for example) has the dollar, while country B has the euro. If the price of a hamburger in country A is P_a, in dollars, and the price of a hamburger in country B is P_b, in euros, the PPP of a hamburger between country A and country B will still be equal to P_b/P_a. In this case, however, the PPP is expressed as a currency ratio, since it equates to an amount in euros per dollar. How should it then be interpreted? It is the amount in euros that has to be spent in country B to obtain the same quantity of hamburgers that can be bought with a dollar in country A. The PPP is therefore equal to the conversion rate that equalises the purchasing power of the two currencies. When we divide the GDP of country B by the PPP, we kill two birds with one stone: we eliminate the differences between the price levels in the two countries; and we express the two amounts in the same currency unit, that of the base country.

Why not simply use the actual exchange rate seen on the currency markets? Because the market rate does not properly adjust for the difference in price levels between two countries and therefore does not provide a true comparison of the volume of goods and services produced per head. Let us try to compare GDP per head in Sweden and in the United States using just the exchange rate. First, divide GDP per head in Sweden expressed in Swedish kronor by the krona/dollar exchange rate. What we get is the Swedish GDP per head expressed in dollars. For a direct comparison with United States GDP, this magnitude (now expressed in dollars) is divided by the GDP per head in dollars of the United States (and multiplied by 100). This gives the continuous curve in Figure 3, which is a percentage index giving the size of Swedish GDP per head relative to that of the United States (which, by convention, is equal to 100). The value of this index can be read on the left hand axis of the chart.

The shape of the curve clearly shows that this calculation is not a proper indicator of relative GDP in volume. It is definitely not true that Swedish GDP per head in volume was 90% of that of the United States around 1970, before briskly rising to 120% in the latter part

INTERNATIONAL COMPARISONS
4. The spatial volume/price breakdown:
    purchasing power parities

3

Figure 3. **GDP per capita using exchange rate**

Sweden GDP per capita as a percentage of USA GDP per capita and US dollar per Swedish krona

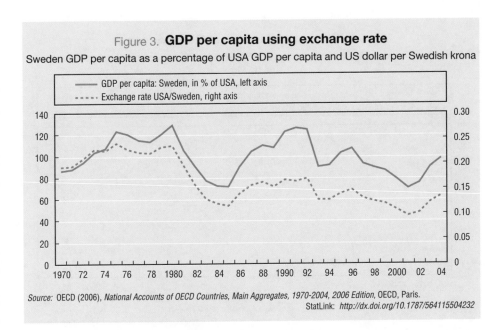

Source: OECD (2006), *National Accounts of OECD Countries, Main Aggregates, 1970-2004, 2006 Edition,* OECD, Paris.
StatLink: *http://dx.doi.org/10.1787/564115504232*

of the 1970s and then falling back to 70% in the mid-1980s. Where does this volatility come from? Clearly, from the exchange rate, shown by the dotted curve (values on the right-hand axis). The correlation between the two curves shows that the volatility of the first (Swedish GDP per head in volume) stems essentially from the volatility of the second (the exchange rate), and therefore the currency exchange rate is not a good relative deflator.

So it is not possible to use market exchange rates. Instead, it is necessary to construct specific indices for the spatial volume/price breakdown, or purchasing power parity (PPP). These PPP indices are price ratios for identical products, the basic building block being the ratio discussed earlier. Indices of this kind can be calculated for each of the major items in GDP (final consumption, GFCF, exports, imports). The overall mean of these PPP indices constitutes the purchasing power parity of GDP. Therefore, PPP is a spatial deflator of GDP, making it possible to compare absolute volumes between countries by eliminating the difference in national price levels. As we have seen, such a deflator is not restricted to countries with different currencies. It is equally valid for use between countries with the same currency (for example between countries in the euro area) or even between regions within a country, quite simply because price levels can differ appreciably between geographic regions, even if they have the same currency unit. To take the case of France, the same wage in euros is worth more in the French provinces than in Paris, simply because the cost of housing is much higher in Paris.

3 INTERNATIONAL COMPARISONS
4. The spatial volume/price breakdown:
purchasing power parities

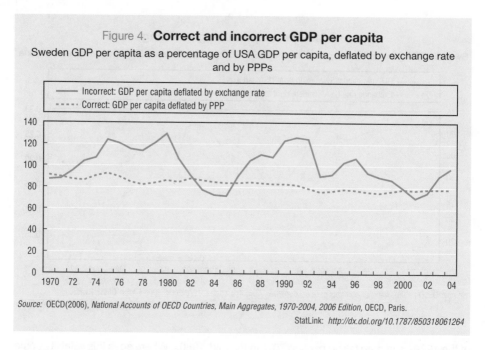

Figure 4. **Correct and incorrect GDP per capita**

Sweden GDP per capita as a percentage of USA GDP per capita, deflated by exchange rate and by PPPs

Source: OECD(2006), *National Accounts of OECD Countries, Main Aggregates, 1970-2004, 2006 Edition*, OECD, Paris.

StatLink: *http://dx.doi.org/10.1787/850318061264*

Figure 4 shows the Swedish GDP per head in relation to that of the United States using two different methods. The first, shown by the continuous line, is the one already seen in Figure 3. This is the incorrect method, consisting of dividing Swedish GDP per head by the exchange rate. The second, shown by the dotted line, consists of dividing the same figures by the PPP for Swedish GDP, with USA = 1. This method – the correct one – makes it possible to conclude that Swedish GDP per head in volume has remained quite stable at around 80% that of the United States, showing a slight tendency to decline over the period 1970-2003.

The question might be asked: what is the relationship between the PPP and the exchange rate? In Figure 5 below, Sweden's PPP relative to the United States is shown by the continuous line, and the exchange rate between the US dollar and the Swedish krona by the broken line. ▶ **IV.** Both are expressed in the same unit, *i.e.* an amount of Swedish kronor per United States dollar. However, the PPP represents the amount in kronor that has to be spent in Sweden to obtain the same quantity of goods and services that a dollar will obtain in the United States, whereas the

IV. The exchange rates shown in this chart are the inverse (1/x) of those in Figure 3

exchange rate is the result of supply and demand between Swedish kronor and dollars on the currency market. It has been sometimes argued that the PPP is a sort of equilibrium exchange rate. One could even say that if the exchange rate seen on the currency markets is below the PPP, the exchange rate can be expected to rise (and *vice versa*), since in that case holders of dollars would have an interest in going and spending them in Sweden, or *vice versa*.

INTERNATIONAL COMPARISONS
4. The spatial volume/price breakdown:
   purchasing power parities

3

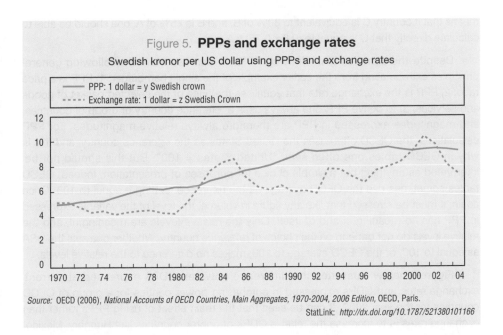

Figure 5. **PPPs and exchange rates**

Swedish kronor per US dollar using PPPs and exchange rates

Source: OECD (2006), *National Accounts of OECD Countries, Main Aggregates, 1970-2004, 2006 Edition*, OECD, Paris.

StatLink: *http://dx.doi.org/10.1787/521380101166*

However, even though the graph shows that the exchange rate has been fluctuating around the PPP, it is necessary to guard against a simplistic interpretation of this comparison. Fluctuations on currency markets depend on many other factors. It would therefore be most imprudent to speculate ("take a position") on a currency solely on the basis of its comparison with the PPP calculated by the OECD. Furthermore, trade in currencies is dominated by exports and imports and capital movements, whereas the PPP is calculated for all goods and services, including those that are neither imported nor exported.

In real life, calculating PPP is a complex matter. It is initially based on surveys to ascertain prices for a representative sample of comparable products in each country. The main difficulty lies in the choice of products. They must be both comparable and representative (*i.e.* the kind that are commonly purchased in each country). This is easy for a certain type of hamburger but more difficult for other goods and services, which are often different from one country to another. Next, price ratios have to be compiled for a large number of products and several regions or countries. If there are multiple products and regions, the overall purchasing power parity is a weighted mean of the price ratios among several countries (zones or regions) for a basket of comparable goods and services. This basket covers all the components of final demand (consumption, investment, net exports). Also, the formula for deriving PPP is more complex than that used to calculate the volume/price breakdown over time. That is because one wants to arrive at a measure that is both "symmetrical" and "transitive". Symmetrical means the relative volume for country B with respect to country A equals the inverse: that of country A with respect to B. Transitivity

3

INTERNATIONAL COMPARISONS
4. The spatial volume/price breakdown:
   purchasing power parities

means that if country C is equivalent to 80% of B, and B is 75% of A, one should be able to calculate directly that C is equal to (0.8 x 0.75) x A.

Despite the complexity of deriving PPP, we can ascertain the following general principles extrapolating from the earlier example of the single hamburger: 1) PPP is a price ratio; 2) PPP is the exchange rate that equalises the price of the selected basket of goods and services; 3) to derive PPP, one always uses a reference country or group of countries, and magnitudes expressed in PPP are therefore always relative magnitudes. For PPP calculations, the OECD often uses the United States as the reference country, and this is why in OECD tables one often sees "United States = 100". But this should not be interpreted as anything but a simple choice for purposes of presentation. Indeed, OECD tables sometimes use the OECD average as the reference, setting it equal to 100. Once again, it must be stressed that like any figure in volume, the level of the variable expressed in PPP has no meaning in and of itself. Only the *relative* levels are meaningful, and the relative levels do not depend on the choice of reference country. Whether one sets the USA as equal to 100, or the OECD average to 100, makes no difference to the relative levels.

Figure 6 below illustrates the difference between GDPs expressed at current exchange rates and GDPs expressed in purchasing power parities for a group of OECD countries for the year 2002. It can be seen that the main effect of using PPPs rather than exchange rates is to increase the relative GDPs of poorer countries like Hungary, Mexico,

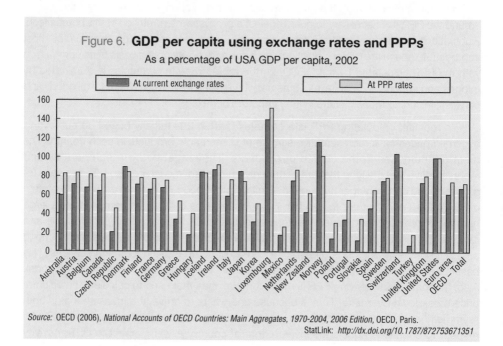

Figure 6. **GDP per capita using exchange rates and PPPs**

As a percentage of USA GDP per capita, 2002

Source: OECD (2006), *National Accounts of OECD Countries: Main Aggregates, 1970-2004, 2006 Edition*, OECD, Paris.
StatLink: *http://dx.doi.org/10.1787/872753671351*

UNDERSTANDING NATIONAL ACCOUNTS – ISBN 92-64-02566-9 – © OECD 2006

INTERNATIONAL COMPARISONS
4. The spatial volume/price breakdown:
   purchasing power parities

3

Poland and Turkey. Why is this? Because the relative level of prices in poorer countries is below that in rich countries, and this difference is not fully incorporated into market exchange rates. Another factor is that PPP covers all goods, including those that are not internationally traded, such as housing. And housing in poor countries is cheaper than in rich countries. Using PPP as the deflator therefore gives a better picture of each country's actual income, especially in the case of the poorer countries.

Although PPPs are more suitable than exchange rates for purposes of international volume comparison, they are a statistical construct rather than a precise measure. In particular, it is more difficult to calculate PPPs than to calculate price indices over time. It is relatively easy to calculate rent increases over time, but how is one to compare the rent of an apartment in London with that of apartments in Warsaw or Madrid? Another difficulty is that the budgets allocated to the price inquiries needed for PPP calculations are limited, with the result that the number of observations is small compared with those done for the calculation of a price index over time. Generally speaking, the variance from one year to another in the PPP calculations is quite large. Therefore, for temporal comparisons of volume GDP, the OECD recommends not deflating the GDP per head series by the "current" PPP series. The results lack homogeneity over time, even though theoretically they have the advantage of using a price structure that is constantly updated.

It is better to use the national series for GDP in volume at the prices of a common base year (for example 2000) and to deflate these by the PPP for a fixed year (for example 2000), although it is not necessary to use the same year. In this way, one obtains series that are doubly in volume: volume over time and spatial volume. These have the precise advantage of presenting the volume growth of GDP per head in each country, while at the same time making it possible to make inter-country comparisons of volume levels. ▶ V. It is this method, sometimes known as "constant PPP", which is used in Figure 2 of this chapter, and hence the title of the chart includes the phrase "based on 2000 PPPs". In fact, although the chart shows the series for GDP per head relative to that of the United States for the period from 1970 to 2003, the PPP used is only for the year 2000. The figures for other years are obtained by applying to the levels for 2000 the changes in GDP per head in volume for the country concerned. Exercise 1, at the end of this chapter, explains how to use this method. More details can be found in the following documents: *Purchasing power parities – measurement and use*, Statistics brief n°3, *www.oecd.org/std/ statisticsbrief*, and *GDP per capita volume indices based on constant and on current PPPs* in OECD's *Main Economic Indicators,found in the sources and methods section of www.oecd.org/std/mei*.

V. On the other hand, they have the disadvantage of using fixed price indices. For example, they overstate the most recent relative GDP in volume of countries that are large producers of computers, whose prices tend to fall over time. By relying on price indices based on a time period in the past, they therefore tend to attribute a larger weighting to computers than the use of more recent time periods does.

5. Comparison of variables in absolute terms: household consumption

In addition to the problem of finding a suitable spatial price index to use as a deflator, the inter-country comparison of absolute levels of variables poses other difficulties, related to institutional differences between countries. For example, inter-country comparisons of absolute levels of household consumption contain a trap into which it is all too easy to fall. As explained in Chapter 5, there are two possible definitions of household consumption in national accounts:

● *Household final consumption expenditure* corresponds to the purchase of goods and services by households.

● *Household actual individual consumption*. This equals household consumption expenditure (above) plus "individual consumption", which is the amount spent by general government and the NPISHs (non-profit institutions serving households) on things that directly benefit households, such as healthcare and education. Households do not pay directly for these services (they pay for them indirectly through taxes), but they benefit from them.

International comparisons of consumption per head are meaningful only if based on actual individual consumption and not consumption expenditure. This is because there are significant differences between countries regarding the proportion of expenditure carried out directly by households for healthcare and education and the proportion carried out on their behalf by government. If one uses expenditure and not actual consumption, one falls into the trap of understating consumption per head in countries that "socialise" this type of expenditure to a greater extent (the countries of western Europe in particular) compared with countries that leave this expenditure more to the private sector (United States). This is why in its volume series in national accounts, the OECD publishes a comparative series of actual *individual consumption* per head deflated by a suitable PPP.

Figure 7 shows the percentage of GDP accounted for by consumption expenditure and actual individual consumption for 10 countries in 2002 (current prices, in national currencies). For these 10 countries, household final consumption expenditure ranges from 45% to 60% of GDP, whereas actual individual consumption is roughly 70%. The largest differences are for France and Denmark, two countries that have to a greater extent "socialised" their expenditure on healthcare and education.

Generally speaking, therefore, international comparisons of absolute levels of variables in the national accounts are problematic. For one thing, countries do not all use exactly the same conventions. As was shown in the first section of this chapter, this has little impact on comparisons of growth rates but can affect comparisons of absolute levels to the tune of several GDP percentage points. In addition to these differences, there are wide variations in the quality of the underlying statistical systems. Some statistical offices have very

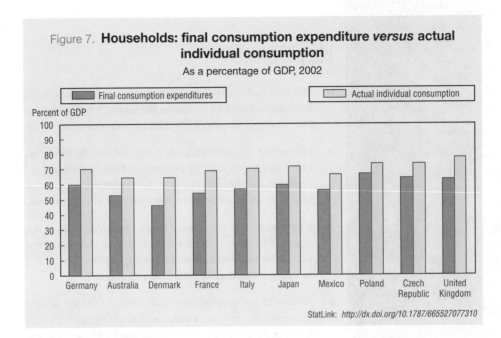

Figure 7. **Households: final consumption expenditure *versus* actual individual consumption**

As a percentage of GDP, 2002

StatLink: *http://dx.doi.org/10.1787/665527077310*

comprehensive listings of firms and/or access to exhaustive tax declarations by firms (by agreement with their tax authorities). These statistical offices therefore have statistics covering most parts of their economies. Other countries, by contrast, do not have such exhaustive basic data at their disposal. In principle, countries are expected to adjust their GDPs to take account of this "non-observed" economy (see Chapter 4). However, it would be pretentious to claim that these adjustments are based on exactly the same methods in each country. All things considered, it would be an illusion to think that the degree of precision regarding GDP levels is less than several percentage points.

In addition to these problems, when one takes into account the lack of precision in the calculation of purchasing power parities, the conclusion is that it is not possible to have unlimited confidence in comparisons of absolute levels. At the OECD, for example, a difference of less than 5% between the GDP per head of two different countries is not considered really significant. Remember, however, that a difference between *growth rates in volume* of 0.2%, for its part, is indeed significant. One often sees journalists making great play of the fact that a given country's GDP per head has exceeded that of another by even less than a single percentage point. Information of this kind has to be treated with caution, and if the difference remains very small, one should check whether the volume growth trends confirm this result. If they do not, it would be more reasonable to say that the GDPs per head of the two countries are "approximately the same".

Key Points

▶ The definitions and conventions used in national accounts are international. In principle, therefore, it is possible to compare national accounts data among countries.

▶ In practice, the methods used are not exactly the same and countries' institutions are different. In the final analysis, the growth rates of the variables in national accounts are more comparable than their absolute levels.

▶ It is necessary in the case of certain variables to carry out appropriate transformations: for example, dividing by the size of the population (resulting in aggregates "per head") or taking institutional differences into account.

▶ In order to compare levels of GDP per head among several countries or regions in volume, it is essential to deflate them by the purchasing power parities (PPP) for GDP, and not by actual market exchange rates.

▶ By dividing GDP (or another variable) by the suitable PPP, one eliminates differences in price levels between two countries, making it possible to compare the variables in volume.

▶ PPP is also calculated between different countries with the same currency (or between regions in the same country), since the same currency does not necessarily have the same purchasing power in different geographical regions.

   UNDERSTANDING NATIONAL ACCOUNTS – ISBN 92-64-02566-9 – © OECD 2006

Exercises
Answers at www.SourceOECD.org/understandingnationalaccounts

Exercise 1: Calculations of GDP per head in constant PPP and comparison with current PPP

Question 1: Table 1 below shows PPP for the United States, Sweden and Japan; Table 2 shows GDP in volume (at 2000 prices) for the same countries; and Table 3 shows their populations. Using data from these three tables, create a new table of relative indices of *GDP per head in volume (USA = 100), at constant 2000 PPP also called "at constant prices and PPPs of 2000"*. Based on the results, draw a chart similar to Figure 2 in this chapter.

Question 2: Table 4 presents the GDP of these same countries but this time at current prices. Calculate a series for GDP per head deflated by *current PPP*. Compare the results with the table you created to Question 1. Comment on the differences.

Table 1. **Purchasing power parities of GDP**

	1995	1996	1997	1998	1999	2000	2001	2002	2003
Japan	175.49	170.87	168.68	166.54	162.04	154.82	149.22	143.67	139.14
Sweden	9.41	9.3	9.38	9.48	9.34	9.19	9.34	9.36	9.39
USA	1	1	1	1	1	1	1	1	1

Table 2. **GDP in volume, at 2000 prices, billion units of national currency**

	1995	1996	1997	1998	1999	2000	2001	2002	2003
Japan	480 223	496 718	505 517	500 224	499 546	511 462	512 501	510 949	517 619
Sweden	1 870.72	1 894.87	1 941.06	2 011.82	2 103.93	2 194.97	2 217.95	2 261.77	2 294.94
USA	7 972.80	8 271.40	8 647.60	9 012.50	9 417.10	9 764.80	9 838.90	10 023.50	10 330.00

Table 3. **Population, in thousands**

	1995	1996	1997	1998	1999	2000	2001	2002	2003
Japan	125 570	125 864	126 166	126 486	126 686	126 926	127 291	127 435	127 619
Sweden	8 827	8 841	8 846	8 851	8 858	8 872	8 896	8 925	8 958
USA	266 588	269 714	272 958	276 154	279 328	282 429	285 366	288 217	291 073

Table 4. **GDP at current prices, billion units of national currency**

	1995	1996	1997	1998	1999	2000	2001	2002	2003
Japan	496 922	509 983	520 939	514 595	507 224	511 462	505 847	497 896	497 485
Sweden	1 770.25	1 815.14	1 888.23	1 971.87	2 076.53	2 194.97	2 269.15	2 352.94	2 438.45
USA	7 342.30	7 762.30	8 250.90	8 694.60	9 216.20	9 764.80	10 075.90	10 434.80	10 951.30

StatLink: *http://dx.doi.org/10.1787/154437888722*

Chapter **4**

PRODUCTION: WHAT IT INCLUDES AND EXCLUDES

Production is what leads to "output" (as it is termed in the national accounts), creating jobs, generating income for workers and owners of capital, and resulting in the goods and services found in our stores. Output is a central concept in economics. It is essentially used by economists *in volume* terms (*i.e.* not at current prices).

Output results from the three *factors of production:* labour, capital and intermediate consumption (inputs). Standard macroeconomic presentations often use a measure based on value added (rather than output) making it possible to dispense with intermediate consumption and hence show only labour and capital as the factors of production. When modelling the growth of output in volume (or, rather, the growth of value added when intermediate consumption has been deducted from both sides of the equation), OECD economists use the following formula:

$$Y' = [f(L, K) \times MFP]',$$

Y' is the growth rate of value added; L stands for labour and K for capital; f is the production function; and the sign ' means the derivative. The term "MFP" stands for "multifactor productivity", which is that part of the change in value added that cannot be attributed to changes in the volume of labour or to capital inputs in production. Its rate of change represents the contribution to value added growth of a more productive combination of labour and capital (for example, improved organisation of work or new techniques). MFP is sometimes called "disembodied technological progress", since it is the result of technical progress that is not reflected in the measurement of capital and labour. MFP is not directly measurable and can only be obtained as a residual from the above formula. Despite its elusive nature, MFP provides the main driving force behind long-term increases in the standard of living. In recent years, numerous studies have shown that MFP has been growing faster in the United States, Canada, Australia and nordic European countries compared with France, Germany and Italy. Within continental Europe, this has triggered an awareness of the need to invest in new technologies and R&D and to carry out structural reform.

OECD economists also use output statistics, again in volume terms, to estimate the "output gap". They do so as part of the regular monitoring of the economic situation in member countries. The basic idea is simple. Given the quantity of labour and capital available at a given moment, what is the maximum growth rate of GDP in volume that can be obtained without fuelling inflation? The corresponding level is known as "potential GDP". When the demand for goods and services exceeds potential GDP, various constraints emerge in the economy: firms have to offer higher wages to attract or retain the workers they need, higher consumption and investment pushes up prices of goods and services, and competition between borrowers forces up interest rates, which constitute part of the price of capital. Potential GDP is compared with observed GDP. If observed GDP is lower than potential GDP, there is said to be a "negative output gap". In this situation, governments often resort try to stimulate demand, either by tax cuts or by additional public spending (major infrastructure projects, and/or recruitment of civil servants, for example). The Central Bank, for its part, may decide to reduce its key interest rates. If there is a "positive output gap" – actual growth exceeds potential growth – it may then be difficult to raise public spending or lower taxes without automatically generating inflation, and the most common response is for the Central Bank to raise its key interest rates.

Although the idea itself is simple, the calculation of potential GDP is a complex matter, since it requires measuring the stock of capital and the value of the services provided by this capital, as well as measuring the labour factor. The latter is not simply the number of workers but rather the number of hours worked, adjusted for the qualitative composition (skill levels) of the workforce. Next, it is necessary to estimate the macroeconomic production function that relates these production factors to output. Despite these difficulties, the OECD evaluates the potential GDP growth rate for its members and regularly publishes the resulting "output gaps". For example, in 2005, OECD economists thought that the United States output gap was almost nil (meaning that growth was at its potential level), whereas it was negative in France (–1.4 points), Germany (–2.1 points) and Japan (–0.4 of a point).* These figures vary according to the current phase of the economic cycle. ▶ I. Non-inflationary growth above potential GDP can only be obtained by increasing the apparent productivity of capital and labour (see Box 1), and one of the ways to achieve this is via structural reforms.

> **I.** It turns out that growth is not steady but follows "economic cycles". Following a recession (a decline in GDP), the economy driven by corporate investment picks up again, reaches a peak and then declines, falling back again into a recession. The whole cycle lasts between 6 and 10 years. And then a new cycle starts again.

Box 1. **Apparent labour productivity**

Apparent labour productivity is defined as the ratio of output to labour. If Y denotes the volume of output and L the volume of labour, labour productivity is equal to Y/L, *i.e.* the quantity of output per unit of labour. For macroeconomic work, economists prefer to use value added in volume (*i.e.* GDP) as the numerator rather than output. The denominator used is the volume of labour, measured by the number of workers multiplied by average working hours (ideally adjusted for the skill level). In practice, one is usually more interested in growth in labour productivity than in its absolute level. This means calculating Y'-L' (rather than Y/L), where Y' is the growth in volume of value added, and L' is the growth in the volume of labour.

---

* *Source: OECD Economic Outlook*, N°78, November 2005.

Studies published by the OECD systematically include major sections on the progress made by member countries in regard to "structural reforms". This expression often arouses suspicion on the part of the trade unions, who see it as a code word for attacks on acquired social rights, such as guaranteed minimum wages, employment-protection legislation and the entitlement to unemployment benefits following the loss of a job. However, this is a one-sided view of the matter, since structural reform involves deregulating markets for goods and services in addition to the labour market. Structural reform of product markets involves increased competition between producers through, for example, the opening up of markets to foreign competitors, the abolition of cartels and other anti-competitive arrangements, and the abandonment of state monopolies, especially in such fields as rail and air transport, telecommunications, electricity, gas and water.

In order to identify which sectors of the economy are particularly in need of structural reform, OECD economists compare the productivity of various industries in different member countries. They pay particular attention to the growth of certain sectors, such as carmakers, airlines and electricity companies. They then try to ascertain the institutional structures in countries with the fastest growth. What apparently works in these countries can be tried in others. All these analyses are largely based on the data for output, or value added in volume, provided by national accounts.

1. The production frontier

II. However the concept of output is foreign to business accounting.

Output is therefore a central concept for national accountants aiming to compile useful data. ▶ II. But it remains to be seen precisely what output covers. To do that, we need to trace the "production frontier," deciding what to *include* in GDP and what to *exclude*. Most of what to include in GDP is non-controversial. For a start, output as measured in the national accounts includes what creates the goods and services that households buy for their everyday needs and that firms buy to be able to produce these goods and services. The important word in this last sentence is "buy", implying that all transactions that are "monetised" are included in GDP. But what about the activity of civil servants and members of the armed forces? Nobody buys the output of ministries or of the army. Another grey area is that of household services rendered free of charge. If one person pays another to clean his windows, this is output, since a service has been sold. But what if people clean their own windows? Does this lie within the production frontier?

As we shall see later, there is general consensus favouring the inclusion in GDP of the services provided by general government. Although these services are not sold, they are included as output (value added) in the national accounts and called non-market services produced by general government. This value added is very substantial, since it represents roughly 15% to 20% of GDP, depending on the OECD country concerned. By contrast, the "non-traded output" of households – cooking, cleaning, childcare, etc. – is, with one exception, not included in the national accounts. The exception consists of the housing that homeowners implicitly provide for themselves. The national accounts act *as if* the owner-occupiers provided housing services (a dwelling to live in) to themselves. These notional, or in national accounts jargon "imputed" transactions, are estimated to be equal to the rents that homeowners would have paid to live in dwellings of the same type, in the same district and with the same service facilities. These imputed rents are added to actual rents to calculate the total output of "housing services".

Imputations are carried out only when they are absolutely necessary for the analysis of changes over time in macroeconomic aggregates or for comparisons between several countries. This is the case for these imputed rents of owner-occupiers. If this output were not included by imputation, the result would be a structural decline over time in GDP, because the long-term upwards trend in home ownership would automatically produce a downward trend in the total value of actual rents (and thus in GDP, all things being equal). It would also make it difficult to compare the GDPs of different countries because the rate of home ownership varies markedly among countries.

Another example of imputation in national accounts is that of goods (mainly food) that some households produce for their own consumption. This represents only a very small part of output in OECD countries, but in developing countries, where farmers consume much of their own production, the proportion is very much higher. In some countries, farmers and other households even produce their tools, houses, outbuildings or their own clothes. As a result, the convention adopted in national accounts has been to impute in the calculation of GDP the output of all **goods** going into households' own consumption, attributing to them the market price of an identical good. On the other hand, as we saw earlier, the **services** households produce for themselves are not imputed in the national accounts, with the notable exception of housing services in the case of owner-occupiers. Nor is any account taken of the services some households provide to others free of charge (repairing a neighbour's dripping tap for nothing). ▶ **III.** Such exclusions may seem arbitrary, but they at least have the merit of avoiding having to make too many imputations, some of them extremely hazardous (see "Household Services" in the Section "Going further").

III. When services between households are provided for payment, attempts are made to include them in output by estimating, for example, the value of paid lessons or paid baby-sitting services.

In conclusion, national accounts define output as the result of the utilisation of one, or more, of the three factors of production: labour, capital and intermediate consumption (material inputs). This necessary condition leads to a very broad definition of output. However, this is later narrowed down by the imposition of other criteria, as the following "decision tree" shows (start reading the diagram from the top left-hand corner). The most important arrow in the diagram, which one could regard as the heart of national accounts, is in the top right-hand corner. It indicates that output consists essentially of the value of goods and services produced by certain economic agents *for sale* to other economic agents (monetary exchange, or in exceptional cases, barter). In the economies of the OECD countries, this constitutes the bulk of output. However, one must not overlook the non-market services produced by general government and the imputed housing services enjoyed by owner-occupiers.

The production decision tree

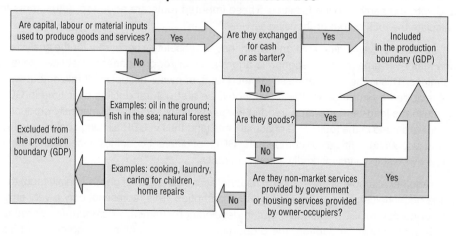

Before going into more detail, it is important to note that output in the national accounts is the output of productive activity *during* a period, which can be a year or a quarter. It is described as a "flow variable" as opposed a "stock variable", which measures a stock, such as the stock of finished products on the 31 December of a given year. Flow variables can be summed; in other words the output for a given year is the sum of the output of the individual quarters. This is not true of stock variables.

2. The illegal economy and the underground economy

In the diagram shown above, there is no distinction made between legal and illegal production. One can therefore conclude that illegal activities are within the production frontier and are hence included in GDP. Such activities are of two types: 1) illegal, such as trading in stolen goods, organised prostitution (in countries where it is illegal) and drug production and drug-dealing; and 2) legal but illegally conducted, such as plumbing or repair work paid in cash and not declared to the tax authorities.

In the OECD countries, illegal activities are marginal in macroeconomic terms. Most estimates have put them at less than 1% of GDP. Although theoretically included in GDP, in practice they are often not estimated and can therefore be considered not to figure in GDP. However, an increasing number of EU countries are now including them. On the other hand,

PRODUCTION: WHAT IT INCLUDES AND EXCLUDES
3. Measurement of output and of value added:
    the general case

4

legal activities carried out illegally (in order to avoid paying taxes and social contributions) constitute what is known as the "**underground**" or "black" or "hidden" economy and are estimated to be anywhere from 2% to 15% of GDP in OECD countries. This proportion is so large that national accountants have had to develop special techniques to ensure they are included in GDP estimates. Figure 1 shows the share of GDP generated by hidden or underground activities. In the chart, these are referred to as the "non-observed" economy because they cannot be observed by the usual types of surveys. In Hungary, for example, the non-observed economy represented at that time 16% of official GDP. This is the share of value added that has been added to the official statistical sources using these special techniques. It is therefore not true to say that the national accounts do not include the "underground" economy. For a concrete example of how this is done, see "The adjustments for the underground economy in the case of France" in the section "Going further".

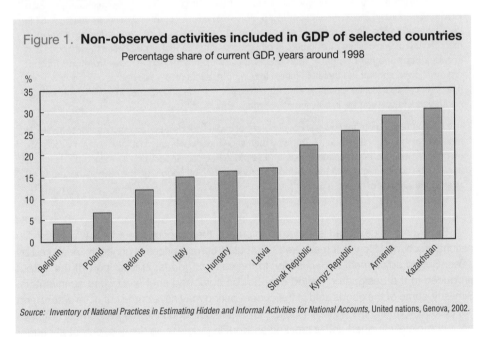

Figure 1. **Non-observed activities included in GDP of selected countries**

Percentage share of current GDP, years around 1998

Source: Inventory of National Practices in Estimating Hidden and Informal Activities for National Accounts, United nations, Genova, 2002.

3. Measurement of output and of value added: the general case

As we saw earlier, output in the national accounts mainly consists of the value of goods and services produced in order to be *sold* to other agents (output not intended for sale is not recorded, with certain exceptions). As pointed out in Chapter 1, this poses a problem of aggregation, in that the sum of output measured in this way can change over

4 PRODUCTION: WHAT IT INCLUDES AND EXCLUDES
3. Measurement of output and of value added:
the general case

time, not because more goods and services are produced but because firms are able to outsource certain activities previously carried out in-house (see Box 2 "The trap of internalisation and externalisation"). National accountants have therefore created the concept of value added. We shall be returning to this later.

Box 2. **The trap of internalisation and externalisation**

In the measurement of output, national accounts do not include "own-account" production – that is, the intermediate goods and services produced and consumed by companies internally. National accounts record own-account production of firms only when the goods are intended for investment. For example, if a company makes cars, the national accounts will not record the production of the engines that power these cars, if they are manufactured by the same company. Similarly, national accounts will not include the personnel services of this carmaker, if these services are provided internally. Recording the "own-account" output of intermediate goods and services would result in unduly inflating the figure for total output. On the other hand, if personnel services and the manufacture of engines are outsourced, in other words if the carmaker purchases these goods and services from another company, then this output will be recorded. A move from one form of organisation to another will therefore inflate total output, although in reality no new good or service has been created. Hence the attraction of the concept of value added (see Chapter 1), whose total is independent of a change in how firms are organised.

It is important to note that own-account output of capital goods, such as machines or software, is recorded in the national accounts. But why then is own-account output of intermediate goods not recorded? Because intermediate goods and services have no impact on GDP, since by definition they will be consumed during the production process. Capital goods, on the other hand, are used over longer periods of time.

But even if value added is preferred to output, the concept of output is widely used in national accounts. How is it measured? Output at current prices is generally measured by sales. But an adjustment is necessary. In the case of goods, at least part of the output produced in the designated period may not be sold, and so it is stocked as inventory. Similarly, some of the goods sold in the current period may have come out of inventory (and not produced during the period). Finally, part of the output during the period may not have been completely finished and is stocked as work in progress. In the end, output at current prices is measured as: sales plus the change (positive or negative) in inventories of finished products or work in progress. This formula is regularly used to calculate output, since the data required exist in company accounts, albeit not always in easily usable form (see Box 3 "The problem of changes in the value of inventories").

IV. An exception among OECD countries is the USA, which calculates its output and value added at market prices (i.e. including taxes on products). See Chapter 12.

As for the prices at which output is measured, these are the "basic prices" corresponding to the revenue per unit of products sold that remain in the hands of the producer. ▶ IV. Basic price therefore does not

PRODUCTION: WHAT IT INCLUDES AND EXCLUDES
3. Measurement of output and of value added:
   the general case

4

Box 3. **The problem of changes in the value of inventories**

One might think it a simple matter to use data in company accounts to determine inventory changes. However, in practice it is not so easy, because inventories generate holding gains when prices are rising and holding losses when they are falling. It is a fundamental principle of national accounts to exclude holding gains and losses in the measurement of output. Indeed, if a firm makes a holding gain by merely keeping products in inventories, this does not constitute a productive process and therefore cannot be included in GDP.* As a result, it is necessary to adjust the figures for inventory changes obtained from company accounts in order to eliminate holding gains and losses on inventories.

* The fact that holding gains and losses do not form part of output and GDP does not mean that they are ignored in the national accounts. They certainly exist and represent an important economic development when prices of goods rise or fall. Expectations of holding gains or losses and their realization can have a major impact on the behaviour of producers and consumers. For this reason, the national accounts record them in the revaluation account (see Chapter 8), but they are not an element of GDP.

include taxes on products (for example, value-added taxes or special taxes on petroleum products or alcoholic beverages), because these amounts do not remain with the producer but are paid to the tax authorities. On the other hand, the basic price includes the subsidies received on products. Therefore, in the national accounts, the prices for exported agricultural products are not the low prices made possible by the export subsidies granted to farmers of OECD countries but the actual sales prices plus the subsidies, thus a price that is closer to the real costs of production. Finally, output in volume is compiled as output at current prices deflated by the appropriate price index.

Intermediate consumption represents the value of the basic materials, components and semi-manufactured goods going into the product, as well as the value of the electricity, the cost of rents, IT services, insurance, legal and accounting services, etc., used in the production of a good or a service. In short, intermediate consumption consists of everything needed to produce other goods and services intended for sale, other than the labour of the workforce and the services provided by plant and machinery, offices and factory buildings.

Just as output is not equal to sales, intermediate consumption is not equal to the purchases of goods and services intended to be intermediately consumed. This is because certain intermediate goods used in the production during the period may have been bought and stocked in a previous period. Similarly, some purchases during the period may be consumed after it has ended, having been stocked in the meantime. In the end, intermediate consumption is equal to the purchases during the period *minus* the change (positive or negative) in the value of the inventories of goods and services for intermediate consumption. Firms often refer to these inventories as "materials inventories". Like output, intermediate consumption is a flow, corresponding to what has been consumed *during* a period (a year or a quarter). This leads to the exclusion from the definition of intermediate consumption of the goods used for production but not entirely consumed during the period, such as machinery or software. These capital goods are classified as "gross fixed capital formation" or GFCF.

Value added, as its name implies, measures the value the firm adds to the products used to manufacture the output and is equal to: output *minus* intermediate consumption. It can be deduced, using the definitions given earlier for the measurement of output and intermediate consumption, that value added at current prices is equal to: sales *minus* purchases *plus* total inventory changes (finished products, work in progress and materials). Value added is a central concept in national accounts. However, because it is defined as a difference between two monetary values (output *minus* intermediate consumption), it is not clear at first sight exactly what it represents. A useful way of defining valued added at current prices is to consider it as the amount of money generated by production that remains available to pay:

● wages and salaries and social contributions (*compensation of employees*);

● production taxes (other than that on products) net of operating subsidies;

● replacement of equipment gradually worn out during production (*consumption of fixed capital*);

● interest payments on loans;

● dividends paid to shareholders;

● purchase of new equipment; and

● financial saving – or the firms' investment in financial products.

It is sometimes this approach that is used in practice to measure firms' value added at current prices in the national accounts (see "The data sources for the value added of non-financial enterprises in France" in the Section "Going further"). Value added in volume is the difference in output in volume and intermediate consumption in volume.

4. The measurement of output and of value added: special cases

The definition of output at current prices as equal to sales + changes in inventories of finished products and work in progress is applicable to virtually the totality of the business sector in the national accounts. This sector is also known as the **market sector,** for which there exists a market with recorded sales, transactions and prices that permit the direct measurement of output. Note however that, even in the market sector, there are activities whose output is difficult to measure or even identify such as banks, insurance companies and retail distributors for which the definition of output based on sales does not work very well. They are all market activities, but their output is mainly purchased indirectly. Therefore an alternative measure of output is needed. Furthermore, there are large activities for which the notion of sales is non-existent, and these constitute the **non-market sector,** covering mainly services provided by general government. The organisations concerned do not sell their services, and it is therefore necessary to find a different measure of their output.

Non-market producers are those that provide services, and in some cases goods, either free of charge or at prices that are not economically significant, meaning in practice prices that cover less than half the cost of production. General government bodies constitute the bulk of the non-market producers, but there are others, like the non-profit institutions (see Chapter 5). Most of the services provided by general government – defence, economic policy, foreign policy, public education and public health care – are provided to the general public without charge. These services are obviously financed through taxation and social contributions, but there is no direct link between the payment of the tax and the level of services received. Citizens or firms are not entitled, for example, to vary their taxes based on the amount of defence or policing they want to consume. A tax is a compulsory transfer to general government and is not the price of a public service.

Certain services provided by general government, like education and healthcare, are provided to households on an individualised basis, meaning that it is possible to know who consumes them. For instance, a family sends its children to the state school, and one therefore knows that it is a consumer of these services. Other services are provided only on a collective basis, meaning it is impossible to know who consumes what. An example is policing: all economic agents, households and firms consume part of the services of the police, but it is impossible to know how much each consumes. In the case of the individualised services, government can sometimes charge part of the price to the consumer (for example, the contribution to the cost of a hospital bed), but this price is usually well below the production costs of the services consumed, and the services are therefore considered non-market.

Whether individual or collective, as there are practically no sales, non-market output at current prices is conventionally measured as equal to the sum of its production costs, including: a) the intermediate consumption; b) the compensation of employees; c) the consumption of fixed capital, which is the utilisation cost of the equipment used by non-market producers (see Box 4); and, in rare cases d) the other taxes paid on production. Exercise 4, at the end of this chapter, shows that measurement of non-market output in the national accounts basically assumes that these are non-profit activities, a very reasonable assumption.

The general formula for measuring output from sales cannot be used to measure the *output of banks*, because banks invoice directly only a very limited portion of their services (for example, foreign exchange commissions, cheque-handling fees, stock-market transaction fees, separately-charged financial advice), but not the bulk of their service, which is making loans. Measurement using the general formula would result in their value added being very small, if not negative; in other words, their intermediate consumption would be greater than their sales! Because banks are obviously profit-making enterprises, there is something wrong here. The fact is that banks make the bulk of their profits by borrowing at low interest rates from depositors and then lending the proceeds to other

Box 4. **Is the output of general government understated?**

Before a firm decides to buy capital goods, it calculates the return, or yield, on the funds it will be investing. This return must be sufficient to cover wear and tear (the consumption of fixed capital) plus a net income that is at least equal to the interest that could be obtained by investing the funds in financial products (bonds, for example). If the return is not sufficient to cover these two elements, a rational entrepreneur will buy the financial products rather than the physical capital. The sum of the consumption of fixed capital and this net return is known as services from capital.

In the case of general government, the production costs used to evaluate output include consumption of fixed capital, but they omit the net return. For a firm, the net return is close to its net operating surplus (see Chapter 7). Because government services are not sold (or only to a marginal extent), it is not possible to calculate the net operating surplus, but the net return could be estimated by applying an appropriate rate of interest to the value of the general government's capital. Views may differ regarding the appropriate interest rate, but it can be said that the present method of valuing non-market output significantly understates the contribution of general government to GDP. For example, the present method implies that scanners or x-ray machines produce no net return when they are used in a public hospital but do so when used in a private clinic. The new national accounts system (SNA 2008), to be introduced starting around 2010-2012, will most probably recommend taking into account the totality of the cost of capital services to evaluate the output of general government. It should result in an increase of several percentage points in the GDP level of all OECD countries, but it will probably not have much impact on growth rates.

borrowers at a higher interest rate. The difference between these two interest rates, which provides the essential part of banks' remuneration, is interpreted in national accounts as their financial intermediation service. The banks are in fact intermediaries between those who want to save – mainly households – and those who want to borrow – mainly firms. Without the banks, these agents would have greater difficulty in coming together. The national accounts therefore measure the output at current prices of banks as the sum of their sales *plus*, approximately, the difference between the interest received from borrowers and the interest paid to lenders. This difference, which forms the bulk of the total, is known as financial intermediation services indirectly measured, or FISIM (see "Going further: FISIM").

Measuring the output of *insurance companies* is even more problematical than in the case of the banks. For the sake of simplicity, we shall deal here only with non-life (property) insurance (automobile insurance, home insurance, etc.). The money received by these non-life insurers in the form of premiums does not only constitute payment for an insurance service but instead mainly goes into a fund from which indemnities will be paid in the event of claims. This being said, insurance premiums cover these indemnities *plus* claim management expenses *plus* the profits of insurance firms. The output at current prices of insurance companies corresponds to these two last items: management expenses and profits. The output will therefore be measured in the national accounts as *the difference between premiums received and indemnities paid out*, this being mathematically equal to management expenses plus profits. Things are in fact slightly more complicated than this, because insurance companies immediately invest the premiums received and leave them invested until such time as they are paid out in the form of indemnities. They therefore derive incomes which, economically speaking, belong to the insured and not to the insurance companies. Therefore, the national accountants impute a repayment of this income from the insurance companies to the insured (households or firms), which then pay them back to the insurance companies, the sums involved still being imputed. It is as if households paid not only premiums but also the investment income. In the end, the output at current prices of insurance companies is equal to the premiums *plus* the investment income *minus* the indemnities.

When measuring output for the national accounts, distribution (both wholesale and retail) also constitutes a special category. This is because if the general formula were applied the results would significantly overestimate total output, since sales in the distribution channel are already recorded as the value of the goods created by the actual producers. Therefore, the output for distribution is measured as the margin obtained on the products sold. So the output at current prices of distributors is equal to the value of their sales minus the value of the products bought for resale. ▶ V. This is known as their distribution margin. The intermediate consumption of distributors therefore excludes their purchases for resale; it consists only of rent, electricity, advertising, packaging and other operating expenses. Their value added is calculated in the usual way, by deducting their intermediate consumption from their output.

> V. This is made on the assumption that inflation is low and hence that there are no significant rises in market prices between the time of purchase and the time of resale. If this assumption does not hold, the rises must be taken into account and the sums involved deducted from the margin. Remember that holding gains or losses are not included in the measure of output in national accounts.

5. Nomenclatures and classifications

The broad nature of the production frontier used in national accounts has several advantages. It provides a useful, albeit approximate, measure of total production (or rather total value added) that is reasonably comparable between countries and over time. However, it is too global for certain economists, who would prefer to concentrate on more narrowly defined parts of the economy. For example, studies of productivity normally concentrate solely on the market sector, excluding the output of general government and eliminating imputations such as the output of housing services by owner-occupiers. In other cases, the economic researcher will want to focus on, for example, agriculture, the metalworking industries or business services.

VI. Note that the term "industry" is used either as a synonym of branch (as it is here) or to indicate the entire grouping of industrial branches – as opposed to agriculture and services.

VII. The reference product classification at international level is the CPC (Central Product Classification) and is described in Chapter 11.

To meet these specific needs, national accountants have compiled classifications (sometimes known as nomenclatures) of *industries.* ▶ **VI.** (also called *branches*). A branch of activity is defined as a grouping of homogeneous production units. Branches are identified by reference to a product classification, so that a branch produces only the goods or services described under a given heading of the product classification. The international reference classification for branches is the ISIC Revision 3 (International Standard Industry Classification, soon to be replaced by ISIC Rev 4). ▶ **VII.**

Table 1 shows percentages of total value added for major branches in four OECD countries. The classification used is the international industry classification in the national accounts (which is based on the ISIC) at the so-called A6 level (6 major branches shown in bold type in the table), and at the A17 level (the branches lettered from A to Q). For example, the A6 level "Industry" is broken down into three A17 levels: C Mining and quarrying; D Manufacturing; E Electricity, gas, and water supply. Firms often operate in several branches, since many of them are diversified. In this case, they are broken down into virtual units producing a homogeneous good. For example, the "Industry" branch includes all productive units producing industrial goods, whether these units be entire firms or parts of firms, known as "establishments". Differences in structure can be seen between highly developed countries, such as the United States and France, where services are very substantial, and less advanced countries like Korea where industry is still very important. Note that the total of values added is not called GDP in the table. This is not an omission; GDP is not equal to the sum of gross values added. GDP is equal to the sum of gross value added plus taxes net of subsidies on products (see Chapters 1 and 10).

For a yet more detailed picture, look at Table 2, based on the "A31" level of the international classification. This gives output, intermediate consumption and value added for Belgium in 2002, broken down by sub-branches of manufacturing.

Table 1. **Value added by industry at current prices**

As a percentage of total value added

Industry code and title		France	Korea	Portugal	USA
	Agriculture and fishing	**2.7**	**4.1**	**3.6**	**0.9**
A	Agriculture, hunting and forestry	2.6	3.8	3.2	0.9
B	Fishing	0.1	0.3	0.4	0.0
	Industry	**16.6**	**29.9**	**19.7**	**17.0**
C	Mining and quarrying	0.2	0.3	0.3	1.0
D	Manufacturing	14.7	26.9	16.8	14.0
E	Electricity, gas and water supply	1.7	2.6	2.6	2.0
F	**Construction**	**5.3**	**8.6**	**7.6**	**4.6**
	Trade	**19.5**	**18.3**	**23.9**	**22.0**
G	Wholesale and retail trade; repair of motor vehicles and household goods	10.8	7.8	14.3	13.1
H	Hotels and restaurants	2.3	3.0	3.0	2.7
I	Transport, storage and communication	6.4	7.5	6.6	6.2
	Business activities	**30.7**	**21.9**	**19.0**	**32.2**
J	Financial intermediation	4.8	9.1	6.0	7.8
K	Real estate, renting and business activities	26.0	12.8	13.0	24.3
	Other services	**25.2**	**17.3**	**26.3**	**23.3**
L	Public administration and defence; compulsory social security	7.6	5.9	9.3	7.4
M	Education	5.6	5.4	7.3	5.1
N	Health and social work	7.9	2.9	6.1	6.8
O	Other community, social and personal service activities	3.4	3.0	3.0	3.9
P	Private households with employed persons	0.5	0.1	0.7	0.1
Q	Extra-territorial organisations and bodies	0.0	0.0	0.0	0.0
	Total value added	**100.0**	**100.0**	**100.0**	**100.0**

Source: OECD (2006), *National Accounts of OECD Countries, Main Aggregates, 1970-2004, 2006 Edition,* OECD, Paris.

StatLink: *http://dx.doi.org/10.1787/417223344147*

Table 2. **Output, intermediate consumption and value added
of manufacturing branches**

Belgium, 2002, current prices, million euros.

Industry code		Output	Intermediate consumption	Gross value added
D	Manufacturing	171 163	127 135	44 028
DA	Manufacture of food products, beverages and tobacco	26 541	20 672	5 868
DB	Manufacture of textiles and textile products	8 364	6 125	2 239
DC	Manufacture of leather and leather products	313	217	96
DD	Manufacture of wood and wood products	2 780	2 042	737
DE	Manufacture of pulp, paper and paper products; publishing and printing	10 166	6 784	3 382
DF	Manufacture of coke, refined petroleum products and nuclear fuel	12 955	11 776	1 179
DG	Manufacture of chemicals, chemical products and man-made fibres	28 893	20 183	8 710
DH	Manufacture of rubber and plastic products	5 186	3 373	1 813
DI	Manufacture of other non-metallic mineral products	6 917	4 513	2 405
DJ	Manufacture of basic metals and fabricated metal products	24 006	17 797	6 209
DK	Manufacture of machinery and equipment n.e.c.	8 016	5 183	2 833
DL	Manufacture of electrical and optical equipment	9 537	6 264	3 273
DM	Manufacture of transport equipment	22 340	18 430	3 910
DN	Manufacturing n.e.c.	5 150	3 775	1 375

Source: OECD (2006), *National Accounts of OECD Countries, Main Aggregates, 1970-2004, 2006 Edition*, OECD, Paris.

StatLink: *http://dx.doi.org/10.1787/547506450686*

Key Points

The production frontier used for national accounts includes:

▶ The production of goods and services intended to be sold, known as market output.

▶ Unsold production, known as non-market output, of general government and non profit institutions.

▶ Production of goods by households for their own consumption, and the own-account production of capital goods by businesses.

▶ The housing services (imputed rents) of homeowner-occupiers, not including the other services produced by households for their own account.

Market output at current prices is measured as: sales plus changes in inventories of finished products and work in progress.

Output is measured at the basic price, which equals the per-unit revenue received by the producer, excluding taxes on products but including subsidies on products.

Non-market output (that of general government and non-profit organisations) is measured by the sum of its costs, including intermediate consumption, compensation of employees, consumption of fixed capital and other taxes on production.

Housing services provided by homeowner-occupiers are imputed as being equal to the rents they would have paid for comparable housing.

The output of banks is measured, for simplification, as the difference between interest received and interest paid, plus the sales of directly invoiced services.

The output of insurance companies is measured as the difference between premiums and indemnities, plus investment income.

The output of the distribution sector is measured by the distribution margin.

Going further

Household services

Official national accounts do not include the domestic and personal services provided by members of a household for their own consumption. This means that activities like cooking, housecleaning, washing clothes and looking after children or elderly people are excluded from GDP unless these activities are carried out by people paid for doing so. This had led John Hicks, the famous economist and national accounts pioneer, to remark that it was possible to reduce GDP by marrying one's cook.

National accountants have rejected the idea of including these services in GDP for practical reasons: the difficulty of imputing values to such services, and to the consequences this would have for the analysis of variations in GDP, which would then contain a substantial portion that is completely "invented". How indeed can one value the service provided by a mother making meals for her family? At the price of an employee in a fast-food preparing a hamburger or at the price of a chef in a three-star restaurant? Some people have suggested estimating the price of the imputed salary at its "opportunity cost", in other words what the mother would have earned had she been working outside the household. This estimation method would produce widely differing results. For example, if the mother is a senior executive, the opportunity cost will be much higher than if she is a cashier in a supermarket. Another difficulty is how to distinguish between activities when there is joint production. A father is simultaneously peeling vegetables for the family meal, keeping an eye on the baby and helping another child with homework. How much time should one allocate to the cooking, to looking after the baby and to the education of the other child? Should the value of these activities be reduced because they are being carried out at the same time?

The decision to place unpaid domestic services outside the production frontier of the national accounts has been quasi-controversial. In most countries, these unpaid services are mainly carried out by women and are manifestly just as important for the general welfare as many of the paid services that are within the production frontier. Looking after children or elderly parents, housecleaning and feeding the family are activities with as much value added (if not more) as those of professional footballers or casino-managers, which are placed within the production frontier. Some people have even gone as far as to accuse national accounts of being the product of a macho conspiracy, aimed at reinforcing the idea that women's work in the home is of no value.

Nothing could be further from the truth; it is purely for practical reasons that the activities are excluded. Moreover, in order to provide the public with better information, several statistical offices compile so-called satellite accounts containing an estimate of this unpaid domestic work. These statistics, forming an annex to the national accounts, show what GDP would have been had unpaid domestic work been included. Figure 2 shows estimates for five countries. These are for 1990 and taken from an OECD report titled *Measurement of Unpaid Household Production. Paris, 1997*. The estimates of the total value of unpaid services range from around 35% of GDP in Germany to more than 50% of GDP in Australia. In any case, women produce almost two thirds of the unpaid domestic work. Clearly, women are worth a lot.

Figure 2. **Unpaid household production**

As per cent of GDP

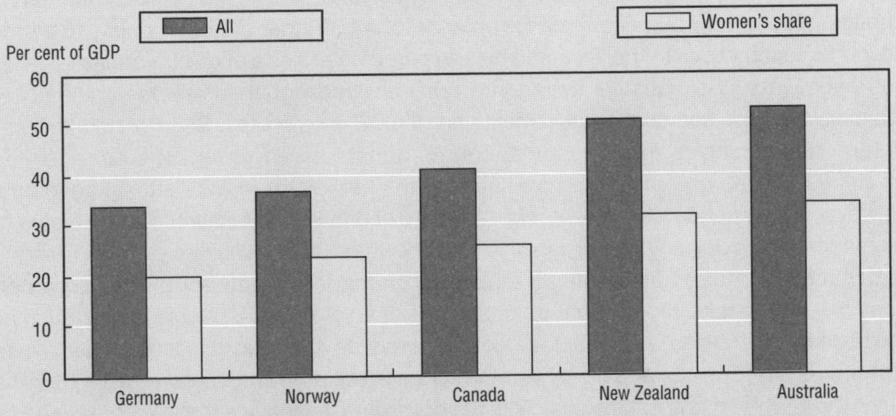

The adjustments for the underground economy in the case of France

To account for the underground economy, all OECD countries make substantial adjustments to the officially obtained GDP. In the case of France, this adjustment amounts to around +4%. It must be made clear, however, that this figure is just an approximation. What INSEE (the French statistical office) calls the underground economy comprises three sub-groupings: illegal activities (drug dealing, organised prostitution, etc.); black labour (clandestine enterprises); and tax fraud. INSEE, like other statistical institutes, does not try to evaluate illicit activities. To account for black labour, it adjusts GDP by roughly +1%. The approach adopted is highly empirical: on the basis of official investigations and socio-economic research, INSEE has picked out sectors where there is a strong presumption of underground work and then estimated, very crudely, sector by sector, the scale of this activity, based on expert opinion.

In the case of tax fraud and tax evasion, INSEE adjusts the accounts by around +3%, of which 2.5% is for dissimulation of receipts and 0.5% for unpaid VAT (Value-Added Tax).

As regards the dissimulation of receipts, the sources used are official figures from the tax authorities compiled on the basis of sample tax investigations. For VAT, the source is a comparison between the theoretical VAT amount calculated on recorded taxable transactions, and the VAT actually recovered by the government, together with several minor adjustments. In addition to these adjustments, there are accounting adjustments for undeclared gratuities and benefits in kind. Each of these represents roughly 0.5% of GDP.

Data sources for the value added of non-financial enterprises: the example of France

One of the drivers that enhances the quality of national accounts is that they are based on the extensive aggregation of individual firms' accounts. In the case of France (but this is applicable to other countries) INSEE has access, albeit after a certain delay, to all the accounts sent by firms to the tax authorities as part of their declarations for profits tax. This source is virtually exhaustive as regards firms and individual entrepreneurships. It is therefore from this source that the largest part of GDP is estimated. Sales of non-financial enterprises as shown in company accounts constitute an essential source for the calculation of the output of the non-financial market sector in the national accounts. However, this is not as simple as it might seem, since there are numerous adjustments to be made to the company accounts, which do not use exactly the same definitions as the national accounts. Adjustments also have to be made to allow for the underground economy and to take into account other sources of an even more reliable nature, such as those derived from the government budget. For example, the national accountants have to make sure that the taxes paid by enterprises are equal to the taxes received by the authorities. When this is not the case, it is the government accounts that are considered as taking precedence, and the data from the company accounts are altered accordingly. This adjustment clearly modifies the measurement of company profits (the gross operating surplus). Onto these figures have to be added the results of INSEE's direct surveys of enterprises (the EAE, or Enquête Annuelle d'Entreprise), whose results are mainly used to make a detailed breakdown of sales by branch.

FISIM

FISIM (financial intermediation services indirectly measured) is the term used to describe the services that banks provide to their customers but which are not invoiced. For bank depositors, these services generally include the management of current accounts, the sending out of bank statements and fund transfers between accounts. Instead of directly invoicing these services, the banks reduce the interest paid to depositors. This interest is in fact lower than the one customers could have obtained by lending their money directly to borrowers. For bank borrowers, these services include the monitoring of their creditworthiness, financial advice, the smoothing over time of repayments and the recording of these repayments for accounting purposes. The cost of these services is an inseparable part of the interest rate that the bank charges to these borrowers.

FISIM at current prices is calculated using the following (simplified) formula:
$(rl - rr) \times L + (rr-rd) \times D$.

In the formula above, rl is the observed interest rate on loans, rr is the so-called reference rate, rd is the reference rate of deposits, L is the amount of loans, and D is the amount of deposits. The reference rate rr is an estimate of a pure interest rate, involving no risk element, thus corresponding to economics agents' preference for the present. The difference between the interest rate paid by borrowers (rl) and the reference interest rate (rr) is used to measure the price of FISIM for the borrowers. The difference between the reference interest rate (rr) and the rate of interest received on bank deposits (rd) is used as the price of FISIM for depositors. These prices are then multiplied by total borrowing, and by total deposits, in order to arrive at the total FISIM consumed by the various economic agents.

The logic of national accounts requires that if FISIM is counted in the measurement of output it must also be recorded as consumption on the part of those using these services. For a firm borrowing from a bank, FISIM will therefore be intermediate consumption. For a household depositing money with a bank or obtaining a loan from a bank, FISIM will be an element in final consumption expenditure. For a long time, national accountants had found no convincing way of allocating this output to consumers and, except in the United States, Canada and Australia, FISIM was conventionally regarded as intermediate consumption at the level of the economy as a whole. Fortunately, a solution has recently been found and adopted by all OECD countries starting in 2005. This still leaves the problem of the choice of reference interest rate. European countries have chosen a rate that is an average of the short-term inter-bank rate and certain longer-term rates, while the United States has chosen the rate on US Treasury Bonds. The allocation between households and enterprises is made pro rata, based on the respective shares of loans and deposits of these two groups.

Exercises   *Answers at www.SourceOECD.org/understandingnationalaccounts*

Exercise 1. Change in the structure of production

This exercise is based on the Table 3 taken from Austrian national accounts at current prices. Show that the Austrian economy has increasingly become a service economy. Illustrate the result by a graph. In which branches are non-market activities to be found? Which branch contains the imputation of rents for homeowner/occupiers? What difference is there between the sum of the values added in this table and GDP? Which of the large branches has grown most since 1980? Express the result as an annual average growth rate. Which of the large branches has grown the least? Is this result in current prices totally convincing?

Exercise 2. Branches and products

Table 2 in this chapter shows output, intermediate consumption and value added by the manufacturing branch for Belgium. Using examples from this table, reconstitute the fundamental relationship linking these three magnitudes. Illustrate for certain branches the differences in their so-called outsourcing rates (externalisation rates). What differences would have been made to this table if one had wanted to present the data by product, and not by branch?

Exercise 3. Calculation of output

The following are the simplified data for a firm producing cars. Sales of cars: 1 353 500. Purchases: raw materials: 540 000; temporary employment services: 350 500; machine tools: 264 000. Inventories of finished products at the start of the period: 245 000; at the end of the period: 346 700. Inventories of raw materials at the beginning of the period: 73 200; at the end of the period: 43 000. Calculate the output, the intermediate consumption and the value added at current prices, assuming no change in prices during the period. Why is this last condition important?

    UNDERSTANDING NATIONAL ACCOUNTS – ISBN 92-64-02566-9 – © OECD 2006

Exercice 1. Table 3. **Austria: gross value added by branch**

Million current euros	1980	1995	2002
Agriculture and fishing	**3 861**	**4 245**	**4 041**
Agriculture, hunting and forestry	3 858	4 239	4 035
Fishing	3	6	6
Industry	**18 986**	**35 577**	**45 218**
Mining and quarrying	925	575	913
Manufacturing	16 047	30 540	39 644
Electricity, gas and water supply	2 014	4 462	4 661
Construction	**5 544**	**12 383**	**14 653**
Trade	**17 712**	**38 284**	**49 305**
Wholesale and retail trade; repair of motor vehicles and household goods	9 849	20 451	25 975
Hotels and restaurants	2 749	6 148	8 827
Transport, storage and communication	5 114	11 685	14 503
Business services	**8 345**	**31 353**	**44 767**
Financial intermediation	3 390	9 622	11 098
Real estate, renting and business activities	4 955	21 731	33 669
Other services	**13 387**	**36 059**	**39 399**
Public administration and defence; compulsory social security	4 008	10 802	11 888
Education	3 986	8 876	10 599
Health and social work	3 240	9 852	9 148
Other community, social and personal service activities	1 965	6 163	7 285
Private households with employed persons	188	366	479
Total value added	**67 835**	**157 901**	**197 383**
GDP	**76 325**	**175 526**	**220 688**

Exercise 4. Calculation of output: the non-market case

The following are simplified data for a unit of general government. Civil servants' gross wages and salaries: 562 980; employers' social contributions: 65 450; purchases of materials: 85 340; tax revenue: 485 770; depreciation: 124 320. Calculate output, intermediate consumption and value added. Verify that the measure of output corresponds to the assumption that this administrative body is non-profit.

Exercise 5. Calculation of output: the case of banks

The following are the simplified data for a bank: foreign exchange commissions: 32 980; stock-market trading commissions: 23 430; interest received: 357 850; interest paid: 204 650; purchases of materials: 34 520; purchases of IT consultancy services: 32 890; purchases of software: 12 590; inventory of materials at the start of the period: 7 420; inventory of materials at the end of the period: 3 860. Calculate the output, the intermediate consumption and the value added. Assume the figure for FISIM is interest received minus interest paid.

Exercise 6. Calculation of output: the case of distributors

The following are the simplified data for a retail chain: sales: 4 567 800; total purchases: 4 120 500 (of which, goods for resale: 3 987 350); inventories of goods for resale at start of period: 476 000; at end of period: 548 400; inventories of materials at start of period: 120; at end of period: 3 250. Calculate the output, the intermediate consumption and the value added. Inflation is assumed to be negligible.

Exercise 7. Calculation of output: the case of insurance companies

The following are the simplified data for an insurance company: premiums received: 210 400; indemnities paid out on claims: 187 500; income from the investment of reserves: 34 270; purchases of consumables: 24 320; inventories of materials at the start of the period: 5 630; at the end of the period: 20. Calculate the output, the intermediate consumption and the value added. Now suppose that an exceptional claim raises the amount of indemnities for this same period to 245 000. Recalculate the output. How is this result to be interpreted?

   UNDERSTANDING NATIONAL ACCOUNTS – ISBN 92-64-02566-9 – © OECD 2006

Chapter **5**

DEFINING FINAL USES OF GDP

Changes in the final uses of GDP, or demand to use the economists' term, determine the growth of real GDP in the short term. This chapter gives the definition of the components of this demand.

The authors of the OECD *Economic Outlook* for 2005, commenting on recent economic developments in the United Kingdom (the country chosen for illustration in this chapter), wrote: *"UK GDP grew by over 3% in 2004 underpinned by **fixed investment** and **government consumption**, which were up by 5.5% and 4.75%, respectively. On the other hand, the contribution from **consumers' expenditure** is diminishing, with growth of just over 1% at an annualised rate in the fourth quarter of 2004, the lowest growth rate since early 2003 when consumer confidence was affected by concerns about Iraq. With growth stronger than in the main European trading partners, **net exports** have remained a drag on growth in 2004."*

There are three target variables that governments try to influence in order to maintain growth at a rate that keeps inflation and employment at the desired levels: 1) demand from households (or, in the national accounts, "households' consumption expenditure"); 2) public consumption (or "general government consumption expenditure"); and 3) investment (or "gross fixed capital formation"). To influence these variables, governments use fiscal and monetary policy instruments (see "How do monetary and fiscal policies operate?" in the Section "Going further").

The total of these three variables is known as domestic demand. Exports are also a major component of final demand, but in this case external demand. It is conventional to show external demand as being equal to exports *minus* imports, the result being known as net exports.

These are the variables that economists look at when trying to predict future economic developments. At first, macroeconomic forecasts are made by estimating final uses based on their recent movements, taking into account recent and expected changes in monetary and fiscal policy. Once these forecasts have been prepared for each member country, the OECD economists then exploit their knowledge of the financial and trading links between OECD countries to see whether the forecasts for each country are consistent for the OECD area as a whole. This leads to an iterative process in which the individual country forecasts are adjusted to produce a consistent set of forecasts taking into account the probable impact of the monetary and fiscal policies of each country on all the others.

This chapter will look at what is contained in each of the components of final uses. It is essential to bear in mind throughout the chapter, even though we do not always repeat the point, that what interests economists most is the variations in the volume for these variables, and not their movements at current prices. Some tables in this chapter use data at current prices, but the proper definition of the variable in the context of macroeconomic forecasting is the corresponding variable in volume (*i.e.* after deflation of the variable in current prices by the appropriate price index). Exercise 1 at the end of this chapter illustrates how a table of final uses at current prices is converted into volume terms.

1. Final uses in the national accounts

Table 1 shows the principal components of final uses and their importance in relation to GDP for the United Kingdom. An obvious feature is the importance of the item "households' final consumption expenditure". This accounts now for more than 60% of GDP in the United Kingdom, and the percentage is similar in other OECD countries.

Table 1. **United Kingdom: Share of final uses in GDP**
As a percentage of GDP, current prices

SNA Codes		1980	1990	2000	2004
P3-S14	Households' final consumption expenditure	57.5	60.6	63.3	62.9
P3-S13	General government final consumption expenditure	21.5	19.8	18.8	21.1
P3-S15	NPISHs' final consumption expenditure	1.4	2.0	2.4	2.5
P51	Gross fixed capital formation	18.7	20.5	17.0	16.3
P52	Changes in inventories	−1.1	−0.3	0.6	0.4
P53	Acquisition less disposal of valuables	0.0	0.0	0.0	0.0
P6	Exports	27.1	24.0	28.0	25.0
P7	*Minus* Imports	−24.9	−26.6	−30.1	−28.4
	Statistical discrepancy*	−0.3	0.0	0.0	0.1
GDP	Gross domestic product	100.0	100.0	100.0	100.0

* This row is explained in Chapter 11.

Source: OECD (2006), *National Accounts of OECD Countries: Volume I, Main Aggregates,* 1993-2004, 2006 Edition, OECD, Paris.

StatLink: *http://dx.doi.org/10.1787/461347577548*

What does "final uses" mean?

First of all, why "uses"? Quite simply because we are dealing with the use of resources placed on the market, these resources being output, imports and withdrawals from inventories. In large part, these uses consist of *purchases* by economic agents, and this is why one speaks of *final expenditure* as well as *final uses*: these two terms mean the same thing.

And then, why "final"? In the national accounts, the uses of resources are described either as *intermediate* or *final*. Intermediate uses consist of goods and services that are consumed (one could also say used-up or transformed) in a production process within the economic territory and during the accounting period (one year); final uses comprises all other goods and services. Note that it is not the nature of the good or service that determines whether it is intermediate or final. A steak bought by household is "final", but if a restaurant buys the same steak, it is "intermediate". Similarly, a steel sheet will generally be an intermediate good, but it can also become final if it is stocked during the current period to be consumed in a later period, or if it is exported. "Final" therefore simply refers to all the goods and services used during the period that are not entirely consumed (used-up or transformed) in a production process in the course of that same accounting period. It will be seen later that several conventions have had to be introduced in order to distinguish "final" from "intermediate" in practice.

In the case of households, apart from their activities as individual entrepreneurs and excluding the special case of dwellings, all the goods and services they buy are final, because despite the fact that they are in large part consumed during the accounting period, they are not used in a production process. It is necessary to remember the definition of output given in Chapter 4: preparing meals and washing clothes in the home are not considered as output in the national accounts. As a result, a raw steak is not considered as intermediate consumption in the production of a meal by a member of a household. The objection can be raised that certain goods purchased by households are not entirely consumed during the accounting period: wine and tinned preserves, for example, can be stocked for several years, while durable goods like cars, computers and household electronics provide services for their owners over many years. The response to these objections is that *by convention*, all goods and services apart from dwellings are considered to have been entirely consumed once they have been acquired by households.

Another important point is that expenditure by general government and non-profit institutions is classified *by convention* as final, either as final consumption expenditure or as gross capital formation (GCF). It may be asked whether some of these services should not be treated as intermediate. While there is little difficulty in accepting that education and healthcare are of a "final" nature, many public services – ranging from defence and policing to street lighting and road maintenance – have some of the characteristics of the "intermediate" category. They clearly contribute to production, since there would be much less output if the government failed to defend the country against a foreign invasion, to maintain law and order and to keep the road system in good condition. Indeed, the absence of such services can lead to catastrophic slumps in output, as the experience of numerous developing countries can testify.

The problem is that it is not possible to say just how much of these services provided by general government contributes to the output of firms and how much to the general well-being of the population. Both households and firms benefit from public security, the road network and the many other contributions to civilised living provided by general government. And even if it were possible to separate out that part of general government services that contributes to production, one would then be obliged to allocate the production costs in a very arbitrary fashion among the producers. These are the reasons that have led national accountants to treat all services provided by general government as "final".

Conversely, all spending by firms on goods and services is "intermediate" apart from investment (GFCF) and changes in inventories. Purchases of investment goods are recorded as *final* and not intermediate expenditure because the consumption of these goods (referred to as *consumption of fixed capital* by the national accountants and as *depreciation* by economists) takes place over a period of more than one year. Changes in inventories also form part of final uses because inventories remain in existence for many accounting periods – usually for the entire lifetime of the enterprise.

Exports – the goods or services sold abroad – are considered as "final" (even though they may be used in a production process by the importing country) because they are final sales from the point of view of the exporting country. From the point of view of the importing country, the value of these imported goods and services is included either in final goods and services or in intermediate goods and services and has to be subtracted from the total of final goods and services to obtain Gross *Domestic* Product. This is why imports carry a negative sign in Table 1.

To sum up, the definition of "final" goods and services is based on several conventions. Purists may find this unsatisfactory since a different set of conventions would give a different set of national accounts. However, it can definitely be said of the current conventions that they result in a set of statistics that have, over many years, proved useful in describing and managing countries' economies.

2. Households' final consumption expenditure

Households' final consumption expenditure is the largest component of final uses. It includes:

1. *Purchases of the goods and services used by households to meet their everyday needs:* clothing, household durables, rent, transport, personal services and so on. These purchases represent by far the largest part of household consumption expenditure. There are three points to note:

   – Some of these purchases are made on credit. In this case, the national accountant has to break the transaction down into three parts: the price of the good itself (for example, a car); the administrative expenses of the financial company making the loan; and the payment of interest. The first part is assigned to household expenditure in the "cars" category; the second to household expenditure in the "financial services" category, but the third is excluded from household consumption expenditure and counted as an interest payment in the household primary income account (see Chapter 6 which deals with the household account). Note that the expenditure on cars is recorded in its entirety the moment the purchasers take possession of them, and not according to the timing of the loan repayments, even when the purchase is made under a financial lease or hire-purchase arrangement.

– Purchases of dwellings are final uses but are included, not in consumption expenditure, but in gross fixed capital formation. National accountants regard the owners of dwellings as producing housing services either for themselves or for tenants. These households invest (by buying the house) and carry out intermediate expenditure, for example on the purchase of building materials or the services of plumbers and electricians needed to keep the dwelling in good condition. Both the purchase of the dwelling (capital formation) and expenditures for repair and maintenance (intermediate consumption) are excluded from households' final consumption expenditure. The former remains a final use, while the latter is an intermediate use.

– In the national accounts, the household sector includes individual entrepreneurs, also called unincorporated enterprises (see Chapter 6). However, spending by households on goods and services intended for consumption in the production process of the enterprise does not form part of households' final consumption but is considered intermediate consumption by the unincorporated enterprise.

2. *Partial payments for goods and services provided by general government.* This covers cases in which the households have to pay a part of the public services provided – for example, a ticket for entry to a public museum, the price of which covers only a small part of the services provided. If prescription medicines and medical services are partly reimbursed by government, the part actually paid by households is included here.[1] The portion that is reimbursed forms part of expenditure by general government, and of households' *actual* consumption, as will be shown later.

3. Payments to general government for various types of licences and permits, when these are made in exchange for a genuine service. Payments designed merely to produce income for general government are treated as taxes and therefore excluded from households' consumption expenditure. The borderline between the two categories is somewhat arbitrary: licences for owning vehicles, boats or aircraft are treated as taxes, while fees for issuing passports and driving licenses are usually regarded as payments for services. In some countries, licence fees for public service television are treated as household final consumption expenditure, but in the United Kingdom the television licence fee is recorded as a tax. (See "Limitations of national accounts: consumption of television").

Households' consumption expenditure also includes a certain number of imputed expenditures. These are items of expenditure that have not really taken place but for which

UNDERSTANDING NATIONAL ACCOUNTS – ISBN 92-64-02566-9 – © OECD 2006

values are assigned – or "imputed" – in order to improve comparability over time and between countries. The main imputed items of expenditure are:

- *Owner-occupiers' imputed rents.* People living in dwellings they own are considered to be selling housing services to themselves. The rents recorded in the national accounts therefore include both the actual rents paid by tenants and imputed rents in the case of owner-occupiers. In most countries, this is the largest imputed item in households' consumption. The amount of the imputed rent is measured by the rents paid for comparable housing in a similar part of the country.

- *Own-account consumption.* Consumption expenditure includes the value (estimated using the corresponding market prices) of the consumption of goods produced by people for themselves. The most important examples are agricultural products produced by farmers for themselves and their families. Note that imputations are made only for goods. With the exception of the housing services of owner-occupiers, no imputation is made for other services such as cooking, looking after children and cleaning when these are produced and consumed within households.

- *Income in kind.* Employees may receive goods and services either free of charge or at very low prices as part of their wages. For example, railway employees are often entitled to travel by train more or less free of charge, members of the armed forces frequently obtain free meals, etc. In the national accounts, these benefits in kind are valued at their cost to the employer. They are then added to compensation of employees and also appear in households' consumption expenditure.

- *Financial intermediation services indirectly measured (FISIM).* Banks commonly provide their customers with certain services free of charge or at prices that are below the cost of production. In some countries, the handling of cheques, for example, is still free. They cover their production costs by charging higher interest rates on the loans they make than on the deposits they receive. FISIM (see Chapter 4) is essentially measured by the difference between the interest received and the interest paid. Some of this FISIM is consumed by households and so must be included in household final consumption expenditure.

Consumption made outside the home territory

Households' final consumption expenditure must include all consumption expenditure made by households resident in the United Kingdom (to take the country illustrating this chapter), whether this expenditure takes place on UK territory or elsewhere. ▶ I. This means having to add to the consumption carried out on home territory the consumption by UK tourists abroad. Since the national accountants do not know what products tourists have consumed abroad, they record a total amount under "tourist services", which is recorded as an import and added to consumption on home territory (which for its part is available in great

I. For the definitions of "residence" and "economic territory", see Section 9 of this chapter.

detail). Conversely, the consumption recorded on home territory must be reduced by the value of purchases by foreign tourists in the United Kingdom.

The price system applied to final uses

The general rule applied in national accounts is that final uses are valued at the prices agreed to by the parties to the transaction. These prices are described as *market prices* or *acquisition prices*. In the case of payments by households, they correspond to the price paid in stores. Points to note:

- The prices of final uses include non-deductible VAT and other taxes on products, such as sales taxes, specific duties on tobacco, alcoholic beverages or motor fuels. The Box 1 "Typology of taxes" explains the distinction between *taxes on products*, such as sales taxes and VAT, which are included in household consumption expenditure, and *current taxes on income and wealth*, which are excluded.

- The prices of final uses include transport and marketing costs.

- The prices of final uses are net of rebates, meaning that they can be lower than the stated prices (or the "catalogue prices"), whether the reduction was obtained by bargaining or having been spontaneously offered by the seller in order to encourage sales.

- The prices of final uses include the tips paid over and above the stated prices. The most common examples are the tips paid in restaurants, taxis and hairdressers.

Classification of household expenditure

The main classification used for household expenditure is described as a classification according to *purpose* and is known as COICOP – *Classification of Individual Consumption by Purpose*. In this case, the products are classified under major headings that are better suited to the analysis of consumption than the standard classification of products, which is better suited to the analysis of production. Table 2 illustrates the changes in consumption expenditure in the United Kingdom on the basis of this classification by purpose. It shows the spectacular decline in just 25 years in the share of expenditure allocated to everyday purposes (food, alcoholic beverages and tobacco, clothing) in favour of leisure and services in general. This phenomenon is true of all countries where real incomes have been increasing. Economists say that "the income elasticity of the demand for basic goods tends to be lower than the income elasticity of the demand for services". The *elasticity* of one variable in relation to another is measured by the ratio between the index of the growth rate of the first and the index of the growth rate of the second. In this case, the elasticity of the demand for services in relation to income is therefore equal to: (100 + the growth rate in the demand for services)/(100 + the growth rate in income).

Table 2 also illustrates a major problem in looking only at expenditures made directly by households. The shares of healthcare (row 06) and education (row 10) are very small,

Box 1. **Typology of taxes**

National accountants separate the taxes paid by households and other agents into four groups: taxes on products (D21); current taxes on income and wealth (D5); other taxes on production (D29); and capital taxes (D91). Only the first two groups, which are the largest, will be dealt with here. Taxes in the first group are often called "indirect taxes" and those in the second "direct taxes".

In the OECD countries, taxes on products consist mainly of VAT, sales taxes and other specific taxes such as duties on petroleum products, tobacco or alcoholic beverages. To these can be added certain other minor taxes and customs duties. These taxes are collected at the time of the sale of the goods and services concerned and are therefore an integral part of the prices the buyer has to pay to acquire them. Prices "including taxes on product" are the most appropriate from the point of view of the economic analysis of consumption and are therefore the ones used by the national accounts. Sales to foreign tourists that are made free of VAT or sales taxes are recorded excluding these taxes, even if the purchaser initially pays them and is subsequently reimbursed. These taxes are said to be "deductible". Only non-deductible taxes are included in the prices used in the national accounts.

Current taxes on income and wealth for households consist mainly of taxes on incomes and profits of unincorporated enterprises, but also include local taxes, property taxes, other wealth taxes and some less important taxes. These "direct" taxes are not included in consumption expenditure but are treated as **transfers**, *i.e.* a payment for which nothing is directly received in return. These taxes are recorded in the secondary income distribution account, as explained in Chapter 6 on the household account.

since what we have here is only the portions of these services that are directly paid by households. In fact, the bulk of these services are free of charge, albeit financed indirectly by taxes or social contributions. The true consumption by households of health and education services is therefore much larger, but the part provided by government is recorded as *individual consumption of general government* and not as *household consumption expenditure*. We shall return to this point in Section 5.

A final point to note in this table is that the second and third rows from the bottom concern tourist expenditure. As explained earlier, it is necessary to add to consumption on home territory consumption by UK tourists abroad, and deduct the consumption of foreign tourists in the United Kingdom (hence the negative sign in this line) in order to obtain the final consumption expenditure by resident households.

3. Final consumption expenditure by general government

This is the second largest final use after household consumption. Expenditures by general government are considered *by convention* as forming part of the final uses (consumption or GFCF) of general government itself. For example, current expenditure on police and education is regarded as consumption by general government. What lies behind this strange convention,

Table 2. **United Kingdom: share of households' expenditures in classification by purpose**

As a percentage of total final consumption expenditure, current prices

SNA code		1980	2004
P31-S14-01	Food and non-alcoholic beverages	17.8	8.8
P31-S14-02	Alcoholic beverages, tobacco and narcotics	5.7	3.8
P31-S14-03	Clothing and footwear	7.7	6.0
P31-S14-04	Housing, water, electricity, gas and other fuels	16.0	18.5
P31-S14-05	Furnishings, household equipment	6.9	6.3
P31-S14-06	Health	0.9	1.7
P31-S14-07	Transport	15.0	14.8
P31-S14-08	Communications	1.7	2.3
P31-S14-09	Recreation and culture	9.9	12.5
P31-S14-10	Education	0.9	1.4
P31-S14-11	Restaurants and hotels	10.7	11.2
P31-S14-12	Miscellaneous goods and services	7.4	11.2
P33-S14	Final consumption expenditure of resident households abroad	2.0	3.8
P34-S14	Final consumption expenditure of non-resident households on the territory	−2.6	−2.1
P31-S14	Total final consumption expenditure of households	100.0	100.0

Source: OECD (2006), *National Accounts of OECD Countries: Volume I, Main Aggregates,* 1993-2004, 2006 Edition, OECD, Paris.
StatLink: *http://dx.doi.org/10.1787/354836586211*

given that these services benefit households and enterprises? Essentially, it is because no one knows how to attribute this expenditure precisely to the beneficiaries, since they do not buy them, even though they pay the taxes that finance them. It has therefore been agreed not to attempt to allocate these expenditures to their beneficiaries but to attribute all these expenditures to general government itself, by convention. Among other advantages, this makes it possible to remain closer to the actual monetary flows.

In accounting terms, final consumption expenditure by government is equal to its cost, defined by the following sum:

- compensation of employees of the government,

- *plus* purchases by government of materials and other intermediate consumption items,

- *plus* consumption of government fixed capital, ▶ II.

- *plus* the purchases of goods and services by the government for the benefit of households (for example, reimbursement of healthcare services, housing allowances, etc.),

- *plus* other taxes on production (a very small item for government),

- *minus* partial payments by households or firms for services provided by government (entry to museums, sales of government publications, etc.).

II. The new SNA, which will be implemented around 2012, could recommend including here "capital services" rather than only consumption of fixed capital. Capital services cover consumption of fixed capital plus an estimate of the return to capital (see Chapter 4).

Although this expenditure is all recorded as final consumption or GFCF by general government in the standard national accounts tables, national accountants have for some years been distinguishing, within general government consumption expenditure, the part that is "collective" from the part that is "individual". *Individual consumption expenditure* is expenditure that is clearly carried out for the benefit of households. Table 3 shows that individual expenditure now represents more than 60% of total expenditure in the UK, following an appreciable rise in this percentage in the past 25 years. This expenditure mainly covers public education and public healthcare. It is this expenditure that was missing from Table 2 but which is required in order to show the true picture of the goods and services consumed by households. Individual expenditure of government also includes spending on aid for social housing, the operating expenses of museums and other government services to households.

Collective consumption expenditure comprises expenditure related to the activities of general government that are not attributable uniquely to households but also benefit enterprises. This includes expenditure on Congress, National Assemblies, Parliaments, etc., on ministries of foreign affairs, safety and order, defence, home affairs, economic affairs and the protection of the environment, as well as government R&D activities.

There is an important economic distinction between these two categories of expenditure. In the case of individual consumption expenditure, the cost to general government of supplying the services depends more or less directly on the number of households making use of the services. It will cost almost twice as much to teach 10 000 children as 5 000. The cost of collective services, on the other hand, depends much less on the number of "customers". Defence services are available to anyone living in the country. The large countries may need to have larger armies than small countries but there is no direct link between the number of people benefiting from the collective service and the cost of supplying them.

Table 3. **United Kingdom: Breakdown of final consumption expenditure of general government**

As a percentage of final consumption expenditure of general government, current prices

SNA codes		1980	2004
P31-S13	Individual consumption expenditure of general government	51.7	61.4
P32-S13	Collective consumption expenditure of general government	48.3	38.6
P3-S13	Final consumption expenditure of general government	100.0	100.0

Source: OECD (2006), *National Accounts of OECD Countries: Volume I, Main Aggregates,* 1993-2004, 2006 Edition, OECD, Paris.
StatLink: *http://dx.doi.org/10.1787/753878315638*

4. Final consumption expenditure of the NPISHs

Non-profit institutions serving households (NPISHs) are units formed by groups of households in order to supply services to themselves or to other households on a non-commercial basis. NPISHs include political parties, trade unions, religious organisations, sports and bridge clubs, cultural associations, charities and associations with philanthropic aims (Red Cross, etc.), and certain charitable foundations. In some countries, a number of universities are also classified in this sector. It has to be noted, however, that NPISHs do not include all institutions with non-commercial aims – far from it. This is because in order to be defined as NPISHs they have to be mainly financed by households' donations or regular subscriptions. Those non-profit institutions that are not directly financed by households but are, for example, controlled or financed by enterprises (Chambers of Commerce, professional associations, mutual insurance companies, etc.) are classified as being in the enterprise sector. Those controlled or financed by general government are classified in the general government sector. In the end, the NPISHs constitute only a small sector in the national accounts.

Like general government, the NPISHs provide "non-market" services. For this reason, their treatment in the accounts is similar to that of general government. The output of services by NPISHs is valued at cost, and by convention the NPISHs "consume" the services they produce. Final consumption expenditure of the NPISHs is therefore equal to their operating costs. Note that donations to charitable organisations are not payments for services. They are regarded as transfers and are recorded in the household account in the *secondary distribution of income* account (see Chapter 6).

We saw earlier how the consumption expenditure of general government was divided between individual expenditure and collective expenditure. This distinction does not have to be made for the NPISHs, since these organisations are at the service of households and all their expenditure is therefore considered as individual.

5. Moving from consumption expenditure to actual consumption

To improve the analysis of households' consumption by incorporating the individual consumption financed by general government or the NPISHs, the national accountants have invented the concept of **actual consumption**. Households' actual consumption is equal to households' consumption expenditure plus the *individual consumption expenditure* of general government and NPISHs. This individual consumption expenditure is also known as "transfers in kind". Table 4 illustrates this move from the notion of "who spends" to that of "who consumes".

Table 4. **United Kingdom: Moving from "who spends" to "who consumes"**
2004

	(P3) Final consumption expenditure (Who spends?)	*(P4) Actual final consumption* (Who consumes?)
(S14) Households	(P3-S14) £732.3 billion = final consumption expenditure of households.	(P4-S14) £912.3 billion = (P3-S14) final consumption expenditure of households (£732.3 billion); *plus* (P3-S15) final consumption expenditure of the NPISHs (£28.9 billion); *plus* (P31-S13) individual consumption expenditure of general government (£151.1 billion).
(S15) NPISH	(P3-S15) £28.9 billion = final consumption expenditure of the NPISHs.	None (0).
(S13) General government	£246.0 billion = (P31-S13) Individual consumption expenditure of general government (£151.1 billion) also known as "transfers in kind"; *plus* (P32-S13) Collective consumption expenditure of general government (£94.9 billion).	(P42-S13) £94.9 billion = collective consumption expenditure of general government.

However, probably because the series go back only a short time, the statistics of **actual consumption** are little used by economists, despite having two analytical advantages. First, it is a measure that comes closer to households' welfare. To analyse the consumption of healthcare and education, it is not sufficient to use only the *direct* expenditure of households on healthcare or education and omit the expenditure for these purposes made by government for the benefit of households. The use of *actual final consumption by households* makes it possible to circumvent this omission. The second advantage is that international comparisons of households' consumption are meaningful only when they are based on *actual* consumption and not on consumption *expenditures*, as was shown in Chapter 3.

6. Gross fixed capital formation

Investment, or to be more precise, gross fixed capital formation (GFCF), is an essential variable for the purpose of economic analysis of demand. The GFCF of "pure" households (in other words, excluding unincorporated enterprises) consists of the purchase of dwellings. This is a good indicator of households' confidence in the future and can be used to predict movements in consumption expenditure. The GFCF of general government consists mainly of road infrastructure but also of office buildings, schools, hospitals, etc. ▶ III.

III. In a few years from now, it will be necessary to add investment in weapons systems (missiles, warships, military aircraft), which for the moment are classified as current expenditure but will be reclassified as investment in the new national accounts system that will come into use around 2012.

IV. The term "fixed" was chosen in contrast to "variable" capital, which consists of inventories. These expressions probably date as far back as Karl Marx, one of the distant sources of inspiration for several of the ideas in the national accounts.

V. This example illustrates the fact that GFCF includes used capital goods. For some developing countries, most GFCF in the form or machinery and equipment consists of second-hand equipment imported from developed countries.

However, what economists are mainly interested in is the gross fixed capital formation of the business sector (non-financial and financial corporations and unincorporated enterprises). This is the largest single component of investment and its movements trigger off the beginning and the end of economic cycles. It also determines the growth in apparent labour productivity.

Gross fixed capital formation is precisely defined in the national accounts as the *net acquisition of produced fixed assets*, *i.e.* assets intended for use in the production of other goods and services for a period of more than one year: machinery, vehicles, offices, industrial buildings, software, etc. Some clarification is needed regarding the wording of this definition:

- The word *fixed* is used to indicate that additions to inventories are not included in GFCF. It does not mean that the equipment in question cannot move. ▶ IV. For example, transport equipment (cars, trucks, ships, aircraft) are not "fixed" in the normal meaning of the word, but they are nevertheless included in GFCF. The same is true of livestock (notably milking cows), which are also included in GFCF.

- *Net acquisitions* signifies that GFCF records the *purchases* of fixed assets after deduction of *sales* of fixed assets on the second-hand market. It is therefore not impossible, theoretically, for GFCF to be negative. For example, car rental firms "turn over" their fleets very rapidly. They buy large numbers of cars, making a positive contribution to GFCF, but at the same time they sell them very rapidly, thus making a negative contribution. For a given period, therefore, it is quite possible that the value of their purchases is smaller than that of their sales. However, such a situation is very unlikely to occur at the macroeconomic level, because one firm's sales of second-hand equipment are often another firm's purchases. ▶ V.

- The term *produced assets* signifies that only those assets are included in GFCF that are the result of a production process recognised by the national accounts. The national accounts also record transactions in *non-produced* assets such as land, primary forests and oil and mineral reserves. These *non-produced* assets are included in the balance sheet accounts but are not included in GFCF because they have been produced by nature and not by human activity. Nature is not a producer in the eyes of national accountants.

Box 2. **A special case: financial leasing**

Rather than buy a capital good outright, some firms prefer to use financial leasing arrangements, consisting of regular rental payments followed by a purchase at the end of the rental period. For example, many airlines acquire their aircraft through financial leases. There are financial companies specialising in this type of arrangement. These companies are the legal owners of numerous capital goods that they do not actually use but make available for others to operate. Economically speaking, it makes more sense to treat the airlines as owners of these assets even though this is not legally true. National accountants, who systematically give economic aspects precedence over legal aspects, record these assets as being on the books of the non-financial corporations that are the actual users, *i.e.* the airlines in this example.

The GFCF borderline

Economists, national accountants and company accountants have spent considerable time discussing the definition of fixed assets, because GFCF determines the measurement of their stock of capital (see Chapter 8), which in turn determines growth. In principle, the more capital there is, the greater the growth.

There is general agreement concerning most kinds of capital goods. Transport equipment, machinery, offices, warehouses, factories and major civil engineering works are clearly fixed assets. But there is still disagreement regarding certain types of expenditure (software, trademarks) that are in the "grey area" between GFCF and intermediate consumption. In principle, the difference between these two factors of production is the fact that the former is not entirely consumed in the annual process of production, while the latter is. Where exactly does the borderline run?

Traditionally, only material goods (also called "physical" goods or "tangibles") were considered as fixed assets. These are the items listed at the beginning of the previous paragraph. However, more and more accountants and economists recognise that several expenditures that do not take material form are not entirely consumed in the productive process during the year. Thus, these expenditures should be therefore "capitalised" and are known as "intangible assets".

Expenditure on mineral exploration is an example. Although accountants in mining firms have long regarded this expenditure as capital (GFCF) rather than current use (intermediate consumption), it is only recently that national accountants have agreed to do the same. Their reluctance stemmed from the fact that mineral exploration is entirely an acquisition of knowledge. (Is there ore in a given geographic area or not?). This change was undertaken, however, in the SNA 1993 and now all expenditure on mineral exploration is regarded as GFCF, *even when the search is unfruitful*. This last point is not as strange as it might seem, because modern exploration technology more or less guarantees a constant success rate: for a given outlay on mineral prospecting, the companies know from experience what percentage will result in exploitable discoveries.

Some other types of intangible asset are now included in GFCF in the national accounts. These are *software, databases* and *entertainment originals* (artistic or literary). The purchase or creation of software is expenditure that is not consumed in the period in which it takes place, since a programme is used for a period of several years. These expenditures, whether on an "in-house" software programme (such as a reservation system for an airline) or original software designed to be reproduced (such as Windows®, owned by Microsoft®), or reproductions (the rights to use Windows® that firms buy from Microsoft®) are all included in GFCF.

The difficulty from the point of view of national accounts is less a question of principle but of practicality, given that they have now diverged from the conventions used in business accounts. In their own accounts, firms treat the purchase or creation of software only partially as capital expenditure, and the firms' accounts are a common statistical source for the national accounts. Why is this? First, because of the application of the cautionary principle by company accountants: when it is not certain that a computer programme will have real value on the market, accounting standards recommend considering the expenditure as Research and Development and therefore not as investment in fixed assets. For this reason, software-producing firms like Microsoft® include no software among the assets on their balance sheets. Second, because firms often have an interest in treating software as a current expenditure so that it can be deducted immediately from their profits, thus reducing their taxes. In the end, national accountants are left with no satisfactory statistical sources for evaluating capital investment in software and are obligated to find substitute sources that are fairly approximate.

Entertainment originals take material form as hard-copy novels, films, CD-ROMs or tapes. But these forms have economic value only when protected by copyright. It is this protection that gives them their value and explains their classification as intangible assets. Their evaluation by the national accountants is even more problematical in practice than for software, and it is reasonable to think that the current national accounts statistics fail to estimate this type of GFCF correctly.

R&D expenditure has not yet been included in GFCF but will most probably be in a few years' time (after 2012), since it has been recommended to capitalise R&D spending in the next national accounts system (see Chapter 8 "The exclusions from the balance sheet accounts").

The GFCF classification

In the national accounts, data on GFCF are presented in several ways. First, GFCF can be broken down by the nature of the product, using the standard product classification. However, this is not the most useful classification, since it is better suited to analysing output than investment. Second, it can be broken down according to the industry or sector making the investment. For example, in the case of the United Kingdom, GFCF (plus changes in inventories) are shown by investing industry in Table 5. As can be seen, manufacturing is far from being the largest investing industry; investment by business services, transport and communications firms, as well as by distribution, hotels and catering businesses were substantially higher in 2003.

Table 5. **United Kingdom: Capital formation (P5) by industry**

Millions of pounds sterling, current prices, 2003

Agriculture, hunting, forestry and fishing	2 578
Mining and quarrying	4 146
Manufacturing	12 605
Electricity, gas and water supply	5 178
Construction	4 727
Distribution, hotels and catering	17 886
Transport, storage and communication	22 053
Business services and finance	29 711
Public administration and defence	10 879
Education, health and social work	9 002
Other services	10 391
Not allocated to industries[*]	50 956
All industries	180 112

* Investment in dwellings, transfer costs of land and existing buildings, and valuables.

Source: OECD (2006), National Accounts of OECD Countries: Volume I, Main Aggregates, 1993-2004, 2006 Edition, OECD, Paris.

StatLink: http://dx.doi.org/10.1787/170138546481

But it is also possible to show a matrix combining two categories: by nature of product and by investing sector. Table 6 shows United Kingdom GFCF broken down by institutional sector and by type of asset, using a classification suited to assets and distinguishing between:

- Material fixed assets:

  1. Dwellings (excluding land).

  2. Other buildings and structures.

  3. Machinery and equipment.

  4. Cultivated assets. These are the trees, bushes and vines making it possible to produce fruit, rubber, wine, tea and other products over a period of several years; they also include livestock raised for the production of milk or wool and animals bred for reproduction.

- Intangible fixed assets:

  1. Mineral exploration – spending on the search for oil or mineral deposits.

  2. Software – standard or developed in-house, originals or copies of originals.

  3. Literary and artistic originals, such as films, novels or music. These assets earn royalties.

It is important to note that GFCF in dwellings and other buildings does not include the value of the land on which they are situated. This is because land is not a produced asset. While *non-produced* assets are excluded from GFCF, the costs associated with the transfer of ownership of *non-produced* assets (transport and installation costs), as well as administrative expenses (lawyers' fees or taxes related to the purchase of these goods) are included in GFCF, as a separate category in the United Kingdom accounts. In the case of *produced* assets, these expenses are included in the prices of the assets themselves.

The price system used

Like all final uses, *Gross Fixed Capital Formation* is valued at acquisition prices. In most cases, this amounts to recording it excluding VAT, since VAT is generally entirely deductible in the case of firms' investments. However, the acquisition prices of capital goods include transport and installation charges, as well as all specific taxes associated with the purchase of these goods. For example, lawyers' fees are included in the value of the purchase of a dwelling (but not the value of the land on which it is built).

Table 6. **United Kingdom: Gross fixed capital formation by type of asset and institutional sector**

Millions of pounds sterling, current prices, 2004

	Public non financial corporations	Private non financial corporations	Financial corporations	Central government	Local government	Households and NPISHs	Total
Dwellings, excluding land	0	502	0	122	3 347	40 425	44 396
Other buildings and structures	1 274	34 085	1 609	5 978	10 002	2 689	55 637
Transport equipment	100	12 392	108	638	315	1 099	14 652
Other machinery and cultivated assets	1 006	42 963	2 655	1 715	1 418	4 646	54 403
Intangible fixed assets	737	3 726	1 230	0	351	351	6 395
Ownership transfer costs on non produced assets	−266	6 706	−1 562	995	−4 226	12 936	14 583
Total GFCF (P51)	2 851	100 374	4 040	9 448	11 207	62 146	190 066

StatLink: *http://dx.doi.org/10.1787/072364437200*

7. Changes in inventories

The next item appearing in the final uses table is the *change in inventories*, *i.e.* the difference between additions to and withdrawals from inventories. In common economic parlance, one might use the terms "stockbuilding" or "changes in stocks" for this entry, but the official name in the national accounts is "changes in inventories". In principle, only the additions to inventories should be part of final uses, and withdrawals from inventories should be classified as resources. However, in order to have accounts that are more compact, it was decided to count withdrawals from inventories as negative contributions to inventories and to combine the two flows.

First, inventories consist of the stocks of inputs intended to be used later as intermediate consumption in a production process (in companies' accounts these are known as "material inventories"). Second, they include stocks of finished goods that have not yet been sold. Third, they include stocks of merchandise purchased for resale, these being found mainly in wholesale and retail distribution. Fourth, they also comprise the strategic stocks (food, oil, stocks for intervention on agricultural markets) managed by government authorities. Lastly, they can also be "work in progress", which consists of goods being processed but which cannot yet be delivered to the user at the end of the accounting period. The value of these goods is therefore included in inventories. An important component of work in progress are goods such as ships, oil-drilling platforms and buildings that may take several months or even years to complete.

One might think it would be an easy matter to calculate changes in inventories by taking the value of inventories at the end of the accounting period and subtracting the value at the beginning, this information being available in companies' accounts. In practice, however, evaluating changes in inventories on the basis of companies' accounting data is difficult because inventories generate holding gains or losses as the market prices of the goods held in stock rise or fall. These gains or losses are not the result of a production process and thus cannot contribute to GDP, which is fundamentally an indicator of production. ▶ VI.

VI. The fact that these holding gains and losses are eliminated from GDP does not mean that they are ignored in the national accounts. They may have an important impact in perceived incomes when the prices of goods rise or fall. Expectations of holding gains or losses and their realization can have a substantial impact on the behaviour of producers and consumers. However, national accountants record them, not as elements of GDP, but instead in a "revaluation account" (see Chapter 8).

VII. This paragraph illustrates the case of an increase in the price of inventories, but there are of course quite common cases of decreases in the price of inventories, which should be treated symmetrically. In this case, it would be more accurate to refer to "holding loss on inventories" and "stock depreciation".

Let us suppose that prices are rising and that the change in inventories is calculated by taking the value of inventories at the end of the period *minus* the value at the beginning. The value obtained in this way will include a capital gain ("stock appreciation") that has to be eliminated in order to obtain the correct valuation of the changes in inventories for the purposes of the national accounts. ▶ VII. If the inventories at the end of the period consisted only of products that were already in inventory at the beginning of the period, in other words, if no new article had been added to the inventories during the period and no article withdrawn, it would be an easy matter to eliminate the holding gain, since it would be equal to the inflation rate times the opening value of the inventory. In reality, goods enter and are withdrawn from inventories at different moments in the accounting period, and it is quite possible that at the end of the period none of the original articles are still present.

When prices change and when products are continually being put into and withdrawn from inventory, there are three ways of evaluating the changes in inventories in the national accounts. The first is theoretically correct but impossible to apply in practice. The second is widely used, although it is in fact a very imperfect approximation. The third is easy, but very indirect and hence should be used with caution.

● The theoretically correct method consists of evaluating the goods coming into inventories at the market prices prevalent at the time of entry, and evaluating the withdrawals from inventories at the market prices ruling at the time of withdrawal. The algebraic sum of these entry and withdrawal values then gives the correct measure of the changes in inventories for the purposes of the national accounts. Unfortunately, this information is simply not available in practice.

● As a result, this theoretical method is replaced by an approximate method consisting of evaluating the value of the changes in inventories by applying to the quantities held at the beginning and at the end of the period either the average prices for the period or the mid-period prices (see Exercise 3).

● The third method is very indirect, consisting of calculating all the other items in supply-use accounts (see Chapter 10) and arriving at the changes in inventories as a residual of this accounting equation. This method is theoretically exact, but it leads to incorporating into the "changes in inventories" item all the errors contained in the other items.

The economic analysis of changes in inventories

Changes in inventories constitute a highly important indicator of possible changes in the growth rate. Nevertheless, the overall change in inventories remains difficult to interpret, because it includes two different types of goods: inputs and finished products. A positive change in inventories of inputs is a good sign since it signifies that producers are expecting an increase in future production. Conversely, an increase in inventories of finished products may indicate that the producers are having difficulty in selling their output and may therefore be about to cut back production and lay off staff. The interpretation of these figures can usefully be complemented by other information, such as industrial business surveys. Note that changes in inventories expressed in volume terms is always shown in terms of contributions to growth and has therefore become more difficult to manipulate in the context of chain-linked volumes (see Chapter 2).

8. Net acquisitions of valuables

This item is very small (see Table 1) and is therefore no more than a curiosity for the macroeconomist. Valuables are goods that are bought not to be consumed or used in production, but in the expectation that they will increase (or at least at least retain) their value over time. Examples include gem-stones, precious metals and paintings by old masters. In general, transactions in these objects take place between households and are therefore consolidated (in other words, cancel out) in the national accounts, except in cases where the goods cross frontiers. In certain countries – notably the United Kingdom and Hong Kong – commercial banks invest in precious metals and these are also classified as valuables. Note, though, that gold stocks held by central banks are classified as "monetary gold" and are shown as financial assets and not as valuables.

9. Exports and imports of goods and services

Exports and imports are key aggregates in the analysis of a country's economic situation. In today's extremely globalised world, whenever the United States (the world's largest national economy, accounting for more than 20% of world GDP) slows down or accelerates, all other economies are affected. The same relationship applies to all other countries because they are all exchanging an increasing amount of goods and services. Exchange rates play an important role here. If the pound sterling or the euro appreciates *versus* the dollar, exports from the United Kingdom or the euro area to the dollar countries suffer as a result. (Note however, that the price of their oil imports will decline, since oil is priced in dollars.) As can be seen in Figure 1, the United Kingdom's "degree of openness" reaches 25%, but this is still low compared with that of a small European country such as Belgium, which is even more open to exports and imports. The "degree of openness" is usually calculated as the following ratio: [(Exports + Imports)/GDP] x 100. It measures the extent to which a country is dependent on trade flows with its trading partners. The evolution in the degree of openness in the case of Belgium is a clear reflection of the country's growing openness to foreign trade, especially after 1993, when the single European Market was put in place.

VIII. In the national accounts, "foreign trade" means foreign trade in goods *and* services. However, since figures for foreign trade in goods were available long before figures for foreign trade in services, a tradition – disputable, admittedly – has been built up of sometimes applying the term "foreign trade" solely to trade in goods. Caution is therefore needed. Customs statistics generally do not cover services and therefore foreign trade on a customs basis may cover only goods; external trade figures in the balance of payments or the national accounts include both goods and services.

All these remarks point to the analytical importance of exports and imports for users of the national accounts. These flows are traditionally broken down into four parts: foreign trade in goods; foreign trade in services; ▶ **VIII.** direct purchases by non-residents in the economic territory (considered as exports of services); and direct purchases by residents in the rest of the world (considered as imports of services). These two latter items in fact cover, if we continue to use United Kingdom as an illustration, spending by foreign tourists in the UK as well as by UK tourists in foreign countries, as discussed in Section 2 of this chapter. We shall not return to the calculation of exports/imports, but we do need to define three important concepts: *economic territory*, *residence* and the *rest of the world*. These concepts are necessary to a precise definition of exports and imports.

A country's economic territory is the geographic area corresponding to the nation state. It includes its air space, its territorial waters, its territorial enclaves in the rest of the world (UK embassies in foreign countries, to take our current example) and free zones. Conversely, it excludes foreign embassies located in the UK. The definition of economic territory is important because only output taking place within the economic territory is recorded in the national accounts. A foreign subsidiary of a UK multinational is not productive in the sense used to draw up the UK national accounts, and its output is included in the national accounts of the country in which the subsidiary is located.

There have been changes in the economic territory covered in certain national accounts. For example, it is only recently (in 1999) that the French national accounts have included the overseas departments in French economic territory.[2] Previously, the economic territory in the French national accounts had been limited to metropolitan France. Because these departments were not included in the territory, the

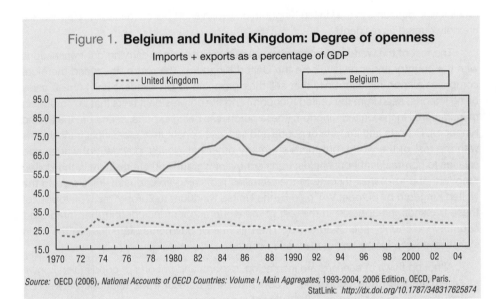

Figure 1. **Belgium and United Kingdom: Degree of openness**

Imports + exports as a percentage of GDP

Source: OECD (2006), *National Accounts of OECD Countries: Volume I, Main Aggregates,* 1993-2004, 2006 Edition, OECD, Paris.
StatLink: *http://dx.doi.org/10.1787/348317625874*

national accounts did not include the output of firms situated in these departments, and therefore recorded exports and imports to and from these overseas departments. Now that these departments are included, the French national accounts include the output of firms installed in these departments; therefore, they do not record transactions between these departments and metropolitan France as exports and imports. This type of mismatch between the official definition of a country and its economic definition in the national accounts is quite frequent; for example, the US national accounts do not include Puerto Rico. Generally, however, the quantitative impact on the accounts is negligible.

The concept of residence is associated with that of economic territory in the national accounts. A unit is said to be resident in a country when its "centre of economic interest" is situated in that country's economic territory. This is usually taken to mean that the unit has carried out economic activity there for more than one year. Only resident units are included in the institutional sectors of the national accounts. Most firms, including unincorporated enterprises that have an activity in the territory, are regarded as resident. For households, the test is where they spend their income. Only those households that make most of their consumption expenditures on the territory are regarded as resident. Households whose members work in the country but make most of their consumption expenditures abroad are excluded. This means, for example, that seasonal workers coming from another country to work for a few months a year in the United Kingdom are not regarded as resident, and their disposable income is not included in household disposable income in the UK national accounts. Conversely, certain British workers living and consuming in the United Kingdom while working in Ireland or another country are included as resident households. Foreign tourists who consume in the United Kingdom only for a short period (generally a few weeks) are not counted as resident.

The rest of the world is composed of all non-resident units carrying out transactions with the country under review, here the United Kingdom. The rest of the world therefore comprises all non-resident units that sell their products to UK resident units (these sales being imports, seen from the United Kingdom) and the non-resident units that buy products manufactured in the United Kingdom (these purchases being exports, seen from the United Kingdom). Exports and imports of goods and services constitute the principal transactions with the rest of the world, but there are many other categories: payment of wages and salaries to non-resident households; transfers by immigrant workers resident in the United Kingdom of part of their income to their families remaining abroad; subsidies paid to the United Kingdom by Europe; VAT paid by the United Kingdom to Europe, etc. The totality of these transactions appears in the rest of the world account included in the "integrated economic account" (see Chapter 10). The balance of payments statistics are the main statistical source for the rest of the world account.

Although flows of services are increasing, exports and imports of goods (also known as "merchandise trade") continue to constitute the core of trade relations between a country and the rest of the world. Statistics of exports and imports of goods were for a long time the best statistics available for the national accounts because customs services needed them for the collection of duties and the monitoring of trade in goods. The quality of these statistics has recently deteriorated in Europe as a result of the introduction of the single market, because there is no longer any legal control by customs services over merchandise moving within the European Union. However, the statistical services or the customs services of individual European countries have introduced surveys of the major exporters and importers in order to be able to continue to monitor these movements. In the absence of these surveys, it would no longer be possible to compile the national accounts in Europe.

These customs statistics show not only the amounts of exports and imports but also give information on the quantities traded – tonnage, number of units, etc. – for a highly detailed list of products (customs classifications typically contain several thousand items). This information is used by national accountants to calculate export and import prices by dividing the values by quantities. These price indices are known as "unit value indices". This procedure is sometimes criticised because, despite being based on quite detailed statistics, it mixes together prices of products of different qualities. In practice, the result is that unit value indices can vary considerably from one period to another, so that the national accountants must apply a smoothing process to make them intelligible. Some countries have developed special price surveys covering exporters and importers to replace these imperfect "unit value indices".

In the national accounts, detailed figures for imports of goods are valued at "cif" prices, meaning that the prices of the goods include "cost, insurance, freight" when they enter the frontier of the United Kingdom. Exports, for their part, are valued at "fob" prices, a maritime term that stands for "free on board", signifying that the prices of the goods include transport and insurance costs when they arrive at the country's frontier but not the transport and insurance costs further to the frontier. This is why one frequently sees in the national accounts tables that specify "imports cif" or "exports fob". To complicate things further, *total* imports in the national accounts are calculated at fob prices, in other words excluding the cost of transport to the frontier. The conversion to fob prices facilitates comparison with the balance of payments and results in an item called "cif-fob adjustment", which is explained in Chapter 10.

Differences in the movements of import and export prices are used to calculate terms of trade indices. The terms of trade are defined as the ratio between the index of export prices and the index of import prices. Exercise 4 gives an example of how these indices are calculated.

The amounts involved in *foreign trade in services* are much smaller than for trade in goods. However, these flows are rising sharply as the result of the increasing outsourcing of service activities. Until recently, exports and imports of services mainly consisted of transport services (sea, air) and insurance (reinsurance is frequently outsourced). It should also be remembered that, conventionally, expenditure by tourists is classified as trade in "tourist services". However, there is now, notably through the Internet, increasing overseas outsourcing of services to businesses and individuals ("call centres", trade in software, data processing). "Medical tourism" is also expanding, with people travelling abroad to receive treatment that is illegal or too expensive in their home countries.

The statistical sources for trade in services are of mediocre quality because this trade is difficult to identify. A very long time ago, the principal source was based on declarations made by banks to their central banks, which monitored all transactions made with the rest of the world in order to keep a check on the country's foreign-currency reserves situation. However, these declarations have been discarded in many countries and it is now necessary to carry out surveys of the principal operators dealing with the rest of the world. Monitoring external trade in services in an increasingly globalized world is a challenge that national accountants will have to face in coming decades.

Notes

1. The portion reimbursed by mutual institutions or private insurance companies is also included in households' consumption expenditure.

2. These are the islands of Guadeloupe, Martinique, La Réunion and Guyane.

Key points

▶ Economists use the word "demand" to cover what are known as final uses in the national accounts: consumption expenditure by households and general government; investment (GFCF); changes in inventories; and net exports (exports *minus* imports).

▶ In the case of producing units, uses may be "final" or "intermediate". Final refers to goods and services that are not entirely consumed during the period in a production process – *i.e.* GFCF and change in inventories. Intermediate refers to goods and services that are entirely consumed in a production process during the period.

▶ By convention, all goods and services bought by households other than dwellings are considered as final consumption, even if they are durable goods and are not entirely consumed during the period. Purchases of dwellings by households are GFCF.

▶ By convention, general government is considered to consume the services it produces. Final consumption expenditure by general government is equal to the compensation of employees, *plus* intermediate consumption, *plus* consumption of fixed capital, *plus* expenditure on market goods and services by general government on the behalf of households, *minus* partial payments.

▶ The price applied in the case of final uses is the market (or acquisition) price, including trade and transport margins and also non-deductible VAT and other taxes on products.

▶ Actual individual consumption is equal to households' consumption expenditure *plus* the individual portion of the consumption expenditures of general government and NPISHs.

▶ Gross fixed capital formation, often known more briefly as investment, is defined as net purchases of produced fixed assets.

▶ Changes in inventories are equal to additions to inventories *minus* withdrawals from inventories. Evaluating these variations on the basis of the inventories at the beginning and at the end of firms' accounting periods is problematical because of the existence of holding gains or losses on the inventories. These have to be excluded from the measure of change in inventories in national accounts.

▶ A distinction is often made between the exports and imports of goods and the exports and imports of services. Detailed imports are valued "cif". Total imports and detailed exports are both valued "fob".

 UNDERSTANDING NATIONAL ACCOUNTS – ISBN 92-64-02566-9 – © OECD 2006

Going further

How do monetary and fiscal policies operate?

Monetary policy consists of the central bank influencing interest rates, either directly or by affecting the money supply. Fiscal policy consists of the government modifying tax rates and increasing or reducing public expenditure.

Concerning monetary policy, a rise in interest rates will tend to reduce consumption expenditure by households because it increases the cost of consumer borrowing and makes saving more attractive. It will also tend to reduce gross fixed capital formation, first because the reduction in household spending reduces firms' incentive to invest in new plant and equipment, and second because it increases their borrowing costs. For equivalent reasons, a decline in interest rates will stimulate household spending and corporate investment.

In the past, many governments tried to encourage exports and reduce imports by means of a different instrument of monetary policy, namely manipulation of exchange rates. More recently, however, most OECD governments have tried to hold their exchange rates stable *versus* their trading partners, with the euro-area countries going so far as to fix exchange rates with each other once and for all.

Fiscal policy operates through two channels: increasing or reducing revenue and increasing or reducing expenditure. Cutting income-tax rates has an immediate impact on household spending and a secondary impact on capital formation (with firms investing more to meet the higher demand). Cutting profit-taxes encourages producers to increase output either by more investment or by higher utilisation of existing capacity.

General government makes both current expenditures (mainly civil service salaries) and expenditures on capital formation (roads, railways, urban development, etc.). Raising these two types of expenditure automatically increases GDP and also produces secondary effects inasmuch as a higher government wage bill will increase household consumption expenditure, and the demand for construction materials stimulates activity in the industries supplying them.

The euro-area countries now have much less freedom in regard to monetary and fiscal policy. They no longer have any possibility of modifying their exchange rates and have very little control over the exchange rate of the euro. Interest rates are set uniquely by the European Central Bank. While fiscal policy is somewhat less restricted, the European Stability and Growth Pact limits the possibilities in this respect by setting a ceiling of 3% of GDP on the difference between revenue and expenditure. Governments can reduce taxes but are then obliged to make corresponding cuts in expenditure, hence cancelling out the global impact on the economy.

The limitations of the national accounts: Consumption of television or of services financed by advertising

In most countries, consumption of television services in terms of viewing hours is large and rising – especially in households with young children. However, this is very poorly reflected in national accounts statistics on household consumption. These only show the payments made by households for access to cable TV networks, and in some countries, charges levied by government to finance public broadcasting. "Consumption" of television by households in the national accounts does not reflect television services that are financed by advertising. It is true that the cost of advertising is included in the price of the goods or services advertised and thus will "appear" as part of final consumption in the national accounts but not as consumption of television, and especially not in volume terms. In the national accounts, commercial television stations are regarded solely as sellers of advertising media. (Some cynics would maintain that this is fairly close to reality...).

The picture is complicated as regards the fees levied by some governments to finance public television services. France regards these fees as a payment for services, and so they are included in households' consumption expenditure. The UK, on the other hand, regards them as a direct tax and so they are excluded from households' consumption expenditure. In countries, such as France, where governments levy charges for public television, an interesting paradox would occur if the government were to abolish the charge and either replace it by budgetary financing or privatise the public channels. Household consumption of television, and hence GDP, would be reduced despite the fact that the only thing that had changed was the source of finance. To solve the problem of this lack of recording of free television services, it would be necessary to impute a value to the "free" services and include this in household final consumption expenditure. However, national accountants have not gone as far as this, despite the fact that practical solutions have been proposed.* One issue is that this type of free service financed by advertising is expanding, notably in the form of Internet services.

Data sources: How are the figures obtained?

As in the other chapters, the French annual accounts are used as an example of the kinds of sources and methods used to estimate final uses of the GDP. We will start with the easiest case and then go on to the more difficult areas.

---

* On this point, the reader may be interested to read Box 28 of the monumental work by André Vanoli: *A History of National Accounting*, IOS press, 2005.

The statistics for foreign trade (from the customs service) and for the balance of payments (from the Banque de France, the French Central Bank) provide information not only on exports and imports of goods but also on exports and imports of services. Through their traditional function of controlling all movements of goods at the frontier, the French Customs Service had an excellent information system that was ideal for the national accounts. However, as noted earlier, the introduction of the single European market in 1993 abolished the obligation to declare trade flows within Europe.

In its place a quasi-exhaustive survey is carried out by the customs services of exporting and importing countries. At the European level, a significant "asymmetry" has opened up in the case of trade within the region, in that total recorded exports are now roughly 5% higher than total recorded imports. It has been deduced from this that certain countries must be overstating their exports and/or understating their imports. Some observers have evoked the possibility of export fraud (inflation of export declarations, since exports are not subject to VAT). While the result has been to cast doubt on this source, national accountants continue to rely on it entirely, as it is all that is available, and despite its shortcomings it remains one of the best sources for the national accounts.

Until now, the balance of payments data published by the Banque de France included all transactions with the rest of the world made by the commercial banks and the largest industrial firms. The compulsory collection of this data made it possible to have quasi-exhaustive coverage of all financial transactions with the rest of the world. By then sorting these transactions by type, it was possible to provide statistics on purchases and sales of services, particularly international transport and insurance.

The Banque de France also calculates the tourist balance, *i.e.,* spending by French tourists abroad and by foreign tourists in France. However, as in the case of goods, this information system has been somewhat destabilised by the ending of the compulsory declaration by banks regarding intra-European flows and by the introduction of the euro, which eliminated one of the sources used for the evaluation of the tourist balance – namely statistics on purchases of foreign currencies for francs (the former French national currency) and *vice versa*. Like the Customs Service, the Banque de France has introduced surveys making it possible to ensure the continuity of the data on which national accountants continue to rely, although they also use other sources where they are available.

This shows that it will be increasingly difficult to compile national accounts in a Europe that has become more and more unified and multinational. One day perhaps, the national accounts of each European country will become the regional accounts of the national accounts of a United Europe. But this day is a long way off. In the meantime, the present national accounts will continue to be published, at the cost of a gradual deterioration in their quality, particularly in regard to transactions with the rest of the world

Consumption expenditure by general government is evaluated on the basis of government accounts. These accounts are very complete and of high quality (see Chapter 9). They provide a very good picture of wages and salaries, intermediate consumption and transfers in kind. The evaluation of the consumption of fixed capital of general government, which is an imputed component of government final consumption expenditure, is made using estimates of the stock of government capital to which depreciation rules are applied taking into account the expected lifetimes of these assets. It is obviously much more of an approximation.

The principal source for gross fixed capital formation is additions to fixed capital, *minus* disposals, reported by firms in their tax declarations. As we saw earlier, INSEE (the French statistical office) has access to nearly all tax declarations by firms and these cover the variables required. The source is therefore a good one. However, it has its limitations in the case of intangible assets such as software, for which firms do not follow the requirements of the national accounts.

The same source is used for changes in inventories. However, the problem of "stock appreciation" makes its use somewhat problematical.

In the case of household consumption expenditure, the source is rather indirect. For most goods the starting point is retail sales, from which are deducted, often using somewhat bold assumptions, the portion of sales that go to firms. These will be either intermediate consumption or GFCF. For other products, use is made of various corporate and government sources, such as car registrations, tax data on sales of tobacco and alcoholic beverages, sales by the state-owned quasi-monopoly for gas and electricity, and sales figures for the transport companies. Relatively little use is made of INSEE's survey of households' budget. INSEE has been obliged to reduce the frequency and the sample size of this survey of household income and expenditure, which is extremely costly and not very well received by the respondent households.

These various sources of information are compared with each other in the supply and use tables which reconcile the total supply of goods and services with their final and intermediate uses. This estimation mechanism is described in Chapter 10.

Exercises   *Answers at www.SourceOECD.org/understandingnationalaccounts*

Exercise 1: Final uses in volume

(This exercise uses the knowledge gained in Chapter 2.)

The following table is the French version in billion euros at current prices of Table 1 in the present Chapter. The second table shows the corresponding price indices. For the analysis of growth, why must preference be given to accounts in volume rather than at current prices?

On the basis of these two tables, calculate the table of final uses in volume at 1995 prices. The sum of final uses in volume in 1995 and 1996 is equal to GDP in volume for 1995 and 1996, but why is this not precisely the case for 1997?

In the remainder of the exercise, the assumption will be made that volumes are additive. Using this assumption, calculate domestic demand and external demand. Calculate the contribution to GDP growth made by final domestic demand and final external demand in 1996 and then in 1997.

Final uses

Billions of euros, current prices

	1995	1996	1997
Household final consumption expenditure	649.03	669.64	679.96
Final consumption expenditure by general government	282.16	293.19	302.89
Final consumption expenditure by non-profit institutions serving households (NPISHs)	7.03	7.30	7.62
Gross fixed capital formation	222.10	223.98	224.59
Net acquisitions of valuables	0.92	0.89	0.99
Changes in inventories	4.41	−2.95	−2.29
Exports	265.97	279.76	319.09
Minus Imports	−249.76	−259.63	−281.68
Gross domestic product	1 181.85	1 212.18	1 251.16

Price indices of final uses

1995 = 100

	1995	1996	1997
Household final consumption expenditure	100.00	101.88	103.30
Final consumption expenditure by general government	100.00	101.61	102.78
Final consumption expenditure by non-profit institutions serving households (NPISHs)	100.00	101.91	103.15
Gross fixed capital formation	100.00	100.86	101.19
Net acquisitions of valuables	100.00	100.68	99.49
Changes in inventories	100.00	114.86	112.07
Exports	100.00	101.65	103.70
Imports	100.00	102.32	103.87
Gross domestic product	100.00	101.45	102.75

Exercise 2: True, false or choose from the list

a) Which of the following are included in household consumption expenditures: fees levied by government for the public television service; the purchase of apartments; interest paid on loans; parking fines; driving licence fees?

b) A farmer produces 300 litres of wine each year. He sells 160 litres to his neighbours and stocks 140 litres for his own consumption. Which figure should be included in household consumption: 160 litres or 300 litres?

c) Total consumption expenditure by households includes expenditure by foreign tourists in France. True or false?

d) Actual household consumption is equal to household consumption expenditure plus that of general government. True or false?

e) Actual consumption of general government is equal to its collective consumption expenditure. True or false?

f) Which of the following items of expenditure are "collective" and which are "individual": primary education; medical research; reimbursement of medicines; police and fire brigades; operating costs of pension funds; cost of free concerts in municipal parks; expenses of troops serving with United Nations forces.

g) Fixed capital formation excludes transport equipment and live cattle. True or false?

Exercise 3: Evaluation of changes in inventories excluding stock appreciation

The first row of the following table shows the price of an item held in inventories in each of six sub-periods. The following rows show the quantities. Fill in the shaded cells/

rows, remembering that the *correct method* consists of evaluating each addition to, and withdrawal from, inventories at the price of the sub-period concerned. The *approximate method* consists of using the average price for the totality of the sub-periods and applying this to the changes in inventories expressed in quantities. The *wrong method* consists of calculating the difference between the values at the beginning and end of the whole period. Comment on the differences. Calculate the "stock appreciation".

Sub-period	1	2	3	4	5	6
Price	4	5	5	7	6	9
Quantities:						
Inventory at the beginning of the sub-period	10					
Additions to inventories during the sub-period (+)	3			1	6	3
Withdrawals from inventories during the sub-period (−)		2	7		4	
Inventory at the end of the sub-period						
Value of additions (prices x quantities)						
Value of withdrawals (prices x quantities)						

Average price over the totality of the sub-periods: ▢

Wrong method

a) Value of inventory at the beginning of the period in current prices: ▢

b) Value of inventory at the end of the period in current prices: ▢

c) Difference (b) – (a), including stock appreciation: ▢

Correct method

a) Total value of additions: ▢

b) Total value of withdrawals: ▢

c) Correct measurement of the changes in inventories (excluding stock appreciation): ▢

Approximate method

d) Quantity at the beginning of the period: ▢

e) Quantity at the end of the period: ▢

f) Approximate measure of the change in inventories (excluding stock appreciation): ▢

Exercise 4: The terms of trade

Using the following tables (showing French imports and exports of goods and services at current prices and in volume), you are asked to:

a) Derive the export price index for the period 1995-2002.

b) Derive the import price index for the period 1995-2002.

c) From these, deduce the terms of trade for the period.

Imports and exports at current prices

Billions of euros

	1995	1996	1997	1998	1999	2000	2001	2002
Imports	249.8	259.6	281.7	306.4	320.8	387.8	388.7	380.2
Exports	266.0	279.8	319.1	341.0	351.6	405.4	412.1	411.6

Source: INSEE, National Accounts.

Imports and exports in volume

	1995	1996	1997	1998	1999	2000	2001	2002
Imports	249.8	253.8	271.2	302.6	321.3	368.2	373.0	375.2
Exports	266.0	275.2	307.7	333.3	347.6	391.3	397.7	403.7

Source: INSEE, National Accounts.

Chapter 6

THE HOUSEHOLD ACCOUNT

1. The three key indicators in the household account

2. The household sector accounts

3. An alternative way to measure household disposable income and consumption

THE HOUSEHOLD ACCOUNT

A household is a group of people collectively taking responsibility to feed and house themselves. A household can consist of a single person or of two or more people living under the same roof, these people generally being linked by family ties. However, there are also "institutional households" consisting of, for example, members of the armed forces living in a barracks or on board a ship, people detained in prison, or nuns living in a convent. National accounts make no distinction between these different categories of "household", and they are all lumped together in what is known as the "household sector", carrying the code S14. In practice, however, the bulk of the household sector consists of families.

The other sectors described in the national accounts – *corporations*, *general government* and *non-profit institutions* – pursue a single goal, namely the production of goods and services. For households, on the other hand, things are more complicated. Members of a household, if they are employed, earn an income that they use to buy everyday goods and services or for investing in financial assets. However, members of a household can also, as is frequently the case, run a family business such as a shop, a cafe, a taxi firm or a farm. In the national accounts, these various enterprises are described by the term *unincorporated enterprises*; they have no shareholders and their responsibility is not limited in the case of payment default (see Chapter 7 on the business sector). Households also produce housing services (real or imputed).

As a consequence, the accounts of the household sector cover two quite different functions: the output of goods and services, on the one hand, and the allocation of an income to consumption and to saving, on the other. It is partly for statistical reasons that no distinction is made between these two functions. It is in fact generally possible to separate out transactions (relating to production, intermediate consumption, compensation and taxes on production) between "pure" households and unincorporated enterprises. Indeed, in certain countries (France, United States), a partial account of this kind is published for unincorporated enterprises. Nevertheless, it is impossible in practice to distinguish other transactions, meaning that there are no complete accounts for unincorporated enterprises nor are there complete accounts for "pure" households.

Certain other OECD countries publish accounts bringing together households and non-profit institutions serving households (NPISHs). This aggregation is based on the notion that, because these institutions are largely financed by households and because their purpose is to serve households, their accounts can be assimilated to those of households. Moreover, the NPISHs constitute a small sector, and their inclusion in the household account makes little difference to the final result. In the end, even though the international system of national accounts recommends that NPISHs should be shown

UNDERSTANDING NATIONAL ACCOUNTS – ISBN 92-64-02566-9 – © OECD 2006

separately from households, in practice users of national accounts who want to make international comparisons will often have to compare "households + NPISHs" (*i.e.*, S14 + S15) rather than the S14 sector alone.

For economists, the "consumer" function of the household sector is of particular interest in that economic growth is influenced directly and immediately by growth in *household final consumption expenditure*, which in turn is determined by *household disposable income* and by the way in which this income is divided between consumption and *saving*. The expressions in italics in this last sentence identify the three key indicators in the household account that we shall be defining in this chapter.

1. The three key indicators in the household account

Table 1 shows, as percentages of GDP, the corresponding expenditure items in the case of Japan, the main ones being: *household final consumption expenditure*; *government final consumption expenditure*; *gross capital formation*; and, lastly, *exports*. An increase or decrease in GDP can be a consequence of variations in one or other of these components. In describing the evolution in the Japanese economy, economists have at various times been able to say that growth has been "driven by exports", "driven" or "slowed down" by consumption, or even sometimes that it was influenced or not by a combination of these factors. Table 1 nevertheless clearly brings out the predominant role played by household final consumption expenditure. Given that this expenditure contributes more than 55% of GDP, a change in this aggregate is bound to have a major influence on GDP growth.

Obviously, all kinds of reasons may prompt a household to increase or reduce its consumption. In the first place, there are the variations in income, or the realisation of holding gains or losses on financial or real estate investments. However, the level of

Table 1. **Japan: final uses**
As a percentage of GDP

Codes		2002	2003	2004
GDP	Gross domestic product	100.0	100.0	100.0
P31-S14	Household final consumption expenditure	55.8	55.6	55.3
P31-S15	Final consumption expenditure of NPISHs	1.3	1.3	1.3
P3-S13	Government final consumption expenditure	17.7	17.7	17.7
P5	Gross capital formation	24.0	23.9	23.9
P6	Exports of goods and services	11.2	11.8	13.1
P7	(–) Imports of goods and services	9.9	10.2	11.2

Source: OECD (2006), *National Accounts of OECD Countries: Volume I, Main Aggregates*, 1993-2004, 2006 Edition, OECD, Paris.
StatLink: *http://dx.doi.org/10.1787/304253524140*

consumption is also influenced by the way in which the household sees its immediate future: likelihood of an increase or decrease in income; perception of the risk of unemployment; expectations regarding inflation. The influence of consumer behaviour on GDP leads economists to keep a close eye on the indicators of "household morale" derived from opinion surveys in which consumers are asked questions such as whether they have confidence in the future, whether they expect to make major purchases soon and whether they think their financial situation has improved or deteriorated over the recent past.

I. The United States is an exception. Since the end of World War II, the US household saving ratio has been relatively low, in contrast to the high GFCF rate that has enabled GDP to grow more or less constantly throughout this period. This situation is explained by the powerful attraction the American economy holds for foreign investors. In other words, the US has been able to finance its investment with the savings of foreign households.

A second notable feature is the importance of gross capital formation. A substantial part of this is directly related to households, since it consists of purchases of housing, which are counted as household GFCF (gross fixed capital formation). This investment is partly financed by household saving.

Household **saving**, the second key indicator, accounts for a large proportion (more than 50%) of total saving in the OECD economies. Table 2 shows for Japan the proportion of total saving originating with households (and NPISHs). This proportion reached 75% in 2003, at a time when the economic climate in Japan was somewhat unique, with a high level of corporate saving and a substantially negative level of public saving. The sums saved by households are available to finance the gross fixed capital formation of other sectors (machinery, factories, transport equipment, roads, railways, communication networks, etc.) and also, in part, the GFCF of households themselves (purchases of housing). Since the end of World War II, there has been a noticeable causal link between the level of household saving and the size of the rise in GDP. ▶ I.

At the microeconomic level, saving is also important in that it provides families with financial security in the event of job loss or falling ill, and it also covers part of the retirement pension. The social security systems that had previously managed to provide adequate protection against these risks are now, because of the ageing of the population, in a difficult financial situation in many OECD countries. In recent years, OECD economists in the various Economic Surveys of member countries have been recommending that the authorities offer incentives to households to save more and thus finance more of their retirement requirements themselves.

The third key indicator, household disposable income, is the sum of *household final consumption expenditure* and *saving*. As we have seen, rises in these two components are desirable for several reasons: an increase in household final consumption expenditure stimulates GDP growth, while an increase in saving permits the partial financing of investment and at the same time eases the burden on the social security system. It seems evident that this result can only be achieved if household income increases, and this

Table 2. Japan: Breakdown of total net saving in the domestic economy by sector

As a percentage of total net saving

		1980	1990	2000	2003
B8N-S1	Total domestic economy	100.0	100.0	100.0	100.0
B8N-S11_S12	Corporations	28.3	14.7	61.3	111.6
B8N-S13	General government	10.1	34.8	−29.0	−86.6
B8N-S14_15	Households and NPISHs	61.5	50.5	67.7	75.0

Source: OECD (2006), *National Accounts of OECD Countries: Volume II, Detailed Tables,* 1993-2004, 2006 Edition, OECD, Paris.

StatLink: *http://dx.doi.org/10.1787/612461403758*

increase is largely a function of the economy's capacity to achieve productivity gains through more efficient use of the labour and capital factors of production.

2. The household sector accounts

These three indicators are explicitly identified in the household sector accounts. It is essential to bear in mind that from now on in this textbook, these accounts and these indicators are expressed at current prices and not in volume.

The sequence of accounts for households is divided into "non-financial" and "financial" accounts. The financial accounts are examined in Chapter 8. At this stage, we shall look only at the sequence of non-financial accounts, starting with the *production account* and ending with the *capital account*. The accounts we shall show here are in T-account form, the "T" referring to their aspect. This is in fact the presentation adopted by most households in keeping track of their receipts and expenditure:

Expenditure	Receipts
a)	a)
b)	b)
c) etc.	c) etc.

In the national accounts, the receipts are known as *"resources"* and are set out in the right-hand column. Expenditure is known as *uses* and is set out in the left-hand column. The final item in the *uses* column is a "balancing item". This is the amount needed to bring *uses* and *resources* into balance. The balancing items of the various accounts (*value added, operating surplus, disposable income, saving* and *net lending/net borrowing*) are particularly interesting aggregates for the purpose of analysis. In the presentation of accounts adopted hereafter, these balancing items are shown in bold type.

II. The initial letter of each code is based on "Eurospeak" terminology: "**P**" indicates products; "**D**" redistribution transactions; "**F**" financial transactions; "**B**" balancing items; and "**K**" (for the German word "kapital") indicates capital accumulation items. These short and precisely defined codes are very useful.

Note that the only way to fully understand what is contained in any given balancing item is to examine the sequence of accounts leading up to it. For example, in order to reply to the question "what is household saving?" it is imperative to examine the series of items that have been added to, or deducted, from the value of the initial item in the sequence of accounts. This notion will become clearer as we progress with the examination the household sector accounts.

To give an idea of the relative importance of the various items, we have chosen the example of the accounts of Italian households in 2003 (in billion euros, at current prices). The tables give the code of each transaction (for example, P1 for output). These are the codes used in international manuals (SNA 93 and ESA 95). ▶ II.

The production account

The first account in the sequence is the *production account* reflecting in particular the function of production of unincorporated enterprises. This very summary account initially consists of three items: *output*, *intermediate consumption* and the first balancing item, *gross value added*, which is the difference between the other two items. In Table 3, we have used the combined grouping "Households plus NPISHs" to illustrate the fact that certain countries publish accounts for these two sectors only in aggregate. A possible variation is the inclusion of "net value added", which is equal to gross value added *minus* the consumption of fixed capital.

If one excludes the NPISHs and looks at the production account of households on their own (S14), Table 4 is obtained. It can be verified, by difference, that the share of NPISHs is very small, and therefore they will be ignored from now on.

The headings in this production account for households show the activities of unincorporated enterprises: farms, retail outlets, taxi firms, beauty parlours, etc. But they also include own-account production of goods by households, and the housing services "produced" by people who rent accommodation to others, or who own their accommodation (apartments or houses). As a consequence, the *output* item on the right hand side of the account includes the imputed rents of these "homeowner-occupiers", while the intermediate consumption in the left hand side includes (in addition to the intermediate consumption of unincorporated enterprises) the expenditure these owners have to make for the upkeep of their accommodation.

Generation of income account

The next account in the sequence is the *generation of income account*, which shows how the value added is distributed between remuneration of the labour and capital factors of production.

Table 3. **Italy: Production account for households and NPISHs (S14 + S15)**

Billion euros, 2003

Uses		Resources	
P2. Intermediate consumption	151.8	P1. Output	501.9
B1. Value added, gross	350.1		
K1. Consumption of fixed capital	57.5		
B1N. Value added, net	292.5		

Source: OECD (2006), *National Accounts of OECD Countries: Volume II, Detailed Tables*, 1993-2004, 2006 Edition, OECD, Paris.

StatLink: *http://dx.doi.org/10.1787/162677411762*

Table 4. **Italy: Production account for households (S14)**

Billion euros, 2003

Uses		Resources	
P2. Intermediate consumption	149.8	P1. Output	495.3
B1. Value added, gross	345.6		
K1. Consumption of fixed capital	57.3		
B1N. Value added, net	288.3		

Source: OECD (2006), *National Accounts of OECD Countries: Volume II, Detailed Tables*, 1993-2004, 2006 Edition, OECD, Paris.

StatLink: *http://dx.doi.org/10.1787/843724311422*

Table 5. **Italy: Generation of income account for households (S14)**

Billion euros, 2003

Uses		Resources	
D1. Compensation of employees	47.0	B1N. Value added, net	288.3
D11. Gross wages and salaries	38.6		
D121. Employers' social contributions	8.4		
D29. Net taxes on production	9.6		
B2N. Operating surplus, net	58.7		
B3N. Mixed income, net	173.2		

Source: OECD (2006), *National Accounts of OECD Countries: Volume II, Detailed Tables*, 1993-2004, 2006 Edition, OECD, Paris.

StatLink: *http://dx.doi.org/10.1787/644667343231*

It starts by showing on the right-hand side, in the resources column, the balancing item from the previous account, in this case, the net value added.

The *uses* column contains two main items: *"compensation of employees"* and *"net taxes on production"*. When the value of these is deducted from *value added*, we have two balancing items, namely the *net operating surplus* and the *net mixed income*.

The *compensation of employees* item in this case covers the employees of the unincorporated enterprises. Compensation consists of wages and salaries in cash, income in kind (free board and lodging, for instance) and the social contributions paid by the owners of unincorporated enterprises on behalf of their employees. It can therefore be seen that compensation of employees is not merely wages and salaries but represents the total cost of labour.

The *net taxes on production* item consists of the taxes payable for the ownership or utilisation of factors of production (labour and capital) – for example, the property taxes paid by owners of dwellings. The word "net" signifies that subsidies on production have been deducted. The subsidies obviously result in an increase in the size of the balancing items, *mixed income* and *operating surplus*. In the *generation of income account* for households, the subsidies are mainly those paid to farmers.

For the financial and non-financial corporate sectors, the balancing item of the account consists entirely of the *net operating surplus*, which measures the remuneration of the capital used in the production process or, in other words, the principal measure of "profit" in the national accounts (see Chapter 7). However, the situation is more complicated for the unincorporated enterprises sector, for which it is often impossible to separate out the remuneration of capital and the remuneration of labour. Take the example of a family retail business or a family taxi firm: once the value added has been reduced by the compensation of employees and by the net taxes on production, what remains is both the remuneration of the capital invested (in this case, the premises, equipment and stock or the vehicles) and also the remuneration of the work done by the owners of the enterprises and their families. Unlike the owners of financial and non-financial corporations, the owners of family firms are not obligated to show in their balance sheet the value of the fixed capital used – and it would in fact be virtually impossible to force them to do so. A taxi can be used as a family car when not needed for professional purposes, just as business premises can also provide accommodation for the family.

This explains why, when it is not possible to distinguish between income from capital and income from labour, the remuneration is described as "mixed" and the balancing item in the *production account* is entitled *net mixed income*. This is what we find recorded as €173.2 billion in the above *generation of income account*. However, there is one case in which there is no doubt that what we have is income from capital and is therefore a balancing item that can be called *operating surplus, net*. This is the activity imputed to homeowner-occupiers consisting of providing housing services to themselves as occupiers of the accommodation concerned. This accounts for the bulk of the € 58.7 billion shown above.

Within mixed income, macroeconomists sometimes need to clearly distinguish between remuneration of the capital used in production and remuneration of the labour used in production. There exist at least two methods for doing this (see section "Going a step further: the breakdown of gross mixed income").

Distribution of primary income account

The next account in the sequence is the *distribution of primary income account* (Table 6). "Primary" income means the income generated by a production process itself or by a closely related process. By contrast, "secondary" income consists of money transferred to, or from, households without being related to a productive activity.

Starting as usual on the side of resources, we have at the top of the column the balancing item from the previous account, *net mixed income/net operating surplus.*

Under resources, the *compensation of employees* item is much larger than the corresponding item in the previous account. This is because in this case it covers the compensation received by all employees in all firms, in general government or in non-profit institutions – and not merely those in unincorporated enterprises. This is the largest item of household income. As seen earlier, compensation of employees represents the total cost of labour and includes the social contributions paid by employers on behalf of their employees and even the "imputed" contributions. It may seem strange to record social contributions as being received by households. To understand the reasons, the reader is referred to the section "Going a step further: actual and imputed social contributions".

The "interest" item (D41) in the resources column for households includes the interest received on households' financial investments. The item D42 corresponds to the dividends paid by companies to households and to the "withdrawals from income of quasi-corporations" (D42) by households. This latter item is in principle reserved for recording payments to the owners of units known as "quasi-corporations", which are not corporations in the legal sense (and therefore pay no dividends in the legal sense, either) but

Table 6. **Italy: Primary income account for households (S14)**

Billion euros, 2003

Uses		Resources	
D4. Property income		B2-3N. Mixed income, net/Operating surplus, net	231.9
D41. Interest	20.3	D1. Compensation of employees	
D45. Rents on land and sub-soil assets	3.1	D11. Wages and salaries	392.8
		D12. Employers' social contributions	149.9
		D4. Property income	
		D41. Interest	55.4
		D42. Distributed income of corporations	149.3
		D44-D45. Other	13.0
B5N. Balance of primary incomes	968.9		

Source: OECD (2006), *National Accounts of OECD Countries: Volume II, Detailed Tables,* 1993-2004, 2006 Edition, OECD, Paris.

StatLink: *http://dx.doi.org/10.1787/833750586632*

which have similarities with corporations. This item is normally very small because quasi-corporations are fairly rare. However, the Italian national accounts are unusual, in that unincorporated enterprises with more than five employees are considered as "quasi-corporations" and are therefore classified in the corporate sector. Item D42 in the Italian case therefore refers to the gross mixed income of a very substantial group of small individual enterprises that in other countries are classified in the household account.

Item D44 consists of imputed interest received by households on their life insurance policies, even though (unlike the interest earned on bonds or savings accounts) they are not able to use the interest freely. The section "Going a step further: insurance" explains the way in which life insurance and other types of insurance are treated. Finally, item D45 is composed of rents received for land or sub-soil assets (deposits of coal or other ores, for example). If the owners of this land or these deposits decide to allow them to be used by others in a production process, they are regarded as beneficiaries of a primary income. On the other hand, rents received for making a dwelling available (or for the temporary use of some other type of fixed capital, such as personal goods or vehicle) are considered as payments for the purchase of services. Therefore, they are included as output in the *production account*, and do not appear in item D45.

The *uses* column of the account includes item D4 "property income" paid by households. Note that the *interest* sub-item includes both the interest paid by households when they take out consumer or housing loans and the interest paid by unincorporated enterprises on their borrowings, notably for the acquisition of machinery or premises.

When the uses are subtracted from the resources, the result is the next balancing item: *balance of primary incomes*. This item is then carried to the top of the resources column in the fourth account, entitled *secondary distribution of income account*.

Secondary distribution of income account

The *secondary distribution of income* account (Table 7) traces the various transfers that take place subsequent to the distribution of primary income, with these transfers mainly aimed at correcting social inequalities. One could equally call this the "*redistribution account*". The most important of these transfers result when government policies redistribute income from well-off households to poorer households, but the transfers appearing in this account can also include private initiatives, notably gifts to charities and repatriation of funds by immigrant workers from poorer countries to their families.

The transfers recorded here are called "current" (as opposed to "capital" transfers), either because they are taken out of income (and not out of capital) or because the beneficiaries regard them as part of current income.

The third item in the resources column is *D62 Social benefits other than social transfers in kind*. These are current social transfers benefiting households (retirement

Table 7. **Italy: Secondary distribution of income account for Households (S14)**

Billion euros, 2003

Uses		Resources	
D5. Current taxes on income, wealth, etc.	145.4	B5N .Balance of primary incomes, net	968.9
D61. Social contributions:		D61. Social contributions	2.3
Employers' social contributions	137.2	D62. Social benefits other than social transfers in kind:	250.4
Employees' social contributions	33.4		
Social contributions by self-employed persons	19.2		
Imputed social contributions	12.7		
D62. Social benefits	1.8		
Other current transfers:		Other current transfers:	
D71. Net non-life insurance premiums	11.9	D72. Non-life insurance claims	13.6
D75. Miscellaneous current transfers	13.2	D75. Miscellaneous current transfers	5.2
B6N. Disposable income, net	865.5		
+ K1. Consumption of fixed capital	+57.3		
= B6. Disposable income, gross	922.8		

Source: OECD (2006), National Accounts of OECD Countries: Volume II, Detailed Tables, 1993-2004, 2006 Edition, OECD, Paris.

StatLink: *http://dx.doi.org/10.1787/204106786502*

pensions, unemployment allowances, family and maternity allowances, sick-leave per diem allowances). Note that these transfers include neither the reimbursement of medicines and medical services nor housing allowances, which are considered as social transfers in kind and recorded in a different account as part of adjusted disposable income. We shall return to this latter concept at the end of the chapter.

Social benefits (D62) break down into "social insurance benefits" and "social assistance benefits". Social insurance benefits are paid out by social security plans organised by government and by private pension plans in return for prior contributions. Social assistance benefits may also meet the same types of needs as the social security benefits, but the recipients have not paid contributions, and these benefits are not provided as a matter of right. Certain subsistence allowances paid to asylum-seekers or minimum incomes provided to very poor people are examples of social assistance benefits.

The final two items in the resources column of this account fall under the heading *other current transfers*. These transfers are of two types: settlements of accident insurance claims by households (fire, theft, road accidents, etc.) and miscellaneous current transfers (money sent by relatives living abroad, grants by non-profit institutions to handicapped people or to disadvantaged families, aid given by the government to households that are victims of floods or other natural catastrophes).

In the uses column of this account, the first item is titled *D5 current taxes on income and wealth*. Current taxes on income include personal income tax and taxes paid on the "mixed income" of unincorporated enterprises. Current taxes on wealth cover the regular tax payments (usually annual) paid on household net wealth (in the French case, for example, the "*impôt de solidarité sur la fortune*"). Note that inheritance taxes are not included, being exceptional payments and therefore treated as capital transfers.

The next item in the uses column is titled *social contributions*. As explained in the section at the end of the chapter ("Going a step further: actual and imputed social contributions"), this item covers the contributions to a social security fund paid by employers on behalf of their employees, the contributions paid by the employees themselves, the imputed social contributions and the contributions paid by the owners of unincorporated enterprises (also called "self-employed").

The last item in the uses column is *other current transfers*. The net non-life insurance premiums are the premiums paid on non-life insurance policies, *minus* the estimated remuneration that the insured pay for the management services of the insurance company (for more details, see the section "insurance" at end of this chapter). The *miscellaneous current transfers* item covers the financial transfers made by migrant workers to their families in their home countries, gifts to non-profit institutions and parking and other fines.

The difference between uses and resources is equal to **net disposable income (NDI)**, a key indicator that represents the amount left at the disposal of households for either consumption or saving, over and above the replacement of the existing capital stock. It is called "net" because the amounts needed for the replacement of capital assets (dwellings and equipment of unincorporated enterprises) have already been deducted. However, certain analysts prefer to use the *gross disposable income* (GDI), which is equal to the previous figure plus the consumption of fixed capital. One reason is because there is uncertainty in the calculation of consumption of fixed capital and, in particular, in the international comparability of this calculation. Another reason to prefer GDI is that it can be better analysed than NDI in terms of purchasing power and correlated to final consumption in volume. The *purchasing power of GDI* is equal to GDI deflated by the price index of household consumption expenditure. If the purchasing power of GDI increases, this means that GDI is rising faster than inflation, and therefore there is a chance that households will consume more in real terms.

Another thing to note about NDI is that this household income aggregate includes sub-items that are already earmarked for particular uses and are therefore not open to a trade-off by households between consumption and saving. For example:

- The *output* item in the *production account* includes agricultural products held back by their producers for their own consumption and the imputed rents of homeowner-occupiers. As a result, the value added derived from these activities, which eventually becomes an element in disposable income, can clearly not be allocated to uses other than the consumption of the farm products and of housing services, respectively. In the OECD countries, own-account consumption of agricultural products is fairly negligible, but the imputed rents represent very substantial sums.

- The *compensation of employees* item in the *primary income distribution account* includes income in kind, but this income has already been "spent" on the corresponding goods and services provided to the employees.

- One part of the *property income interest* (D41) in the *Primary income distribution account* covers imputed interest on the reserves managed by the non-life insurance companies on behalf of policy holders. This imputed interest is earmarked as part of consumption of services provided by the non-life insurance companies.

The final point to note about NDI is that the concept of disposable income used in the national accounts is different from the theoretical concept as defined by certain economists (see section "The relationship to economic theory"). In particular, it does not include the holding gains or losses on shares or on real estate.

Use of disposable income account

The balancing item *net disposable income* is shown at the top of the resources column in the following account, the *use of disposable income account*.

Table 8. **Italy: Use of income account for households (S14)**
Billion euros, 2003

Uses		Resources	
P31. Household final consumption expenditure	780.4	B6. Net disposable income	865.5
		D8. Adjustment for the change in net equity of households in pension fund reserves	7.5
B8N. Net saving	92.7		

Source: OECD (2006), *National Accounts of OECD Countries: Volume II, Detailed Tables*, 1993-2004, 2006 Edition, OECD, Paris.
StatLink: *http://dx.doi.org/10.1787/066546721580*

The adjustment required in the second item of the resources column (coded D8) is necessary because of the way contributions paid to pension funds, as well as the pensions paid out by these funds, are treated in the *secondary distribution of income account*. They are in fact assimilated as contributions to, and benefits from, the social security system, even though they should be treated in the same way as transactions with the life insurance companies. This special treatment has been adopted because contributions paid to pension funds (and the pensions paid out by these funds) are generally regarded by households as similar to the contributions paid to social security funds and the benefits paid by these funds. If one regards them as having the same impact on consumer behaviour, it seems logical to apply the same treatment. However, transactions with pension funds are also recorded in the financial accounts (see Chapter 9). Therefore, it is necessary to make an adjustment in the non-financial account so that the value of the balancing item (*saving*) carried forward into the financial accounts is correct. The adjustment equals the change in the net equity of households in pension fund reserves, thus its name. When calculating the household saving ratio, it is important to recall that item D8 should be added to the denominator of this ratio (disposable income) since it is included in the numerator (saving).

The uses column within the "use of disposable income" account contains only two important items, namely *household final consumption expenditure* and the balancing item *net saving*. A complete definition of household final consumption expenditure was already given in Chapter 4, but it is worthwhile recalling that household final consumption expenditure consists mainly of purchases of everyday goods and services (clothing, food, durable consumer goods, rents, transport, personal services, etc.) *plus*:

- The imputed rents "paid" by homeowner-occupiers.
- The estimated value of in-household output, especially crops and livestock consumed by households owning an agricultural holding.
- The estimated value of goods and services received by employees by way of remuneration in kind.

On the other hand, household final consumption expenditure does not include:

- Purchases of housing – dwellings are fixed assets used to produce the provision of housing services: they are therefore recorded in the capital account (GFCF) and are not considered consumption.
- Purchases of other types of buildings and equipment used mainly for production by family enterprises are also GFCF (agricultural equipment, business premises, taxis, goods vehicles, etc.).
- Purchases by family firms of intermediate consumption goods (seeds and fertilisers in the case of farmers, paint and brushes in the case of decorators, fuels and maintenance for taxi drivers, etc.) are intermediate consumption and not final consumption.
- Purchases (less sales) of "valuables" – including gold coins, antiques, rare stamps and works of art – purchased to serve as "stores of value", are regarded as investments by the purchasers who hope their value will increase over time (or, at the very least, not diminish).

The balancing item, *net saving,* is the difference between NDI and consumption expenditures. This is our third key indicator. Because it is obtained as the difference between two very large aggregates, it is almost invariably tainted by errors. Even a relatively small adjustment in one or the other of the two contributing aggregates – disposable income and household final consumption expenditure – automatically leads to a relatively substantial adjustment in the balance. As a consequence, it is necessary to be wary of the initial published estimates of saving, as these will certainly be substantially readjusted in the following two or three years.

In practice, analysts are not interested in the level of household saving as much as in the household saving ratio, which is the ratio of household saving to disposable income (to which is added the adjustment D8). For the purpose of international comparison, it is essential to use the same definitions. The method preferred by the OECD is to take the *net* saving ratio. Table 9 shows the net household saving ratio in Italy and in other industrialised countries in recent years.

Table 9. **Net household saving ratios**
As a percentage of disposable income

	1998	1999	2000	2001	2002	2003
France	11.9	11.5	11.4	12.2	13.3	12.4
Germany	10.1	9.5	9.2	9.4	9.9	10.3
Italy	12.2	9.8	9.2	10.1	10.5	10.7
Japan	11.0	10.7	9.5	6.6	7.2	7.4
USA	4.3	2.4	2.3	1.8	2.4	2.1

Source: OECD (2005), *OECD Economic Outlook,* December No. 78, Volume 2005, Issue 2, OECD, Paris.

StatLink: *http://dx.doi.org/10.1787/788276117017*

On first sight, the much lower figures in this table for the United States suggest that American households are much more spendthrift than those of other countries. This difference could be due to statistical or institutional differences making the saving ratios not strictly comparable. However, as was seen in Chapter 3, recent studies have shown that the gap remains even when adjustment is made for these statistical or institutional differences.

Capital account

The balancing item *net saving* is forwarded to the top of the resources column in the *capital accumulation account,* which is the last non-financial account in the sequence (Table 10). Because of the presence of "gross fixed capital formation" under the uses, it is preferable that this account be on a gross basis. This is why we have also included *gross saving* under resources, this aggregate being equal to net saving plus consumption of fixed capital.

The only other item in the resources column is *D9 net capital transfers received.* The use of the word "net" refers to the fact that capital transfers paid have been deducted from the capital transfers received. The receipts include investment aids. The payments

6

THE HOUSEHOLD ACCOUNT
3. An alternative way to measure household
   disposable income and consumption

Table 10. Italy: Capital accumulation account for households (S14)

Billion euros, 2003

Uses		Resources	
P51. Gross fixed capital formation	84.1	B8N. Saving, net	92.7
P52. Variations in inventories	0.7	K1. Consumption of fixed capital	57.3
P53. Acquisitions less disposals of valuables	2.0	B8. Saving, gross	150.0
K22. Acquisitions less disposals of intangible non-produced assets	0.1	D9. Net capital transfers received	–8.5
B9 .Net lending (+)/Net borrowing (–)	54.6		

Source: OECD (2006), *National Accounts of OECD Countries: Volume II, Detailed Tables*, 1993-2004, 2006 Edition, OECD, Paris.

StatLink: *http://dx.doi.org/10.1787/726016723234*

mainly consist of inheritance tax. In some countries, capital transfers received also include an adjustment between social contributions due and social contributions paid.

Gross saving is used to acquire financial and non-financial assets. The first four items in the uses column correspond to the acquisition of non-financial assets. The first of these, *gross fixed capital formation,* includes purchases of housing or of equipment (by unincorporated enterprises) and the planting of orchards, vineyards or forests, among other things. The *variations in inventories* item covers stocks of finished products and intermediate consumption goods held by unincorporated enterprises. *Valuables* are objects such as precious metals, antiques and works of art purchased to serve as stores of value, and their purchase is considered as "investment", being often made with the intent to resell. The *intangible non-produced assets* cover patents, copyrights, leaseholds and other assignable contracts entitling the holder to use land, buildings or mineral deposits.

The balancing item *B9 Net lending (+)/net borrowing (–)* is the amount available for the purchase of financial assets (for example, to be deposited in a savings account) or for debt repayment (paying off a car loan or a house mortgage, for example) and is almost always positive for the household sector as a whole. The "net lending" is also sometimes called "financial saving". Some countries publish a "financial saving ratio", which is equal to net lending divided by Gross Disposable Income of households (and multiplied by 100).

3. An alternative way to measure household disposable income and consumption

The international system of national accounts SNA 93 proposes an alternative method of measuring household disposable income and consumption that takes into account spending by general government and NPISHs for the benefit of households.

THE HOUSEHOLD ACCOUNT
3. An alternative way to measure household
   disposable income and consumption

6

The underlying idea is that final consumption expenditure by general government and by NPISHs finances two quite different categories of services: collective services intended to benefit society as a whole, and services used by members of household on an individual basis. Examples of *collective services* are defence, law and order, tax collection, control of public spending, supervision of air quality and water pollution, drafting and promulgation of legislation, and public management in general. In theory, it is society as a whole that benefits from these services, and it is impossible to calculate the extent to which an individual household uses them.

The "individual services" supplied by general government include healthcare, education, social services, housing services, recreational and cultural services. In these cases, it is possible in principle to calculate the extent to which any individual household makes use of them. Households use these services to differing degrees, depending on their situation. For example, childless households will not make great use of education services, in contrast to families with numerous children. Similarly, the consumption of healthcare services depends on the frequency with which members of a household fall ill.

SNA 93 includes these individual services, along with other transfers, in an alternative household income account titled *redistribution of income in kind account* (Table 11). In this account, they are recorded in the resources column under the title *social transfers in kind*.

Table 11. **Italy: Redistribution of income in kind account for Households (S14)**

Billion euros, 2003

Uses		Resources	
		B6N. Net disposable income	865.5
B7N. Net adjusted disposable income	1 026.0	D63. Social transfers in kind	160.5

Source: OECD (2006), *National Accounts of OECD Countries: Volume II, Detailed Tables*, 1993-2004, 2006 Edition, OECD, Paris.
StatLink: *http://dx.doi.org/10.1787/285048651075*

Social transfers in kind include the expenditure by general government and NPISHs on the provision of the various individual services mentioned above (healthcare, education, etc.), but also the reimbursement of purchases of goods and services, such as medical consultations and medicines, as well as housing allowances. The balancing item *net adjusted disposable income* is equal to disposable income, as usually measured, plus the social transfers in kind.

Given the existence of this alternative method of measuring disposable income, it was only logical that a new account be created illustrating the use of this new measure of income. This new account is called the *use of adjusted disposable income account* (Table 12).

6

THE HOUSEHOLD ACCOUNT
3. An alternative way to measure household
   disposable income and consumption

Table 12. **Italy: Use of adjusted disposable income account for households (S14)**

Billion euros, 2003

Uses		Resources	
P31. Household actual individual consumption	940.9	B7N. Net adjusted disposable income	1 026.0
		D8. Adjustment for the change in net equity of households in pension fund reserves	7.5
B8N Saving, net	92.7		

StatLink: *http://dx.doi.org/10.1787/425548518164*

The first item in the uses column is *actual individual consumption.* Note that there is now no mention of "expenditure". Actual individual consumption measures the value of the goods and services actually consumed by households, including the goods and services financed by general government or NPISHs. This additional value is equal to the part of consumption of general government and NPISHs that can be considered "individual" as described in previous chapters.

It is important to note that the balancing item of this alternative account, *net saving,* remains strictly identical to the balancing item in the traditional presentation of the household accounts. This is because *adjusted disposable income* and *actual final consumption* have both been increased by the same amount (the value of social transfers in kind) so that the difference between the two, *i.e., saving,* remains unchanged. As mentioned in Chapter 3, the concepts of *adjusted disposable income* and *actual individual consumption* are mainly of interest in international comparisons.

UNDERSTANDING NATIONAL ACCOUNTS – ISBN 92-64-02566-9 – © OECD 2006

Key points

▶ A household is a group of people who collectively take responsibility for feeding and housing themselves. A household can consist of a single person or two or more people living under the same roof, these people generally being linked by family ties.

▶ The principal function of the household sector is consumption, but it also has a productive function.

▶ The output of the household sector includes that of unincorporated enterprises and households producing housing services for themselves (homeowner-occupiers).

▶ "Gross disposable income" and "net disposable income" (GDI and NDI) are the most important balances for analysing the situation of households, measuring the sum available for consumption and saving.

▶ Changes in the purchasing power of gross disposable income is the main factor determining the change in the volume of goods and services consumed by households.

▶ Saving is equal to disposable income *minus* consumption expenditure; or, alternatively, adjusted disposable income *minus* actual individual consumption. Financial saving is the same thing as the net lending of households.

▶ The gross saving ratio is equal to gross saving divided by GDI (plus item D8). The net saving ratio is equal to net saving divided by net disposable income (plus item D8).

▶ Social transfers in kind are equal to the "individual" consumption of general government and the NPISHs.

Going further

The breakdown of gross mixed income

Economists rely on national accounts to measure changes in the share of value added between wages and profits and, also, to measure changes in productivity over time and among countries (see introduction to Chapter 4). Economists find it hard to make their analyses unless they are able to distinguish in the national accounts between the returns to these two factors of production both for unincorporated enterprises as well as for corporations. This is why they usually try to break mixed income down into its two components: the implicit salary of the owner(s) and the return to capital.

There are two ways of doing this for unincorporated enterprises. The first consists of estimating the compensation of the self-employed in the case of unincorporated enterprises. The return to capital is then the difference between the mixed income and this figure. The second method consists of estimating the return to capital and assuming that the rest of mixed income is the return to labour. The first method is generally based on the number of independent workers as reported in surveys of family employees or in the population census, on the assumption that they receive the same average compensation as dependent workers employed in similar activities. The second method takes as its starting point an estimate of the stock of fixed capital used by unincorporated enterprises, sometimes adjusting this stock downward to allow for the fact that this capital can also be used for private purposes. The observed average rates of return for similar assets in corporate enterprises are then applied to the assets of unincorporated enterprises to get the return to capital.

While in theory these two methods are equally valid, in practice it is the first that is mainly used, probably because the data needed are easier to obtain. These two methods can obviously be used simultaneously, but in this case the total obtained is often larger – sometimes considerably larger – than the mixed income recorded in the accounts. One possible explanation is that the owners of unincorporated enterprises earn a "psychological income" in the form of satisfaction at being their own masters and so accept lower remuneration for their labour and capital investment than would be true of a corporation.

Actual and imputed social contributions

"Compensation of employees" is defined in the national accounts in way that shows explicitly the full cost of labour as a factor of production. For example, whereas in the real world social contributions are paid directly by the employers to the social funds and are never seen by the employees, the national accounts treat them as part of wages paid to households. As a result, the "compensation of employees" item includes all contributions, including imputed contributions (see below), and therefore reflects the total cost of labour. So that things should come out right in the end, the "secondary distribution of income account" contains another fictitious flow, this time from households to the social funds. What we then have is the following fictitious circuit for social contributions: Employer –> Households –> Social insurance funds. It is essential to keep this circuit in mind when interpreting the household account.

In most countries, employees and employers are obliged to make regular contributions to a social security plan that usually reimburses employees for medical costs, pays out unemployment benefits and provides retirement pensions. However, certain employers pay social security benefits directly to their employees without going through a social security fund. In this situation, national accountants consider that these employees and employers pay an "imputed" social contribution. They estimate the sum the workers would have had to pay to receive the social benefits paid to them, and these imputed contributions are included in "compensation of employees". Thus, the full cost of labour can be recorded in the accounts. The benefits they receive are recorded in the resources column of the "secondary distribution of income account" alongside the other social benefits. Because it is difficult to estimate the hypothetical contributions that these workers would have had to pay to receive benefits, national accountants often start from the principle that the imputed social contributions are equivalent to the benefits actually received. This simplification is apt to disappear in the case of pension contributions because the new SNA 2008 will probably recommend the application of so-called actuarial methods in estimating pension contributions (see next section).

Pension funds and social security plans

One difficult issue, especially for international comparisons, is the recording of pension contributions and pension benefits of employees. One can distinguish two main types of pension systems: those functioning as "savings plans" (also called "by capitalisation") and those functioning as "transfer plans" (also called "by repartition" or "pay-as-you-go"). If the pension plan is a saving plan (often called a "pension fund"), each employee contributes to a fund from which his or her future pension benefit will be paid. Thus, the national accounts record all the contributions to the plan (both those of employers and of employees) as a form of saving (i.e. an increase in the pension asset of employees) and pension benefits as "dis-saving", or a decrease of the pension asset.

By contrast, a pension plan is a transfer plan (rather than a saving plan) when the pension contributions of current employees are used to pay the pension benefits of current retirees. In this case (which is typical of social security pension systems), the national accounts deduct pension contributions from income (and thus they are also deducted from saving), and pension benefits are considered part of income (and thus included in saving). Thus, there is a significant difference in impact between these two methods of financing the retirement of employees. To harmonise the measure of income, the SNA 93 recommended recording also (in parallel) the pension contributions and benefits of saving plans (i.e. pension funds) as if they were transfer plans (i.e. social security). However, this creates a dissymmetry in the accounts, which has to be corrected by item "D8 net equity in pension funds" in the "use of disposable income account." It is interesting to note, however, that the US, Canada and Australia – three major countries with pension funds – do not record this item because they do not use the parallel accounting that generates it.

Because of the dramatic financing problem caused by the forthcoming retirement of the "baby-boom" generation (those born between 1945 and 1960), significant reforms of pension systems are under way in many countries. These reforms are in two directions: first, reduce the pension promises and/or raise contributions; second, transform "defined benefits plans" in "defined contribution plans". This last sentence needs some explanation.

A defined benefit plan is a pension plan for which the pension benefit is calculated in terms of a percentage of final salary. In this type of plan, it is the sponsor of the plan, often the employer, who bears the financial risk of the pension benefit. Defined benefits plans are often "pay as you go" and thus unfunded. Typically, the social security retirement systems of continental European countries are unfunded defined-benefits plans.

On contrary, defined contribution plans are saving plans: the pension benefit is the result of the accumulated contributions of the employee and the employer on behalf the employee. Thus, the employer does not bear the financial risk of the pension promise. Defined contribution plans are, by definition, funded, meaning that they hold a reserve of non-financial or financial assets that results from the investment of the accumulated contributions. It is from this reserve that the pension benefits are paid.

The new SNA (edited in 2008 but scheduled to be implemented in 2012) will recommend, in line with business accounting recommendations, that all unfunded employer-defined benefits plans should be recorded as if they are saving plans. (In principle, this should also apply to government plans for their employees, but this is still in discussion.) This recommendation will require the calculation of a pension liability for these plans (and thus a pension asset for the employees) using what is called actuarial methods. The objective is to harmonise the recording of the different types of plans despite their different mode of financing. In this context, the contributions of defined benefits plans will not equal the contributions paid by the employers, but the value of the change in the pension promise incurred by the employer during the period. This will improve the measure of employers' full labour costs. Actuarial methods for pension accounting consist in estimating the pension liability of defined benefits plans based on employee demographics and calculating from that the employer's expected outflows for pension payments. These outflows are transformed into a current liability and discounted using a discount rate.

Insurance

A distinction is made between two types of insurance: non-life (often described as accident insurance) and life insurance. With non-life insurance, the policyholder is compensated for theft, road accidents, fire, natural catastrophes, bodily injury, income loss, etc. Non-life insurance also covers a type of "life" insurance that would be more appropriately called "death" insurance. This is an insurance policy in which the insurance company agrees to pay the beneficiaries named by the insured person a predetermined sum in the event of his/her death (before a predetermined age in the case of "term" life insurance and at any date in the case of "whole life insurance"). Term life insurance is simply a wager between the policyholder and the insurance company. If the policyholder dies before the pre-agreed age, he "wins" in the sense that the insurance company will be obligated to pay a certain capital to the beneficiaries. On the other hand, if the policyholder is still alive at the predetermined age, it is the insurance company that "wins" since it will not have to pay out the premiums paid in by the policyholder during the duration of the policy. This insurance functions in a similar manner to non-life insurance and is quite different from life insurance as described below.

In the case of non-life insurance, national accountants divide the premium paid by the policyholder into two parts: the remuneration for the service provided, and the net premium, *i.e.,* the remainder. The remuneration for the service corresponds to the estimated payment by the policyholder to the insurance company for the management of the funds collected in the form of premiums, the processing of claims, advisory services, publicity and other current expenditures. By assumption, the amount of the remuneration for the service is equal to the difference between the premiums received and the claims paid out plus what is known as the "premium supplement". This supplement corresponds to the property income received by the insurance company from investing the premiums in financial and other assets. National accountants regard this income as belonging to the policyholders. They therefore show it as "received" by the policyholders (in the resources column of the distribution of primary income account) before being "paid back" to the insurance company as part of the remuneration of the service. Remuneration for the service is part of household final consumption expenditure. The net premiums (premiums *minus* remuneration for the service) are treated as a transfer between the policyholders paying the premiums and the policyholders eligible for receipt of claims. The net premiums are recorded in the "other current transfers" item in the uses column of the secondary distribution of income account, while the repaid claims are recorded in the "other current transfers" item in the resources column of the same account.

Life insurance works very differently from non-life insurance. A life insurance policy, or contract, is one of many ways in which a person can build up capital that will be repaid at a pre-agreed date, increased by the interest earned on invested premiums. A life insurance policy usually involves the regular payment of premiums or contributions. Life insurance defined here is thus a saving plan as defined in the previous section and is thus similar to any other financial investment (a savings account, share purchases, stuffing gold coins in the mattress, for example).

The contributions and the withdrawals made when the policy/contract matures are financial transactions and recorded in the financial accounts (see Chapter 8). Life insurance nevertheless requires two non-financial transactions that must be recorded in the non-financial accounts. First, as in the case of non-life insurance, the policyholder has to pay the insurance company for the service rendered in managing the funds collected. Most of the time, insurance companies record this remuneration for service separately, and it is therefore unnecessary to make estimates of the amount concerned. It is included in household final consumption expenditure as remuneration for services. Second, even though the insurance companies retain the interest received from investing the insurance premiums, and even though policyholders have no access to this interest before the policy matures, this interest, legally speaking, is the "property" of the policyholders. For this reason, it is recorded in the "property income" item in the resources column of the primary distribution of income account. This manner of proceeding has a legal justification but also an economic one. When a life insurance policy/contract offers a higher yield than usual, the policyholder feels richer and increases his consumption (the so-called "wealth effect"), even though the money will not be received before the pre-determined date. If the yield offered is lower than usual, he or she will be inclined to reduce consumption.

Income in national accounts and in economic theory

The national accounts define income as the flow of net resources arising directly, or through redistribution, from normal productive activities and potentially available for consumption. On the other hand, some economists (Hicks in particular) define income as the maximum sum that can be consumed in a given period without reducing a household's real net worth (net worth is the difference between assets and liabilities; real net worth is this difference deflated by the price index for final consumption). It is therefore important to have a clear understanding of the differences that exist between the two definitions:

Capital gains and losses, known as "holding gains/losses" in the national accounts, are related to changes in the prices either of fixed assets (notably housing) or of financial assets (notably shares). Households in OECD countries have on several occasions in the recent past benefited from rises, or suffered from falls, in the prices of these two types of assets. One remembers in particular the stock market bubble toward the end of the 1990s and the steep drop in stock prices starting in 2000. When the price changes are positive, the holding gains enable households to consume far more than their disposable income without eating into their net worth. Conversely, negative holding gains (*i.e.*, losses) prompt households to consume distinctly less than their disposable income to compensate for the decline in their net worth. These amounts may therefore be included in the economists' definition of income, but they are not included in the national accounts definition of income.

A second difference is that theoretical income (the economists' definition) includes capital transfers. But in the national accounts, only current transfers are included in the calculation of disposable income.

Lastly, a household's net worth can be affected by events totally unrelated to the economic activities that constitute the principal subject of the national accounts. Floods, forest fires, gales and earthquakes reduce net worth by destroying buildings or other types of property. Conversely, net worth takes on increased value when, for example, a farmer finds oil on his land. The changes in asset values following events of this type are recorded under "other changes" in the volume of assets account, but they are not considered income in the national accounts.

By combining several different accounts, the national accounts system allows for the calculation of household net worth based on the theoretical concept of income, rather than disposable income, but a special calculation is needed to obtain this result.

Exercises   *Answers at www.SourceOECD.org/understandingnationalaccounts*

Exercise 1: True or False?

a) When share prices rise:

i) household disposable income increases;

ii) household saving declines.

b) When a tenant buys the apartment he/she had previously been renting, GDP increases because it now includes an imputed rental income of homeowner-occupiers.

c) When, in a given year, the number of road accidents is higher than usual, household *disposable income* also tends to be higher than usual.

d) A rise in the rate of income tax automatically leads to a decline in household disposable income.

e) A farmer whose olive plantation is destroyed in a storm automatically suffers a decline in his disposable income.

f) A cut in the rate of inheritance tax automatically leads to a decline in household saving.

g) A cut in the rate of reimbursement of dental care leads to:

i) a rise in GDP;

ii) a decline in household disposable income.

Exercise 2: Test your knowledge of the household account

Enter the transactions described below in the sequence of accounts starting with the *production account* and going through to the *utilisation of disposable income account*.

The Devant household consists of Jacques, his wife Monique, their daughter Nicole, Monique's mother Simone, and Jacques' brother Xavier. During the year:

● Jacques receives a salary of 2 000 for his job as store manager. His employer pays 20 in social contributions. Jacques pays 25 in income tax and 15 in social contributions. He spends 100 on meals and transport and 280 to buy a new car. He finances this purchase with a loan and pays 5 in interest during the year as a whole. He hands over the rest of his salary to Monique, who is responsible for the household's accounts.

● Monique is unemployed throughout the year, receiving 350 in unemployment benefit. She spends 1 900 on food, 120 on rent and 15 on household insurance. (Even though Monique is unaware of this, 5 out of this 15 corresponds to remuneration for the service provided by the insurance company).

- Simone receives 45 from a pension fund to which her late husband was affiliated, as well as 265 in the form of a social security pension. She spends 130 on clothes and gives Nicole 25 in pocket money.

- Nicole spends all the pocket money received from her grandmother on sweets. She also receives 30 in pocket money from her parents but saves this in order to buy a bicycle.

- Xavier has no fixed employment, but carries out undeclared painting jobs for neighbours. This brings him 1 500 during the year, but he spends 400 of this on paint and brushes. He occasionally calls on a friend to help him and pays him 40. Once when on a worksite, he parked in an unauthorised space and his van was clamped, costing him 20 to have the clamp removed. He spends 450 on cigarettes, beer and football match tickets. He pays 60 in alimony to his ex-wife.

Production account

Uses	Resources
Intermediate consumption	Gross output
Value added	

Primary distribution of income account

Uses	Resources
Compensation of employees	Value added
Wages and salaries	
Employers' social contributions	
Net taxes on production	
Mixed income/operating surplus	

Allocation of primary income account

Uses	Resources
Property income	Mixed income/operating surplus
Interest	Compensation of employees
Rents	Wages and salaries
	Employers' social contributions
	Property income
	Interest and dividends
	Rents
Balance of primary incomes	

Secondary distribution of income account

Uses	Resources
Current taxes on income and wealth, etc.	Balance of primary incomes
Social contributions	Social benefits other than social transfers in kind
Employers' social contributions	Social security benefits in cash
Employees' social contributions	Social assistance benefits in cash
Social contributions by self-employed persons	
Other current transfers	Other current transfers
Net non-life insurance premiums	Non-life insurance claims
Miscellaneous current transfers	Miscellaneous current transfers
Disposable income	

Use of disposable income account

Uses	Resources
Household final consumption expenditure	Disposable income
	Adjustment for the change in net equity of households on pension funds
Saving	

UNDERSTANDING NATIONAL ACCOUNTS – ISBN 92-64-02566-9 – © OECD 2006

Chapter 7

BUSINESS ACCOUNTS

1. The relationship between the firm (enterprise) and the corporation

2. The structure of corporate-sector accounts

3. From corporations to firms

OECD economists are particularly interested in the institutional framework in which enterprises (firms) operate, in order to identify how to improve firms' performance and generate an increase in employment, among other benefits. In recent OECD reports on France, for example, the authors have suggested a certain number of structural reforms intended to improve the performance of French firms. For example:

● ease the employment regulations that hinder layoffs and discriminate against small innovative units that need to be able to adjust their scale and the composition of their workforce;

● further deregulate the markets for goods and services, which remain highly regulated in France and hamper competition. The OECD economists cite the example of retail distribution, where the legislation was initially designed to prevent the large firms from wiping out the small ones, but it has on the contrary discouraged new entrants and handed over domination to a few large firms;

● improve the efficiency of the public sector, in other words general government and firms controlled by general government, which remains very large in France and partly explains the high rate of corporate tax compared with other OECD countries, acting as a brake on direct investment by foreign firms in France; and

● complete the establishment of a competitive market for network industries. Under pressure from Europe, France has liberalised its transport and telecommunications networks, but has not yet fully done so for energy.

In the national accounts, firms are classified into two sub-sectors: corporations and "unincorporated enterprises" (or "individual entrepreneurs"). Individual entrepreneurs are firms, usually small in size, that do not have corporate status or do not have complete sets of accounts. They are themselves grouped with households, and in many cases the national accounts, unfortunately, do not identify them separately. The fact that they are grouped with households means that economic analysis often has to be confined to corporations, despite the fact that unincorporated enterprises also make a significant contribution to total value added. Table 1 shows the importance in terms of value added of the different institutional sectors in certain OECD countries.

As can be seen from these few examples, it is the corporate sector that is the largest contributor to value added, far ahead of general government. But it can also be seen that value added for households is substantial, with much of this stemming from the imputation of output (imputed rents) for owner-occupied housing. However, a further appreciable

Table 1. **Breakdown of gross value added by sector**

As a percentage of total gross value added, 2003

		France	Greece	Netherlands	Switzerland
S11-S12	Corporations	60.7	32.1	70.0	71.7
S13	General government	18.0	13.7	14.0	11.5
S14-S15	Households *	21.2	54.2	15.9	16.8
S1	Total economy	100.0	100.0	100.0	100.0

* Including unincorporated enterprises and NPISHs.

Source: OECD (2006), *National Accounts of OECD Countries: Volume II, Detailed Tables*, 1993-2004, 2006 Edition, OECD, Paris.

StatLink: *http://dx.doi.org/10.1787/667355442012*

portion is in the form of value added of unincorporated enterprises. In particular, the fact that in Greece household value added accounts for more than 50% of total value added can be explained by the very large number of firms that do not have corporate status and are thus grouped with households in the national accounts.

As for the corporations themselves, the national accounts break them down into two main sub-categories: non-financial corporations (S11) and financial corporations (S12). Financial corporations (banks, insurance companies) play a key role in the economy, but their accounts are not as easy to analyse as those of non-financial corporations, and it is for this reason that the national accounts show them separately. The definition of financial corporations can be found in Chapter 10.

Table 2 shows that, in France, 56% of the total value added came from non-financial corporations in 2003.

This table also shows that 9.2% of gross value added was accounted for by unincorporated enterprises, a larger figure even than that for financial corporations.

Table 2. **France: breakdown of gross value added by sector**

As a percentage of total gross value added, 2003

S11	Non-financial corporations	56.1
S14A	Unincorporated enterprises	9.2
S12	Financial corporations	4.7
S13	General government	18.0
S14B	"Pure" households	10.9
S15	NPISHs	1.2
S1	Domestic economy	100.0

Source: OECD (2006), *National Accounts of OECD Countries: Volume II, Detailed Tables*, 1993-2004, 2006 Edition, OECD, Paris.

StatLink: *http://dx.doi.org/10.1787/371418181211*

7 BUSINESS ACCOUNTS
1. The relationship between the firm (enterprise)
   and the corporation

Decision-makers have always paid great attention to the small and medium-sized enterprises (SMEs). Some SMEs are not corporations as legally defined, and they are therefore not classified in the corporate sector but as unincorporated enterprises. These small units play a very important role in agriculture and the liberal professions and sometimes as "start-ups" in industry (after all, Microsoft® began life as an unincorporated enterprise). However, their contribution to total value added remains limited by the fact that as they expand, small firms tend to be transformed into corporations. It is therefore the corporate sector, particularly non-financial corporations, that provides the backbone of economic growth in most developed countries. This chapter will look first at the accounts of non-financial corporations and then return to the accounts of unincorporated enterprises.

1. The relationship between the firm (enterprise) and the corporation

For the national accounts, an enterprise is an *institutional unit*, in other words an economic agent having independent economic decision-making power, whose aim is to *produce market goods and services.* The word "market" is very important; it means that the products are sold on the *market* at *economically significant prices*. One of the criteria used by national accountants to determine whether a firm sells its products at an economically significant price is to see whether the value of its sales is equivalent on a lasting basis to more than 50% of its production costs. This definition therefore excludes, for example, general government units that provide products free, or almost free. Although it is far from being based on "profit-seeking" (if a firm's sales cover only 51% of its costs, it will have to be heavily subsidised to continue to exist), this definition nevertheless implies that the behaviour of the firm as viewed by the national accounts is not based on altruism, in contrast to general government and NPISHs.

A *corporation* is a form of enterprise having a legal identity separate from that of its owners. This separation gives the owners the important advantage that in the event of failure of the business their responsibility toward those to whom the firm owes money is limited to the amounts they have invested in the business and does not extend to their personal assets (except in the case of an offence such as embezzlement, but that is another story). In the case of unincorporated enterprises, there is no legal distinction between the firm and its owners, and the latter are personally responsible for all debts in the event of business failure. In order to become a *corporation*, a firm has to submit to a certain number of legal conditions, some of them costly, and this explains why owners of very small firms do not apply for these advantages.

One of the major legal requirements for corporations is the publication of a complete set of accounts recording the value of the financial and non-financial wealth at the start of the period (one talks of an "opening balance sheet") and at the end of the period ("closing balance sheet"), as well as the receipts and payments made between these two dates.

The period is generally one year and often corresponds to the calendar year. These accounts are the source enabling national accountants to calculate the macroeconomic accounts of the corporate sector.

By contrast, most of the unincorporated enterprises do not have complete sets of accounts. Some of the transactions cannot be separated from those of their owners in their capacity as households. It is for this reason that the national accounts include them in the household sector.

Two points to note:

- Certain non-financial corporations can be wholly or partially owned by the State (or other parts of general government). These are then known as public enterprises. Even so, they are not classified under general government, since they sell their products at prices close to their real costs. There is, however, a problem for analysts in that these firms can sometimes behave differently from private corporations. For example, certain public enterprises have a so-called public service function that often prevents them from charging their customers on the basis of actual marginal cost. Since some public enterprises do not therefore carry out their production according to quite the same rules as private corporations, the SNA recommends that national accountants draw up a special account in their case. In practice, however, very few OECD countries do so.

- In principle, the crucial distinction between corporations and unincorporated enterprises as far as the national accountants are concerned is not so much their legal status but as to whether or not they publish a complete set of accounts. A certain number of large units (for example NGOs, large legal firms, medical practices or co-operatives) are not legally constituted as corporations but nevertheless publish accounts showing their balance sheet and their transactions. These units are sometimes described as "quasi-corporations" and are then classified within the corporate sector.

2. The structure of corporate-sector accounts

As with all institutional units, the sequence of national accounts for the corporate sector is divided into *non-financial accounts* and *financial accounts*. The financial accounts will be described in Chapter 8. Here, we shall look only at the sequence of non-financial accounts, starting with the *production account* and ending with the *capital account*. These accounts show the following: how the income derived from production is divided between the factors of production (labour and capital); the amount by which this income is increased or reduced by "property income" or by various kinds of transfer (mainly taxes); and finally, how much is left to the firm for the acquisition of tangible or financial capital. All this information is valued at current prices.

In the presentations of the production and income accounts, the receipts, designated as *resources*, are shown in the right-hand column of each account. The expenditure items are designated as *uses* and shown in the left-hand column. The capital account shows how capital formation is financed, so the *changes in assets* are shown on the left-hand side and *changes in liabilities and net worth* are shown on the right-hand side. The last item on the left-hand side is known as the *accounting balance* and is equal to the difference between total resources (or changes in liabilities and net worth) and total uses (or changes in assets). The accounts are designed to produce accounting balances such as *value added, operating surplus, saving* or *net lending/net borrowing*, aggregates that are of particular interest for economic analysis. In the accounts set out below, the accounting balances are shown in bold type. In order to give an idea of the relative importance of the different items, their values in billions of euros or dollars are shown for the year 2004. We have chosen to illustrate this chapter by taking first the non-financial corporation sector for France and then continuing with the non-financial corporation sector for Australia.

The corporation sector's production account

The first account in the sequence is the *production account* (Table 3). This contains just three items: *output* on the right (in other words under *resources*); *intermediate consumption* on the left (in other words under *uses*); and the accounting balance (on the left, equal to the difference between the other two items) resulting in the *gross value added*.

The output of non-financial corporations amounted to 2 061.9 billion euros in France in 2004, a figure much higher than French GDP (1 648.4 billion euros). This should no longer come as a surprise at this point in the textbook, because it is clear by now that this output includes substantial double counting, since the output of one firm is the intermediate consumption of others. This figure for total output is therefore not a macroeconomic aggregate to be used for most analytical purposes. Instead, use is generally made of the gross value added of non-financial corporations, which is equal to 828.5 billion euros.

The output of firms is divided into market output and output for own final use. With the exception of certain service industries (*e.g.* retail trade) for which special conventions apply, market output, which constitutes the bulk of the total, is measured as the sum of sales and the changes in inventories of finished products and work-in-progress. For non-financial corporations, the output for own final use consists of the value of the non-financial assets made by the firm for its own use (in particular in-house software). The amount involved is very small (roughly 1% of total output). Intermediate consumption is measured as the difference between the purchases of goods and services needed for production and the change in inventories of these products.

Note that it is also necessary to take into account, among uses, the depreciation of the capital used (*consumption of fixed capital* in national accounts terminology). The consumption of fixed capital is the reduction in the value of produced capital (other than inventories) due to wear and tear and obsolescence. It is a production cost and its amount therefore appears in the left-hand column (in the same way as intermediate consumption),

UNDERSTANDING NATIONAL ACCOUNTS – ISBN 92-64-02566-9 – © OECD 2006

Table 3. **France: Production account for non-financial corporations (S11)**

Billion euros, 2004

Uses		Resources	
P2. Intermediate consumption	1 233.5	P1. Output	2 061.9
B1. Gross value added	828.5		
K1. Consumption of fixed capital	121.1		
B1N. Net value added	707.4		

Source: OECD (2006), *National Accounts of OECD Countries: Volume II, Detailed Tables*, 1993-2004, 2006 Edition, OECD, Paris.

StatLink: *http://dx.doi.org/10.1787/351084305031*

as a deduction from output to obtain the "true" figure for corporate value added, known as *net value added*. It is probably because of the difficulty of estimating the consumption of fixed capital (see section "Going a step further") that INSEE, the French statistical office, prefers to publish "gross" rather than "net" figures in the corporate sector accounts. However, from the point of view of analysing firms, it is the net accounting balance that is more suitable. Exercise 1 at the end of this chapter shows how one can easily move from the gross balances and accounting ratios to the net equivalents.

The corporation sector's generation of income account

The next account in the sequence is the generation of income account (Table 4). This shows how the value added that has been created is distributed between the two factors of production: the labour factor (compensation of employees) and the capital factor (gross operating surplus). The account begins on the right with the gross value added (this is for the French accounts, but one could also use *net* value added). Under uses, one finds compensation of employees, itself broken down between wages and salaries and employers' social contributions. One should note that wages and salaries include employees' contributions, or income tax withheld at source. Similarly, although employees do not in practice receive the employers' social contributions (which, like the employees' contributions, are paid directly to social insurance plans, tax authorities, etc.), the national accounts treat them *as if* employees did receive them, in such a way as to show the total cost of the labour factor to the employers. The contributions included comprise both those actually paid by the employers and the so-called imputed contributions. The contribution circuit is explained in detail in Chapter 6.

Before arriving at the gross operating surplus, which represents the remuneration of the capital factor, account has to be taken of other taxes on production and other subsidies on production. These taxes on production are made up of taxes on wages or capital paid by firms (in France, consisting mainly of the "taxe professionnelle" – a local business tax).

Table 4. **France: Generation of income account for non-financial corporations (S11)**

Billion euros, 2004

Uses		Resources	
D1. Compensation of employees:		B1. Gross value added	828.5
D11. Wages and salaries	401.7		
D121. Employers' actual social contributions	124.3		
D122. Employers' imputed social contributions	13.2		
D29. Other taxes on production	44.4		
D39. Other subsidies on production	−10.3		
B2. Gross operating surplus	255.2		
K1. Consumption of fixed capital	121.1		
B2N. Net operating surplus	134.1		

Source: OECD (2006), *National Accounts of OECD Countries: Volume II, Detailed Tables*, 1993-2004, 2006 Edition, OECD, Paris.

StatLink: *http://dx.doi.org/10.1787/501842372545*

I. These other taxes and other subsidies on production (D29 and D39) are the difference between total taxes and subsidies on production *less* taxes and subsidies on products (D21 and D31), respectively. The latter (which include VAT) do not appear in the accounts for corporations even if corporations are, in practice, collecting these taxes, because production in the national accounts is valued at basic prices, *i.e.* excluding taxes on products and including subsidies on products.

II. An advantage of this way of recording is that other taxes and subsidies can be combined as one item, *i.e.* "other taxes *less*

▶ I. The subsidies on production in the case of firms are subsidies paid by the government to help firms to produce, and they are small. The main subsidies on production in France are in fact paid to farmers, who are for the most part not classified as corporations but as unincorporated enterprises. Notice that the minds of national accountants sometimes work in a complicated fashion. In this case, subsidies are not shown as receipts but as negative uses. ▶ II.

The *gross operating surplus* (or, after deduction of the consumption of fixed capital, the *net operating surplus*) is the principal measure of firms' performance in terms of operating profits. This measure differs from profits as calculated in company accounts, as explained in "Going further: Profits and gross operating surplus: not to be confused" toward the end of this chapter. This explains why the national accountants have chosen to give this item a name other than "profit".

It is possible to calculate from these results a *profit share* (also called sometimes in France, "margin rate" – "taux de marge"), equal to the gross operating surplus as a percentage of gross value added. This is a key indicator of firms' performance in the national accounts. In line with what was said earlier, it is preferable to use a net profit share, *i.e.* the net operating surplus divided by the net value added, although INSEE in France prefers to stick to the gross aggregates. The following graph shows the evolution in French net and gross profit share since 1978. The two move virtually in parallel, although in the recent period the net share declines slightly more markedly than the gross share.

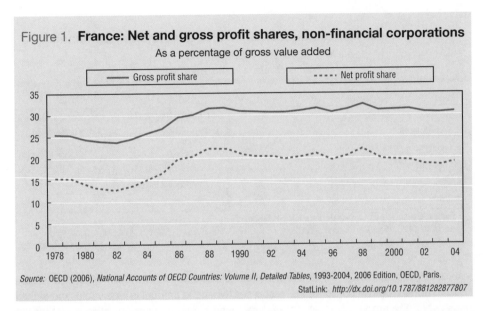

Figure 1. **France: Net and gross profit shares, non-financial corporations**
As a percentage of gross value added

Source: OECD (2006), *National Accounts of OECD Countries: Volume II, Detailed Tables,* 1993-2004, 2006 Edition, OECD, Paris.
StatLink: *http://dx.doi.org/10.1787/881282877807*

The choice between gross and net profit shares is therefore mainly of importance in international comparisons, when comparing more the levels of variables than their changes. When one looks at an individual country, it is rather the change in the profit share that is of interest. On either a gross or a net basis, the profit share for non-financial corporations in France rose strongly between 1982 and 1986 before levelling off. Among the quarterly national accounts tables published for France there are two particularly interesting ones that analyze the origin of the change in profit shares. These tables are the subject of Exercises 4 and 5 (since these are difficult Exercises, it is therefore advised to look directly at the answers).

Distribution of income account

Leaving France aside, let us continue to explore the accounts of the corporate sector, but now taking the example of Australia. Although situated on opposite sides of the world, the two countries use the same system of national accounts. However, Australia does not calculate the production account and the generation of income account for corporations; it starts to calculate the accounts of the corporate sector only at the third stage, the one known as the *distribution of income account*. This distribution of income account starts with the operating surplus. It then shows all the current transfers carried out by corporations either as uses or as resources.

These transfers include, in the first place, *property income*. While only the total (D4) appears in Table 5, there are five types of property income: interest (D41); dividends (D421); reinvested earnings on direct foreign investment (D43); property income attributed to

Table 5. **Australia: distribution of income account for non-financial corporations (S11)**

Billions of Australian dollars, 2004[*]

Uses		Resources	
		B2N. Net operating surplus	115.1
D4. Property income	83.4	D4. Property income	23.6
D5. Current taxes on income	37.7		
D62. Social benefits		D61. Social contributions	
D7. Other current transfers	9.3	D7. Other current transfers	5.9
B6N Net Disposable Income = B8N Net Saving	14.1		

[*] Fiscal year beginning on 1 July 2004 and ending on 30 June 2005.

Source: OECD (2006), *National Accounts of OECD Countries: Volume II, Detailed Tables*, 1993-2004, 2006 Edition, OECD, Paris.

StatLink: *http://dx.doi.org/10.1787/167874565301*

insurance policyholders (D44); and rent on land and sub-soil assets (D45). Most of these are liable to appear both in corporations' resources (when the amount is receivable) and in their uses (when the amount is due). To analyse these items, it is important to note that the corporation accounts are not "consolidated" in the national accounts (unlike the household account, which is consolidated by definition). "Consolidation" means eliminating, when aggregating the accounts of the many units of the sector, the transactions among units of the same sector being aggregated. This therefore leaves only transactions between units of the sector in question with units of *other* sectors. On the contrary, not consolidating means not carrying out this elimination, in other words simply summing up all transactions, whether internal or external to the sector in question.

In this particular example of non-consolidated accounts, the amount of 23.6 billion Australian dollars of property income receivable by Australian non-financial corporations in 2004 includes the dividends payable by certain corporations *to other corporations*. It is in fact very difficult to consolidate the accounts of corporations because, while one knows whether a corporation is the payer or the recipient, one does not know to whom this amount is paid, or from whom it is received. Thus, in the non-consolidated non-financial corporation accounts for Australia, the property income payable by non-financial corporations (83.4 billion Australian dollars) is not payable solely to agents other than non-financial corporations (*i.e.* financial corporations, households, general government and the rest of the world). Much of this property income is payable to other non-financial corporations, and this explains the size of the item for property income receivable (23.6 billion Australian dollars). To obtain the approximate amount of net property income receivable by other agents (financial corporations, households, general government, rest of the world) it is necessary to calculate the difference between the property income payable (83.4) and the property income receivable (23.6), *i.e.* 49.8 billion Australian dollars.

- *Interest.* This is the interest paid on loans obtained by non-financial corporations from banks (financial corporations).

- *Dividends.* These are the portions of profits paid out by firms to their shareholders. At the same time, corporations receive dividends on their holdings in other corporations. "Dividends" in this case include all types of methods used by corporations to distribute part of their profits, including the issuance of new shares.

- *Reinvested earnings on direct foreign investment.* This item is interesting in that it reflects a fresh example of imputation in the national accounts, in this case stemming from taking into account the phenomenon of *control* by certain multinational firms (known as parent companies) of other firms (known as subsidiaries) located abroad. A firm is deemed to control another when it is capable of significantly influencing the decisions of the latter, notably as regards dividend distribution. In this case, the parent company has a completely free choice of whether to have a dividend distributed to itself or to retain this dividend in its subsidiary. To reflect the genuine degree of enrichment (or impoverishment, if the subsidiary is making losses), what is recorded in this row is the amount of profits that is not redistributed in the form of dividends but retained in the subsidiary. ▶ III. Despite being described as "reinvested profits", this item can be negative when the subsidiary is making losses. It is to be found in both resources and uses. In resources, the amount is the profits reinvested by Australian multinational corporations in their overseas subsidiaries; in uses, the amount represents the profits reinvested by foreign multinational corporations in their Australian subsidiaries. This item, despite being of interest, is probably very inaccurately captured, since information on foreign subsidiaries of multinational corporations is of mediocre quality. Another special feature of the item is that the reasoning is applied only to multinational corporations: national accountants do not apply it between Australian parent companies and Australian subsidiaries.

> III. Note for experts: the counterpart of this flow appears in item F5 of the financial accounts (shares and other equities).

- *Property income attributed to insurance policyholders.* This is an imputed flow corresponding to the property income obtained by insurance companies investing their technical reserves. Since these technical reserves belong not to the insurance companies, but to the policyholders (in this case, the policyholders are the non-financial corporations), the national accounts are compiled as if the property income was paid back to the policyholders and then paid out again in the form of consumption of insurance services.

- *Rent from land and sub-soil assets.* This fifth type of property income consists of rent received by owners of land or sub-soil assets (oil, coal, mineral deposits) in cases where the exploitation is entrusted to others. Note that this very small item does not include rentals from office buildings or from rental cars used by corporations, which are purchases of services recorded as intermediate consumption in the production account.

The next item in the "uses" part of the distribution of income account is taxes on income (D5). This item mainly consists of corporation tax, which amounted to 37.7 billion Australian dollars in 2004. The distribution of income account also includes social contributions received (D61) and social benefits paid (D62). This may seem surprising, given that most social contributions are paid to social insurance plans, and that the benefits are received from these same plans, although they are not classified in the corporate sector. The reason for the existence of these flows is that large firms sometimes set up their own systems of pensions or social insurance. In this case, the benefits are paid directly by the firm to its current or former employees. However, the national accounts act as if the imputed contributions corresponding to these benefits were paid to employees as part of their compensation (in the generation of income account) and then paid back by these same employees to these same corporations, which then use them to pay out the social benefits. As we have already seen, this complicated system is aimed at bringing out the totality of the cost of labour in the generation of income account. However, Australia does not follow the 1993 SNA in this regard. While its national accounts act as if the imputed contributions by employers were paid to employees, it does not show them being paid back to the employers. Hence, there are no entries to be made for social benefits (D61 and D62). Australia is not alone in deviating from the 1993 SNA in this respect.

The other items in this account are "other current transfers". In particular, these consist of flows related to corporations' non-life insurance policies. Corporations receive compensation for non-life claims and pay net non-life insurance premiums. Since the national accounts are based on the accrual accounting principle (see Chapter 10), it is not the claims *paid* to the corporations during the period that are recorded but the claims *due* during the period. And why is the word "net" attached to the insurance premiums? The answer is because the national accounts distinguish three elements in the payment of an insurance premium: 1) the payment for an insurance management service; 2) the participation of each policyholder in the claims paid out; 3) the VAT and the specific taxes payable on insurance. The net premium corresponds only to the second element, the first being treated as intermediate consumption of insurance services in the production account of non-financial corporations. The third element is collected by the insurance companies but does not appear in their accounts for national accounts purposes; instead, it is recorded as being received directly by government, without showing who the payer is. For a better understanding of the recording of insurance-related flows, the reader is referred to the section "Going a step further – Insurance: are net premiums equal to the claims paid out?"

The balancing item of the account is known as *net disposable income*. This balancing item is exactly equal, in the case of corporations, to their *net saving* because by definition corporations have no consumption.

The capital account

We now come to the last of the accounts for non-financial corporations, namely the *capital account*. This account describes how saving is used by corporations for financing investment (GFCF) in capital goods and changes in their inventories. Hence, rather than "uses", on the left-hand side of Table 6, we now have "changes in assets"; and rather than "resources" on the right-hand side of the table we now have "changes in liabilities and net worth".

As can be seen in Table 6, Australian firms had net saving of 14.1 billion Australian dollars in 2004. However, it is necessary to reconstitute on the right-hand side of the table (changes in liabilities and net worth) *gross* saving, by adding consumption of fixed capital, in order to compare it with *gross* fixed capital formation on the left-hand side of the table. If we had put *net* fixed capital formation on the left-hand side (under changes in assets), there would have been no need for this adjustment. However, it is the tradition to show gross fixed capital formation under changes in assets. According to these figures, there was a sum of 75.8 billion Australian dollars in gross saving that was used by firms to finance their fixed investment of 102.7 billion Australian dollars. Most of the shortfall was financed by net borrowing of 26 billion Australian dollars. This explains why gross saving is sometimes referred to as "self-financing", in other words, the financing of investment using the firm's own resources. It is possible to calculate a "self-financing ratio" by dividing gross saving by gross fixed capital formation. This ratio expresses the amount (in %) of the GFCF, which is financed by the saving generated by the firms themselves, without using credits from banks

Capital transfers receivable (D9) include such things as building and equipment grants from general government to research laboratories. Capital transfers payable include contributions to local government by real estate developers towards the cost of the construction of roads on their subdivisions and contributions by coal mining companies towards the cost of constructing railway lines.

Table 6. **Australia: Capital account for non-financial corporations (S11)**

Billions of Australian dollars, 2004

Changes in assets		Changes in liabilities and net worth	
		B8N. Net saving	14.1
P51. Gross fixed capital formation	102.7	K1. Consumption of fixed capital	61.6
P52. Changes in inventories	0.0	B8. Gross saving	75.8
P53. Acquisition less disposal of valuables	0.0	D9. Capital transfers receivable	2.3
K2. Acquisition less disposal of non-produced non-financial assets	0.1	D9. Capital transfers payable	−1.2
B9. Net lending/borrowing	−26.0		

Source: OECD (2006), *National Accounts of OECD Countries: Volume II, Detailed Tables*, 1993-2004, 2006 Edition, OECD, Paris.

StatLink: *http://dx.doi.org/10.1787/854583015531*

The balancing item of the capital account is the item **B9 net lending/net borrowing** – "net lending" when it is positive and "net borrowing" when it is negative. In the case of *non-financial* corporations, it is in fact usually negative. It is indeed common practice for non-financial corporations to call on the saving of households (intermediated by banks) to finance investment they are unable to make out of their own resources. This is traditionally done through borrowing from the banks.

If one turns to the Australian *financial* accounts, the estimate for the net borrowing of *non-financial* corporations is 55.0 billion Australian dollars, somewhat higher than the 26 billion Australian dollar figure in the capital account. It is not uncommon to see statistical discrepancies of this magnitude between the estimates of net lending/borrowing in the capital and financial accounts. In both accounts, net lending/borrowing is obtained as a balancing item, and so the statistical discrepancy reflects inconsistencies between the estimates relating to the "real" economy as portrayed in the capital account and the financial data in the financial account. As will be seen in Chapter 8, the financial accounts use different data sources (mainly data from banks) than the non-financial accounts (corporate accounts).

3. From corporations to firms

We have now seen in some detail the accounts of corporations. In practice, however, macroeconomists are more interested in having at their disposal accounts for all enterprises, whether incorporated or not, since they are more interested in economic rather than legal criteria when carrying out their analyses. Unincorporated enterprises are producers like any others. Unfortunately, the national accounts are not currently capable of providing the full set of accounts for all firms, because unincorporated enterprises, by definition, do not have complete sets of accounts. However, some countries like France and the United States calculate partial accounts for all firms including unincorporated enterprises. In France, this grouping is known as "NFCs-Ues" (in French: "SNFEI"), standing for "non-financial corporations and unincorporated enterprises" ("sociétés non financières et enterprises individuelles"). This grouping excludes financial corporations. A similar sector in United States is the "business sector", which includes financial corporations (see Chapter 12).

Who are these individual entrepreneurs with their unincorporated enterprises (UEs)? They are generally members of a household who manage family firms such as a retail store, a taxi company, a farm or a medical or legal firm, provided that these firms do not have corporate status. Farmers make up a substantial portion of the UEs, but self-employed doctors, lawyers and architects are another significant constituent group. Note that the national accounts do not go so far as to classify homeowner-occupiers as individual entrepreneurs. The imputed output of housing services and all the related transactions form part of the "pure" household sector. This is also the case for the non-imputed output of housing services when a household that owns another dwelling in addition to its own rents it out directly to tenants. Notwithstanding the fact that housing services are being produced by one unit for the consumption of another, these households are not regarded as individual entrepreneurs.

From an economic standpoint, the UEs are producers as much as corporations are. Statistically, however, it is impossible to distinguish certain transactions of UEs that are linked to their entrepreneurial activity from transactions relating to their functions as households. This explains why it is not possible to draw up a complete set of accounts for UEs, nor for "pure" households (*i.e.* excluding transactions related to the UEs' productive activities).

France nevertheless has a partial set of accounts for the UEs. All that is then needed is to add this to the accounts for the non-financial corporations (NFCs) to obtain a set of accounts for NFCs-UEs, *i.e.* for all non-financial market producers. This partial account makes it possible to calculate, for example, the gross profit share (or, if preferred, the net profit share) that was discussed earlier, but this time in a version extended to the UEs.

It can be seen that the profit share of NFCs-UEs is roughly seven percentage points higher than that of the NFCs. One might be tempted to deduce from this that unincorporated enterprises are distinctly better performers than corporations, since it is their inclusion that brings about this leap in the profit share. However, this is not the case. The profit share of NFCs-UEs is higher because, by definition, the "profits" of unincorporated enterprises include the implicit remuneration of the work performed by the individual entrepreneurs. This remuneration is a very high percentage (around 80%), and this pushes up the overall profit share. Because of this, the analytical information content of this indicator is severely reduced. In fact, the balance of the generation of income account for the UEs is known as "mixed income" (carrying the code B3), whereas the balancing item of the generation of income account for corporations is known as the "operating surplus" (carrying the code B2). The use of the term "mixed income" reflects the notion that this form of operating profit is not comparable with that of corporations since it "mixes" the remuneration of the capital factor and the labour of the owner of the unincorporated enterprise.

Table 7. **France: Comparison of the profit shares of non-financial corporations and non-financial corporations plus unincorporated enterprises**

As a percentage of value added

	2001	2002	2003	2004
Profit share of NFCs (S11)	31.3	30.7	30.6	30.8
Profit share of NFCs-UEs (S11 + S14A)	38.5	37.8	37.8	38.0

Source: INSEE.

Key points

▶ An enterprise is an institutional unit whose objective is to produce market goods and services; in other words, to sell its products on the market at an economically significant price.

▶ One of the criteria used by national accountants to decide whether a price is economically significant is to calculate a sales/costs ratio. If this ratio is higher than 50%, the enterprise is regarded as being "market".

▶ The corporate sector is made up of firms that are legally constituted as corporations and produce complete sets of accounts, unlike the unincorporated enterprises. The non-financial corporations sector excludes banks, insurance companies and other financial intermediaries, but includes the public-sector enterprises.

▶ Some countries calculate accounts for the grouping consisting of corporations and unincorporated enterprises. This grouping is sometimes called the "business sector". However, it is not possible to calculate more than a partial account for this grouping, since by definition unincorporated enterprises do not have complete sets of accounts separate from those of their owners.

▶ The profit share is the principal indicator of performance as regards the profits of non-financial corporations in the national accounts. It is most often calculated in its "net" version, *i.e.* as the net operating surplus divided by the net value added (and multiplied by 100). Theoretically speaking, this net profit share (net of consumption of fixed capital) is analytically preferable to the gross profit share (gross operating surplus/gross value added), since it takes into account depreciation (*i.e.* consumption of fixed capital).

▶ The "self-financing ratio" measures the proportion of fixed investment financed by the saving generated by the firms themselves, as opposed to external financing (bank loans or the issuance of shares or bonds). It is calculated as gross saving divided by GFCF (and multiplied by 100).

 UNDERSTANDING NATIONAL ACCOUNTS – ISBN 92-64-02566-9 – © OECD 2006

Going further

Consumption of fixed capital and amortisation

Consumption of fixed capital is defined in the SNA 1993 as "the decline, during the course of the accounting period, in the current value of the stock of fixed assets owned and used by a producer as a result of physical deterioration, normal obsolescence or normal accidental damage" (SNA 1993, paragraph 6.178). This is what economists refer to as "depreciation". In the n ational accounts, therefore, the consumption of fixed capital can be regarded as a synonym for depreciation. Company accountants, on the other hand, use the term "amortisation", which covers the same concept but measures it in a slightly different way compared with the national accounts. This section explains the difference.

A key part of the definition quoted above is "decline ... in the current value". National accountants measure the consumption of fixed capital by applying a "depreciation coefficient" to the current value of each capital asset, that is to say to its current market price, whereas company accountants apply a depreciation coefficient to the value of the capital good at its *original purchase price* (they call this "historic cost"). When the prices of capital goods rise, the difference can therefore be very significant. This method of business accounting is partly explained by tax considerations. The rules binding company accountants do in fact authorise the re-evaluation of assets, but since this re-evaluation is taxed, they generally avoid doing so, and their assets in most cases continue to be valued at their purchase price. The national accounts, which are not affected by tax rules, prefer to evaluate these items at their current market value.

Company accountants and national accountants both often make the assumption that capital goods lose their value in a constant manner each year. This is known as "straight-line" depreciation. For example, if one considers that the service life of a certain capital asset is 10 years, it will be assumed that it loses 1/10 of its value each year. Now suppose that the asset is in its ninth year of life and that it cost 100 when it was purchased eight years ago. Suppose also that, as a result of inflation, the market price of this asset had been rising by 4% each year since it was purchased. In this situation:

- The accountant of the commercial firm calculates its depreciation in the ninth year of its life by taking 100/10 = 10.

- The national accountant calculates the consumption of fixed capital in the ninth year of its life as $[100 \times (1.04)^8]/10 = 13.7$. In other words, he revalues the asset by the cumulative rate of inflation before calculating the depreciation.

There is an economic explanation for this difference. Because of inflation, the real utilisation cost of this asset during its ninth year is not 10, but 13.7, since this is the amount the firm has to set aside to replace this asset when it comes to the end of its productive life. There is another important difference between the two accounting systems, which is that company accountants apply the mortality rates for the asset that are most favourable to them from a tax standpoint, whereas the national accountants do their best to apply physical and economic laws. For example, if the tax authorities allow a truck to be depreciated in three years, the company accountants will do just that, while the national accountants will take the view that in fact a truck lasts 10 years and will depreciate it over this longer period. In the final analysis, national accountants cannot calculate the consumption of fixed capital simply by taking the sum of the amortisation declared by firms in their accounts. They have therefore designed their own method, which is known as the "perpetual inventory method" or PIM (see Chapter 8). Currently, this method is the best available for calculating the consumption of fixed capital, but it involves numerous assumptions regarding service lives and rates of depreciation. This probably explains why certain national accountants prefer to publish incomplete accounting balances (gross and not net) on the grounds that they are more reliable, instead of the net figures that are more correct but less reliable.

Profits and gross operating surplus: not to be confused

In the national accounts, the operating surplus is the portion of the income derived from production that is earned by the capital factor. It differs from the profit figure shown in the company accounts for several reasons. The following diagram (which remains approximate) shows the reconciliation of the two:

> net operating surplus (national accounts)
> *plus* consumption of fixed capital
> = gross operating surplus (national accounts)
> *minus* amortisation (company accounts)
> *plus* inventory appreciation (national accounts)
> *minus* conceptual or practical differences (treatment of software, fraud, leasing arrangements)
> *minus* property income paid (national accounts)
> *plus* property income received (national accounts)
> *plus* exceptional losses and profits, in particular capital gains and losses
> = pre-tax profit (company accounts)
> *minus* taxes on profits
> = after-tax profit (company accounts)

The first stage in this reconciliation consists of adding the consumption of fixed capital in order to obtain the gross operating surplus. Then we subtract the company accountants' measure of depreciation (amortisation). It is then necessary to add the holding gains and losses from owning inventories, known as the "inventory appreciation" or "inventory valuation adjustment". For the company accountants, this item is included in the profit calculation, whereas in the national accounts it is excluded from the measurement of output, and hence from the operating surplus. Next, it is necessary to adjust for certain other conceptual differences. For example, the national accountants treat most spending on software as investment and not as intermediate consumption. This is done so that the software expenditure does not affect the operating surplus (except for depreciation), whereas it generally affects directly the calculation of company profits. Similarly, the national accountants adjust the figures supplied by firms to take into account the understatement of profit for reason of fraud in certain sectors. Finally, leasing arrangements are treated differently in the two accounting systems.

The next stage is to add property income received (interest) and deduct property income paid. Profit as measured by company accountants is calculated taking these flows into account. Finally, company accounting rules permit certain "exceptional" transactions to be taken into consideration in calculating profits. For example, company profits can include the capital gains realised on the sale of subsidiaries or on currency transactions. Adding these exceptional elements can lead to substantial differences – in either direction – between the measurement of profits in the national accounts and in the company accounts.

Finally, and this is not the least of the practical differences, it must never be forgotten that the national accounts retrace only the operating profit of firms carrying out their activities on the economic territory. It is therefore impossible to compare the profits announced by the large multinational firms quoted on the stock markets with what is included in the national accounts, since the profits of the multinationals include those made by their overseas subsidiaries.

Insurance: are net premiums equal to the claims paid out?

The modelling of transactions relating to non-life insurance in the national accounts can be summarised using the following notations: GP denotes gross premiums, in other words the sum of money appearing on your insurance invoice (however, in this simplified example, we will exclude taxes such as VAT); S represents the insurance service (*i.e.* the output of non-life insurance in the national accounts, measured by the administrative expenses *plus* the operating profit of the insurance companies*); II represents investment income; and C represents claims payable. The net premiums, NP, are defined as equal to the gross premiums *plus* the investment income *minus* the insurance service, and this gives us the first equation: 1) NP = GP + II – S. The insurance service is measured by GP + II – C, *i.e.* the gross premiums *plus* the investment income *minus* the claims payable, giving us the second equation: 2) S = GP + II – C. Rearranging the two equations gives NP = C, so that the net premiums are equal to the claims. This "accounting identity" calls for two remarks.

First, the identity holds good only for the economy as a whole and not for individual institutional sectors, let alone individual customers. For example, in France in 2002, total net non-life insurance premiums amounted to € 33 billion and total claims to € 32.8 billion (the difference being explained by flows to and from the rest of the world). However, this does not

* See Chapter 4 for a more complete description of the output of insurance companies.

imply that the net premiums paid by non-financial corporations are equal to the claims owed to non-financial corporations. It is quite possible that in that year they suffered fewer accidents of various kinds than other agents did. This is indeed what seems to have happened in France in 2002, since the net premiums of non-financial corporations were € 8.6 billion and their claims were only € 5.3 billion. However, such a situation is unlikely to last: if for structural reasons non-financial corporations have fewer expenses due to accidents than they pay out in premiums, it would be logical for the premiums to decline.

The second remark is that this equality is logically dubious. By what miracle should claims be identically equal to premiums when the insurance business is itself inherently unpredictable? Some years are catastrophic; others have relatively few claims. It is all a matter of probability – the theory that lies at the heart of the insurance profession. Obviously, the so-called law of averages operates in favour of a certain regularity. But in practice the volatility of accidents, and hence of claims, means that premiums and claims are only rarely equal. In the national accounts, however, the miracle is achieved in a simple manner: this volatile difference is allocated, by construct, to the output consisting of the insurance service S, as shown by equation (2). The counterpart of the accounting identity NP = C is therefore the volatility of the output of the insurance service. After long discussions among national accountants, it has been proposed that this construct should be inverted by allocating the volatility, no longer to S, but to a transfer in the distribution of income account. The proposal for change was prompted by the fact that the current volatility of S was adversely affecting the interpretation of GDP. This reform has already been introduced in the United States and is expected to be generalised in the update of the 1993 SNA, scheduled for 2008.

Exercises   *Answers at www.SourceOECD.org/understandingnationalaccounts*

Exercise 1. Accounting balances and ratios: from gross to net

This exercise is based on the French national accounts. It consists of calculating the net accounting balances and ratios starting from the gross balances they provide. First question: find on the INSEE website (*www.insee.fr*) the annual national accounts table that gives the consumption of fixed capital ("consommation de capital fixe") by non-financial corporations ("sociétés non financières") between 2001 and 2003. Second question: find on the INSEE website the principal gross accounting balances for non-financial corporations over the same period (gross value added – "valeur ajoutée brute" – and gross operating surplus – "excédent brut d'exploitation"). Calculate the net balances. Deduce from these the gross and net profit ratios.

Exercise 2. To see whether you have understood the accounts system

The following is a list of transactions made by an advertising firm. Place these various transactions correctly in the structure of accounts shown further below, and show that the firm's gross saving amounted to 620 K$ (1 K$ = 1 000$).

Revenue	K$
1. Sales to customers	4 500
2. Interest on bank account	30
3. Payment of claim for fire damage	10

Expenditure	K$
4. Paper, Ink and other office supplies used during the year	380
5. Rent paid for additional office space	150
6. Cost of electricity and telephones	60
7. CEO's remuneration	300
8. Gross staff wages and salaries	1 500
9. Employers' social security contributions on staff wages and salaries	800
10. Dividend paid to shareholders	420
11. Profits tax payable	180
13. Purchase of computers and software	240
14. Interest on the bank loan for the purchase of computers	40
15. Payment to the security company for the protection of buildings	70
16. Property tax on office buildings	20

Uses	Resources
P2. Intermediate consumption	P1. Output:
	P11. Market
B1. Gross value added	P12. For own final use

Generation of income account

Uses	Resources
DI. Compensation of employees:	
D11. Wages and salaries	B1. Gross value added
D121. Employers' actual social contributions	
D122. Employers' imputed social contributions	
D29. Other taxes on production	
D39. Other subsidies on production	
B2. Gross operating surplus	

Allocation of primary income account

Uses	Resources
	B2. Gross operating surplus
D4. Property income:	D4. Property income:
D41. Interest	D41. Interest
D421. Dividends	D421. Dividends
D43. Reinvested earnings on direct foreign investment	D43. Reinvested earnings on direct foreign investment
D45. Rents on land and sub-soil assets	D45. Rents on land and sub-soil assets
B5. Balance of primary incomes	

Secondary distribution of income account

Uses	Resources
D51. Taxes on income	B5. Balance of gross primary incomes
	D61. Social contributions:
D622. Private funded social benefits	D611. Actual social contributions
D71. Net non-life insurance premiums	D612. Imputed social contributions
D75. Miscellaneous current transfers	D72. Non-life insurance claims
B6. Gross disposable income	D75. Other current transfers

Use of disposable income account

Uses	Resources
B8. Gross saving	
	B6. Gross disposable income

Exercise 3. Some international comparisons for corporations, year 2000

Using the first five rows, calculate three significant corporate ratios for each country: the net profit share (NOS/NVA); the investment rate (GFCF/GVA); and the self-financing ratio (Gross saving/GFCF). Be careful: the profit share you are being asked for is a net rate, whereas the investment rate and the self-financing ratio are gross rates.

	Germany M euros	United States Billion $	France M euros	United Kingdom M £
Gross value added	1 133 570	6 151	770 000	637 967
Gross operating surplus	357 370	1 709	231 576	213 014
Saving, net	–13 620	137	22 737	19 674
Consumption of fixed capital	180 800	740.2	118 782	70 076
GFCF	246 320	1 104.3	161 041	110 259
Profit share (net)				
Investment ratio				
Self-financing ratio				

Exercise 4. (Difficult) The calculation of the profit share for non-financial corporations

Table 27 of the "Informations Rapides", which is the main publication of the French quarterly national accounts (detailed results) contains the following table:

	2001	2002
Profit share (%)	39.9	39.6
Change in the profit share	–0.1	–0.3
Contributions to the change in the profit share		
Labour productivity* (+)	–0.4	0.2
Real wages and salaries (–)	0.0	0.5
Other elements (+)	0.3	0.0

* Productivity is defined here in terms of value added.

Explain how the change in the profit share can be expressed as a function of the change in labour productivity and growth in real wages and salaries (*plus* other elements). For this purpose, start with the definition of the profit share and the equation GVA = CE + GOS + TNS, where GVA is the gross value added, GOS the gross operating surplus, CE the compensation of employees (including employers' social contributions) and TNS the taxes net of subsidies on production (from now on this last item will not be shown separately but will be included under "other elements"). Use the definition of productivity (value added in volume/employment) and real wage rate (the hourly wage rate divided by the price of value added). Based on these variables, comment on the change in the profit share in 2002. Make the link with the economic principle governing wage bargaining, which says that real wage rates (including employers' social contributions) can increase by the amount of productivity gains.

Exercise 5 (Difficult): Producer prices and production costs

Table 26 of the "Informations Rapides" of the French quarterly national accounts (detailed results) includes the following table.

Change in production costs

%

Non-financial corporations	2001	2002
Producer prices	1.6	0.3
Total unit cost	1.4	0.2
Of which, intermediate consumption	0.6	−0.7
Taxes related to production	−1.3	1.4
Wage cost	3.5	2.0
Components of the unit wage cost		
Average wage per head (+)	3.3	2.4
Productivity * (−)	−0.8	0.4

* Productivity is defined here in terms of output.

What is the implicit definition of total cost in this table? How can one deduce from it total unit cost? How does the analysis of total unit cost make it possible to understand the evolution in producer prices? Write down the formula for the relationship between total unit cost and its components. Write down the relationship between unit wage costs and its three component variables (average wage per head, productivity, employers' social contributions). Justify the (+) and the (−). Why does the footnote relating to the productivity variable mention "in terms of production", whereas in the table for the previous exercise it mentioned "in terms of value added"?

Chapter **8**

THE FINANCIAL AND BALANCE SHEET ACCOUNTS

1. The importance of household wealth for the analysis of the current economic situation

2. The principle of quadruple-entry bookkeeping

3. Financial assets and liabilities

4. The link between financial flows and financial stocks

5. The non-financial assets

6. The complete sequence of accounts of an institutional sector

8 THE FINANCIAL AND BALANCE SHEET ACCOUNTS
1. The importance of household wealth for the analysis
of the current economic situation

Household final consumption expenditure accounts for 60% of GDP, so that a change of one or two percentage points in this aggregate can decide whether the economy does well or badly. The OECD economists therefore keep a close eye on the factors that influence household consumption. The most important of these is their disposable income during the period in question, but it is not the only one. Another variable influencing consumption is the change in household wealth.

1. The importance of household wealth for the analysis of the current economic situation

Households own financial and non-financial assets that constitute their "wealth". When the value of these assets increases due to a rise in share prices, or a rise in land values above the rise of prices of other goods and services, households feel richer and hence are more inclined to save less and spend more. It is wealth in the form of stocks that is most sensitive to these capital gains, or "holding gains" (see "Going a step further: Holding gains or losses and market prices in the national accounts"). These gains were particularly spectacular toward the end of the 1990s, thanks to the so-called new economy phenomenon. This influence on household behaviour is known as the "wealth effect". It is particularly visible in the United States, where a large percentage of households own financial wealth in the form of securities (*i.e.* stock market shares, unquoted shares, bonds and other equities).

The OECD regularly publishes indicators of the changes in household wealth. The following table, extracted from a recent publication, deals with Canada, the United Kingdom and the United States.

The figures in Table 1 are expressed as percentages of **net disposable income**, making it possible to evaluate the wealth in terms of the number of years of annual income. For example, in Canada in 2004 households' net worth was equivalent to 523.1% of their net annual disposable income, *i.e.* more than five years worth of income. The wealth comprises financial assets (bank accounts, savings accounts, stock market shares, other shares, bonds, etc.) and non-financial assets (land, housing, productive assets of individual entrepreneurs). But households also have debts (mortgages, consumer loans, etc.), and you are not truly rich if you own substantial financial wealth but at the same time have considerable debts. This is why economists look at net worth, which is equal to total assets

THE FINANCIAL AND BALANCE SHEET ACCOUNTS
1. The importance of household wealth for the
analysis of the current economic situation

8

Table 1. **Household wealth and indebtedness**

As a percentage of nominal net disposable income

	Canada			United Kingdom			USA		
	1993	2000	2004	1993	2000	2004	1993	2000	2004
Net worth	459.1	509.0	523.1	583.0	727.4	741.3	490.6	579.5	557.8
Net financial worth	203.8	246.7	220.2	278.7	364.0	253.0	280.8	360.2	297.8
Non-financial assets	255.3	262.2	302.9	304.3	363.4	488.3	209.8	219.3	260.0
Financial assets	303.4	359.4	343.6	385.2	476.2	405.3	370.5	463.0	421.3
Of which shares	56.0	90.3	83.9	73.6	108.7	64.0	92.3	154.7	116.2
Liabilities	99.5	112.6	123.4	106.5	112.2	152.3	89.6	102.8	123.5

Source: OECD (2005), *OECD Economic Outlook,* December No. 78, Volume 2005, Issue 2, OECD, Paris.

StatLink: *http://dx.doi.org/10.1787/626746050668*

minus total liabilities. For example, the total financial and non-financial assets of Canadian households in 2004 came to 646.5% (302.9% + 343.6%), but after deduction of liabilities equivalent to 123.4%, the net worth was only 523.1%, well below the equivalent figure for United Kingdom households and slightly less than that of United States households.

Table 1 also illustrates the impact of the speculative bubble in the latter part of the 1990s on household wealth. In the United States, the value of shares held by households rose from 92.3% to 154.7% of disposable income in just seven years. To some extent, this increase was due to an increase in the volume of shares bought by households, but mainly it was caused by a rise in shares' prices. However, the 2001 downturn on Wall Street wiped out half the potential gains accrued between 1993 and 2000, and unrealised holding gains were just as rapidly replaced by unrealised holding losses. Stock markets have their ups and downs. This would matter less were it not for the impact on growth, notably via the "wealth effect". Fortunately, the spectacular rise in real estate prices compensated in the early 2000s for the slump in the stock market. This can be seen by the surge in non-financial wealth, for example in the United Kingdom, where it rose from 363.4% to 488.3% of household disposable income in the space of four years. It was certainly this additional non-financial wealth that enabled UK and American households to maintain their high level of consumption and low level of saving in the recent period.

The financial accounts and the balance sheet accounts in the national accounts constitute the source for the household data we have just commented on. However, the financial accounts also cover financial and non-financial corporations, and general government. These accounts make it possible to calculate not only the net worth of various groups of agents at a given moment, but also how this has evolved over time. This chapter describes the organisation of these accounts.

2. The principle of quadruple-entry bookkeeping

Preceding chapters have shown how the national accounts record transactions relating to production, consumption and distribution between the various institutional sectors. At the end of all these transactions, economic agents are either in a borrower situation, meaning that they have spent more than they have received, or in a lender situation, meaning that they have spent less than they have received. The financial accounts show how the borrower sectors obtain the financial resources they need, and how the lender sectors allocate their surpluses. In general, non-financial corporations are globally borrowers while households are globally lenders. Globally, means for the sector as a whole, and not unit per unit (*i.e.* many poor households are not lenders).

We shall see here, in a section in which anyone who has worked on company accounts will recognise some familiar conventions, that each transaction can be recorded twice: once as a transaction related to production, consumption, etc., and once as a monetary transaction – national accountants would say once as a non-financial transaction and once as a financial transaction. This system shows the high degree of integration within national accounts.

In our money-based societies, every transaction has as a counterpart movement of funds (except for barter transactions, which are recorded solely as non-financial transactions). National accountants say that *each non-financial transaction has a financial "counterpart"*. Take a very simple example. Household H buys a television set for $300. This will be recorded as consumption of $300 in the form of a non-financial transaction. Because of the purchase, the household's bank balance is reduced by $300, the result being a reduction of $300 in the financial accounts. Every transaction by an agent therefore gives rise to two entries: one in the non-financial accounts; the other in the financial accounts, as shown in the summary T-account below.

Accounts of household H					
Non-financial transaction			Financial transaction		
Uses		Resources	Uses		Resources
Consumption	300		Reduction in bank balance	300	

We shall now record the same transaction, but this time from the point of view of corporation C, which sold the television set. As with the household, there are two entries, but for the corporation both entries are under "resources": one as an output among non-financial transactions; and one as an increase in the company's bank balance among financial transactions.

This means that, in total, a single transaction is recorded four times in the national accounts, hence the term quadruple-entry bookkeeping. Put another way, two entries are made for each of the two sectors involved in a transaction.

Accounts of corporation C					
Non-financial transaction			Financial transaction		
Uses	Resources		Uses	Resources	
	Output	300		Increase in bank balance	300

In practice, the financial accounts are somewhat more complicated than we have just shown. For one thing, instead of recording movements in funds under uses or resources depending on whether they correspond to an increase or decrease in a bank balance, all the transactions on the bank accounts, are entered on the same side of the T-account. Moreover, the equivalent of the "uses" column is renamed "change in assets" (denoted by Δ Assets) and the "resources" column is renamed "change in liabilities" (denoted by Δ Liabilities). Our earlier example then gives the following entries:

Accounts of household H				
Non-financial transaction			Financial transaction	
Uses	Resources		Δ Assets	Δ Liabilities
Consumption	300		Bank balance	−300

Accounts of corporation C				
Non-financial transaction			Financial transaction	
Uses	Resources		Uses	Δ Liabilities
	Output	300	Bank balance	+300

It will be seen that this leads to the existence in the financial accounts of transactions carrying a negative sign. For instance, the reduction of $300 in the household's bank balance is recorded as − 300 under changes in assets. This complicates things somewhat, but remains easily understandable, since a negative number indicates a decrease in the financial asset in question – in this case a decline in the bank balance. Since a given period will see numerous movements in bank accounts, some positive and some negative, the financial account will record only the algebraic (net) sum of all these movements taken together.

On the liability side, we find the debts. To complicate our example slightly more, as illustrated below, if our household had taken out a loan of $300 to pay for its television set, we would find on the "change in liabilities" side a debt increase of $300, matched by an increase in the bank balance of the household. Note that it is quite possible to find a negative number among the changes in liabilities. For example, if a household repays a debt, this will be recorded as a negative number in the right-hand column "changes in liabilities" (for a more comprehensive example, see section "Going a step further: a more complete example of entries in the financial accounts"). A final change in presentation involves placing the accounts of each agent one below the other and not side-by-side.

Accounts of household H		Accounts of corporation C	
Non-financial transaction		Non-financial transaction	
Uses	Resources	Uses	Resources
Consumption 300			Output 300

Accounts of household H		Accounts of corporation C	
Financial transaction		Financial transaction	
Δ Assets	Δ Liabilities	Δ Assets	Δ Liabilities
Bank balance (money obtained from the loan taken out) +300	Loan taken out +300	Bank balance +300	
(money paid for the TV set) −300			

The T-accounts make it easier to visualise all the accounting relationships involved in the quadruple entry. We will call them "accounting identities". The *first accounting identity* is the cancelling out along the row of the non-financial transactions, with the consumption of $300 under uses matched by output of $300 under resources. In contrast to the financial accounts, there are no figures with negative signs in the non-financial accounts (although there are exceptions). However, it is valid to place a "virtual" negative sign on a transaction in the uses column and a "virtual" positive sign on a transaction in the resources column. Thus, one can place a negative sign on the consumption of $300 and a positive sign on the output of $300. This gives (−300 + 300) = 0, so the first accounting identity is respected.

If we forget the complication introduced by the loan, the *second accounting relationship* is the cancelling out along the row of the financial transactions, with the − $300 in the household's bank balance matched by +$300 in the company's bank balance: (−300 + 300) = 0.

To better visualise these two accounting relationships, one can introduce a crucial balancing item providing the link between the non-financial and the financial transactions. This is **net lending/net borrowing**, carrying the code **B9**.

The net lending/net borrowing is the balance of all the non-financial transactions. Once agents have produced their output, been paid for their work, consumed, paid their taxes, received their benefits, etc., they have either underspent their receipts, in which case they are said to have generated "net lending", or overspent their receipts, in which case they need to borrow and so are in a "net borrowing situation". This balancing item, like all similar balancing items in the non-financial accounts, is conventionally entered in the uses column and is calculated as the sum of the resources *minus* the sum of the uses. If the result is positive, there is net lending; if it is negative there is net borrowing. For the sake of simplicity in the national accounts, "net lending/net borrowing" is presented as a single item;

a positive sign is attached to net lending and a negative sign to net borrowing. The following table shows the accounts of the above example (whithout the complication of the loan) including the balancing item B9.

Accounts of household H		
Non-financial transaction		
Uses		Resources
Consumption	300	
B9 Net lending/net borrowing	−300	

Financial transaction		
Δ Assets		Δ Liabilities
Bank balance	−300	
		B9 Net lending/net borrowing −300

Accounts of corporation C		
Non-financial transaction		
Uses		Resources
		Output 300
B9 Net lending/net borrowing	+300	

Financial transaction		
Δ Assets		Δ Liabilities
Bank balance	+300	
		B9 Net lending /net borrowing +300

B9 is also the balance on all the financial movements. We accordingly find the same number at the bottom of the financial transactions account, but in this case it is conventionally placed in the right-hand column and is calculated as the sum of the changes in assets *minus* the sum of the changes in liabilities. From the point of view of the financial accounts, this balancing item can be interpreted as a change in financial net worth. If an agent is in a net lending situation, this means that, other things being equal, he or she has become financially richer during the period. Note that this can be due to several different factors. The agent may either have increased his/her claims on other agents or reduced his debts, or performed a mixture of both. Conversely, if an agent is in a net borrowing situation, his/her financial net worth has decreased (leaving aside price movements and other changes in volume).

The *final accounting identity* results from the (theoretically) strict accounting identity between the balance on the financial accounts and the balance on the non-financial accounts. By definition, these two "B9s" are equal. For each of the two agents – corporation and household – this equality is respected in our example. Unfortunately, however, it is not respected in the actual national accounts tables. This is not because there are exceptions to the general rule but because the statistical sources used for the calculation of the non-financial accounts are different from those used for the financial accounts. The resulting divergence is known as a "statistical discrepancy", and its existence explains why the B9 of the non-financial accounts is sometimes coded "B9A" and that of the financial accounts "B9B" (or called "net financial transactions") so as to differentiate them. Only the general government sector has at times no statistical discrepancy between B9A and B9B, thanks partly to the quality and consistency of the information available for the accounts of this sector but also, in Europe, to the need to produce the "cleanest" accounts possible, given that they are closely monitored by the European Commission (see Chapter 9). In the general government case, therefore, B9A is often equal to B9B.

It is essential to have a firm grasp of these *three accounting identities* to be able to record in a convincing manner certain complex operations (see Exercises 2 and 3 at the end of this chapter). An important corollary of these three accounting identities – one might even call it a theorem – is that in a closed economy (one that has no relations with the rest of the world) the sum of the net lending and the net borrowing is zero by definition. In other words, one agent's lending is necessarily another agent's borrowing (see box below "Saving and investment"). In an open economy, the sum of the net lending and net borrowing of resident agents is equal to the net lending or net borrowing of the rest of the world, but carries the opposite sign.

Box 1. **Saving and investment**

The basic Keynesian model taught in elementary macroeconomics classes is: $Y = C + I$; $R = Y$. These equations are to be read as follows: demand Y is equal to consumption C *plus* investment I; income R is equal to output Y, which is itself equal to demand. From this is derived the well-known equation:

$$Saving = R - C = I$$

stating the basic rule that saving equals investment. If one assumes that firms do not self-finance any of their investment and that households do not invest, this is tantamount to restating our "theorem" that the sum of agents' net lending/net borrowing is zero in a closed economy. Indeed, households save and in this way are net lenders. Firms, for their part, have to find funding for their investment. Under the simplified conditions presented here, households' net lending exactly covers, by definition, firms' net borrowing. This illustrates the convergence that exists between the national accounts model and the Keynesian model.

It is strongly recommended that Exercise 2 be done after a first reading of this chapter. In addition to providing an illustration of these accounting identities, it will demonstrate that some transactions are purely financial, in the sense that they involve no non-financial transactions. For example, if a household sells shares only the two movements in financial assets are recorded, with no corresponding entry in the non-financial accounts.

3. Financial assets and liabilities

In our very simple example, we have introduced only one type of financial asset (the bank account) and only two agents. In reality, there is a very wide variety of claims and debt and also a wide variety of institutional sectors. In particular, there is considerable detail in the financial accounts regarding the different categories of *financial* corporations. The complete list of these financial subsectors is given in Chapter 10.

The entire scope of the information provided by the financial accounts can be seen by referring to the "table of financial transactions" (also called "flow of funds") toward the end of this chapter. However, before going into all these details, it is useful to start with a stylised presentation of the financial accounts, to show that things are not as complicated as they look in the detailed table.

Stylised presentation of the financial accounts

	Assets		Liabilities	
	Financial institutions (FI)	Non-financial agents (NFA)	Financial institutions (FI)	Non-financial agents (NFA)
Deposits		W	W	
Loans	X			X
Interbank refinancing	Y		Y	
Securities	Z1	Z2	Z3	Z4

In this stylised presentation, we have indicated by capital letters the cells in the table where the bulk of the transactions and the major accounting equalities are to be found. As the presentation shows, the financial accounts trace out the assets and liabilities and the changes in these taking place between the *financial institutions* (mainly banks) and the *non-financial agents* (households, corporations, general government). The principal financial assets are shown in the left-hand column: *deposits* (including bank accounts), *loans* (*i.e.* bank loans to corporations and households), *interbank refinancing* (all the transactions between banks that are necessary for the financial system to function properly) and *securities* (bonds and shares).

For example, the deposits (W) are assets for the non-financial agents and liabilities for the financial institutions, and the total of the one is equal to the total of the other. The loans (X) are mainly assets for the financial institutions and liabilities for the non-financial institutions, and again the two totals are equal. The amounts involved in interbank refinancing (Y) are sometimes astronomical, but it will be seen that this is in fact internal to the financial sector, with roughly the same amounts recorded as assets and liabilities. Only the securities (Z) are recorded on both the assets and liabilities sides for virtually all the institutional sectors. The exception is the household sector, since households do not issue securities. As for other lines, total securities issued (Z3 + Z4) equals total securities acquired (Z1 + Z2).

There are in fact many more columns and rows in the real table of financial transactions in the national accounts. In particular, financial assets are broken down by their degree of "liquidity" (a financial term measuring the rapidity and facility with which an asset can be transformed into cash or another generally accepted means of payment: a bank account is highly liquid, but a share is less liquid because it first has to be sold, requiring payment of a commission). The following is the list of the principal financial assets recorded in the national accounts. The list of financial liabilities is identical, since one agent's financial asset is necessarily another agent's liability (see box "Tricks of the trade").

Box 2. Tricks of the trade: how to distinguish a financial asset from a non-financial asset

A financial asset for one agent always is a corresponding liability for another agent. For example, a bank account is an asset for a household and a liability for the bank. Banknotes are assets for those who own them and a liability for the central bank that issues them. A loan is an asset for the lender and a liability for the borrower, and so on. The only exception to this rule is "monetary" gold held by central banks. Non-financial assets, on the other hand, have no identifiable counterpart. If a household owns a dwelling, this appears among its assets, but it is no one's liability. A firm owns a machine that appears among its assets but no other agent has a corresponding liability.

The list of financial assets is as follows:

1. F1 – Monetary gold and SDRs. This item usually only concerns central banks. It reflects the gold held as a monetary reserve by a central bank *plus* Special Drawing Rights. SDRs are special assets created by the International Monetary Fund and held by central banks. There are two exceptions: in the United Kingdom, F1 is recorded for the sector S1311 (central government), while in the United States, it is split between S121 (central bank) and S1311 (central government).

2. F2 – Currency and deposits. This item includes "currency", code F21 (which is an asset for the holders and a liability for the issuers, mainly central banks). It also includes "transferable deposits", code F22, which includes current bank accounts, as well as "other deposits" (F29). Item F2 does not exactly correspond to the so-called monetary aggregates (see section "Going a stage further: financial accounts and money supply").

3. F3 – Securities other than shares. This item is broken down into two sub-items: F33 "securities other than shares, except financial derivatives" and F34 "financial derivatives". Item F33 is sub-classified by maturity into short-term and long-term and includes, in particular, the securities issued by the public treasury to finance the public deficit. It also includes all other bonds, including those issued by corporations. Item F34[1] "financial derivatives" is a large item but is almost exclusively concerned with interbank refinancing. The description of financial derivatives is somewhat too technical for this textbook.

4. F4 – Loans. This item contains all the financial assets that are created when creditors lend money directly to debtors. This item includes consumer loans, housing loans and loans to businesses. Like item F3, it is broken down into two sub-items: short-term

UNDERSTANDING NATIONAL ACCOUNTS – ISBN 92-64-02566-9 – © OECD 2006

loans (for less than one year) and long-term loans (for more than one year). This breakdown has its limitations. For one thing, loans are now sometimes renegotiable. For another, a long-term loan nearing the end of its life becomes a short-term loan.

5. F5 – Shares and other equity (including shares issued by investment funds, such as mutual funds). This item includes shares in both quoted and unquoted companies. How to value the latter is the Achilles' heel of financial national accounts. It is in fact very difficult to estimate what their market price would be, since by definition there is no market for them. Note, moreover, that shares are shown as liabilities of corporations in the national accounts, even though they are not a debt of companies but form part of their "own funds". Shares in investment funds are shares held indirectly, through portfolios managed by banks and financial corporations (including property portfolios). This item is increasingly important, since households apparently prefer this type of product to direct holding of shares and bonds.

6. F6 – Insurance technical reserves. This item is broken down between F61 "net equity of households in life insurance reserves and in pension fund" and F62 "prepayments of insurance premiums and reserves for outstanding claims". In terms of holdings, item F61 represents the cumulative value of the savings invested by households in life insurance contracts and in capitalisation pension funds. The value of these assets is attributed to households in the national accounts, despite the fact that these assets in company accounting appear in the balance sheets of the companies managing these funds. This attribution is a correct representation of economic reality, since the savings belong to the households and not to the companies managing them. Indeed, at some stage, these sums will be returned to the households in the form of annuities or retirement pensions. The implicit debts of the pension plans known as "pay-as-you-go" (often social security or civil service pension plans) are not recorded in the national accounts, although there is a debate among national accountants on this point. For the time being, the institutional differences among countries regarding pension plans (capitalisation *versus* pay-as-you-go) generate very significant differences in the financial accounts, making international comparisons difficult. In particular, pension assets (in other words, future pension rights) in countries with mainly capitalisation systems are recorded as households' assets, while the value of future pension rights in countries with pay-as-you-go public systems (like France, Germany, Italy and Spain) are not recorded. Item F62 represents the prepayments of non-life insurance premiums and outstanding claims on insurance companies.

7. F7[2] – Other accounts receivable/payable. This item contains two sub-items: F71 "trade credits and advances" and F79 "other accounts receivable/payable, except trade credits and advances". The first of these is a substantial item, which includes credits related to commercial transactions (in France, for example, payments between firms for goods and services are frequently on a 60-days basis, meaning that the seller delivers the product while accepting payment 60 days later). The second sub-item includes, in particular, all the implicit credits relating to wages and salaries, taxes, rents,

etc. The national accounts record transactions on the basis of "accrual accounting", as do company accounts. This means that a transaction must be recorded in such a way that the accounts reflect at any moment the value of agents' entitlements and obligations. For example, even if an employee's salary is paid two or three months late, the salary will be entered in the month during which the work was carried out, because this is when an obligation to pay was generated by the employer. Since the salary is entered but has not been paid, there is a claim by the employee on the firm, which is entered in item F79. A similar entry will be made for tax due to the government but not yet paid.

4. The link between financial flows and financial stocks

As was pointed out at the beginning of this chapter, the purpose of financial accounts is mainly to provide figures on the net worth – *i.e.* assets *minus* liabilities – of institutional sectors. The stock of assets and liabilities is recorded at a given moment in time. In the national accounts, this is usually 31 December, but there are also quarterly financial accounts. Take the example of a UK household H, which on 31 December of year A, has £2 000 in its bank account, owns £13 500 of shares and £23 000 of bonds, while its short-term debts amount to £3 500 (consumer credit) and its long-term debts to £7 500 (mortgages).

Stocks of assets and liabilities at 31/12/A

Assets	
F2. Currency and deposits	2 000
F5. Shares	13 500
F3. Securities other than shares	23 000
Liabilities	
F41. S-T Loans	3 500
F42. L-T Loans	7 500

Starting with this situation at 31/12/A, let us suppose that a household performs the following series of financial transactions during year A + 1. It spends £35 000 on consumption, receives £37 000 in wages and salaries, sells £6 500 of shares and repays £1 500 of its short-term debt and £2 500 of its long-term debt. These transactions (*i.e.* these financial *flows*) will be traced out in the financial accounts, as movements between two financial stock situations).

Financial flows are recorded at the prices actually paid, *i.e.* in current pounds sterling. In the case of transactions using payment instruments denominated in other currencies (euros, dollars, yen, etc.) and transactions in shares and bonds, whose market prices are subject to change, the actual prices at the time of sale or purchase and the currency rates prevalent on the day of the transaction are applied.

Financial accounts for the year A + 1

	Δ Assets	During A + 1
F2. Currency and deposits		−35 000
		+37 000
		+6 500
		−1 500
		−2 500
		= 4 500
F4. Shares		−6 500
F3. Securities other than shares		
	Δ Liabilities	During A + 1
F41. S-T Loans		−1 500
F42. L-T Loans		−2 500

One would be forgiven for thinking that the situation at 31/12/A + 1 would therefore be equal to the situation at 31/12/A *plus* the movements carried out during year A + 1. However, this is only approximately the case, since it does not allow for the impact of changes in asset prices. Applying the general principles of the national accounts, financial (and non-financial) stocks of assets and liabilities are valued at the market prices ruling on the day the accounts are drawn up, usually on the 31 December. But market prices of shares and bonds change (for example, the value of a bond changes in inverse proportion to changes in interest rates – see "Going a step further: The valuation of assets and its relationship to economic theory"). The value of an asset held by an agent can therefore change between 31/12/A and 31/12/A + 1, even in the absence of any transaction carried out by the agent, simply through the operation of price changes on the market, leading to holding gains in the case of upward movements and holding losses in the case of downward movements.

Returning to the example of our household, let us suppose that the average price of the shares it owns falls by 20% between 31/12/A and 31/12/A + 1. One can also suppose that it was in anticipation of this fall that the household sold a substantial portion of its shares (let us assume that this took place at the very beginning of the year, before the price fall, so as to simplify matters). A household will therefore have suffered a holding loss of 20% on the remaining £7 000 held in shares, *i.e.* a loss of £1 400. Let us at the same time suppose that the bond portfolio of the household consists of 6% Treasury bonds and that during the year the market rate of interest on Treasury bonds fell to 4%. In this case, the market value of the bonds will have risen (see Exercise 4 for the calculation of bond values). Let us suppose that this produced a holding gain of £3 200. All these changes in the price of assets are recorded in a special account known as the "revaluation account". Because on the asset side the cash holdings (or on the liability side the loans) are not subject to revaluation, no revaluations are required for these items.

Revaluation account for year A + 1

	Δ Assets	During A + 1
F4. Shares		−1 400
F3. Securities other than shares		+3 200

We are now in a position to find the value of the financial holdings at the end of period A + 1, which equals the initial stock at end of year A (or at the beginning of year A + 1), *plus* the flow of transactions in assets or liabilities during the year *plus* the revaluations. For example, the amount of shares at 31/12/A + 1 is equal to £13 500 (stock at 31/12/A) *minus* £6 500 (sales of shares) *minus* £1 400 (holding losses on the remaining shares), which gives £5 600.

	Financial Assets and liabilities 31/12/A	Financial transactions During A + 1	Revaluations During A + 1	Financial Assets and liabilities 31/12/A + 1
Assets				
F2. Currency and deposits	2 000	4 500		6 500
F5. Shares	13 500	−6 500	−1 400	5 600
F3. Securities other than shares	23 000		+3 200	26 200
Liabilities				
F41. S-T Loans	3 500	−1 500		2 000
F42. L-T Loans	7 500	−2 500		5 000

This example presents the complete information available for households in the financial accounts (with the exception of a special account called "*other changes in volume*", see below). The complete financial accounts show the financial flow, revaluation and financial stock accounts for all the institutional sectors – households, corporations, general government, and NPISHs. As might be expected, they are particularly detailed for the financial corporations, which play a critical role in the management of financial relations and constitute the prime statistical source for the financial accounts.

The complete financial accounts are in three parts. First, there are the financial flows, which are brought together in the table "Flows of Funds" (FoF). An example of this table is given at the end of this chapter, for Spain and extracted from an OECD publication. This shows the financial transactions of general government, corporations (in particular, financial corporations) and transactions with the rest of the world (corresponding to the financial account of the balance of payments). Next, there are the revaluation accounts (and the accounts showing other changes in assets) and, finally, the financial balance sheet accounts, which show the stocks. These financial stock accounts are themselves part of the balance sheet accounts described in the final section of this chapter.

Taken together, these tables show for each institutional sector the details of the financial counterpart of its net lending/net borrowing and the composition of its financial net worth. Conversely, for a given financial asset – shares, for example – it is possible to know the net issue flows and the purchasing sectors, and finally, in the stock accounts, the total value of the shares issued in the economy and the sectors holding these shares. The financial accounts are drawn up mainly on the basis of financial corporations' published accounts (central bank, banks, financial intermediaries – see section "Data sources").

5. The non-financial assets

The net worth of the various agents, and especially of households, is not made up solely of *financial* assets and liabilities but also includes *non-financial* assets. For the household sector, non financial assets include dwellings and in some countries assets in the form of housing are greater than households' financial assets. Many households prefer to put their savings into "bricks and mortar". Households' non-financial assets also include the plant and equipment and the software owned by individual entrepreneurs (who are classified in the household sector).

The national accounts list a wide variety of non-financial assets: buildings and other structures; machinery and other equipment; inventories; valuables; land; mineral deposits; non-cultivated biological resources; reserves of water whose ownership can be established and transferred; and certain intangible assets (software, patents, licences, assignable contracts). One curious feature is that the national accounts distinguish between the value of land and the structures built on this land, although in practice the two are indivisible.

However, the definition of assets in the SNA is restricted to *"assets functioning as a store of value over which ownership rights are enforced by institutional units, individually or collectively, and from which economic benefits may be derived by their owners by holding them or using them over a period of time."* This definition excludes, for example, the so-called human capital, as discussed in the section "Limitations of the national accounts: The exclusions from the balance sheet accounts".

The value of non-financial assets (also called **capital stock**) is usually estimated by the *perpetual inventory method* (PIM). The PIM method is based on data for past flows of GFCF in volume and applies the simple principle that today's stock is equal to what was previously invested *minus* what has since been used up. Applying assumptions regarding physical deterioration and decommissioning, this method is therefore based solely on very long series of GFCF that are, in principle, available to the national accountants. Each annual investment is an addition to the stock, while each decommissioning (retirement from the stock of capital) or element of physical deterioration (consumption of fixed capital) is a deduction.

Using this method, it is possible to calculate the gross (or net) stock of fixed capital at the end of period n, with GC(n) then being equal to the gross (or net) stock of fixed capital at the end of the previous period GC(n – 1) *plus* the GFCF in period n, GFCF(n), *minus* the decommissioned items DEC(n) (or, respectively, the consumption of fixed capital CFC(n)).

This gives, for the gross capital stock: $GC(n) = GC(n-1) + GFCF(n) - DEC(n)$, and, for the net capital stock: $NC(n) = NC(n-1) + GFCF(n) - CFC(n)$. Measured in this way, the *net capital stock* is the market value of the stock of fixed assets and is a major component of the net worth of the nation and of the institutional sectors that own these assets. The *gross capital stock* does not have any clear economic meaning: it has been sometimes used in estimates of the production function (see introduction to Chapter 4) but most economists now use measures of capital services for this purpose rather than the capital stock whether on a net or gross basis.[3]

By developing these formulae, it can be seen that the stock of capital is a function of past investment, decommissioning and physical deterioration. If the series for past GFCF is sufficiently long, the initial GC or NC is no longer of any importance, since at the end of a finite time all the initial assets will have been retired from the capital stock. Everything depends, however, on the estimations of DEC(n) and of CFC (n), which are themselves based on assumptions relating to the average service lives of different kinds of assets, "mortality functions" which describe the distribution of decommissionings around these averages, and physical deterioration (also known as "wear and tear"). OECD countries use several different types of mortality functions. Many European countries use a log-normal mortality function while other OECD countries prefer Weibull or Winfrey functions. Physical deterioration is usually assumed to be "straight-line" meaning that it occurs in equal amounts over the lifetime of the asset, although some countries, including the United States, assume that it occurs at a constant rate. Estimates of the average service lives of different kinds of assets are clearly very important in applying the PIM. In certain countries, these parameters are derived from a survey of enterprises. The following are examples in the case of France: it has been estimated that IT hardware has an average service life of five years; transport equipment between seven and 15 years; a building 25 years and public infrastructure 60 years. On the basis of these assumptions, one obtains discard rates D_i, such that $DEC(n) = \Sigma_i GFCF(n-i) \cdot D_i$. The rates of consumption of fixed capital C_i are calculated as a linear smoothing of these past discard rates, and this gives $CFC(n) = \Sigma_i GFCF(n-i) \cdot C_i$. Taken together, this makes it possible to calculate the stocks of capital GC(n) and NC(n) in volume. The same formulae are then used, but with the introduction of price indices, to obtain the stock of capital at current prices and the consumption of fixed capital at current prices.

The balance sheet accounts

The balance sheet accounts are a synthesis of the tables of financial and non-financial stocks for the various institutional sectors. They make it possible to see in a single table all the assets and liabilities of each sector and hence measure the total wealth of macroeconomic agents at a given date (generally 31 December). The estimates are made at market prices and hence provide the best measure of this wealth (even though it is potential because unrealised) at this date. The estimation of this wealth is nevertheless limited to the items that the national accountants consider as eligible to be considered as assets or liabilities (see section "Limitations of the national accounts").

The following is a summary model of the balance sheet account that we shall use to introduce the definition of "net worth", which is the most all-embracing heading in the national accounts.

Simplified balance sheet account at 31/12/A for a given sector

Assets		Liabilities	
Non-financial assets	NFA	Net worth (including shares and other equity)	$C = A - L$
Financial assets	FA	Liabilities (excluding shares and other equity)	L
Total	$A = NFA + FA$	Total	A

As the table shows, the net worth of an institutional sector is equal to the total assets A (financial assets FA and non-financial assets NFA) *minus* total liabilities L (excluding shares and other equity appearing under liabilities). Since households have no shares on the liability side of their accounts, the net worth in their case is equal to assets *minus* liabilities. In the case of corporations, the net worth includes shares, because the recording of shares in the liabilities column is conventional and does not mean that the corporations owe these sums. In other words, shares are not debt of the companies. By their nature, holders of shares (households or other corporations) cannot demand their repayment from the company as long as the latter remains in activity. Shares appear in the liabilities column but form part of the "own funds" of the companies, hence their inclusion in their net worth.

One sometimes hears mention of *financial* net worth. This is a net worth figure but limited in scope to financial assets and liabilities and taking no account of non-financial assets. This is a somewhat narrow concept, since non-financial assets play just as important a role as financial assets in agents' behaviour.

The tables in the balance sheet accounts make it possible to explain how the net worth is created, in other words the way in which the stock of net worth at the end of a given period is arrived at from the stock of net worth at the end of the previous period. Changes in stocks can be due to several factors.

1. Consumption of fixed capital: this measures the physical depreciation and the obsolescence of the non financial assets.

2. Actual changes in non-financial and financial assets: these are made up of gross capital formation in the case of non-financial assets, and for financial assets, of the financial account flows described earlier.

3. Revaluations: these measure the holding gains or losses during the period that have affected assets and liabilities held by the sector under review.

4. Other changes in volume: This account covers exceptional transactions, generally of non-economic origin, that can affect the wealth of an institutional sector. For example, the destruction of buildings as the result of a natural catastrophe or a war is recorded negatively in this item; the discovery of new exploitable oil reserves will also be recorded there but this time positively. This item is also the place where the effects of changes in the sectoral classification of certain units will be recorded.

Taken together, these changes lead to the table on balance sheet accounts as shown at the end of the next section.

6. The complete sequence of accounts of an institutional sector

We are now in a position to visualise the entire set of accounts of an institutional sector (corporations, for example) right through from the production account to the balance sheet account, using the simplified diagram set out below. Note the organisation of the accounts in "T" form, with the early tables showing uses on the left and resources on the right and subsequent financial tables showing "changes in assets" on the left and "changes in liabilities" on the right. Last comes the balance sheet account in the very compact presentation we have just seen.

	Uses	Resources
Production account	P2. Intermediate consumption	P1. Output
	B1. Value added, gross	
Generation of income account	D1. Compensation of employees	B1. Value added, gross
	D29. Other taxes on production (*minus* subsidies)	
	K1. Consumption of fixed capital	
	B2N. Operating surplus, net	
Distribution of income account	D4. Property income	B2N. Operating surplus, net
	D5. Current taxes on income, wealth, etc.	D4. Property income
	D6. Social benefits (from employers)	D6. Social contributions (by employers)
	D7. Current transfers	D7. Current transfers
	B8N. Saving, net	

UNDERSTANDING NATIONAL ACCOUNTS – ISBN 92-64-02566-9 – © OECD 2006

	Uses	Resources
Capital account	P5. Gross capital formation	B8N. Saving, net
	K1. Consumption of fixed capital (with a minus sign)	D9. Capital transfers
	B9A. Net lending/net borrowing	
	Δ Assets	Δ Liabilities
Financial accounts	F1. Monetary gold and SDRs *	F1. Monetary gold and SDRs
	F2. Currency and deposits	F2. Currency and deposits
	F3. Securities other than shares	F3. Securities other than shares
	F4. Loans	F4. Loans
	F5. Shares and other equity (including investment funds)	F5. Shares and other equity (including investment funds)
	F6. Insurance technical reserves	
	F7. Other accounts receivable	F7. Other accounts payable
		B9B. Net lending/net borrowing

* "Monetary" gold and SDRs will appear only for central banks or similar institutions.

Balance sheet accounts	Stock at 31/12/ previous year	*Minus* Consumption of fixed capital	*Plus* GFCF for non-financial assets *or plus* financial transactions	*Plus* Revaluations	*Plus* Other changes in volume	= Stock at 31/12/ current year
Financial assets						
Non-financial assets						
Liabilities in the form of shares						
Liabilities (excluding shares)						
Net worth (including shares)						

Notes

1. The classification code for this item will be changed to F7 in 2012.

2. The classification code for this item will be changed to F8 in 2012.

3. For further details see OECD (2001), *Measuring Capital, an OECD Manual: Measurement of Capital Stocks, Consumption of Fixed Capital and Capital Services,* OECD, Paris.

Key points

▶ Generally speaking, in the national accounts a transaction by an agent is recorded twice: once in the non-financial accounts and once in the financial accounts. However, when the transactions are purely financial, they are recorded twice in the financial accounts, and in this case without any impact on net lending/net borrowing.

▶ Since a transaction involves two agents, it is therefore recorded four times, *i.e.* two entries for each agent.

▶ The financial accounts trace out first the flows and then the stocks of agents' financial assets and liabilities. The balancing item of the flows is item B9B "net lending/net borrowing"; the balancing item of the stocks is the financial net worth.

▶ If an agent is in a net lending position, his financial net worth, ignoring revaluations and other volume changes, has risen during the period. If he is a net borrower, his financial net worth has diminished (again ignoring revaluations and other volume changes).

▶ The item B9B (net financial transactions) is in theory equal, by definition, to the balancing item of the non-financial accounts, *i.e.* item B9A. In practice, there is a difference between the two, called "statistical discrepancy".

▶ Theorem: in a closed economy, the sum of the B9 items for various agents is zero.

▶ The balance sheet accounts give an estimate of the net worth of the institutional sectors at a given date

▶ Stocks and flows of financial and non-financial assets and liabilities are valued at market prices (the prices prevalent on the day the accounts are drawn up in the case of the financial stocks, and the prices prevalent on the date of the transaction in the case of financial flows).

▶ Two successive evaluations of financial stocks will differ by the intervening flows, revaluations and other volume changes.

▶ The net worth of an institutional sector is equal to total financial and non-financial assets, *minus* liabilities (excluding shares and other equity, in the case of corporations). This is the broadest measure of the net wealth of institutional sectors at a given date.

 UNDERSTANDING NATIONAL ACCOUNTS – ISBN 92-64-02566-9 – © OECD 2006

Going further

Holding gains or losses and market prices in the national accounts

The prices of the assets held by households and corporations vary over time. Share prices can rise and fall on the stock market, just as prices of buildings and dwellings vary in response to the law of supply and demand and the current business climate. When the prices of assets held by economic agents rise, the agents concerned have a holding gain; when they fall they have a holding loss. A distinction is made between "unrealised" gains and losses and "realised" gains and losses. A typical unrealised gain or loss occurs when the price of a share held by an agent changes but when the agent has not yet sold his holding. By contrast, realised gains and losses result from the sale of the shares (or of dwellings). The agent has then received the proceeds of the holding gain (which is in most cases subject to tax). His unrealised gain has then become a realised gain. However, national accountants are only interested in the unrealised holding gains, partly because economic agents feel richer when the prices of their assets rise, whether they sell them or not. In any case, the realised holding gains are difficult to measure.

The prices at which assets (and liabilities) are valued in the national accounts are the prices on the day in question (generally 31 December). This is the rule for both financial and non-financial assets and liabilities. The difference between the opening value (1 January) and the closing value twelve months later (31 December) therefore includes the holding gains and losses. These are recorded in the national accounts, and the data can be used by economists to calculate the "wealth effect". However, these changes in value are not recorded in the income account but in a special "revaluation account" that comes after the income account in the sequence of accounts. As a consequence, these holding gains and losses, whether unrealised or realised, do not affect the measurement of agents' income in the national accounts, in contrast to the practice adopted for company accounts. In the national accounts, agents' incomes come almost entirely from output and from the redistribution of the proceeds of this output, and not from holding gains. This convention has its advantages. It avoids introducing into the measurement of income an element that is volatile and may be only potential. It also has disadvantages. Agents modify their behaviour in light of holding gains. In fact, as they see it, there is no real difference between a realised capital gain and, for example, income from labour, apart from the fact that it is less predictable (although some salaries and entrepreneurial income can also be difficult to predict). Moreover, there is a certain contradiction in the national accounts in that the tax on realised capital gains is deducted from disposable income, whereas the capital gain on which the tax is based is not itself part of this disposable income.

The systematic valuation in the national accounts of assets and liabilities at market prices is also open to discussion. For one thing, this "wealth" may be only potential. For example, the mere suggestion that a large holder of shares in a firm might dispose of his holding can lead to a fall in the price of the shares capable of reducing this same holder's potential realised holding gain. Much the same is true of the sale of property by a large institutional owner (an insurance company or a bank). For this reason, company accountants are more cautious than national accountants and apply the principle of valuation at the purchase price (except in the case of some quoted shares, for which the potential holding gain is practically certain to become a real gain). This caution leads to difficulty in interpreting total assets and liabilities in company accounts. These totals do not reflect economic reality since they add together assets or liabilities valued at very different dates. This difference in relation to the national accounts makes it difficult to use company balance sheets in the calculation of the balance sheet accounts. However, it is possible that the two sets of accounts could come into line in the near future with the application of the principle of "fair value" in company accounts. This "fair value" puts the prices at which valuation is made on the same footing as in the national accounts. This new approach is being recommended by the International Accounting Standards Board.

A final detail regarding valuation prices for financial assets is that they exclude taxes, fees and expenses, unlike the prices of non-financial assets, which include all of these. In both cases, the fees and expenses correspond to payment for a service. In the case of financial assets, the service is explicitly consumed as such; in the case of non-financial assets, it is consumed in the form of a capital good, since it is included in the price.

A more complete example of entries in the financial accounts

Another example than in the Section 2 of this chapter can be used to illustrate the difference between uses/resources entry and entry as "change in assets/change in liabilities." Suppose that an agent (for example, a bank) in a given period borrows 100, repays 20 on a previous borrowing, lends 50 and is repaid 10 on loans made earlier.

With uses/resources recording, this would give:

Resources: 110 (100 + 10)

Uses: 70 (20 + 50)

This is because the agent receives 100 through borrowing and 10 from the repayment of the loan, resulting in resources of 110. It pays out 20 in loan repayment and lends 50, resulting in uses equal to 70.

But the recording in the national accounts will be as follows:

Change in assets: 40 (50 – 10)

Change in liabilities: 80 (100 – 20)

Let us see how to interpret the figures in the national accounts. The agent lends 50 and so increases his assets in the form of loans made. He receives a repayment of 10 on an earlier loan, which reduces the value of his assets because the earlier loan has been reduced by the amount of this repayment. He borrows 100, which will increase his liabilities in the form of loans. He repays 20, which reduces his liabilities since he now owes 20 less.

Only the figures in the national accounts give real information regarding the situation in terms of assets and liabilities, in other words on the change in the agent's financial wealth. This is in contrast to the analysis simply in terms of uses/resources, which merely records the agent's cash position.

Financial accounts and money supply: the example of the euro area

One often hears of "the money supply", defined more or less broadly as the aggregates known as M1, M2 or M3. These "M" aggregates correspond to progressively broader definitions of money as explained below. Currently, in the euro area, only the money supply of the area as a whole has any economic significance (Some central banks in the euro area continue to publish a figure for money supply, but this only shows their country's contribution to the euro-area money supply). The European Central Bank (ECB) follows these aggregates closely, using principally a measure of type "M3", even though since 2003 this has been of secondary importance for the ECB compared with the inflation indicator. If M3 evolves too rapidly, the ECB may decide to raise its interest rates

There is obviously a relationship between the financial accounts and the money supply aggregate and its counterparts. Starting with the stylised diagram of the financial accounts shown in the text, extraction of the column "financial institutions" gives the following:

Simplified balance sheet of financial institutions (FI)

	Assets	Liabilities
	Financial institutions (FI)	Financial institutions (FI)
Deposits		W
Loans	X	
Interbank refinancing	Y	Y
Securities	Z1	Z3

Knowing that total interbank refinancing is roughly equal on the assets and liabilities sides, this row can be eliminated. Furthermore, it is assumed that the securities in the liabilities column are there only by convention, and so the preference is to show them in the assets column, with a negative sign, under the term "stable resources". We then have the following table:

Money supply and its counterparts

	Assets	Liabilities
	Financial institutions (FI)	Financial institutions (FI)
Deposits		W
Loans	X	
Securities	Z1	
Stable resources	−Z3	

The money supply aggregate is then equal to total deposits W on the liability side of financial institutions. Its counterparts are the three items in the assets column: loans *plus* securities *minus* stable resources (securities on the liability side for financial institutions). The precise definitions of the money supply depend on the breadth of the definition of deposits. The following, in decreasing order of liquidity, are the definitions of M1, M2 and M3, according to the content of the items included in W:

M1 = currency in circulation (F21) + sight deposits (F22).

M2 =M1 + deposits repayable on less than three months' notice (including the products classified in F29) + term deposits with an initial maturity of less than two years.

M3 =M2 + repurchase agreements + holdings in monetary mutual funds + money market instruments (short-term securities for less than one year issued by financial institutions) + debt instruments with an initial maturity of less than two years.

Certain items in M2 and M3 have definitions that do not match categories in the financial accounts (notably the reference to maturities of less than two years). It is therefore not easy for anyone who is not an expert to make the precise reconciliation between the financial accounts and the monetary aggregates.

Data sources: the statistical sources for the financial accounts

We will illustrate the sources of financial accounts using the case of Canada. The statistical sources for the Canadian financial accounts consist mainly of the financial balance sheets of banks, statistical surveys of other types of financial institutions and non-financial corporations, as well as administrative and survey data on governments and their agencies. Data on non-residents are a re-arrangement of the balance of payments and international investment position accounts. Data on households are largely derived as counterpart entries from the source data of other sectors, in particular from financial institutions. The role of the financial accounts is to analyze for coherence and integrate data coming from various sources to produce comprehensive, accurate and reliable estimates of financial transactions and positions. Data from the "chartered"(commercial) banks form an integral part of the data in the financial account. Chartered bank data arise from a tri-party arrangement (central bank, regulator of financial institutions and Statistics Canada) whereby the banks submit to Statistics Canada on a quarterly basis booked-in-Canada income statement and balance sheet data along with a number of detailed supplementary schedules. The supplementary schedules provide crucial information on deposit-taking and lending activities with the sectors/industries/agents in the economy. For example, counterpart household borrowing/debt estimates (the bulk of these funds provided by chartered banks) are mainly constructed from banking loan asset detail. A periodic review of bank reporting is currently underway. Comprehensive surveys of other types of financial institutions are conducted by Statistics Canada mainly as part of the quarterly enterprise survey program in the economic statistics field. Near-banks (by sub-industry), life insurance business (by segment), investment funds, sales finance companies, consumer loan companies, issuers of asset-backed securities, investment dealers, investment management and holding companies, etc. are all part of this survey.

Questionnaires are sufficiently detailed to provide considerable asset breakdowns and to provide for reliable counterpart entry estimates in non-financial sectors (borrowing and investing) – in particular, in the household sector. For example, the survey on investment funds permits calculation of the mutual fund assets of households. Non-financial corporations' estimates are derived from quarterly enterprise survey program in the economic statistics field. While only total non-financial corporations are published in the financial accounts, the survey covers the underlying industries in considerable detail. Detailed quarterly surveys of pension funds are conducted as part of the social statistics program at Statistics Canada, and they make up an important share of institutional investors assets. The net pension assets of these surveyed plans provide the bulk of the employer-sponsored pension plan assets of the household sector. Government sector data (federal, provincial and local) are compiled from the annual audited Public Accounts as well as from sub-annual administrative sources and survey data. Government business enterprises are based principally on quarterly surveys. Detailed databases on liability-side issues/positions in securities (i.e. shares, corporate and government bonds) are also maintained as part of the supporting detail in the financial accounts. Comprehensive coverage of issues of securities and their details form the basis of these databases, which are used to supplement the survey-based information.

Financial transactions' asset-side information is mainly derived from adjusted (for capital gains, foreign currency adjustments, etc.) balance sheet survey data, discussed above. Adjustments are, to a significant extent, based on enterprise supplementary survey schedules of revaluations of assets-liabilities by instrument. In addition to asset side transactions, the balance of payments group also makes use of a database derived from investment dealers' administrative information on new purchases of securities.

The household sector is constructed using indirect methods. Estimates are based largely on counterpart information from financial institutions for major asset holdings (deposits, pension assets, investment fund assets, life insurance assets, saving bonds) and for liabilities. However, selected financial assets are calculated using residual derivation. In particular, this is the case for marketable securities. While holdings of marketable debt instruments are not significant in the household sector, marketable shareholdings are, and depend on the quality of the information recorded elsewhere in the system. Non-marketable shareholdings are similarly derived. Household survey data are just starting to be used in the context of national financial accounts.

In many countries, as in Canada, financial accounts are mainly compiled based on banking statistics regarding the financing of the economy, whereas the non-financial accounts are based on the statistics of non-financial corporations. Therefore, it is hardly surprising that the two B9 balances, B9A and B9B, do not coincide in practice, and that a row showing a statistical discrepancy has to be introduced. In Europe, one exception is the account for general government, for which the banking sources and the administrative sources have been thoroughly standardized with the result that sometimes a statistical discrepancy can be avoided. Lastly, in financial accounts, source data is in some countries provided only in the form of outstanding amounts, or stocks. In this case, flow data have to be calculated by difference, imputing when necessary a valuation change in the amounts outstanding (see Exercise 6).

The valuation of assets and its relationship to economic theory

In the national accounts, an economic asset is defined as a tangible or intangible good on which right of ownership is exercised and whose holding or use procures economic advantages for the owner.

In economic theory, the value of such an asset is equal to the "present value" of the future income it will bring in for its holder. Suppose that the asset brings in a sum of S_t each year (t representing the year) until year T. Then, if all the conditions of perfect information and perfect competition are met, the market price of the asset is equal to $\Sigma\, S_t/(1 + r_t)^t$, summed from 1 to T, where r_t denotes the discount rate, in other words agents' preference for the present (an interest rate containing no risk premium). This method could in theory have been used to calculate asset values in the national accounts, but it is difficult to apply in practice and so other methods are used. Even so, the calculation of present values is useful in helping to understand certain entries in the national accounts.

Take the case of a bond purchased at 1 000 and bringing in 10% a year, or 100, for five years. Its value is equal to the sum of the present values of each annual flow, in other words to the annual flow divided by the discount rate raised to the power of the number of the period. It can be verified that this value is equal to 1 000, the purchase price of the bond.

Period t	Annual flow	Discount rate or Interest rate (1 + 10%) raised to the power t	Present value (column 2 divided by column 3)
1	100	1.1	90.90909
2	100	1.21	82.64463
3	100	1.331	75.13148
4	100	1.4641	68.30135
5	1 100	1.61051	683.0135
		Sum of the present values:	1 000

Let us now suppose that interest rates fall on the capital markets. For example, suppose that at the end of Period 3 they fall suddenly to 5%. The value of the bond calculated using present values will rise simultaneously to 1 136.162, as shown in the following table. It is not surprising that it is at this new value that the markets find equilibrium. This is because the bond brings in 10%, twice the return on a newly issued bond. It is therefore normal that its price on the secondary bond market should rise. The national accounts record the increase (or the decrease, in the event of a rise in interest rates) in the value of the bond in its revaluation accounts as a holding gain (or loss). Exercise 4 illustrates this case, extending it to the even more complex cases of bonds issued below par, or with a zero coupon.

Period t	Annual flow	Discount rate OR Interest rate (1 + 5%) raised to the power t	Present value
3	100	1.05	95.2381
4	100	1.1025	90.70295
5	1 100	1.157625	950.2214
		Sum of the present values:	1 136.162

The irrefutable logic of the calculation based on the sum of present values has numerous applications in national accounts. Let us suppose that an agent, for example a central government, undertakes to pay St per year for 10 years in the form of retirement benefits in return for the receipt in the current year of a sum A, which can be regarded as an advance payment of pension contributions. Exercise 3 shows that recording this transaction in the national accounts necessarily requires an interest element.

Limitations of the national accounts: The exclusions from the balance sheet accounts

A very broad definition of investment as "expenditure made today that will provide income tomorrow" could have led to the use of an extensive notion of assets. The national accounts have not gone as far as this, so the following assets that meet this broad definition are excluded from the national accounts balance sheets: 1) human capital, which can be defined as the cumulative expenditure on the training of individuals; 2) research and development; 3) natural capital, which can be defined as the value of non-mineral natural resources (naturally-occurring water, air, etc.); 4) public monuments (the Château de Versailles in France, Stonehenge in England, the Forum in Italy, etc.); 5) household durable goods, which are conventionally recorded as consumption although their service life is longer than one year; 6) military "hardware" (aircraft carriers, military aircraft, nuclear missiles, etc.); 7) pension rights in pay-as-you-go plans; 8) certain intangible assets such as trademarks, customer goodwill, etc. On the liability side, conditional financial liabilities such as debt guarantees or provisions built up by firms are not included as liabilities in the national accounts. For example, the debt of public-sector enterprises guaranteed by the State is not recorded as a liability for central government in the national accounts.

The above limitations are regularly criticised because intangible assets are becoming increasingly more important in our sophisticated economies. The exclusion of R&D, for example, leads to the fact that national accounts ignore the output of all the innovators at work within companies. There are several reasons for these exclusions, in particular the difficulty of estimating some of the concepts involved. However, this boundary is not fixed for all time. There are ongoing discussions among national accounts experts concerning possible changes. In particular, the next system will most probably recognise R&D expenditure as investment and therefore as giving rise to assets. The same is true of military hardware. However, these changes will not take place before 2012.

In recent years, economic research has paid considerable attention to the idea of measuring human capital. This involves attaching a market value to each member of the population, especially as a function of his/her education. Studies on the application of this principle have calculated the economic value of qualifications as the present value of the additional salaries that can be expected during a person's lifetime as a result of obtaining a higher diploma. The 1993 SNA (§ 1.52) explains why it would be difficult to include this value in the national accounts:

"However, while knowledge, skills and qualifications are clearly assets in a broad sense of the term, they cannot be equated with fixed assets as understood in the System. They are not produced because they are acquired through learning, studying and practising – activities that are not themselves processes of production. The education services produced by schools, colleges, universities, etc., are consumed by students in the process of their acquiring knowledge and skills. Education assets are embodied in individuals as persons. They cannot be transferred to others and cannot be shown in the balance sheets of the enterprises in which the individuals work (except in rare cases when certain highly skilled individuals are under contract to work for particular employees for specified periods)."

This final sentence explains why certain footballers are included as assets in the accounts of English football clubs. It is clearly the contracts with the players that are the assets and not the players themselves.

The Flow of Funds

The table on the following pages is taken from the consolidated financial accounts published by the OECD for Spain. The table on the first page shows changes in assets; the table on the following page shows changes in liabilities.

A specific example will illustrate how to read this table, which covers transactions carried out during 2004. Spanish households (and NPISHs) "acquired" (in quotes because the figure is a net flow, *i.e.* the sum of acquisitions of financial assets and of the incurrence of liabilities) shares and other equity (F5) – including mutual funds shares – for a total of € 13.5 billion. During the same time period, non-financial corporations acquired € 28.5 billion, financial corporations € 33.1 billion and the rest of the world € 16.2 billion. The second part of the table identifies the issuers: € 16.1 billion by non-financial corporations; € 29.0 billion by financial corporations; and € 47.3 billion by foreign companies (these are shares in foreign companies bought by Spanish residents, households or corporations).

This table calls for these final remarks: Note that the balancing item is not called "net lending/net borrowing" but "net financial transactions". This is because while in principle the balancing item *net financial transactions* (net acquisition of financial assets *minus* net incurrence of liabilities) should correspond to the balancing item *net lending (+)/net borrowing (–) (B9)* in the capital account, this is not the case in practice; they are likely to diverge significantly because of differences in sources and errors of measurement. This is why in several parts of this chapter we have coded differently the two entries: one as "B9A", the other as "B9B". The latter can also be referred to as "net financial transactions".

Spain, Consolidated Flows, by instrument and by sector, 2004

Million EUR

		Total economy	Non-financial corporations	Financial corporations	General government	Households and NPISH	Rest of the world
		S1	S11	S12	S13	S14+S15	S2
	Net acquisition of financial	371 966	60 163	218 327	9 880	83 596	145 522
F.1	Monetary gold and SDRs	−73	..	−73	..	..	73
F.2	Currency and deposits	89 461	11 837	25 331	6 131	46 161	14 090
F.21	Currency	12 265	608	−10	−	11 667	−
F.22	Transferable deposits	20 250	7 785	−	3 597	8 869	78
F.29	Other deposits	56 946	3 444	25 341	2 535	25 626	14 012
F.3	Securities other than shares	−2 264	5 009	−10 902	802	2 826	101 847
F.33	Securities other than shares, except financial derivatives	−1 432	3 264	−8 325	802	2 826	102 863
F.331	Short-term	−2 832	−2 411	89	−	−510	392
F.332	Long-term	1 399	5 675	−8 414	802	3 337	102 471
F.34	Financial derivatives	−832	1 746	−2 578	−	−	−1 017
F.4	Loans	175 760	3 892	170 612	1 256	−	8 702
F.41	Short-term	24 555	−78	24 633	−	−	1 042
F.42	Long-term	151 205	3 969	145 979	1 256	−	7 659
F.5	Shares and other equity	76 200	28 517	33 063	1 068	13 552	16 195
F.51	Shares and other equity, except mutual funds shares	60 704	25 891	33 063	1 040	710	15 583
F.511	Quoted shares	16 624	3 594	14 114	−	−1 084	5 894
F.512	Unquoted shares	30 195	10 110	18 603	588	894	3 061
F.513	Other equity	13 884	12 186	346	452	901	6 627
F.52	Mutual funds shares	15 496	2 626	−	28	12 841	612
F.6	Insurance technical reserves	17 249	1 848	408	−	14 993	−
F.61	Net equity of households in technical reserves	13 130	−	−	..	13 130	..
F.611	In life insurance reserves	5 860	..		..	5 860	..
F.612	In pension funds	7 270	..		..	7 270	..
F.62	Prepayments of premiums and reserves for outstanding claims	4 119	1 848	408	..	1 863	..
F.7	Other accounts receivable	15 634	9 060	−112	622	6 064	4 616
F.71	Trade credits and advances	7 762	5 502	−	−	2 260	4 646
F.79	Other	7 872	3 557	−112	622	3 804	−30

StatLink: *http://dx.doi.org/10.1787/114767212178*

Spain, Consolidated Flows, by instrument and by sector, 2004 *(cont.)*

Million EUR

		Total economy	Non-financial corporations	Financial corporations	General government	Households and NPISH	Rest of the world
		S1	S11	S12	S13	S14+S15	S2
Net incurrence of liabilities		406 121	97 553	212 181	12 264	84 123	111 367
F.2	Currency and deposits	73 228	–	72 992	236	–	30 323
F.21	Currency	8 078	..	7 842	236	..	4 187
F.22	Transferable deposits	20 328	..	20 328	–	..	–
F.29	Other deposits	44 822	..	44 822	–	..	26 136
F.3	Securities other than shares	85 760	957	82 381	2 421	–	13 823
F.33	Securities other than shares, except financial derivatives	85 245	957	81 867	2 421		16 186
F.331	Short-term	–2 440	793	–783	–2 450	..	–
F.332	Long-term	87 685	164	82 650	4 871	..	16 186
F.34	Financial derivatives	514	–	541	–	..	–2 363
F.4	Loans	177 782	82 709	–314	7 527	87 860	6 680
F.41	Short-term	23 992	21 416	–83	37	2 623	1 605
F.42	Long-term	153 789	61 293	–231	7 490	85 237	5 075
F.5	Shares and other equity	45 050	16 057	28 993	–	–	47 345
F.51	Shares and other equity, except mutual funds shares	28 942	16 057	12 885	..	..	47 345
F.511	Quoted shares	11 045	–1 466	12 511	..	..	11 473
F.512	Unquoted shares	10 169	8 956	1 214			23 088
F.513	Other equity	7 728	8 567	–840	..	..	12 784
F.52	Mutual funds shares	16 108	–	16 108	..	..	–
F.6	Insurance technical reserves	16 841	–449	17 290	–	–	408
F.61	Net equity of households in technical reserves	13 130	–449	13 579	..	..	–
F.611	In life insurance reserves	5 860	–	5 860	..	..	..
F.612	In pension funds	7 270	–449	7 720	..	..	..
F.62	Prepayments of premiums and reserves for outstanding claims	3 711	–	3 711	..	..	408
F.7	Other accounts payable	7 462	–1 720	10 839	2 080	–3 737	12 788
F.71	Trade credits and advances	7 074	6 906	1 214	506	–338	5 334
F.79	Other	387	–8 627	10 839	1 574	–3 399	7 454
	Net financial transactions	–34 155	–37 390	6 146	–2 384	–527	34 155

StatLink: *http://dx.doi.org/10.1787/114767212178*

Exercises   *Answers at www.SourceOECD.org/understandingnationalaccounts*

Exercise 1: Say whether the following affirmations are true or false

In the national accounts: *a)* a holding gain adds to agents' income; *b)* a holding loss reduces agents' income; *c)* a transaction is generally recorded four times; *d)* every non-financial transaction has a counterpart recorded as a financial transaction; *e)* every financial transaction has a counterpart recorded in the non-financial accounts,; *f)* the price of an asset remains constant, at its purchase price; *g)* human capital is included in the evaluation of national accounts wealth; *h)* in a closed economy, the sum of the balancing items B9 is zero; *i)* repayment of a loan leads to an increase in recorded assets; *j)* the difference between the net values at 31 December in the current year and 31 December in the previous year is explained entirely by the balancing item B9 of the agents concerned.

Exercise 2: Quadruple entry

Household H is employed by corporation C, a producer/supermarket. To simplify the entries, it will be assumed that all the household's economic relations are with this one corporation. H receives a salary of 40 000 from the corporation and consumes 30 000 in products from the corporation. With the remaining 10 000, the household buys further shares in the corporation for 2 000, and with the remaining 8 000 it pays off part of the debt contracted with the employer the previous year, amounting to 15 000. The corporation pays H a dividend of 200, and H pays the corporation interest on its debt, amounting to 300. Lastly, the corporation grants H another loan of 9 000. Draw up the financial and non-financial T-accounts. Check the accounting identities. Would the recording of the credit of 9 000 to H have been the same if the corporation had been a bank? Among these transactions, find one that is purely financial, and demonstrate that it has no impact on B9 and hence no impact on net worth.

Exercise 3 (difficult): Application of accrual accounting

Let us suppose that an agent, the central government in this case, undertakes to pay retirement benefits amounting to S for a period of 10 years, in return for the payment by households in year 0 of a sum A, which can be assimilated to a contribution. The aim of the exercise is to record this transaction in the national accounts on an accrual basis.

Question 1: show the relationship between A and the series of payments S, using the calculation of the present value.

Question 2: record the initial transaction and the series of payments S using the T-shaped financial accounts without the introduction of interest.

Question 3: calculate the residual debt of central government at the end of the first period of payment of benefits and show that it is different from the present value of this residual debt. Deduce from this that it is necessary to record interest. Draw up all the corresponding T-shaped accounts. Draw a parallel with a loan. Justify the fact that the B9 of central government is negative. Conclude from this that if interest is recorded the transaction will be neutral as regards agents' wealth.

Exercise 4: Calculation of the value of a bond

This exercise is a direct application of the section "Going a step further: the valuation of assets and its relationship to economic theory". The market rate of interest is 4%. Let there be a Treasury bond of $1 500 issued in 2004 and carrying a coupon of $60 per year for 10 years.

Question 1: verify that the bond was issued at the market rate and that the issue price of this bond corresponds to the present value of the future income from it.

Question 2: suppose that, in 2007, the interest rate for these same Treasury bonds increases to 6%. What will be the new price of the bond on the secondary market? How will the national accounts record this difference in price for the bondholder and for the issuer of the bond? Comment.

Question 3: return to question 1. Let us suppose that the government issues the same bond at a price of $1 250. How should the difference versus the market price be treated in the national accounts?

Question 4: let us suppose that the government issues this bond in the form of a zero-coupon bond, putting it on sale at a price of $1 014. How should this case be treated in the national accounts?

Exercise 5: Treatment of debt cancellation

Using the principles of quadruple entry, record the transaction by which the Spanish government cancels a debt of 1 000 that it had granted to a corporation that had not paid its taxes. Draw up a simplified financial T-account for the two agents before the transaction, and then describe the transaction in terms of flows. Identify the impact on the B9s of central government and the firm. Justify this economically. Deduce from the accounting identity of the non-financial and financial B9s that it is imperative to enter a counterpart in the non-financial transactions (D99, a capital transfer).

Draw conclusions for the impact on the central government resulting from a debt cancellation granted by Spain to a developing country. Discuss.

Exercise 6: Calculations of flows using stocks at market value

The sources for the financial accounts are largely bank balance sheets. The difference from one year to another in these balance sheets ($S^t - S^{t-1}$) can be used to calculate the flow (F), but as we have seen, it is necessary to make a distinction between a flow and a revaluation. Each of these two elements has to be estimated, using simple assumptions. This exercise will illustrate the calculation. The starting point is the following equation: $S^t = S^{t-1} + vS^{t-1} + F + (v/2)F$, where v denotes the change in price between $t-1$ and t. This equation expresses the fact that the stock at the end of the period S^t is equal to the stock at the beginning of the period S^{t-1} *plus* the revaluation of the stock held at the beginning of the period vS^{t-1} *plus* the transaction (F) *plus* the revaluation for the transaction (v/2)F. The assumption is made that transaction F takes place in the middle of the period, hence the term v/2.

Use this equation to calculate F in the following case of loans denominated in US$. We suppose S^{t-1} (in euros) = 1 000; S^t = 1 500; US$/euro exchange rate in $t-1$ = 1; US$/euro exchange rate in t = 0.8.

UNDERSTANDING NATIONAL ACCOUNTS – ISBN 92-64-02566-9 – © OECD 2006

Chapter **9**

THE GENERAL GOVERNMENT ACCOUNT

OECD Economic Surveys on individual member countries always contain in-depth analysis of fiscal data, and they sometimes criticise government fiscal policy. Here are some extracts from the July 2003 report on France:

"France faces a daunting task in meeting the fiscal challenge posed by the ageing of its population, which is expected to result in the ratio of people retired to those employed doubling by 2030. [...] The long-run fiscal challenge amplifies the need to strengthen the budget in the shorter term. The authorities will need to quickly redress the recent fiscal slippage and make progress towards re-establishing medium-term budgetary equilibrium in line with official objectives. Unfortunately, [...], the OECD expects the deficit to exceed 3.5 per cent of GDP in 2003. While this represents a broadly neutral stance on a structurally adjusted basis and notwithstanding the current cyclical slump, the failure to reduce the structural deficit during recent years of fast growth requires policy to be more rigorous now. In this regard, the authorities' decision to seek a 0.5 per cent of GDP reduction in the structural deficit in 2004 is appropriate."

It turns out that the condition of the French public accounts was even more worrisome than the OECD had expected in 2003. Indeed, as shown in Table 1 below (published by INSEE, the French statistical office), the French public deficit was 4.2% of GDP in 2003, considerably higher than the 3.5% predicted by the OECD. Although the situation improved in 2004 (a deficit of 3.6%), this was still above the 3% ceiling set by the Maastricht Treaty for EU member countries. In addition, French public debt exceeded the other Maastricht ceiling of 60% of GDP in 2003 and rose further in 2004. These results are due to the continuing upward drift in public spending (53.7% of GDP in 2003), while compulsory levies (taxes and social contributions), the main source of revenue for general government, declined as a percentage of GDP (43.1% in 2002) before rising again in 2004 (43.4%).

All the indicators cited above (with the exception of the structural deficit, see Box 1 "The cyclically adjusted financial balance") come directly from the national accounts published by INSEE for the general government sector. This is not surprising. Because the central government is the major macroeconomic agent, it is normal to use macroeconomic accounts for analysing its policy. But it is the Maastricht Treaty criteria, which are based on definitions contained in the national accounts, that intensified the use of national accounts by EU member countries to analyze their public finances (see at the end of this chapter "Going a step further: The Maastricht criteria"). Since then, compilation of the general government accounts has become a very significant part of the work of European national accountants. Macroeconomists should gain thorough knowledge of these definitions or risk talking nonsense.

In this chapter, we start by describing the general government account via a simplified diagram. Then, we outline the composition of general government, and we end with how to calculate the four major public-finance indicators shown above in Table 1.

Table 1. **The French general government account for 2004 (as recorded in May 2005)**

Percentages of GDP	2001	2002	2003	2004
General Government deficit *	−1.5	−3.2	−4.2	−3.6
General Government debt *	56.2	58.2	62.8	64.7
General government expenditure	51.7	52.7	53.7	53.5
Taxes and compulsory social contributions	43.8	43.1	43.1	43.4

* As defined in the Maastricht Treaty.
Source: INSEE, National Accounts.

Box 1. **The cyclically adjusted financial balance (or "structural" balance)**

General government spending and revenues are often highly sensitive to economic developments. Tax revenues tend to decline during economic downturns as income and consumption slow down, while at the same time public spending may increase as more people become unemployed and qualify for social assistance or unemployment benefits. On the other hand, during upturns, public finances improve as tax revenues boom and the number of those receiving social benefits usually declines. These fluctuations in tax revenue and public expenditure – in the absence of any discretionary change in policy – make it difficult to assess whether the fiscal stance is expansionary, neutral or restrictive for a given period, and to judge whether fiscal balances are sustainable in the long run.

To respond to these key questions, economists have developed the concept of cyclically adjusted fiscal balances – often called "structural balances" or "structural deficits" when negative – by untangling structural and cyclical components of the general government balances of the national accounts. To derive these cyclically adjusted fiscal balances, one has to: 1) define what would be the potential (or structural) output of a country (see Chapter 3); and 2) estimate how tax revenue and public spending react when the actual output deviates from its potential during the economic cycle. Girouard and André (2005) provide a detailed view on the methodology used at the OECD.* One should note that some one-off factors may make comparisons of cyclically adjusted public finance data across time and countries dubious. Examples include the transfer of future pension liabilities from a public enterprise to the general government sector accompanied by a transfer of existing pension fund assets from the enterprise to the general government sector. This would improve the cyclically adjusted balance at the time of the transfer but result in deterioration in the longer-term. The cyclically adjusted financial balance removes the impact of the economic cycle, but not the impact of these one-offs or any other changes in structural policy.

* N. Girouard and C. André, "Measuring cyclically adjusted budget balances for OECD countries", OECD Economics Department Working Papers No. 434, 2005.

1. A simplified diagram for general government

General government (GG) constitutes a very important institutional sector, including central government, local authorities and the social security funds. In federal countries (such as Germany) state authorities (called "Länder" in Germany) are also included. The official code for general government in the national accounts is "S13". Put simply, this sector has two functions: the production of non-market services (education, health care, defence, policing, etc.) and the redistribution of income (social benefits, subsidies). To finance the cost of these functions, general government levies taxes and social contributions. Part of these resources is used to pay public employees' salaries, as well as the intermediate consumption and investment needed to produce non-market services supplied free of charge. The rest is redistributed in the form of social benefits or subsidies.

National accountants use a common accounting framework for all the institutional sectors, be they private companies or government. However, it is worth remembering that government agencies are structured differently than firms. For one thing, government services have no selling prices, since they are free of charge. For another, most general government agencies are not aiming to make an operating profit. Economists in fact use different aggregates depending on whether they are looking at firms or at general government: in the case of firms, they look mainly at the profit ratio (net operating surplus/value added), while for general government they look mainly at net lending/net borrowing (which is coded as "B9").

Box 2. **Why is such importance attached to item B9?**

For general government, B9 (net lending/borrowing) is equal to revenue *minus* expenditure. A negative B9 shows the existence of net borrowing, or a public deficit. General government must strive not to spend more than it earns, on a structural basis. In general, net borrowing leads to an increase in the public debt and hence in the interest charges that have to be borne by future generations. A positive B9 means the existence of net lending, or a "surplus", enabling the government to reduce its debt. B9 is one of the main criteria in the Maastricht Treaty (see section at the end of the chapter). As a result, European countries pay a lot of attention to this balance.

Several non-European countries – for example, the United States – prefer to use a different balance, namely net saving (B8N). The disadvantage of the B9 aggregate is that it can become negative as a result of investment by government, which, in most cases, is positive in nature because it can contribute to future output. Net saving (B8N) has the advantage of being unaffected by a particular amount of investment in a given period, reflecting solely current operations, namely current revenue and current expenditure (including consumption of fixed capital). The rule that countries using this balance B8N set for themselves is that current revenue should, on average, cover current expenditure, allowing that investment can be financed through borrowing. This is often referred to as the "golden rule".

The following simplified picture of the general government account illustrates how national accounts manage to bring the specific "non-market" operations of general government into the common framework. As in the case of the other institutional sectors, the account is in traditional "T" form, with "Uses" on the left and "Resources" on the right. The shaded areas of the account represent the monetary flows actually recorded (in other words, the revenues and expenditures) which are: taxes and social contributions under "resources"; employee compensation, intermediate consumption, subsidies, social benefits, interest on the public debt and GFCF under "uses". At the bottom of this shaded section, there is a row showing the balance representing net borrowing/net lending. All these amounts are calculated at current prices.

General government account: simplified diagram

The shaded areas show monetary flows, the un-shaded areas imputed flows

Uses	Resources
	Output of non-market services
Compensation of employees	
Intermediate consumption	
Consumption of fixed capital	*Profit =NOS =0*
Subsidies	Taxes
Social benefits	
Debt interest	
	Social contributions
Final consumption equal (with some simplification) to Output of non-market services	
GFCF	
Net lending/net borrowing	

We now have to add to this framework items that are not based on monetary transactions (since prices are zero). This invented (or "imputed") portion is shown in italics in the un-shaded areas. In the top right-hand corner of the account, as resources, we see output of non-market services defined as equal to total costs (compensation *plus* intermediate consumption *plus* consumption of fixed capital – see Chapter 4). As a result, the profit – or to be more precise, the net operating surplus (NOS) – is zero, which should come as no surprise when dealing with non-profit institutions. This non-market output is provided to households and firms, but it is not recorded as consumption by these sectors but as consumption by the government itself. Thus, to counterbalance this "imputed" output of general-government resources, the "Uses" section of general government includes an entry for final consumption by general government, which equals non-market output (simplifying somewhat – see Box 4 "Definition of final consumption expenditure of general government" further down the Chapter).

It is very important to note that "final consumption by general government" is an accounting convention. General government does not actually consume its output. Households and firms consume that output as public services. However, because there are no observable monetary transactions (the services are free of charge), national accountants have given up on the idea of attributing this consumption specifically to households or to firms, and they have attributed it to general government itself. Note also, however, that the addition of the "imputed" items (output of non-market services and final consumption) makes no difference to the bottom line of the account (*i.e.* net lending/net borrowing), because the addition to resources is exactly offset by the addition to uses. In the end, net lending/net borrowing remains equal to the difference between actual revenue and expenditure.

I. There are exceptions to the rule that only actual flows affect the calculation of net lending/net borrowing. For example, when a government writes off debt owed by a developing country, no payment is made, but the amount is still recorded as a capital transfer expenditure in the national accounts, and thus affects net lending/borrowing.

To conclude, note that the simplified diagram of the government account presents four major quasi-principles: 1) the important balance is net lending/net borrowing, which is the difference between actual revenue and expenditure, ▶ I. 2) non-market output by definition equals total costs; 3) the net operating surplus of general government is zero; 4) by convention, general government consumes what it produces.

2. Detailed structure of the general government account

A complete set of accounts for France in 2003 (including the financial accounts and balance sheets) is shown on the following Table 2. These accounts illustrate how the general government accounts are integrated into the national accounts, from production to balance sheet. In contrast to the earlier T-shaped model, with uses on the left and resources on the right, we have in this case shown the uses below the resources. However, this is merely a matter of presentation and does not affect the analysis.

As is typical, each account ends with a balance, which is coded with an initial capital B (for example, "B1 Value added, gross") shown under uses in the upper part of the account and under resources in the lower part. For example, the balance of the production account is gross value added, which is then shown again under resources in the generation of income account. Certain intermediate balances (disposable income, for example) are shown even though they have little meaning in the case of general government and are only rarely commented on by economists. By contrast, the final balance, "B9 net lending/net borrowing" is highly significant. Certain secondary transactions are grouped together under miscellaneous, because they are marginal and of interest only to specialists.

Let us start by taking the upper part of the accounts. The output of general government consists essentially of **non-market output** ▶ **II.** (€ 294.4 billion in 2003), whose definition and evaluation have been explained in the diagram and in Chapter 4. But there is also a certain amount of market output, and output for own final use (together amounting to € 44.7 billion). The former consists of sales by general government (publications, sales of medicines by hospitals, exports of warships from naval shipyards, sales of water supply by communal syndicates). Output for own final use consists mainly of the costs of producing in-house software.

> **II.** The official title of this entry is "Other non-market output", but we have simplified this in the text and in the diagram.

After deducting from total output intermediate consumption of € 82.1 billion (which represents all the current operating costs of functioning, such as paper, telephone, rentals, etc.), general government shows gross value added of € 257.0 billion, equivalent to 16.2% of GDP (see Box 3 "Limitations and pitfalls"). Most of the expenditure in the generation of income account consists of compensation of civil servants (€ 215.6 billion), which includes actual and imputed social contributions (see Chapter 6). The imputed contributions are fairly high for general government because, in France, the state is itself the manager of the pension system for its employees and therefore does not pay employers' contributions. This item therefore has to be imputed in order to evaluate the actual cost of employing civil servants.

The net operating surplus, which measures profit, is equal to –€ 0.9 billion, which is practically zero. This is something of a surprise, since it was stated earlier that the profit of general government was zero by definition. The fact is that the diagram was an oversimplification, since small parts of the government sector operate as market enterprises (for example, certain water-supply units), so they record operating profits or losses. The amounts remain very small, however, and it should be remembered that, as a matter of principle, **the net operating surplus of general government is zero.** One might even call this one of the fundamental equations of the national accounts.

Then we have the two major accounts "allocation of primary income and secondary distribution of income". ▶ **III.** In them are resources commonly called "indirect taxes" but known in the national accounts as "taxes on production and imports" (€ 236.9 billion), most of which in the case of France consist of VAT (Value-Added Tax) and the TIPP (internal tax on petroleum products). Among uses, note the size of the item for interest on the public debt (€ 45.6 billion). Note also, further down, the substantial sum derived from so-called direct taxes, known in the national accounts as "taxes on income and wealth" (174.2), which include income tax and corporate profits tax, as well as numerous other taxes, including, the wealth tax in the case of France. The resources also include the substantial amount of social contributions received by the social security funds (289.3), which are subsequently redistributed to households. Note that social security funds are not financed exclusively through social contributions but also through general taxes, and sometimes through borrowing. Taxes and social contributions are measured on an "accrual basis" (see "Accrual accounting and government accounts" at the end of this chapter).

> **III.** The differentiation between the two accounts ("primary" and "secondary") is somewhat artificial and should not be considered an important feature.

Table 2. **Accounts of general government in billions of euros, France, 2003**

Non-financial accounts of general government

Production account		
Resources		
P11/P12.	Market output and output for own final use	44.7
P13.	Other non-market output	294.4
Uses		
P2.	Intermediate consumption	82.1
B1.	Value added, gross	257.0
K1.	Consumption of fixed capital	38.6
B1n.	Value added, net	218.3
Generation of income account		
Resources		
B1n.	Value added, net	218.3
Uses		
D1.	Compensation of employees	215.6
	Miscellaneous	3.6
B2n.	Operating surplus, net	−0.9
Allocation of primary income account		
Resources		
B2n.	Operating surplus, net	−0.9
D2.	Taxes on production and on imports	236.9
	Miscellaneous	−15.1
Uses		
D41.	Interest	45.6
B5n.	Balance of primary income account, net	175.3
Secondary distribution of income account		
Resources		
B5n.	Balance of primary income account, net	175.3
D5.	Current taxes on income and wealth	174.2
D61.	Social contributions	289.3
	Miscellaneous	10.4
Uses		
D62.	Social benefits	280.2
	Memorandum item D631: social transfers in kind via market producers	88.2
	Miscellaneous	41.9
B6n.	Disposable income, net	326.9
Use of income account		
Resources		
B6n.	Disposable income, net	326.9
Uses		
P3.	Final consumption expenditure	377.4
P31.	Of which, individual	245.6
P32.	Of which, collective	131.8
B8n.	Net saving	−50.5

UNDERSTANDING NATIONAL ACCOUNTS – ISBN 92-64-02566-9 – © OECD 2006

Table 2. **Accounts of general government in billions of euros, France, 2003** *(cont.)*

Non-financial accounts of general government

Capital account		
Resources		
B8n.	Net saving	−50.5
D9.	Capital transfers, net	−3.2
Uses		
	Net capital formation	12.9
P5.	Of which, GFCF	49.6
	Of which, other	1.9
K1.	Of which, Consumption of fixed capital	−38.6
B9A.	Net lending (+)/net borrowing	−66.6

Source: OECD (2006), *National Accounts of OECD Countries: Volume II, Detailed Tables,* 1993-2004, 2006 Edition, OECD, Paris.

Financial accounts of general government

		2003
Changes in liabilities (flows of transactions)		
F1.	Monetary gold and SDRs	0
F2.	Currency and deposits	−6.2
F3.	Securities other than shares	86.0
F4.	Loans	14.8
F7.	Other accounts payable	12.4
B9B.	Balance of transactions in financial assets and liabilities	−66.5
	Statistical discrepancy (B9B − B9A)	0
Changes in assets (flows of transactions)		
F1.	Monetary gold and SDRs	0
F2.	Currency and deposits	12.1
F3.	Securities other than shares	−3.2
F4.	Loans	2.0
F5.	Shares and other equity	18.4
F6.	Insurance technical reserves	0.0
F7.	Other accounts receivable	11.1

Source: OECD (2006), *National Accounts of OECD Countries: Volume IIIa, Financial accounts: Flows,* 1993-2004, 2005 Edition, OECD, Paris.

StatLink: *http://dx.doi.org/10.1787/351156400808*

Table 2. **Balance sheets of general government, France, 2003** (*cont.*)

	Value at beginning of 2003	Transactions	Consumption of fixed capital	Revaluation	Other volume changes and adjustments	Value at end of 2003
Non-financial assets	918.4	51.5 *	−38.6	76.4	0.0	1 007.7
Financial assets (consolidated)	3 87.5	40.5		10.6	0.0	438.5
Financial liabilities (consolidated)	1 033.2	107.0		−1.9	0.0	1 138.3
Net worth	272.7	−15.0	−38.6	88.9	0.0	307.9

* This amount corresponds to gross capital formation.

Box 3. **Limitations and pitfalls of percentages of GDP**

All the main public-finance indicators are normally expressed as percentages of GDP, in other words, the amounts in current prices divided by GDP at current prices and then multiplied by 100. This permits international comparisons, such as comparing countries' deficits (expressed in billion euros or dollars or any other currency), which would otherwise have little meaning, since for the same absolute level of deficit a large country is much more capable of financing its shortfall than a small country with correspondingly smaller taxation and borrowing potential. Presentation as a percentage of GDP is applied to all public finance indicators and especially to total government expenditure and total fiscal burden, which is the sum of taxes and compulsory social contributions. These two latter indicators are widely used to measure the importance of the government's role in the economy, which in France is quite large (largest among the OECD countries). However, this approach is open to criticism. GDP is the sum of the values added. Strictly speaking, therefore, the importance of government activity in relation to GDP should be measured as the contribution of its value added to GDP, that is, 16.1% in the case of France. But even using this more rigorous yardstick, France would still have one of the largest ratios of government activity to GDP in the OECD.

The analysis of social benefits in the national accounts is somewhat complicated. The classification distinguishes social benefits other than social transfers in kind (D62) and social benefits in kind (D631). A large part of the payments to households by social security and other social insurance or social assistance units (pensions, maternity allowances, family allowances, death benefits, etc.) is recorded under D62. It is this part (€ 280.2 billion) that appears as a use in the general government account under "social benefits" (and as a resource in the household account). However, another substantial part (€ 88.2 billion) is classified under D631. This includes repayments from the health sector of social security – medicines, medical visits and costs of transporting patients – payment of household and medical assistance in the home and housing allowances. Somewhat strangely, these are not shown as social benefits received by households but as "social transfers in kind", in a subsidiary account called "adjusted disposable income", and they are counted as final consumption expenditure of general government, and not as consumed by households.

This explains why the sum recorded as (P3) final consumption expenditure of general government (€ 377.4 billion) is higher than the non-market output (€ 294.4 billion), contrary to what was shown in the simplified diagram. The fact is that, as explained in the previous paragraph, the major part of the social benefits in kind, the part corresponding to purchases by general government of goods and services produced by market producers and supplied to households, is recorded as final consumption expenditure by general government and not as social benefits. To complicate matters even more, the national accounts record a small portion of the sales by general government under "partial payments" by households. In the case of France, these consist mainly of daily hospital fees, which in fact represent a very small fraction of hospitalisation costs. This part of the consumption expenditure of general government has to be removed, since it is recorded directly under household consumption. Thus, the formula that precisely defines the final consumption expenditure of general government is therefore more complicated than the one in the simplified diagram:

Box 4. Definition of final consumption expenditure of general government

P3/S13 Final consumption expenditure of general government = P13/S13 Non-market output – P131/S13 Partial payments by households + [D6 311 + D63 121 + D63 131]/S13 Social benefits in kind corresponding to purchases of products supplied to households via market producers. This gives, in billion euros: 294.4 – 5.2 + 88.2 = 377.4. Unfortunately, the last two figures in the bracket are not shown in the main table published by INSEE for general government and one has to go to the subsidiary accounts to find them.

Final consumption expenditure of general government is itself split into individual consumption expenditure (245.6) and collective consumption expenditure (131.8). The former includes expenditure by general government that can be unmistakably attributed to households, consisting essentially of spending on healthcare and education. The latter covers all other expenditure, *i.e.* that part of which it cannot be said with certainty who the consumers are, households or enterprises. These are collective expenditure items, such as general administration, defence, policing, etc. It was shown in Chapters 3 and 5 that by adding together individual consumption expenditure and household expenditure, one obtained households' actual final consumption, a concept used for international comparisons, in particular.

It will be seen from looking at other rows in the account that the column "uses" include net capital formation of general government, which is equal to GCF (€ 49.6 billion +€ 1.9 billion) *minus* consumption of fixed capital (€38.6 billion). Finally, there is the now familiar item net lending/net borrowing of general government (B9A), which in 2003 was a negative € 66.6 billion, representing net borrowing or, in common terms, a public deficit. For

EU countries, this balance is the most important Maastricht criteria. It closes the sequence of accounts known as the **non-financial accounts** of general government.

The non-financial accounts are then followed by the financial accounts, showing how general government has financed the deficit. As can be seen on the side of "changes in liabilities" (see Chapter 8 for definitions), this was done mainly by issuing securities – *i.e.* Treasury bonds, called in France BTF (short-term), BTAN (medium-term) or OAT (long-term) – for a sum of € 86.0 billion. We shall not comment here on the smaller financial transactions of the government, but is worthwhile to comment on the "balance of transactions in financial assets and liabilities", which is another name for net lending/net borrowing (in fact, it has a similar code: B9B). It will be seen that, unlike the household and enterprise accounts, the B9B balance is exactly equal to the B9A balance, demonstrating the higher quality of the general government account (see section "Sources" at the end of this chapter).

As can be seen in the row entitled "financial liabilities" on the balance sheets, the substantial issuance of Treasury bonds has contributed to a rise in the public debt (€ 107.0 billion). The amount of public debt, as defined in the national accounts (which differs from the definition of public debt according to the Maastricht treaty) is € 1 138.3 billion. INSEE estimates that the total assets of general government at current prices amount to € 1 446.2 billion, of which € 1 007.7 billion is non-financial assets (land, buildings, other construction) and € 438.5 billion of financial assets (essentially listed or non-listed shares in public-sector enterprises). It is interesting to note that the net worth of the general government estimated by INSEE actually increases during 2003, while at the same time the government has very significantly increased its debt. These messages are contradictory: the first is positive, the second negative. The positive message should be considered with caution, because the increase in the net worth is essentially due to the estimated re-evaluations of the non-financial assets of the government (+76.4). This probably corresponds to estimated holding gains on government buildings. But these estimates are very approximate, and because it is probably difficult to sell government buildings, this is only "potential" revenue.

3. What does general government include?

The figures shown in the national accounts for the totality of general government clearly depend on the scope of this sector. It is obvious that parts of the administration, like the Finance Ministry or the Education Ministry, are included. In fact, all the units financed through the budget discussed in Parliament are included. But there are many entities, particularly in France, that are commonly said to be "on the border" between public and private. In the national accounts, one says that they are on the frontier "between the market and non-market sectors". For example, are the French public utility Électricité de France (EDF) and the French Post Office, both of which have long exercised a public monopoly, part of general government? Does a university or a secondary school form part of general

THE GENERAL GOVERNMENT ACCOUNT
3. What does general government include?

9

government? Since the net lending/net borrowing of general government is equal to the sum of the net lending/net borrowing of the bodies included in it, knowing which entities are part of general government is essential to reliable calculation of the public deficit and, above all, a calculation that is internationally comparable.

National accountants pay particular attention in deciding which **institutional units** form part of general government. Institutional unit means an economic decision-making centre, characterised by autonomous decision-making in carrying out its principal function, and a complete set of accounts. Autonomy in decision making is judged by the unit's ability to make commitments, take on debts and award contracts in its own name. If a unit does not have these characteristics, it has to be included in the institutional unit that makes these decisions for it.

The general government sector is comprised of institutional units whose main activity is either to produce non-market goods and services or to redistribute income and national wealth. Non-market producers are those that provide services – and sometimes goods – free of charge, or at prices that are **not economically significant**. This original concept plays an important role in determining whether a unit is inside or outside the general government. The international system of national accounts defines prices that are not economically significant as "prices which do not have a significant influence on the amounts the producers are willing to supply, or on the amounts purchasers wish to buy". In practice, many countries interpret this criterion as meaning "prices that cover less than half the cost of production". Take the case of EDF, the large French electricity enterprise. EDF is indisputably an institutional unit (having a complete set of accounts), but it does not produce non-market goods and services, since electricity is sold at economically significant prices (prices cover costs: EDF makes, most often, a profit). Like the other large French public enterprises, (Railways, Post Office) EDF is thus included in the enterprise sector, not the general government. Now take the case of a statistical office like INSEE. It is not an institutional unit because it has very limited financial autonomy and cannot contract significant debts in its own name. It is therefore included as part of its supervisory institutional unit, the Finance Ministry, which is itself included in the unit known as central government. INSEE therefore forms part of general government via the central government unit under which it comes. On the basis of these general principles, national accountants have developed a decision-making tree containing three even more precise questions (see Box 5).

Table 3 shows the general government sector in the case of France (figures in brackets show the total expenditure of each element, in order to give an idea of its importance[1]). As can be seen, the general government sector is itself broken down into three sub-sectors: central government (S1311), local government (S1313) and social security funds (S1314). ▶ **IV.** Central government in the narrow sense of "the State" is the largest unit of general government, and its expenditure and revenue constitute the largest

IV. The international classification contains four subsectors, including S1312, which consists of the "states" level in the case of a federation. For example, in Germany, the subsector S1312 consists of the "Länders".

Box 5. **The decision-making tree regarding inclusion in general government**

The tree is made up of three interlinked questions:

First question: Is the unit an institutional unit? If so, go on to the next question; if not, it is included in the institutional unit it comes under (as we saw in the example of the statistical office discussed earlier in the text).

Second question: Is it public? Meaning is it controlled by a unit that is itself part of general government? If so, go on to the next question; if not, it does not form part of general government.

Third question: does it produce non-market goods and services? This criterion here is whether goods and services are sold at "prices that are not economically significant", a concept that in practice is often measured by whether sales regularly represent less than 50% of the production costs. If so, it is classified in general government.

Let us apply the decision-making process above to a farm. Is it an institutional unit? Yes. Is it controlled by a part of general government? No. Farms, therefore, however much they receive in the way of subsidies in France, do not form part of general government. Now take the case of "Réseau Ferré de France", the public enterprise that manages the railway infrastructure in France (while the SNCF manage transport on that infrastructure). It is an institutional unit. It is controlled by general government (its managers are appointed by central government). However, its sales (tolls paid by SNCF) cover slightly more than 50% of its costs. It is therefore not part of general government. Even using this tree, however, there remain problematical cases, such as that of financial units, because measuring their sales presents practical problems.

---

part of the overall general government account (expenditure amounting to €329 billion). Central government in France also includes the accounts of almost 800 organisations collectively known as "various central government agencies". These are institutional and quasi-institutional units meeting the criteria set out above. They include the universities, all the specialised higher-educational schools, the CEA (Atomic Energy Commissariat) and the CNRS (National Centre for Scientific Research). This clearly shows the importance of the public sector in France in education and research.

The local authorities comprise the regions (22 in number), the "departements" (100) and the "communes" (36 000) together with the numerous and varied bodies attached to them. Lastly, the social security funds include the major funds for employees and independent workers (CNAM: sickness, CNAF: family, CNAVTS: retirement), UNEDIC (unemployment insurance), the supplementary pension schemes (AGIRC, ARRCO), and, the largest item, the public hospitals – or more precisely, the hospitals participating in the public hospital service.

Table 3. **Composition of the French general government sector**

General government (S13) (Total expenditure in 2001: € 772 bn)	Central government (S1311)	State (S13111) (Total expenditure in 2001: € 329 bn)	General budget Special Treasury accounts Ancillary budgets Treasury operations
		Various central government agencies (S13112) (Total expenditure in 2001: € 50.5 bn)	Comprises roughly 800 bodies of varying legal status, in many cases public establishments of an administrative nature, reflecting the tradition of State centralisation and intervention in France, especially in the fields of higher education, research and cultural activities.
	Local government, (S1313) (Total expenditure in 2001: € 147.1 bn)	Local authorities (S13131) (Total expenditure in 2001: € 128.9 bn)	"Commune", "départements", regions, inter-communal syndicates, urban communities and non-market "régies" (semi-official enterprises).
		Various local government agencies (S13132) (Total expenditure in 2001: € 24.6 bn)	Non-market units that are part of communes or locally financed; Chambers of commerce; secondary schools, etc.
	Social security funds (S1314) (Total expenditure in 2001: € 351.2 bn)	Social insurance funds (S13141) (Total expenditure in 2001: € 337.6 bn)	General social security system; special funds; other supplementary pension funds for employees and independent workers
		Bodies controlled by social insurance (S13142) (Total expenditure in 2001: € 56.8 bn)	Public hospitals; other bodies

Source: INSEE.

4. The principal public-finance indicators

These are the four indicators shown in the table at the beginning of this chapter: 1) the public deficit; 2) the public debt; 3) public expenditure; 4) total taxes and social contributions. They are usually shown as percentages of GDP (in other words divided by GDP at current prices and then multiplied by 100). In the case of the EU countries, the first two indicators are among the Maastricht criteria that are reported (or "notified") to the European Commission. The other two are not central to the national accounts but derived from them. They do not form part of the Maastricht criteria.

Public deficit: item B9A "net lending/net borrowing of general government". When the item is negative, it is a public deficit and when positive, a public surplus. A recent complication has arisen from the fact that the deficit reported to the European Commission differs slightly from item B9A in the national accounts because of the treatment of interest on exchange-rate swaps. This highly technical, but marginal, point is not appropriate for discussion in this textbook.

Public debt: the amount of public debt on the balance sheets of general government. In the case of EU countries, the "notified" (or Maastricht-reported) public debt is appreciably different from debt as it appears in the national accounts, for three reasons. First, the notified debt is consolidated, meaning that debts owed by one general government unit to another are cancelled out, for example, the debt of central government *vis-à-vis* local authorities. Second, the notified debt is valued at nominal prices and not at market prices as is done in the national accounts. Finally, the notified debt includes only part of the debt, excluding that relating to pension liabilities, the accrued interest not outstanding and certain very short-term debt (commercial borrowing and advances). Exercise 8, at the end of this chapter, shows the reconciliation of the two definitions.

Public expenditure: this is total actual expenditure, meaning monetary payments by general government.[2] This indicator is widely used to measure the size of the role played by general government in the national economy. French governments of both main political tendencies have always regarded it as an important indicator and tried to reduce it.

Total taxes and social contributions: this indicator has much in common with the previous one, but it is measured by general government revenue and not expenditure. As its name indicates, it reflects the taxes and actual contributions (in other words, not including imputed contributions) that households and firms must pay to various parts of general government. The figure is very high for France by comparison with other countries (see Table 4), and all governments have tried to reduce it. ▶ V. It should

V. In France, this indicator is called "prélèvements obligatoires" translated as "compulsory levies".

Table 4. **Taxes and compulsory contributions**

As a percentage of GDP, 2001

Sweden	51.4
France	45.0
Italy	42.0
Germany	36.8
United States	28.9
OECD average	36.9

Source: OECD (2005), *Revenue Statistics*, 1965-2004, 2005 Edition, OECD, Paris.

StatLink: *http://dx.doi.org/10.1787/758160463051*.

be stressed that, for EU countries, the figures include taxes paid to the EU institutions (including the European Community portion of Value-Added Tax), although these do not form part of general government revenue in the national accounts. For this reason, it is more accurate to refer to taxes and social contributions *payable to general government and EU Institutions.*

Notes

1. It may be noted that, sometimes, the sum of the expenditures of the lower parts is larger than the higher level. This is because, moving up one level, the consolidation of certain cross-transactions means that they cancel each other out. For example, certain transfers between central government and local authorities are counted as expenditure by central government but not by general government, since this expenditure appears elsewhere as revenue for local authorities that are part of general government.

2. In principle only, because in practice it includes some amounts that are not actually paid, such as imputed contributions (included in compensation of employees) or gross fixed capital formation in the form of software produced for own account. Moreover, this amount includes (somewhat bizarrely) certain "negative expenditures", such as the proceeds from the sales of telecommunications licences.

Key Points

▶ The general government sector consists of institutional units producing non-market goods and services or carrying out transactions that redistribute income or national wealth.

▶ Non-market output is the sum of the costs involved: intermediate consumption, compensation of employees, consumption of fixed capital.

▶ The net operating surplus of general government is, by definition, basically zero.

▶ In the national accounts, accounting convention requires that the non-market output of general government be accounted for as if it were consumed by general government itself.

▶ The consumption expenditure of general government is equal to the non-market output (*minus* partial payments) *plus* the social benefits in kind purchased by general government for the benefit of households.

▶ The public deficit is measured by item B9 "net lending/net borrowing" of general government. If this is negative, it means a deficit; if it is positive, a surplus.

▶ Total taxes and social contributions consist of taxes and actual social contributions paid by households and firms to general government, and in the case of the EU countries, to the European institutions.

 UNDERSTANDING NATIONAL ACCOUNTS – ISBN 92-64-02566-9 – © OECD 2006

Going further

The Maastricht criteria

When, in the Dutch town Maastricht, the European countries decided to introduce the euro as a common currency, it was necessary to reach agreement on fiscal policy in order to prevent bad fiscal management in one country from affecting the others. If one country allows deficits to build up and thus increases its public debt at the expense of future generations, it also threatens to raise interest rates on the euro and hence make all the other countries pay the price. So policy makers decided to impose fiscal rules on all EU governments, via the so-called "Maastricht Treaty". Because the national accounts provided the best internationally comparable accounting framework, the Maastricht Treaty outlined criteria based on the definitions in the national accounts. On 1 April and 1 September each year, performance in relation to these criteria is "notified" to the European Commission. The first of these criteria is the notified public deficit, measured approximately by item S13-B9 in the national accounts. This must be less than 3% of GDP. The second criterion is the notified public debt (see definition in the text) which has to be less than 60% of GDP. Since the introduction of these criteria, Eurostat (the EU statistical office) has put considerable effort into recommending comparable treatment among countries, even in the most difficult cases. The financial prowess of government Treasuries is in fact just as great as that of other big players in the financial markets. In the end, the relevance, comparability and transparency of public accounts have benefited considerably from the use of national accounts.

The two Maastricht criteria on the deficit and debt levels are in fact linked, since a deficit can be expected to lead to an increase in debt. Some economists have criticised the Maastricht criteria on the grounds that they should take the economic situation into account. They think it is absurd to ask a country in the throes of a recession to cut expenditure in order to meet the criterion; at time when tax revenue is declining, this would tend to intensify the recession. The European Commission is therefore moving toward an interpretation based more on longer-term trends, by setting a target for a reduction in the structural deficit, in other words the deficit adjusted for the impact of the economic cycle. (The structural deficit is explained in the Box 1 "the Cyclically adjusted financial balance"). At the same time, it is interesting to note that the debt criterion appears to go somewhat against the fundamentals of capital management theory, because it focuses on "gross debt", not taking into account assets held. Capital management theory prefers "net debt", which equals liabilities *minus* assets. This is because for a given amount of gross debt, the diagnosis for two countries can differ widely depending on their assets.

For example, one country may have no assets, while another has considerable shareholdings. By selling these shares, the second government can reduce its debt, which is not true of the first. In practice, however, the financial assets of general government are difficult to measure and some of these assets are not easy to sell. This probably explains why the Maastricht Treaty refers only to gross debt and not net debt. However, this can result in certain paradoxes (see Exercise 7).

Data Sources: How are the figures obtained?

The general government accounts are the most precise of the national accounts. For this sector, unlike the situation for households and firms, national accountants have all the accounts of the institutional units making up the sector and not just a statistical sample. The compilation method used for general government therefore becomes less statistical and more accounting oriented. In France, the accounts of central government, the social security system and the thousands of local entities are transmitted to the "Direction de la Comptabilité Publique" (Public Accounts Directorate) in the Finance Ministry. Here, a special service consisting of some 30 people transforms the thousands of accounts and budget headings into the aggregates used in the national accounts, following the very detailed directives supplied by INSEE. The compilation method nevertheless remains statistical for the initial estimates, at a time when not all the accounts, especially those of the local authorities, are not yet available. For 2005, for example, INSEE published its initial estimates of the accounts of general government at the beginning of March 2006. These initial estimates are then subsequently revised.

There are two fortunate consequences of the excellence of government-accounts data: 1) In most countries, there is no need to reconcile the balances of the non-financial accounts and the financial accounts (B9A and B9B, respectively) for the general government. 2) National accountants can use government data to improve the compilation of accounts for the other sectors. For example, since they include comprehensive data for social contributions received by general government, and since these necessarily correspond to the social contributions paid, the figures can be used to improve the enterprise account, which is not exhaustive in this respect. Because of this, national accountants say that the general government account acts as a "pilot" account.

Tricks of the trade: Above and below the line

For the non-specialist in public finances, analysing the accounts of numerous public entities is a nightmare when it comes to adding together (or "consolidating") several of these. This is because of the numerous flows between these entities, making it easy to get lost in the complexity of relationships, with the result that mistakes can be made in calculating the overall deficit. The national accounts provide a simple benchmark that can even be expressed mathematically: the net lending/net borrowing item is an additive variable. In other words, the overall net lending/net borrowing for a group of units is precisely equal to the sum of their individual net lending/net borrowing. It is therefore easy for national accountants to measure the impact of the reclassification of a government unit. The net lending/net borrowing of this unit can be added to that of general government as a whole, without needing to know anything about its complex relations with others.

 UNDERSTANDING NATIONAL ACCOUNTS – ISBN 92-64-02566-9 – © OECD 2006

Reference is sometimes made to "above-the-line" and "below-the-line" accounting. What do these obtuse terms mean? Are they used to hide something? No. These expressions are used by national accountants to describe whether a given operation will have an impact on the deficit. The "line" in question is item B9A, the net borrowing/net lending of the capital account. An operation is classified as "above" this line (corresponding to its actual location in the sequence of accounts) if B9A is affected, and "below" this line if there is no impact. Let us take an example. Central government can obtain cash (to buy back part of its debt, for example) either by selling shares or by selling property. If it sells shares, the operation is below the line (national accountants also say that it is "entirely financial"). This is because shares constitute a financial asset; financial assets are included in the financial account, *i.e.* below the line, and the money obtained is also a financial asset, treated similarly. The situation is quite different if the government sells property. The money obtained is again shown below the line, but the sale of the property is shown above the line, with the result that the public deficit is correspondingly reduced. Exercise 6 explains this case, which is interesting in that it highlights one of the limitations of the definition of the public deficit. Why should the impact be different between a financial disposal (of shares) and a non-financial disposal (of property)? The answer is that it is based on a convention, and like any convention, the definition of the deficit as the item B9 has advantages and disadvantages.

Accrual accounting in general government accounts

National accounts are drawn up on what is known as the accrual basis (for more on accrual accounting, see section "Going a step further" in Chapter 10, here we shall merely describe the implications for the general government account). Accrual accounting is a basic accounting practice in the private sector, but it has not so far been completely accepted for public accounting except in a few countries. In France, while the social security institutions have adopted it, this is not yet true of the State Budget, which to a great extent remains on a "cash" basis, especially for income. In other words, France records the tax payments received and not the tax due. INSEE, the French statistical office, is therefore obliged to transform the budgetary data in certain cases to adapt it to national accounts, notably for VAT (Value-Added Tax). In practice, VAT generated and collected by firms during a given month is received by the government only six weeks later. INSEE therefore brings forward the VAT recovery by these six weeks (see Exercise 9 at the end of this chapter). For certain other taxes, INSEE records tax assessments and not tax payments, and so has to introduce an adjustment item called "assessed but unlikely to be collected" (see Exercise 5). INSEE is also obliged to make significant modifications in the amount of interest paid by government in order better conform with the accrual concept. For example, some government bonds are "zero-coupon", meaning that interest is not paid annually but in a lump sum at the end of the bond's maturity. INSEE spreads out the interest over the life of the bond in order to give a truer account of government's actual annual charges.

Exercises   *Answers at www.SourceOECD.org/understandingnationalaccounts*

Exercise 1: Updating the first table

Go to the INSEE website, *www.insee.fr*. Using the pages devoted to the annual national accounts for general government, find the amounts in million euros in recent years for the following: general government net lending/borrowing (B9A); the public debt; public expenditure; taxes and compulsory contributions. Also find GDP at current prices. Using these figures, update the four indicators in Table 1 of this chapter.

Exercise 2: MCQ: Are the following propositions true or false?

- The "deficit" is the same as "net lending".
- All output of general government is non-market.
- Social benefits are financed out of social contributions.
- The convention in the national accounts is that general government consumes its non-market output.
- B9A is the official code of the net lending/net borrowing item of the non-financial accounts.
- The sum of the B9 items of the institutional units making up general government is less than the B9 of general government.
- In France, the state monopoly generating and distributing electricity (EDF) is an institutional unit forming part of general government.
- Non-market output is sold at economically significant prices.
- The gross operating surplus of general government is zero.

Exercise 3: Identifying general government expenditure in the general government account (a tricky exercise)

The following table shows INSEE's calculation of total French general government expenditure in 2003. On the basis of this model, find the principal elements of this calculation (those in bold type), using the full set of general government accounts included in the text and other information. Explain why total final consumption expenditure of general government is not included in the expenditure figure, despite being the largest "use" item of general government. Explain why the consumption of fixed capital is not included.

Table of expenditure of general government

2003

Intermediate consumption	82.1
Compensation of employees	215.6
Other taxes on production	7.2
Property income other than interest (D4 excluding D41)	0.0
Current taxes on income, wealth, etc. (D5)	0.0
Interest	45.6
Social benefits other than social transfers in kind (D62)	280.2
Social benefits in kind of market goods and services (D63-part)	88.2
Subsidies (D3)	26.0
Other current transfers (D7)	41.9
Capital transfers (D9 excluding D91, D995)	12.9
Gross fixed capital formation	49.6
Net acquisitions of non-financial assets	1.9
Total expenditure	851.3

Source: INSEE.

Exercise 4. Moving from expenditure to revenue

Total expenditure was shown in the previous exercise (€ 851.3 billion). How can the figure for revenue be very easily obtained from the general government account?

Exercise 5. Moving from revenue to compulsory levies (a tricky exercise)

Compulsory levies are the sums raised by government (and EU institutions, for EU) from households and firms in the form of taxes and compulsory social contributions. They therefore correspond to government revenue. This exercise consists of attempting to move from the general government revenue (shown below) to total compulsory levies in the case of France, using subsidiary information. Use two principles: 1) do not include imputed social contributions; 2) include taxes paid directly to the European institutions. The result you are looking for is € 658.8 billion.

Exercise 6. Deficit and debt as recorded in the T-shaped accounts

The object of this exercise is to illustrate the difference between "above the line" and "below the line" transactions. This exercise is training in the use of T-shaped accounts, which are an excellent instrument that any national accountant should use before replying to what is a difficult question.

Revenue of general government

2001

Output of market branches and residual sales (P11)	45.0
Output for own final use (P12)	1.6
Partial payments by households (P13-part)	6.2
Other subsidies on production (D39)	0.3
Interest (D41)	4.6
Property income other than interest (D4 excluding D41)	4.9
Taxes on production and imports (D2)	221.4
Current taxes on income, wealth, etc. (D5)	185.0
Capital taxes (D91)	8.2
Social contributions (D61)*	267.5
Taxes and social contributions assessed but unlikely to be collected, net (D995)	−5.6
Other current transfers (D7)	12.0
Capital transfers (D9 excluding D91, D995)	0.4
Total revenue	751.3
Including imputed social contributions	
For information:	
Imputed social contributions received by general government	26.6
Customs duties and VAT received by EU institutions	8.9

Source: INSEE.

Let us first suppose that the State sells shares worth € 10 billion in order to pay off part of its debt. Show that this has no impact on the deficit, by completing the non-financial and financial T-shaped accounts below.

Non-financial account of general government

Uses	Resources
B9A Net lending/net borrowing	

Financial account of general government

Changes in assets	Changes in liabilities
Currency and deposits	Currency and deposits
Securities other than shares	Securities other than shares
Shares and other equity	
	B9B Balance on the financial account

Show, using the same accounts, that the sale of property for € 10 billion, again for the purpose of reducing the debt, has an impact on B9A. Draw conclusions.

Exercise 7. (A follow-up to 6, but slightly more complicated)

The object of this exercise is to complete the T-shaped tables below with the following information. The government sells property for € 5 billion and equities for € 3 billion, issues long-term Treasury notes for € 30 billion and buys in short-term Treasury notes for € 10 billion. By how much will its deficit be reduced? How will its debt change? Recapitulate the variation in general government net worth.

Non-financial account of general government

Uses	Resources
GFCF	
B9A Net lending/net borrowing	

Financial account of general government

Change in assets	Change in liabilities
Currency and deposits	Currency and deposits
Short-term securities	Short-term securities
Long-term securities	Long-term securities
Shares and other equity	
	B9B Balance of the financial account

Exercise 8: Converting debt as defined in the national accounts into "Maastricht" debt

Comment on the Table 5 published by INSEE for France.

Exercise 9. Calculation of tax revenue on an accrual basis

The Table 6 shows a quarterly series for the receipts of VAT (Value-Added Tax) by the Treasury. Calculate the amount of VAT as recorded in the national accounts for the year, remembering that it is assumed that there is a lag of six weeks between the generation of the VAT (the purchases by households) and receipt by the Treasury. Suppose that the government raises the VAT rate by 2 percentage points at the beginning of November. Show why the series on an accrual basis is more useful in macroeconomic terms than the series on a cash basis.

Table 5. **(Exercise 8)**

Million euros	2001
Debt as recorded in the national accounts	
Total general government	1 059 401
The move to consolidated debt (1)	
AF 2 Consolidation of deposits	35 419
AF33 Consolidation of securities other than shares	15 780
AF 4 Consolidation of loans	16 214
The move to nominal value (2)	
AF 33 Valuation difference on bonds	39 100
Exclusion of other accounts payable and of accrued interest not paid (3)	
AF 7 Other accounts payable	109 585
AF 28, 38, 48 Accrued interest not paid	3 372
Statistical adjustments (5)	654
Maastricht debt = Debt as recorded in the national accounts *minus* (1) minus (2) minus (3) minus (5)	
Total general government Maastricht debt	839 277

Table 6. **(Exercise 9)**

Q1	Q2	Q3	Q4	Q1	Q2
15 420	16 658	14 548	16 510	18 540	19 870

UNDERSTANDING NATIONAL ACCOUNTS – ISBN 92-64-02566-9 – © OECD 2006

Chapter **10**

THE INPUT-OUTPUT TABLE AND INTEGRATED ECONOMIC ACCOUNTS

According to Edmond Malinvaud, one of the most distinguished contemporary French economists, the national accounts are "the presentation, in a rigorous accounting framework, of all the quantitative information relating to the nation's economic activity".* Here, the importance of the words "rigorous accounting framework" must be stressed. In fact, any macroeconomist carries in his head a simplified model of the economy in which everything made by someone is used by someone else, anything exported by someone is imported by someone else, anything saved by someone is invested by someone else, and so on.

However, basic statistics are not presented in a "rigorous accounting framework". They never precisely tie in together. For example, for a given product, the figures for total output are not going to correspond to the figures for total use. The reason for this is simply that output statistics are compiled differently from those of use: the statistical questionnaires are not addressed to the same people; the classifications are different; statisticians apply different methods; and so on. Some people have even ironically formulated a "theorem" that states if two statisticians are given the same set of data, the aggregate results they provide will necessarily be different!

For these reasons, macroeconomists appreciate that national accounts constitute one of the rare cases in which statisticians provide tables that are (almost) completely consistent. ▶ I. The totals are equal to the sum of the parts, the resources are equal to the uses, and so on. The simple model carried by macroeconomists in their heads is therefore given concrete shape, and it is this that gives national accounts their potency.

Even so, it has to be remembered that there are no miracles in statistics. To obtain consistent tables, national accountants have been obliged to cut here, to re-evaluate there – often arbitrarily – even though they use the best possible methods. The high level of consistency among tables in the national accounts (to within a few million of the national currency) should not be allowed to mask what is still only limited accuracy (see Chapter 11). Some statisticians take the view, however, that it is the attempt to achieve consistency in the statistics that is one of the driving-forces for better quality. This consistency is obtained by using several global tables that we consider in this chapter.

I. "Almost" because there nevertheless remain certain inconsistencies known as "statistical discrepancies" that will be discussed later in this chapter. Some of these we already saw in Chapter 8 as the difference between the "B9" in the non-financial accounts and the "B9" in the financial accounts.

* *Initiation à la comptabilité nationale*, INSEE, 1973. We drew heavily on this text for Section 5 of this chapter.

1. The supply-and-use tables (SUTs)

In the national accounts, the first set of global tables is known as the "supply-and-use tables" (SUTs). A table of this kind applies to each product of the classification, for instance software. The equilibrium for this product can be stated as follows:

Equation 1: Output + Imports = Supply = Uses = Intermediate consumption + Final consumption + GFCF + Changes in inventories + Exports

First, let us interpret this equation in terms of *numbers*. The equation then signifies that the *number* of software programmes produced plus the *number* of software programmes imported is *necessarily* equal to the sum of the *numbers* of software programmes purchased by the user firms. The software is either for: 1) intermediate consumption (the small "disposable" programmes); 2) investment (the large professional programmes); 3) consumption by households (games software, in particular); 4) stocked as inventories by the software-producing firms in the form of work in progress; or 5) exported.

This is an absolute equality: the resources (another name for "supply") are *necessarily* equal to the uses, by definition. This explains why national accountants also refer to this equation as an *accounting identity*. They make constant use of it, mainly to derive one item based on results for the others. For example, suppose there were no statistics concerning changes in inventories of software programmes. No matter: if statistics are available for the other items, the "change in inventories" item can be obtained by making intelligent use of the accounting identity and deriving it as the balance of the other items:

Change in inventories = Supply – Intermediate consumption – Final consumption – GFCF – Exports

In this way, we kill two birds with one stone: we obtain an estimate of the changes in inventories, and at the same time we verify the accounting identity. This example was not chosen at random because in certain countries, like France, this is the way changes in inventories are obtained. Incidentally, this illustrates a paradox of the national accounts, namely that those compiling them are not necessarily anxious to have statistics on every single item in the supply-and-use tables. For one thing, it is certain that in this case the statistics will not spontaneously "tie up". It will be necessary to choose which of the figures to trim, and this is no easy exercise.

Therefore, it should not be thought that the accounting identity method is perfect. If changes in inventories are calculated as the balance between resources and other uses, all the errors of evaluation in any of these items will find their way into the change in inventories, with possibly pernicious results. It is therefore better in this case to have direct statistics in order to make corrections "by hand" of the supply-use balance. As can be seen, while in theory the equilibrium between resources and uses is indisputable, its verification in practice forms part of the "art" of the national accountant. Box 1 explains the statistical sources of the SUTs.

Box 1. **Sources for the supply-and-use tables**

Chapters 1, 3 and 4 have already described the sources for each of the items in the supply and use tables in the case of France. We shall therefore give here only a brief reminder of what these are, still in the case of France. Market output is derived principally from sales statistics. Figures for merchandise imports and exports are taken from customs figures. Imports and exports of services mainly come from the Balance of Payments statistics of the Banque de France. Non-market output and consumption by general government come from the public accounts.

The allocation of uses on the "domestic market" (defined as output + imports – exports) depends on the nature of the product. When the product is an investment, the use will be GFCF. When it is not an investment good, it is either household consumption or intermediate consumption. The nature of the product generally makes it possible to decide whether the sales constitute solely or mainly household consumption, or, by contrast, intermediate consumption. However, in cases where the nature of the product is not a sufficient criterion, bold assumptions have to be made to allocate the sales between final consumption and intermediate consumption. It is the intermediate consumption that is the most difficult to identify. This is because systematic surveys of firms – making it possible to know the nature of their purchases – are no longer done in France. Many of the cells in the intermediate consumption matrix are therefore estimated on the basis of information regarding the past. This is why INSEE, the French statistical office, is reluctant to publish intermediate use tables at detailed level. The changes in inventories are sometimes calculated as the difference between other items.

The estimates are compiled, product by product, at the 472 level of the product classification, meaning that there are 472 SUTs. These are then aggregated and compared with the global estimates derived from statistical processing of the company accounts transmitted by firms to the tax authorities. The art of the national accountant then lies in matching the global estimates and the detailed estimates to obtain the high degree of consistency shown by tables in the national accounts. This operation is known as "arbitration" (see Chapter 11).

Interpreting the accounting identity in terms of the *number* of software programmes was clearly simplistic. In practice, SUTs are drawn up in monetary terms, *i.e.* the amount of software programmes bought or sold *in millions of national currency* – in other words, the quantities multiplied by the prices. When these prices are those of the current period, one speaks of a supply-and-use table at current prices; when they are valued at the prices of a different period (often the previous year), one speaks of a supply-and-use table at constant prices. We saw in Chapter 2 the importance of constant-price data in the national accounts, since they are fundamental to the calculation of GDP growth in volume.

II. The accounting identity holds only in volume based on constant prices. It does not hold using chain-linked volumes, which lead to non-additivity (see Chapter 2).

In both cases, whether at current prices or constant prices, the accounting identity still holds. ▶ **II.** However, the introduction of prices complicates the equilibrium somewhat, because the different transactions are not carried out at the same prices. The following is a more complete version of the full supply-use equilibrium, this time expressed in monetary aggregates:

Equation 2: Output + Imports + non-deductible VAT + Other taxes on products – Subsidies on products + Trade margins + Transport margins = Supply = Uses = Intermediate consumption + Final consumption + GFCF + Changes in inventories + Exports.

Analysis of the complete equation

Compare this second equation with the first. It is in the resources that the differences are to be found. The additions include non-deductible VAT (see section "Going a step further: the treatment of VAT in the national accounts"), other taxes (*minus* subsidies) on products, trade and transport margins. Why these additions? The answer is because of the conventions used to evaluate the price of each transaction. The most important of these conventions are as follows:

1. On the resources side: a unit of output is evaluated at the "basic price", defined as the amount the producer can obtain from the production of this unit. This definition therefore excludes taxes on products invoiced by the producers but then passed on to the government. Imports are valued "cif", in other words, at the price paid for them at the frontier, including cost, insurance and freight (*i.e.* transport) from the country of origin to the importing country's frontier.

2. On the uses side: all domestic uses are valued at their market price, also known as the purchase price, including non-deductible Value-Added Tax (VAT) and other taxes as well as transport and trade margins. Exports are valued "fob" (free on board), meaning the price paid by the customer to have the merchandise loaded on a ship (or a plane or a truck) at the frontier.

It can therefore be seen that the difference between prices applied to resources and prices applied to uses includes the taxes payable on the products. (VAT is one of the most important taxes, but there are also in certain countries specific taxes on petroleum products, alcohol or cigarettes.) In addition to taxes, prices on the resources side include the corresponding subsidies (treated as negative taxes) and the trade and transport margins. For a better understanding, here are some examples:

1. Taxes on products. An oil company produces motor fuel. Its basic price per litre is the proceeds received as refiner, say 20 cents. The purchase price to the consumer will be its market price, which is the refiner's receipts, plus VAT and the specific petroleum-products tax payable to the government on this litre. These taxes amount to 80 cents, meaning that the pump price is 100 cents. The supply-use equilibrium is therefore (per litre): 20 (basic price) + 80 (taxes on products) = 100 (price to the consumer). The taxes are not counted in the basic price, since the producer merely collects them for passing on to government.

2. Trade margins. First, note that by convention national accounts do not consider retail and wholesale services to be consumed directly. Instead, the national accounts register the consumption of retail and wholesale services as the trade margins included in the cost of the products bought. Take the example of computers. Producers are unlikely to sell these directly to households (with one or two major exceptions related to Internet sales). Instead, they sell through a supermarket or another type of retailer. Suppose that the producer sells a computer to the supermarket for 1 000 euros. The supermarket will add its mark-up, say 500 (to cover inventory charges, publicity, etc. and its profit margin). It also has to add VAT of 225 (assuming a VAT rate of 15%). The supply-use equilibrium of the "computer" product will therefore be: 1 000 (basic price of the producer) plus 500 (trade margin) + 225 (VAT) = 1 725 (price to the consumer).

3. An alternative presentation would have been to establish the equilibrium for computers excluding trade margins, as follows: 1 000 (basic price) + 150 (VAT) = 1 150 (price to the consumer excluding trade margins), and in parallel an equilibrium for the "distribution" product: 500 (basic price for the commercial service) + 75 (VAT) = 575 (price to the consumer for the commercial service). This presentation, which is highly artificial, has not been adopted by the national accountants, so that in the end the accounts show no specific consumption of commercial services. And yet there has indeed been output of a retail and wholesale services, equal to the sum of the trade margins. To resolve this contradiction, national accountants add a negative column in the input-output table, which reflects a conventional cancelling out of the output of distribution. We shall come back to this point later in this chapter.

The complete equation in constant prices

The above examples are at current prices. However, Equation 2 can be applied in exactly the same way using prices from a different period, for example the previous year. It can then be used to calculate changes in volume.

The following is a (simplified) balance for year A, at current prices, for a given product, in quantities, prices and monetary aggregates. It can be verified that the monetary aggregates are equal to the unit prices multiplied by the quantities.

	Output	Imports	Trade margins	VAT	Total Resources	Final consumption	GFCF	Exports	Total Uses
Quantity	35 900	12 800			48 700	42 150	854	5 696	48 700
Unit price	15 000	15 000				18 940	16 000	16 000	
Value in millions	538.5	192.0	48.7	123.9	903.1	798.3	13.7	91.1	903.1

The following is the balance, also at current prices, for the following year, A + 1.

	Output	Imports	Trade margins	VAT	Total Resources	Final consumption	GFCF	Exports	Total Uses
Quantity	42 000	14 100			56 100	43 580	950	11 570	56 100
Unit price	15 500	15 500				19 538	16 500	16 500	
Value in millions	651.0	218.6	56.1	132.4	1 058.1	851.5	15.7	190.9	1 058.1

The following is the resource-use balance for year A + 1, at year A's prices (*i.e.* in constant prices), obtained by replacing the prices of year A + 1 by the prices of year A.

	Output	Imports	Trade margins	VAT	Total Resources	Final consumption	GFCF	Exports	Total Uses
Quantity	42 000	14 100			56 100	43 580	950	11 570	56 100
Unit price	15 000	15 000				18 940	16 000	16 000	
Value in millions	630.0	211.5	56.1	128.1	1 025.7	825.4	15.2	185.1	1 025.7

The last row of this table therefore shows the "volumes", at the previous year's prices. All that is then needed to obtain the growth in volume is to divide these volumes for year A + 1 by the corresponding values at current prices for year A. For example, the growth in household consumption *in volume* between year A and year A + 1 is 825.4/798.3 = 1.034, *i.e* an increase of 3.4%.

Special mention should be made of the significance of in-volume figures for VAT and trade margins. These two items (VAT and trade margins) are elements of prices, so how is it possible to speak of volume in their case? This is another example of a national accounting convention one simply has to get used to. The volume of VAT is defined as the monetary amount obtained by applying the growth rate in volume of the use item on which VAT is received to the VAT in value of the previous year. In our example, therefore, the VAT in volume for year A + 1, *i.e.* 128.1, is obtained by applying the growth rate of 3.4% to 123.9, which is the value of VAT in year A. Why 3.4%? Because, this is the increase in volume of household consumption, the item on which the VAT is paid. Similarly, the trade margins in volume for year A + 1 are obtained by multiplying the growth rate in volume of each of the items of demand concerned by the trade margin to the corresponding value of the trade margin in year A.

Although already quite complicated, the above example has deliberately been kept simple in comparison with actual practice. Our main purpose is to illustrate the supply-use balance as an essential building block in national accounts calculations, at both current and constant prices.

2. The aggregate supply and final uses tables

There are as many supply and use tables as there are product categories in the national accounts. In the case of France, for example, 472 detailed SUTs are calculated each year at both current prices and previous year's prices. These detailed tables are then summed up to obtain more aggregated tables.

At aggregate level, the supply-and-use tables are broken down into three parts: the resources table; the intermediate uses table; and the final uses table (final uses being all uses other than intermediate). It has to be recognised, however, that not all countries use this presentation in their national accounts. The following elements are therefore not strictly capable of being generalised to all the OECD countries. They nevertheless make it possible to highlight certain practical presentation problems.

The resources table constitutes the left-hand part of the supply and use table. ▶ III. Table 1 is a version for France based on the highly aggregated so-called E level classification, consisting of 16 product groups. Tables at less aggregated levels would be too large for a single page. This table is to be read as if the resource parts of each SUT had been placed one above the other. For example, the first row shows resources for agricultural products (item EA in the classification), the second shows food products (item EB, Manufacture of food products, beverages and tobacco). For each item, one finds the resource headings set out in Equation 2 of the current chapter: output, imports, margins, taxes, subsidies. ▶ IV.

III. In the US, the resource table is called the "make" table.

IV. The section "Going a step further" explains the rows for the cif-fob adjustment and the territorial adjustment.

Table 2 shows final uses and is the counterpart of the previous table (Table 1). For each product category, it shows each type of final use.

3. Intermediate use table (IUT)

In addition to these two tables – the product supply table and the product final uses table – national accounts break out "intermediate consumption" for a given product into intermediate consumption figures by industry. An industry is defined as the aggregation of firms, or parts of firms, making a given product.

For a better understanding, let us take a fictitious and simplified supply-use balance for the electricity category. In this case, we have Output (250) + Imports (15) = Intermediate consumption (142) + Final consumption (97) + Exports (26). National accountants distribute the amount of 142 for intermediate consumption among detailed industries, recording, for example, 12 for the consumption of electricity by the automobile industry, 9 for the textile industry, 26 for the aluminium industry, and so on.

Table 1. **France: supply table**

Billions of euros, 2002, at current prices[*]

Product		Output of products	Imports	Cif-fob Adjustment	Trade margins	Transport margins	Total taxes on products	Of which, VAT	Subsidies on products	Total resources
EA	Agriculture	71	9	0	18	1	2	2	−8	93
EB	Food products	126	23	0	52	6	23	10	−2	229
EC	Consumer goods	118	57	0	65	5	20	18	0	264
ED	Motor vehicles	94	37	0	16	2	10	9	0	159
EE	Capital goods	156	72	0	29	3	5	5	0	265
EF	Intermediate goods	245	102	0	40	11	6	5	0	403
EG	Energy	92	31	0	11	2	39	11	−1	175
EH	Construction	171	0	0	0	0	16	16	0	187
EJ	Trade	277	4	0	−230	0	2	2	0	53
EK	Transport	127	17	−7	0	−31	3	2	−7	102
EL	Financial activities	137	3	0	0	0	9	2	0	148
EM	Real estate activities	220	0	0	0	0	3	3	0	223
EN	Services to businesses	439	22	0	0	0	24	15	0	484
EP	Personal and domestic serv.	141	2	0	0	0	13	9	0	156
EQ	Educ. health and social work	236	0	0	0	0	1	1	0	237
ER	Administration	142	0	0	0	0	0	0	0	142
PCHTR	Territorial Adjustment	0	21	0	0	0	0	0	0	21
PCIFFOB	Cif-fob Adjustment	0	−7	7	0	0	0	0	0	0
TOTAL		2 792	393	0	0	0	175	109	−19	3 341

* The sums of the columns and the rows may not correspond to the totals shown because of rounding.
Source: INSEE.

In this way, a matrix known as the intermediate uses table (IUT) is compiled, showing consumption *by products* in the rows, and intermediate consumption *by industry* in the columns. Table 3 below is an illustration in the case of France using the E-level classification (16 products/16 industries) for 2002.

Table 3 is to be read as follows: First, along the rows, we find intermediate consumption of a given product by different industries. For example, the row EG Energy (comprising electricity, gas and oil), shows that the French EA industry (Agriculture), shown in the first column, had intermediate consumption of energy products amounting

Table 2. **France: final uses table**

Billions of euros, 2002, at current prices[*]

Product	Final cons. Households	Final cons. General Government	Final cons. NPISH	Total final consumption expenditure	Total GFCF	Valuables	Changes in inventories	Total GCF	Exportations	Total final uses
EA	28	0	0	28	1	0	2	3	10	41
EB	134	0	0	134	0	0	0	0	30	164
EC	121	19	0	140	6	1	1	7	51	198
ED	51	0	0	51	20	0	1	22	48	121
EE	13	3	0	16	56	0	0	56	83	155
EF	34	0	0	34	5	0	0	5	99	139
EG	60	0	0	60	0	0	−1	−1	11	70
EH	9	0	0	9	136	0	−1	135	0	144
EJ	18	0	0	18	0	0	0	0	5	23
EK	23	1	0	25	0	0	0	0	17	42
EL	43	0	0	43	0	0	0	0	4	47
EM	147	11	0	158	16	0	0	16	0	174
EN	41	8	0	49	48	0	0	48	25	121
EP	99	13	4	116	2	0	0	2	2	121
EQ	37	170	14	221	0	0	0	0	0	222
ER	1	136	3	140	0	0	0	0	0	140
PCHTR	−14	0	0	−14	0	0	0	0	34	21
PCIFFOB	0	0	0	0	0	0	0	0	0	0
TOTAL	844	362	22	1 228	291	1	2	294	420	1 942

[*] The sums of the columns and the rows may not correspond to the totals shown because of rounding.
Source: INSEE.

to 4 billion euros; the EB industry (Food products) consumed 3 billion euros (the third column); and the EC Consumer goods industry consumed 1 billion, and so on. Total intermediate consumption of energy products amounted to 105 billion euros, the total of all the figures in this row.

Looking at the columns on Table 3, one can see the intermediate consumption of all product types for any given industry. In the case of "EG Energy", it can be seen that in 2002 its intermediate consumption of capital goods amounted to 1 billion, its consumption of intermediate goods to 4 billion, its consumption of energy products to 41 billion, etc. Its total intermediate consumption amounted to 64 billion euros.

Table 3. **France: intermediate uses table**

Billions of euros, 2002, at current prices*

Products	Industries	EA	EB	EC	ED	EE	EF	EG	EH	EJ	EK	EL	EM	EN	EP	EQ	ER	Total
EA	Agriculture	13	31	0	0	0	3	0	1	0	0	0	0	0	2	0	1	51
EB	Food products	7	28	2	0	0	2	0	0	1	0	0	0	2	17	6	0	65
EC	Consumer goods	1	1	23	3	2	2	0	1	4	1	2	0	10	4	8	4	66
ED	Motor vehicles	0	0	0	29	0	0	0	0	5	1	0	0	1	0	0	0	38
EE	Capital goods	2	1	2	8	47	11	1	11	2	4	0	0	8	1	4	8	110
EF	Intermediate goods	8	8	27	25	33	100	4	32	8	2	1	1	10	3	3	1	264
EG	Energy	4	3	1	1	1	12	41	3	9	11	1	1	5	4	4	3	105
EH	Construction	0	0	0	0	0	1	3	22	1	1	1	4	3	2	2	3	43
EJ	Trade	0	1	2	1	2	2	1	2	9	3	1	1	4	1	1	0	30
EK	Transport	0	1	2	0	1	4	1	1	13	24	1	1	5	2	2	2	60
EL	Financial activities	2	3	2	1	3	4	2	5	15	5	31	8	14	4	2	2	102
EM	Real estate activities	0	1	1	0	1	2	0	0	12	1	4	12	9	3	2	2	50
EN	Services to businesses	2	12	19	9	17	25	9	18	43	12	28	12	114	13	11	18	363
EP	Personal serv.	0	0	1	0	1	1	0	0	5	1	1	3	6	11	2	1	35
EQ	Educ. health and social	0	0	1	0	1	1	0	0	1	1	1	0	2	1	4	1	15
ER	Administration	0	0	0	0	0	0	0	0	0	0	0	0	1	0	0	0	2
PCHTR	Territorial Adjustment	0	0	0	0	0	0	0	0	0	0	0	0	0	0	0	0	0
PCIFFOB	Cif-fob Adjustment	0	0	0	0	0	0	0	0	0	0	0	0	0	0	0	0	0
	TOTAL	41	91	83	77	110	169	64	97	127	67	70	43	194	68	51	47	1 399

* The sums of the columns and the rows may not correspond to the totals shown because of rounding.

Source: INSEE.

Be sure to note the difference between reading the rows, which show figures for a single product category, and the columns, which show a single industry. It is essential not to confuse the two, even if the items in the classification have the same name. In our example, the Energy product category and the Energy industry are both labelled EG, and yet one consists of energy products and the other of the firms producing these energy products. The similarities and differences between product and industry classifications are explained in the section "Going a step further".

4. The input-output table

We can now synthesize the three tables we have just looked at, plus two more. The resulting vast **input-output (IO) table** encompasses what might be called **goods and services accounts**. (This is in contrast to the "institutional sector accounts" that are part of the "integrated economic accounts" presented in Section 7 of this chapter). The organisation of the IO table is shown below. In the middle, we have the intermediate use table; on the left is the product supply table, and on the right is the product final uses table.

Table 4. **Input-output table**

Product supply table	Intermediate use table	Final uses table
	Production account by industry	
	Generation of income account by industry	

Underneath the intermediate use table there are two accounts that we have not yet looked at in this chapter: the production account by industry; and the allocation of income account by industry (see Table 5). These two accounts give for each industry its output, its intermediate consumption and, finally, its value-added, as well as the breakdown of the value-added between compensation of employees and gross operating surplus (or mixed income). All these concepts were examined in Chapters 6, 7 and 9, which focused on the accounts of households, firms and general government. In fact, these tables constitute a breakdown by industry of these accounts.

The input-output (IO) presentation, made up of these five tables, gives both a global and a detailed view of all the economic relationships involving products and industries. To get an idea of the wealth of data in the national accounts, note that the IO table of France is calculated at the G level, in other words 114 products and 116 industries. On its own, the French intermediate uses table therefore contains 13 224 cells (114 x 116) for each year. The whole IO table contains around 17 000 cells, and this for 20 years!

Table 5. France: production and generation of income accounts by industry

Billions of euros, 2002, at current prices[*], at current prices

	EA	EB	EC	ED	EE	EF	EG	EH	EJ	EK	EL	EM	EN	EP	EQ	ER	TOTAL
P2 Intermediate consumption	41	91	83	77	110	169	64	97	127	67	70	43	194	68	51	47	1 399
B1 Value added	38	28	38	17	45	76	27	73	150	59	66	174	226	76	189	110	1 393
P1 Output by industry	79	118	121	94	155	245	91	170	277	126	137	217	419	144	240	157	2 792

Generation of income account by industry

	EA	EB	EC	ED	EE	EF	EG	EH	EJ	EK	EL	EM	EN	EP	EQ	ER	TOTAL
B1 VALUE ADDED	38	28	38	17	45	76	27	73	150	59	66	174	226	76	189	110	1 393
D1 Compensation of employees	8	15	23	9	33	52	11	42	92	40	40	9	154	50	146	89	814
B2 orB3 Gross operating surplus or mixed income	30	11	13	7	10	19	13	29	53	16	22	152	66	27	42	20	532
D29 Other taxes on production	1	2	2	1	2	5	3	2	6	4	5	13	8	2	5	2	63
D39 Operating subsidies	-2	0	0	0	0	-1	0	0	-1	-1	-1	0	-2	-3	-3	-1	-16

* The sums of the columns and the rows may not correspond to the total shown in the columns or the rows because of rounding.

Source: INSEE.

However, INSEE does not publish all the detailed tables. Resources and final uses are made available at the G level, but the input-output table is made available only at the F level (40 products). Unfortunately, even at the most aggregated level, IO would not fit in a page of this book, so we cannot illustrate it here. However, Exercise 1 at the end of this chapter proposes the compilation of an IO table using copy-and-paste. The reader is advised to re-read the preceding paragraphs with a complete IO table of this kind in front of him or her. This will show the high internal consistency of the goods and services accounts much more clearly than any verbal description.

5. The use of the input-output table for economic analysis

What impact will the construction of a new high-speed rail link have on various branches of the national or regional economy? For the construction of the high-speed track, the public works firm will need steel for the rails, electric pylons and also pre-stressed concrete for the bridges and other major construction works. The result will be to increase demand for the products of the steel and concrete industries. But this is not all. The firm will also need to buy new excavators and cranes and the production of these will in turn also require more steel. The steel industry will therefore see demand for its products rise substantially and, since it consumes coal and electricity, demand for the products of these other industries will also increase, and so on.

This is one type of question for which the input-output table can be useful, once one accepts the fairly bold assumptions of a linear production function and, in particular, the fundamental assumption that the "technical coefficients" remain fixed. The "technical coefficients" for industry are the ratios obtained by dividing the value of each of the various products consumed by an industry by the output of that industry. These technical coefficients can be denoted by a_{ji}, where j is the intermediate-consumption product and i is the industry (a_{ji} is therefore "the technical coefficient" of industry i for product j).

It is assumed, in this simplified universe, that the classifications by product and by industry are identical, in other words that the i and the j belong to the same universe, with i and j running from 1 to n. The a_{ji} are equal to X_{ji}/x_i, where X_{ji} is the intermediate consumption of product j by industry i, and x_i is the output of industry i. They are called "technical coefficients" because they are meant to represent a given production technique: tor example, making one tonne of steel requires 5 tonnes of coal, 3 tonnes of iron, 10 megawatts of electricity, etc. The ratio between the value of the five tonnes of coal and the value of the resulting tonne of steel constitutes a coefficient that is representative of this production technique and is assumed to be fixed in volume. ▶ V. For the limitations of these assumptions, see the section "Relationship with economic theory".

V. "Accounting coefficient" would be a better term than "technical coefficient", since what we have are monetary amounts and not quantities. However, the term "technical coefficient" is generally used.

Using these notations, and adding a variable y_j to represent final demand for product j, a simplified supply-use balance can be written as follows:

$$x_j = X_{j1} + X_{j2} + \ldots + X_{jn} + y_j \tag{3}$$

The above indicates that the output of product j is equal to the sum of the intermediate consumption of product j by the various industries 1 to n, *plus* the final demand for this same product j.

As $a_{ji} = X_{ji}/x_i$, equation 3 can be written:

$$x_j = a_{j1}x_1 + a_{j2}x_2 + \ldots + a_{jn}x_n + y_j \tag{4}$$

Using a matrix notation, and denoting by [A] the square matrix of the coefficients [a_{ji}], by [x] the output column vector [x_j] and by [y] the final demand vector [y_j], we have:

$$[x] = [A] . [x] + [y] \tag{5}$$

Reorganising and denoting the diagonal unit matrix by I, and expressing [x] as a function of the remainder, we find:

$$[x] = [I - A]^{-1} . [y] \tag{6}$$

In other words, output is equal to the inverse of matrix [I – A] multiplied by the final demand vector. If one makes the bold assumption that the technical coefficients are fixed, this equation also holds for a variation Δy in demand. We then have:

$$[\Delta x] = [I - A]^{-1} . [\Delta y] \tag{7}$$

and Δx is therefore the value of change in output necessitated by the variation Δy in demand.

The answer to our initial question regarding the impact of a high-speed train link is therefore obtained by a calculation of this kind. One sets a value Δy_j on the variation in final demand necessitated by this project and applies equation 7. Exercise 4 at the end of this chapter is based on a similar simulation.

6. From the sum of the values added to GDP

Table 5, presented earlier, represents the production account by industry and gives the gross value added of each of these industries. We explained in Chapter 1 that GDP is the aggregate of output (free of double counting) obtained from the *sum of the gross values added*. We call this value *GDP output approach*. The total column in the "gross value added" row of the production account in Table 5 gives a value of 1 393. Is this the value of GDP for France?

The answer is no, because the national accountants have chosen to arrange matters so that GDP corresponds *also* to the sum of final uses; in other words, the *GDP output*

VI. The US is an exception regarding this rule. Value added in the NIPA accounts (see Chapter 12) is valued at market price, not at basic price. Thus, in the US national accounts, the sum of values added is, in principle, equal to the GDP expenditure approach.

approach must equal the *GDP expenditure approach*. However, we have seen that both the value added and output approaches to calculating GDP use basic prices, while the final uses approach uses purchase prices, including taxes on products, net of subsidies on products.

This explains why the exact definition of GDP is not the sum of the values added, but the sum of the values added *plus* the taxes on products (D21), *minus* the subsidies on products (D31). ▶ **VI.** This price adjustment makes it possible to bring the GDP output approach and final uses approach into equality.

Table 6 below shows the reconciliation between the output approach for calculating GDP and the expenditure approach, in this case using the case of Korea for 2003. The first part of the table clearly shows the addition to value added at basic prices of taxes on products *minus* subsidies on products (D21 – D31). It is this adjustment that makes it possible to obtain the value of GDP at market prices (as it is often called), and this also equals the figure obtained using the expenditure approach.

Table 6 also illustrates the equality of these two approaches with the "income approach", which is also based on the input-output table. The three GDPs are indeed equal. The generation of income account by industry shown earlier (Table 5) gives, for each industry, the breakdown of value added between the two factors of production – labour ("Compensation of employees", coded as D1) and capital ("Gross operating surplus and mixed income", coded as B2/B3 – *plus* "Other taxes on production" (D29) net of "Other subsidies on production" (D39).

This breakdown is also found in Table 6. Indeed, the gross value added at basic prices used to calculate the output-approach GDP (639 761.90) is equal to the sum of: "D1 Compensation of employees" or 319 891.70; *plus* "B2/B3 Gross operating surplus and mixed income", or 313 613.30; *plus* "D29-39 Other taxes on production", net of subsidies, or 6 256.90. These "other" taxes and subsidies (D29 or D39) should not be confused with taxes and subsidies on products (D21 or D31). D29 and D39 are specific taxes and subsidies, generally for small amounts, not applied to products but to the production process. An example is taxes on the wage bill. The income-approach GDP can also be obtained as the sum of the compensation of factors of production *plus* all taxes on production, and it can be expressed using the codes as: D1 + B2/B3 + D2-D3. We already saw this three-pronged approach to GDP in Chapter 1. Exercise 2 illustrates these calculations.

Table 6 also contains a typical "statistical discrepancy". Korea's GDP using the expenditure approach is equal to the GDPs obtained by the output and income approaches only if an additional 4 928.20, called the "statistical discrepancy", is added to the various elements of demand. The reason is that Korea's national accounts are derived from two distinct statistical sources. The figures for both the output and income accounts come from

Table 6. **Korea: gross domestic product: the three approaches**
Billions of Won, 2003

	2003
Gross Domestic Product (output approach)	724 675.00
B1 Gross Value Added at basic prices	639 761.90
+ D21-31 Taxes less Subsidies on products	84 913.10
Gross Domestic Product (expenditure approach)	724 675.00
P3 Final consumption expenditure	485 380.40
+ P5 Gross capital formation	217 099.00
+ P6 Exports of goods and services	274 995.10
– P7 Imports of goods and services	–257 727.70
+ Statistical discrepancy	4 928.20
Gross Domestic Product (income approach)	724 675.00
D1 Compensation of employees	319 891.70
+ B2/B3 Gross operating surplus and gross mixed income	313 613.30
+ D2-3 Taxes less subsidies on production and imports	91 170.00
of which: D29-39 Other taxes less subsidies on production	6 256.90
of which: D21-31 Taxes less subsidies on products	84 913.10
+ Statistical discrepancy	0

Source: OECD (2006), *National Accounts of OECD Countries: Volume II, Detailed Tables*, 1993-2004, 2006 Edition, OECD, Paris.
StatLink: *http://dx.doi.org/10.1787/845038246065*

the database consisting of the company accounts sent to the tax authorities, whereas the elements of demand (consumption, GFCF) come from surveys.

As a consequence, Korea's GDP obtained using the expenditure approach differs slightly from that obtained using the other approaches. Because the Korean national accountants found no satisfactory method of spreading this difference between the other items, they decided to show it separately in its own right. This practice of maintaining certain "statistical discrepancy" items between the different approaches to GDP has been adopted by several other OECD countries (the United States, in particular). Other countries, by contrast, eliminate these differences by various methods and do not show discrepancies that arise from the different ways of measuring GDP. This difference of methodology between countries does not imply that the statistical sources for the first group of countries are less reliable than for the second group. It is more a practical question and a presentational choice.

These statistical discrepancies are contrary to the "rigorous accounting framework" espoused by Edmond Malinvaud (see beginning of this chapter), but it is reasonable to leave a certain amount of latitude in the national accounts tables. As Alan Greenspan, former Chairman of the US Federal Reserve, used to say: showing statistical discrepancies has the advantage of reminding users that national accounts are far from being 100% reliable. Greenspan even added that the analysis of these discrepancies could itself be a source of information. In fact, some observers have shown a correlation between the value of the statistical discrepancies and the business cycle.

The three approaches to GDP reflect valuation of GDP at market prices as opposed to valuation "at factor cost". In the factor-cost approach, now abandoned, value added was calculated at the prices remunerating each of the factors of production, labour and capital. No taxes were taken into account. Some regret the abandonment of GDP at factor cost as an aggregate indicator of output. Indeed, from the point of view of the producer, taxes on products have no great influence on production decisions. But this has not prevented most economists and national accountant from using GDP at market prices as the main indicator of output, because it is highly practical to have GDP equal to the sum of final uses. However, some people consider that this practice has led to some double counting in GDP (see section "Limitations of the national accounts").

If instead of using the sum of the *gross* values added, one had used the values added *net* of the consumption of fixed capital, one would then have had NDP, standing for Net Domestic Product. This aggregate is unfortunately little used despite being conceptually more correct than GDP, for both the production and income approaches. However, NDP is less robust statistically because of the difficulty of calculating the consumption of fixed capital.

7. The integrated economic account (IEA)

We have just looked at the input-output table, the internally consistent table for the presentation of the goods and services accounts. The second major internally consistent table is known as the integrated economic account (IEA). This provides a synthesis of the entire institutional sector accounts (see Box 2 "Institutional units and institutional sectors"). The IEA table is much too large to be shown on a page of this book. In fact, it spreads over two pages, with the uses on the left and resources on the right, columns for the institutional sectors and rows for the transactions. It can be summarised by saying that it constitutes the juxtaposition of the accounts of households, corporations and general government presented in Chapters 6, 7 and 9. In addition to these sectors, the IEA table shows the account of the whole national economy and the account of the rest of the world (we shall be returning later to these two accounts). The advantage of the IEA account is that it provides an immediate and consistent vision of all the transactions concerning a given operation at current prices. One of the important rules of national accounts as depicted in the IEA is accrual accounting (see section "Going further").

Box 2. Institutional units and institutional sectors

The basic economic unit in the national accounts is known as the **institutional unit**. It is defined as "an elementary economic decision-making centre characterised by uniformity of behaviour and decision-making autonomy in the exercise of its principal function". A household is an institutional unit in the sense that it is within the household that decisions are made regarding the modalities of its principal function, *i.e.*, consumption. For a "legal person" (*i.e.* a corporate body and not a "physical person") to be an institutional unit it must, among other things, have a complete set of accounts. If the unit in question does not have complete accounts, it is considered as forming part of the larger unit that contains it. For example, the French statistical office (INSEE) is not an institutional unit, because it is a directorate of the Finance Ministry, which is itself part of general government. General government has complete accounts but INSEE does not.

The **institutional sectors** are groupings of institutional units. They are six in number: households (S14); non-financial corporations (S11); financial corporations (S12); general government (S13); non-profit institutions serving households (S15); and the rest of the world (S2). The rest of the world is not really an institutional sector since it comprises only that part of the accounts of non-resident units that relates to transactions with resident units. The notion of residence was explained in Chapter 4. The definition of most of the institutional sectors was set out in Chapters 5, 6, 7 and 9, except for financial corporations.

The **financial corporations** are the institutional units specialising in financial intermediation (banks) and in insurance. The financial corporation sector (S12) comprises the central bank, the commercial banks, specialised financial corporations, mutual funds (also called UCITS in Europe – undertakings for collective investment in transferable securities), financial auxiliaries, which comprise certain portfolio management companies, insurance companies and pension funds.

Let us take, among the 60 or so rows in the integrated economic account (IEA) for Denmark, the row for "interest" (D41). In the IEA, this is a single row, with the left side showing the amounts as uses, and the right side showing the amounts as resources. But for space reasons, in Table 7 we show the resources below the uses (even though in the actual table they are side by side).

Here is how to read the table: The first sub-table shows the "uses", *i.e.* the interest *paid* by the institutional sectors. The first group in the column is entitled "National economy" and labelled S1. This is the institutional sector, consisting of the four *resident* institutional sectors, as opposed to the "Rest of the world", consisting of *non-residents*. The four resident sectors are the non-financial corporations, the financial corporations, general government, households and non-profit institutions serving households. The figure of 334.3 billion kroner for interest is therefore the total amount of interest paid by each of the domestic sectors, *i.e.*: 45.2 + 157.9 + 48.0 + 83.1, these figures all appearing in the same row. ▶ VII. Following this,

VII. The equality between S1 and the sum of the resident sectors is a consequence of the national accounts not being "consolidated" (see section "Going further").

Table 7. **Extract from the integrated economic account for Denmark: row "D41 interest"**

Billions of Danish kroner, 2003

		Uses						
		S1 National economy	S11 Non-financial corporations	S12 Financial corporations	S13 General government	S14-S15 Households and NPISHs	S2 Rest of the world	Total
D41.	Interest	334.3	45.2	157.9	48.0	83.1	31.4	365.6

		Resources						
Total	S2 Rest of the world	S14 Households and NPISHs	S13 General government	S12 Financial corporations	S11 Non-financial corporations	S1 National economy		
365.6	47.6	22.5	18.9	237.1	39.6	318.1	D41	Interest

Source: OECD (2006), *National Accounts of OECD Countries: Volume II, Detailed Tables*, 1993-2004, 2006 Edition, OECD, Paris.

StatLink: *http://dx.doi.org/10.1787/252465163805*

the next column indicates the interest paid to Denmark by the rest of the world, amounting to 31.4 billion kroner. In all, 365.6 billion of interest is paid by the various sectors.

The second sub-table ("resources") shows the interest *received*, broken down by institutional sectors. Obviously the total interest received, 365.6 billion, is equal to the total interest paid, in conformity with the principle of consistency of the national accounts. Going along the row, one finds the sums received by each institutional sector.

This table is interesting because it makes it possible to visualise how the interest flows are broken down among agents. It nevertheless has two limitations. The first is that it is not consolidated (see section "Going a step further"), so it is important not to misinterpret the figures. The large sum of interest paid by the financial corporations does not signify that this interest is paid to other institutional sectors – far from it. Most of the interest paid by financial corporations is to other financial corporations, as a result of the complexity of modern financial systems.

The second limitation, linked to the first, is that these tables fail to show what national accountants call the "who-to-whom" element. For example, the table does not show "to whom" the financial corporations pay the 157.9 billion. Most probably, as has just been said, it is paid largely to other financial corporations, but also to households and non-financial corporations. However, these amounts are not known. Only a "who-to-whom" matrix could answer this question. The statistical offices have this type of information for certain transactions but do not generally publish them.

8. The transition from GDP to national income

It would be redundant to comment on all the rows in the integrated economic account (IEA) since the accounts for the main institutional sectors have already been described, one by one, in Chapters 6, 7 and 9. Here we shall only comment on the accounts of the S1 "National economy" sector, which is interesting in that it includes major aggregates such as Gross National Income, Gross Disposable Income, national saving and the nation's net lending/net borrowing.

Gross national income

Since GDP equals the sum of the values added *plus* taxes on products net of subsidies, it has an important place in the production account of sector S1, an extract of which is shown for Korea in Table 8. The second important aggregate in this account is gross national income (GNI), or net national income (NNI), if the consumption of fixed capital is subtracted. This aggregate (GNI) used to be called gross national product (GNP), but too many people confused it with gross domestic product, and it was therefore given a new – and more suitable – name.

Gross domestic product is the economic wealth produced by economic agents within the economic territory. Gross national income is the sum of the primary incomes of the economic agents resident in the territory. In the case of Korea, the difference between the two appears clearly in the first part of Table 8 below. In order to derive GNI from GDP, the following steps are necessary:

1. start with GDP (724 675.0 in 2003);

2. add the primary incomes received from the rest of the world (+9 116.7). These primary incomes consist of wages and salaries, property income (interest, dividends) and taxes and subsidies;

3. deduct the primary incomes paid to the rest of the world (–8 371.4);

4. to finally obtain the GNI (725 420.3).

The above makes it easier to interpret GNI. It is the totality of the primary incomes received by economic agents resident in the territory, regardless of whether these incomes are obtained in the territory or not. In addition to the income derived from production within the territory (already included in GDP), there are the incomes derived from production outside the territory (not included in GDP). This explains the addition of the compensation of employees received from the rest of the world, in all likelihood the wages and salaries of workers resident in Korea but working in neighbouring countries. Conversely, it is necessary to deduct the wages and salaries of workers who are non-resident in Korea but who have come to work there. The same operation is carried out for trans-border flows involving the two other forms of primary income, namely property income and taxes and subsidies on production. And the final result is GNI, which (unlike GDP) is an *income-based* concept and not a *production-based* concept, since it includes income derived from production abroad (and hence not recorded in its totality) and

Table 8. **Korea: the transition from GDP to GNI and other major aggregates**

Billions of Won, 2003, at current prices

B1_G.	Gross domestic product	724 675.00
D1_D4.	+ Primary incomes receivable from the rest of the world	9 116.70
D1_D4.	− Primary incomes payable to the rest of the world	−8 371.40
B5_G.	Gross national income at market prices	725 420.30
K1.	− Consumption of fixed capital	−98 850.60
B5_N.	Net national income at market prices	626 569.70
D5_D7.	+ Current transfers receivable from the rest of the world	9 375.90
D5_D7.	− Current transfers payable to the rest of the world	−12 819.40
B6_N.	Net national disposable income	623 126.20
P3.	−Final consumption expenditures	−485 380.40
B8_N.	Saving, net	137 745.80
D9.	+ Net capital transfers from the rest of the world	−1 601.10
P5.	− Gross capital formation	−217 099.00
K2.	− Acquisitions less disposals of non-produced assets	−66.40
K1.	+ Consumption of fixed capital	98 850.60
B9_S1.	Net lending/net borrowing	17 829.90

StatLink: *http://dx.doi.org/10.1787/671625385132*

excludes the value of output repaid to foreign factors of production. Hence, the use of the word "income" instead of "product" in its name. This being said, in the case of Korea the difference between the GDP and GNI is very small. We saw in Chapter 1 that it is greater for a country such as Luxembourg because of the importance of trans-border workers in relation to the country's economy. ▶ VIII. Given GNI, it is possible to calculate net national income (NNI) by subtracting the consumption of fixed capital.

> **VIII.** GNI is an important aggregate for European Union (EU) countries because it is one of the main indicators used to allocate the operating costs of the EU institutions among member countries.

The rest of Table 8 outlines the transition from NNI to *national saving*. Similar additions and deductions for transactions with the rest of the world are made in order to obtain Net Disposable National Income, from which is deducted total final consumption expenditure in order to obtain National saving, which itself equals the sum of the savings of the different institutional sectors. Finally, one arrives at the *nation's net lending/net borrowing*, essentially by deducting capital formation. It can be seen from Table 8 that in 2003 Korea had net lending of 17 829.9 billion won. In other words, Korea had no need of foreign financing for its investment. On the contrary, Korea globally provided more financing to foreign countries than foreigners did to Korea.

UNDERSTANDING NATIONAL ACCOUNTS – ISBN 92-64-02566-9 – © OECD 2006

Key points

▶ The balances depicted in the supply-and-use tables (SUTs) for products constitute the basic accounting identity for the goods and services accounts. They compare resources (output, imports) with uses (intermediate consumption and final uses). They are calculated at current prices and in volume.

▶ Output is valued at basic prices. Uses are valued at market prices.

▶ Trade and transport margins as well as taxes (net of subsidies) are all included in the calculation of resources for products in the supply-and-use table.

▶ The input-output (IO) table consists of the juxtaposition of the supply-and-use balances (resources table and final uses table) and the matrix of intermediate consumption. This matrix shows in its columns the various intermediate consumptions for a given industry.

▶ The input-output table also includes the production accounts and the generation of income accounts for industries.

▶ The input-output table is available at current prices and in volume.

▶ When value added is calculated at basic prices (which is generally the case), the Gross Domestic Product is the sum of the values added of the industries *plus* taxes on products net of subsidies.

▶ Gross National Income (GNI) is the new name for Gross National Product, which must not be confused with Gross Domestic Product. GNI equals the sum of the primary incomes of economic agents resident in the territory, regardless of whether these incomes were obtained within the territory or not. GNI does not include the primary incomes generated in the territory by non-resident agents.

▶ The integrated economic account is a reorganised grouping of the accounts of the institutional sectors. It shows the amounts of uses and resources of each institutional sector for all transactions. It is calculated only at current prices.

Going further

The treatment of VAT in the national accounts

In many countries, the VAT (Value-Added Tax) is one of the main taxes on products. It is collected in stages by firms for the benefit of government. The principle is as follows. All market producers (including distributors) are obligated to invoice a certain additional VAT percentage on the prices of the goods and services they sell. VAT is identified separately on the invoices of the seller firms so that the buyer firms know how much VAT they have paid. Firms pay to the government only the difference between the VAT they have collected on their sales and the VAT they have paid on their purchases. Hence the description "value-added": the tax relates to the difference between output (sales) and intermediate consumption and investment, a notion that therefore comes close to that of value added in the national accounts. VAT is not invoiced at all on exports. It is applied to imports, however.

Due to this construction, VAT is an economically more rational tax than the old taxes based on sales, which could show an increase, for example, simply if a new intermediary joined the chain from producer to consumer. This cannot happen with VAT. The success of this tax, which is now applied in more than 100 countries, lies also in the fact that it is less open to fraud than traditional taxes. This is because buyer firms have an interest in seeing that the seller firms record VAT correctly, since they are able to claim reimbursement.

The term "deductible VAT" is applied to the VAT payable on firms' intermediate consumption or gross fixed capital formation, since these amounts are deductible from the VAT owed by the firm to government as a result of its sales. Conversely, the term "non-deductible VAT" applies to the VAT that the buyer cannot deduct from his own VAT debt to the state. By definition, therefore, the VAT paid by households is totally non-deductible, since households are final consumers of the goods. On the other hand, also by definition, virtually all the VAT paid by firms on their purchases is deductible. There remain, however, special cases in which firms cannot entirely deduct the VAT on their purchases and are accordingly liable for a small portion of non-deductible VAT. VAT on purchases by non-market producers that are part of general government or NPISHs is often non-deductible.

In the national accounts system, only the non-deductible VAT is recorded. It would have been too complicated, and in the end would have been of little use for the purposes of analysis, to trace the flows of deductible VAT. This decision has three consequences. First, in the national accounts, the VAT paid on household consumption appears in the accounts in its entirety because it is totally non-deductible. By contrast, however, firms' intermediate consumption and investment are subject, in the national accounts, only to a very small amount of VAT, since most of the VAT on these flows is deductible. Lastly, VAT is recorded not as having been received by government from individual firms but as a global receipt from "the total economy".

The brief example given below shows both the actual mechanism for the recovery of VAT and its recording in the national accounts (considering a VAT rate of 20%).

1. Actual VAT mechanism: firm A makes a sale of 120 to firm B, including 20 of VAT, which firm A pays back to the government. Firm B makes a sale of 270 to the final consumer, including 45 of VAT. It therefore pays the government (45 – 20) = 25. In total, the government receives 45 in the form of non-deductible VAT.

2. Corresponding treatment in the national accounts: firm A is recorded as making a sale of 100 to firm B (and not 120, as in reality). The 20 of VAT is not recorded because it is deductible. Firm B makes a sale to the final consumer of 270, including 45 of VAT. This amount of 45 is recorded in its totality, being non-deductible. Moreover, it is recorded as being received by the government not from firm B, but from the total economy.

As can be seen, the treatment in the national accounts does not correspond to the monetary flows. However, the result is the same from the point of view of the government's receipts of VAT. Better still, this presentation is more suited to macroeconomic analysis, because it means that virtually the total amount of VAT in the national accounts is shown as affecting household consumption. The system therefore marks a return to economic reality that might be otherwise masked. The payers of the VAT received by government are the final consumers, or households, and not the firms, which merely collect the tax.

Note that in Europe a small portion of the VAT is paid into the European budget. In practice, this portion is received by the government and then transferred to the European budget. In the national accounts, it is treated as being paid directly to the European institutions.

Industries, products and specific operations in the input-output table

This section explains certain additional notions that are indispensable for a full understanding of the tables making up the input-output table, using the example of France.

The classification of industries is almost the mirror image of the classification of products. In fact, an industry is defined as the totality of firms, or parts of firms, that produce a given product. For a full understanding of the relationship between the two, the best thing is to go to the INSEE website: *www.insee.fr/fr/indicateur/cnat_annu/base_2000/ documentation/methodologie/nomenclatures.htm*.

INSEE presents its classifications as being simultaneously products and industries. From the above website, let us consider a classification at level G, titled "G31 pharmaceutical industry." This is itself contained within level F under "FC3 Pharmaceuticals, perfumes and toilet preparations" and in turn contains another subhead within level H titled "24.4C manufacture of medicines". The terminology used in this last case, including the word "manufacture", seems to suggest that it is an industry. But it is important not to go wrong on this point, since it can also be interpreted as the output of this industry, in this case medicines. It therefore represents simultaneously the activity (industry) and its result (the medicines produced). The principle that has to be kept in mind is that the output of industry X is (virtually) equal, by definition, to the output of product X. The word "virtually" is necessary because the national accounts are somewhat more complicated, and this equality does not hold for certain industries. It would take too long to go into the details here.

There is, however, one case where an industry exists but there is no corresponding product. This is "trade" (retail and wholesale trade). In the national accounts there is indeed output of trade services (measured by the trade margin) but there is no "trade" product, since, as explained in the main text, the trade margin is included in the purchase price of the product being sold. For this reason, the product supply table for France (Table 1) contains a row "EJ trade" with 277 in the output column, but this amount is cancelled out slightly further down by the purely conventional introduction of a negative margin of –230. The two amounts are not exactly equal, since the EJ item in fact contains other sub-headings than pure trade, but the idea is there: there is an output of trade, but no trade product. Although there is not the same dichotomy in the case of transport (for which there is both an industry and a product), a similar conventional cancelling out is applied relating to transport margins on final uses. This explains the figure of –31 appearing in the "transport margins" column for the "EK transport" product in Table 1.

Two other rows in the French input-output table deserve additional explanation. These are the last two rows of Tables 1 and 2: "territorial adjustment" and "cif-fob adjustment". The first concerns products consumed outside the territory, in practice tourism expenditure (see Chapter 5). Spending by French tourists abroad is conventionally recorded as an import of services (worth 21) in the product supply table (Table 1). Spending by foreign tourists in France is recorded as exports (worth 34) in the final uses table (Table 2). The difference between the two (–14) is recorded in the final uses table, in the same row and in the column "household final consumption expenditure". This sum will be added to the other consumption expenditure[1] in order to obtain, at the bottom of this column, the total household final consumption expenditure of households residing in France. This is because the other product rows in the same column of Table 2 include purchases by foreign tourists and these therefore have to be deducted to obtain consumption by residents. Conversely, the other product rows do not contain consumption by French tourists abroad and this has to be added in order to obtain their

UNDERSTANDING NATIONAL ACCOUNTS – ISBN 92-64-02566-9 – © OECD 2006

total consumption. This dual operation is carried out in the input-output table with the help of this row.

The cif-fob adjustment also pertains to relations with the rest of the world. As we saw in the main text, imports of goods are calculated cif, *i.e.* including cost, insurance and freight to the frontier. However, this price includes transport services from the exporting country's frontier to the French frontier. To give a more precise image of the imports of services, it was decided to show the total of imports at fob (free on board) prices, which exclude these transport costs, and to show the imported transport charges in total in the "transport" row. This explains the subtraction of 7 billion euros in the cell at the intersection of the "imports of goods" column and the "cif-fob adjustment" row in Table 1. If the transport service is carried out by a resident transporter, the output of this service will be included in the output of the "EK transport" industry. If it is carried out by a non-resident transporter, it will be included in imports of transport services. In either case, these amounts have to be deducted from the transport product row, since there is no use corresponding to these resources. This explains the entry for the same amount of -7 billion in the cell at the intersection of the "cif-fob adjustment" column and the transport row in Table 1. As for the cell at the intersection of the "cif-fob adjustment" column and the "cif-fob adjustment" row in Table 1, this is purely conventional and serves only to ensure that the row totals and the column totals for this specific operation cancel out. This cif-fob adjustment is quite complicated but has no overall impact. Its sole purpose is to give a clearer picture of the total aggregate imports of goods and services.

Limitations of the national accounts: is there double counting in GDP?

GDP is equal to the sum of the components of final demand, each expressed at their purchase price, including taxes on products such as VAT. At the same time, GDP contains an estimate of the value of the output (and consumption) of non-market services, partly financed by these taxes. In so doing, are we not counting these taxes twice over?

The following simplified example will make it easier to understand the problem. Let us take an elementary economy in which there are only two products, manufactured goods and education. In this economy, the manufactured goods are subject to VAT at 20% and the proceeds are used by the authorities to purchase the services of teachers who provide free education services to households. It is assumed that there is no intermediate consumption in the economy.

The national accountants calculate GDP using the production approach: sum of values added + VAT, resulting in (120 + 20) = 140. This result matches that of the expenditure approach, since the addition of all the components of final demand, reduced in this case to consumption, does in fact give 140. But is there not something strange about including VAT of 20 in the value of final consumption of manufactured goods and also counting this 20 in the consumption of education, although the latter is in fact free?

A simplified economy financing education by VAT on manufactured goods

	Output = Value added	VAT	Final consumption
Manufactured goods	100	20	120
Education	20		20
GDP	140		140

Moreover, is it correct to speak of GDP at market prices when the consumption of education services is valued at a price that is not the one observed on the market, since education is free?

In order to understand the implications of the problem, let us suppose that the authorities decide to abolish VAT and to have the teachers paid directly by households. In addition, it will be assumed that nothing else happens either to volume or to prices. Following this change, we then obtain a GDP of 120 at current prices, representing a drop of 20.

Abolition of VAT, replaced by direct purchase of educational services

	Output = Value added	VAT	Final consumption
Manufactured goods	100		100
Education	20		20
GDP	120		120

This decline is somewhat strange. Seen from the producers' viewpoint, the value of their output has not changed; seen from the consumers' viewpoint, the value of their overall consumption has not changed. There has indeed been a decline in the prices of manufactured goods, thanks to the abolition of VAT, but this decline was offset by the rise in prices of educational services, which were previously free and now have to be paid for. The overall decline in GDP of 20 is therefore difficult to interpret.

Rather than talk of double counting, the conclusion may therefore be that there has been a failure to respect in the present definition of "GDP at market prices" the desired invariability in the face of such an institutional change. Should this be cause for concern? Not fundamentally, since the changes in volume will be unaffected. GDP in volume at the previous year's prices will still equal 140 following the institutional change. The consumption in volume of manufactured goods will also equal 140, since the prices applied are those of the previous period. In total, volume growth will be zero, which is intellectually satisfactory. As regards spatial comparison with another country, if (as is desirable) purchasing power parity (PPP) is applied, the problem will also be solved, since PPPs are calculated after tax and so will automatically correct for any "double counting".

It remains true that direct comparisons of GDP at current prices should not be made in the absence of PPP adjustment, although this is something one sees very often. Also, it is not clear how to interpret the GDP price index in the case of abolition of VAT (the implicit deflator of GDP will decrease, while it should remain constant). Nevertheless, there is no other definition of GDP that makes it possible to verify that GDP = output = income = expenditure. One question could be: is this equation purely theoretical due to the wedge introduced by taxes?

Relationship with economic theory: Wassily Léontieff and the use of input-output tables

The first input-output tables were developed by an American economist of Russian descent, Wassily Léontieff. In the 1930s, he published an input-output table for the United States for the years 1919 and 1926 and used it to describe the structure of the American economy. However, it was in his native country, which had by then become the Soviet Union, that the most extensive use of the table was made. Gosplan, the Soviet Planning Ministry, drew up a five-year plan which set targets for the availability of consumer and capital goods and used input-output tables to evaluate the output needed to reach these targets. Each industry was accordingly given production targets that it was obligated to meet. Other countries like India, Egypt, China, Vietnam and Cuba adopted similar methods.

France and the Netherlands also had their five-year plans, but the purpose of these was not to impose targets on industries but rather to provide benchmarks and incentives. France and the Netherlands are market economies in which industries are not told what to produce. The five-year plans have now totally disappeared. At the same time, use of input-output tables to estimate the output needed to meet a given demand has become rarer but has not completely disappeared.

The assumption of fixed technical coefficients is a limitation of the method, except in the short term. Indeed, relative price movements between intermediate goods are not taken into account while they can generate technical changes that call this assumption into question. Moreover, long-period analysis of technical coefficients shows that they change substantially over time. Indeed, one of the major trends in recent decades has been industrial firms' increasing externalisation of entire portions of their production systems ("outsourcing"). For example, firms have drastically reduced their internal IT services to buy the IT services of specialised outside firms, regarded as giving better value for the money. This same phenomenon has occurred in the case of financial auditing, cleaning services and security, among others. Lastly, more and more industrial firms have been calling on the services of temporary agency staff (seen as being more flexible) even for their core productive activities. In all these cases, this outsourcing increases the intermediate consumption of industrial firms without correspondingly increasing their output. The result is a slow but inexorable increase in technical coefficients.

Although the use of input-output tables for economic analysis has been tending to diminish, there are certain examples to the contrary. The OECD has recently published an interesting study using this technique in an economic/environmental framework.[2] The international Kyoto protocol on the environment sets targets for reductions in emissions of CO_2 (the principal "greenhouse gas") for the industrial countries. Most of the signatories have made progress towards these targets. However, this may not correspond to a genuine reduction in the emissions of CO_2 attributableto a country.

The problem is that the Kyoto protocol focuses on emissions within a country's borders, whereas globalisation means relocation of industries from the rich countries to the poor countries, reducing the emissions of the former but increasing the emissions of the latter, especially as they tend to use inefficient production techniques. In total, CO_2 emissions are higher than before. The OECD study dealt with emissions of CO_2 that are attributable not to the production of the rich countries, but to their consumption. For this purpose, it used input-output tables to determine which industries are involved in meeting certain types of consumption, including industries located in other countries. The study concluded that the emissions of CO_2 attributable to the consumption of the rich countries were 5% greater than the emissions due to their domestic production.

Accrual accounting

The so-called accrual principle is applied throughout the national accounts. It is based on the same method used in company accounts. The principle is as follows: a transaction must be recorded in accordance with the amount and the timing of the creation of the claim (for the creditor) or of the obligation (for the debtor). For example, sales from firm A to firm B will be recorded at the time of change of ownership, in other words, when the sales contract is signed, without waiting for the payment of the money corresponding to the sale. In the period between the time of sale and the time when the money is transferred, the accounts will show a credit by the seller in favour of the buyer. This is the general principle applied in theory to all the series in the national accounts.

There is a dual justification for adopting this principle. First, if one considers that one aim of the national accounts is to show the wealth of economic agents at the end of the period, it is nothing less than indispensable. An agent's wealth at the end of the period must include as positive items all the unconditional claims on other agents (for example, if the sales contracts have been signed and the product delivered, the seller has an unconditional claim on the buyer) and, as negative items, the obligations contracted vis-à-vis other agents (for instance, even if he has not yet paid the government the taxes for the period, he still owes them). Second, its application permits better analytical correspondence among the variations of the macroeconomic series. For example, if the government raises the VAT rate in December of a given year, the repercussions on VAT receipts will be felt in the first quarter of the following year, given the time lag between the payment of VAT by agents and the receipt of these monies by government. However, it would be analytically incorrect to record the rise in VAT only in the following year, whereas some consumption at the new rate has already taken place in the current year. In accountants' jargon, it is said that the VAT receipts have to be "time-adjusted" in order to attach them to the period when the flow was generated (at the time when, for example, a household purchases a product).

In practice, things are not so simple. On the one hand, the national accountants use company accounts, for which accrual accounting is primordial. One might therefore think that the principle is respected. However, this is not totally the case, since in many countries one of the largest macroeconomic agents, *i.e.* government, does not systematically apply this rule. Quite rightly, the national accountants consider that for certain transactions (*e.g.* taxes) government statistics are better than those derived from aggregating the company accounts. The national accounts, which are bound to be internally consistent, therefore replace the accrual-basis tax data supplied by firms with the government statistics, which are better in terms of coverage but worse with respect to the accrual basis. An adjustment is therefore necessary and is made by shifting the timing of the VAT receipts of the government in order to bring them more into line with the timing of the generation of the tax.

Another practical difficulty needs to be pointed out, namely the difficulty experienced by the national accountants in applying this principle without taking into account "provisions". A firm always has to deal with bad payers. While it will therefore record all its claims on its purchasers, it will also, by precaution, set aside a "provision" to cover non-payment and this will be recorded in its income statement. But the national accounts do not allow for the recording of these provisions, which, by definition constitute a view taken by one agent of other agents, entailing a lack of symmetry. The national accounts, for the purpose of internal consistency, record only what is symmetrical. This is a contradiction that needs to be resolved.

What does "consolidation" mean?

There are two ways of aggregating institutional units' accounts. The first is simply to add them together, as do most national accounts systems. The second is to add them together but to eliminate the transactions between individual institutional units involved in the aggregation. This method is known as "consolidation". When consolidation has been carried out, there remain only the transactions between the aggregate grouping created and the units located outside this grouping. For example, in the extract from the integrated economic account concerning interest discussed in the main text (see Table 7), if the total for the national economy (S1) had been calculated by consolidation, the figure would have been much smaller than DKK 334.3 billion, because most of the interest is paid by resident units to other resident units, and so takes place within S1.

It is fairly easy to find a consolidated figure for S1. This is because if one eliminates transactions between resident sectors all that is left, in principle, are the transactions with non-resident sectors, and there is only one such sector, *i.e.* the rest of the world (S2). The "consolidated S1" figures therefore correspond to the counterpart of the figure for S2, and so the consolidated interest paid by "S1 National Economy" is necessarily equal to the interest received by "S2 Rest of the World", *i.e.* DKK 47.6 billion. Note that two sectors are already consolidated. These are the rest of the world and households. The rest of the world by definition because the national accounts for a country take no interest in transactions that are internal to other countries or to transactions between other countries; households by statistical necessity because their accounts are obtained by difference since virtually no direct information is available regarding households. Because they are obtained by difference, household accounts are consolidated out of necessity. However, as it is very difficult to consolidate aggregate business accounts, they are most often not consolidated in the national accounts.

Note also that the items obtained as balancing items in the accounts (value added, operating surplus, saving, net lending/net borrowing) are generally invariant, whether there is consolidation or not. This is because they result from the difference between resources and uses. If the resources consist of transactions internal to the sector, the uses must necessarily include them also.

Notes

1. This value is in fact negative in the case of France and so it would be more correct to say that it is subtracted. It is negative because spending by foreign tourists in France is greater than spending by French tourists abroad. This situation is also described by saying that the tourism balance is positive.

2. Ahmad, Nadim and Wyckoff, Andrew (2003): Carbon Dioxide Emissions Embodied in International Trade of Goods, *OECD Science, Technology and Industry Working Papers,* No. 2003/15, OECD, Paris.

Exercises   *Answers at www.SourceOECD.org/understandingnationalaccounts*

Exercise 1. Reconstitution of an input-output table using "copy and paste"

The aim of this exercise is to compile a life-size input-output table at level E of the French classification (16 products/industries). Go to the INSEE website (insee.fr), find the annual national accounts, and then look for "Synthesis tables" and then "input-output table" ("tableau des entrées et sorties"). This will give you the product supply table ("tableau des ressources en produits"), the final use table ("tableau des emplois finals par produits"), the intermediate use table ("tableau des entrées intermédiaires") and, underneath, the production accounts ("comptes de production") and the generation of income accounts ("comptes d'exploitation") by industry ("branche"). Print out these tables separately. Using copy and paste, reassemble them so as to obtain the picture of the input-output table given in Section 4 of this chapter. Be careful to ensure that both the rows and the columns correspond. Read again Sections 1 to 4 of this chapter with this new set of tables in front of you. For those courageous enough, the INSEE site makes it possible to perform the same manipulation at level F (40 products). The result is a very large table. Imagine how big it would be at level G (114 products)!

Exercise 2. Reconstitution of the accounts of institutional sectors

Take the case of an economy with three institutional sectors: households (including NPISHs), corporations (financial *and* non-financial) and general government.

Various sources have been used and processed according to the definitions in the national accounts, with the following result:

	Corporations	General government	Households
Expenditure			
Interest	162	35	20
Employers' social contributions	129	53	11
Dividends	60		
Other taxes *minus* subsidies on production	54	2	2
Operating surplus	?	?	65
Gross wages and salaries	431	87	51
Withdrawals from income of quasi-corporations	24		
Current taxes on income, wealth, etc.	34		178
Other property income	25		
Income from land and sub-soil assets	31	7	27

	Corporations	General government	Households
Final consumption expenditure		368	1 031
Social security reimbursements		57	
Benefits		162	
Other current transfers	57	159	73
Social benefits other than social transfers in kind	43	289	
Adjustment for the change in net equity of households in pension fund reserves	11		
Resources			
Value added (at basic prices)	780	158	561
Social contributions	54	268	
Dividends	28	5	13
Taxes *minus* subsidies on products		133	
Other current transfers	59	109	72
Income from land and sub-soil assets	44		21
Other property income	16		23
Interest	139	14	56
Withdrawals from income of quasi-corporations		13	44

In addition, the balance of payments supplies the following data:

Debit (resources of the rest of the world)	
Gross wages and salaries	2
Interest	21
Dividends	14
Other current transfers	59
Withdrawals from income of quasi-corporations (located within the economy)	3
Credit (uses of the rest of the world)	
Gross wages and salaries	6
Other property income	14
Interest	13
Withdrawals from income of quasi-corporations (located in other countries)	36
Other current transfers	10

Here are certain indications that will be useful for the exercise:

1. the data shown in the first table above are not complete, and additional figures will have to be reconstituted;

2. the wages and salaries shown in the balance of payments table are by their nature paid to, or received, by the rest of the world, and the remainder are paid to households;

3. social benefits are by definition received by households;

4. social contributions received by corporations and general government are paid by households;

5. the adjustment for the change in the net equity of households in pension fund reserves applies to households, by definition;

6. households' adjusted disposable income is equal to disposable income *plus* social transfers in kind (Social Security reimbursements, other benefits in kind).

This exercise consists of completing the accounts for the three institutional sectors shown on the website.

Households

Generation of income account

Uses	Resources
Compensation of employees	Value added
Gross wages and salaries	
Employers' social contributions	
Other taxes on production, less subsidies	
Operating surplus	
Mixed income	

Allocation of primary income account

Uses	Resources
	Gross operating surplus and mixed income
	Compensation of employees
	Gross wages and salaries
	Employers' social contributions
Property income	Property income
Interest	Interest
Income from land and subsoil assets	Dividends
	Withdrawals from income of quasi-corporations
Balance of primary incomes	Income from land and subsoil assets
	Other property income

Secondary distribution of income account

Uses	Resources
Current taxes on income, wealth, etc.	Balance of primary incomes
Social contributions	Social benefits other than social transfers in kind
Other current transfers	Other current transfers
Disposable income	

Use of income account

Uses	Resources
	Disposable income
Final consumption expenditure	Adjustment for the change in the net equity of households in pension fund reserves
Saving	

Use of adjusted disposable income account

Uses	Resources
	Adjusted disposable income
Actual consumption	Adjustment for the change in the net equity of households in pension fund reserves
Saving	

Corporations

Generation of income account

Uses	Resources
Compensation of employees	Value added
Gross wages and salaries	
Employers' social contributions	
Other taxes on production, less subsidies	
Operating surplus	

Allocation of primary income account

Uses	Resources
	Operating surplus
Property income	Property income
Interest	Interest
Income from land and sub-soil assets	Dividends
Other property income	Withdrawals from income of quasi-corporations
	Other property income
Balance of primary incomes	

Secondary distribution of income account

Uses	Resources
Current taxes on income, wealth, etc.	Balance of primary incomes
Social benefits other than social transfers in kind	Social contributions
Other current transfers	Other current transfers
Disposable income	

Use of income account

Uses	Resources
Adjustment for the change in the net equity of households in pension fund reserves	Disposable income
Saving	

General government
Generation of income account

Uses	Resources
Compensation of employees	Value added
Gross wages and salaries	
Employers' social contributions	
Other taxes on production, less subsidies	
Operating surplus	

Allocation of primary income account

Uses	Resources
Property income	Operating surplus
Interest	
Income from land and sub-soil assets	Taxes *minus* subsidies on production and imports
Other property income	Taxes *minus* subsidies on products
	Other taxes *minus* subsidies on production
	Property income
	Interest
	Dividends
	Withdrawals from income of quasi-corporations
Balance of primary incomes	Other property income

Secondary distribution of income account

Uses	Resources
	Balance of primary incomes
	Current taxes on income, wealth, etc.
Social benefits other than social transfers in kind	Social contributions
Other current transfers	Other current transfe s
Disposable income	

Use of income account

Uses	Resources
Final consumption expenditure	Disposable income
Saving	

Use of adjusted income account

Uses	Resources
Actual consumption	Adjusted disposable income
Saving	

Exercise 3. Creating an integrated economic account

Use the accounts of the three institutional sectors in the previous exercise to complete the integrated economic account in the following pages:

Integrated economic account (extract) (1/3)

Total	Rest of the world	Total economy	Corporations	General government	Households	Production account	Corporations	General government	Households	Total economy	Rest of the world	Total
						Imports					499	499
540	540					Exports						
						Output	1 708	410	1 264	3 382		3 382
1 883		1 883	928	252	703	Intermediate consumption						
						Taxes minus subsidies on products				133		133
1 632		1 632	780	158	561	Value-added/GDP						
−41	−41					Trade balance (goods and services)						
						Generation of income account						
						Value added						
						Compensation of employees						
						Gross wages and salaries						
						Employers' social contributions						
						Taxes *minus* subsidies						
						On products						
						Other taxes						
						Operating surplus						
						Mixed income						

Integrated economic account (extract) (2/3)

Total	Rest of the world	Total economy	Corporations	General government	House-holds	Allocation of primary income account	Corporations	General government	Households	Total economy	Rest of the world	Total
						Operating surplus/mixed income						
						Compensation of employees						
						Gross wages and salaries						
						Employers' social contributions						
						Taxes *minus* subsidies						
						On products						
						Other taxes on production						
						Property income						
						Interest						

UNDERSTANDING NATIONAL ACCOUNTS – ISBN 92-64-02566-9 – © OECD 2006

Integrated economic account (extract) (2/3) *(cont.)*

Total	Rest of the world	Total economy	Corporations	General government	House-holds	Allocation of primary income account	Corporations	General government	Households	Total economy	Rest of the world	Total
						Dividends						
						Income from quasi-corporations						
						Income from land and sub-soil assets						
						Other property income						
						Balance of primary incomes/National						
						Income						

Integrated economic account (extract) (3/3)

Total	Rest of the world	Total economy	Corporations	General government	Households	Secondary distribution of income account	Corporations	General government	Households	Total economy	Rest of the world	Total
						Balance of primary incomes						
						Current taxes on income, wealth, etc.						
						Social contributions						
						Other social benefits						
						Other current transfers						
						Disposable income						
						Use of income account						
						Disposable income						
						Final expenditure						
						Change in pension fund equity						
						Saving						
						Current-account balance						

Exercise 4. Use of the input-output table in a so-called Léontieff model

Take the following input-output table, consisting of: [M] the intermediate consumption matrix; [Y] the vector of final demand for intermediate products, capital goods and consumer products; and, lastly [X], the vector of output from the industries producing these same products (in order, intermediate products, capital goods and consumer products).

	[M]			[Y]
Intermediate products	5	20	20	5
Capital goods	5	10	12	33
Consumer products	10	6	15	89
[X]	50	60	120	
	Intermediate products	Capital goods	Consumer products	

Given the above figures, and with the help of the equations in Section 5 of this chapter, do the following:

1. calculate the matrix [A] of technical coefficients;

2. use Equation 7 to calculate the impact on [X] of an increase of 20 in final demand for consumer products (say, as a result of a tax cut by the government).

UNDERSTANDING NATIONAL ACCOUNTS – ISBN 92-64-02566-9 – © OECD 2006

Chapter 11

THE NATIONAL ACCOUNTS MACHINERY: COMPILATION AND REPORTING

Previous chapters concentrated on the definitions of the variables in the national accounts. This chapter is quite different; its aim is to explain how national accounts are compiled *in practice* and to describe the main consequences of this process for the user. We will start by discussing the quarterly accounts; then we will examine the relationship between quarterly national accounts and annual national accounts. Finally, we will look at ordinary revisions and comprehensive revisions in the national accounts. The example used will be France, but the lessons to be learned apply also to other countries.

1. The quarterly national accounts

In the United States or the United Kingdom, the national accounts have been from the start almost entirely quarterly. In France and in many other countries, they have been essentially annual for a long time but are becoming increasingly quarterly, thanks to the progress made in the collection and processing of statistics. It is therefore essential for the macroeconomist to be well-informed regarding the timing, format and publication of quarterly national accounts.

Why have quarterly accounts?

One of the crucial objectives of macroeconomic statistics is to help the authorities make the right decisions at the right moment. It would not be appropriate to launch a policy boosting the economy when the upswing has already started, or conversely to "cool down" the economy when it is already entering recession. It is therefore desirable to have the most refined possible information regarding the economic cycle and its turning points. In this context, the annual national accounts, which in the French case are published in April of the following year, arrive far too late. Moreover, exclusive reliance on annual averages can in fact be misleading about the true state of the economy (see Exercise 1 at the end of this chapter). Hence, the importance of compiling accounts that are more timely than annual ones. The present situation regarding the resources available and the reliability of statistics limits this effort to quarterly accounts, but some countries such as Canada calculate GDP monthly.

The quarterly national accounts constitute the central instrument for short-term economic analysis at the OECD. The first pages of *Economic Outlook No. 78* dated December 2005 open with the following graph and the attached comment: *"World growth has been broadening over the past few months. Already strong in North America and most of Asia, economic momentum now looks well established in Japan, and continental Europe is progressively recovering from its latest bout of weakness. The fledgling European expansion*

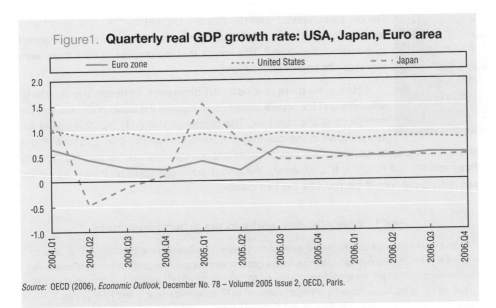

Figure1. **Quarterly real GDP growth rate: USA, Japan, Euro area**

Source: OECD (2006), *Economic Outlook,* December No. 78 – Volume 2005 Issue 2, OECD, Paris.

has been facilitated by low long-term interest rates, euro depreciation and buoyant export markets, although final domestic demand is still growing below trend."

Quarterly accounts are much used by forecasters, whether in the Finance Ministry helping in the preparation of the government budget or in public or private research institutions such as those connected to the large banks. Thanks to the quarterly accounts, these economists are in a position to update their forecasts for the coming year as quarterly information becomes available for the current year. ▶ I. In France, the quarterly accounts are also used in connection with the six-month forecasts made by INSEE's Short-Term Economic Forecasts Department. These are presented in the regular publications entitled *Conjoncture in France*, which contain numerous quarterly figures accompanied by comments regarding average year-on-year changes or statistical carryover (see Box 1 "Annualisation and various growth indicators"). The French INSEE is in fact one of the few statistical institutes that has been given the authority to make forecasts.

good forecast is,
e all, one that is
d on the most recent
figures.

Specific features of the quarterly accounts

In certain countries such as the United States or the United Kingdom, the user of the national accounts sees no real difference between the annual accounts and the quarterly accounts. These are countries where the national accounts were developed *simultaneously* on a quarterly and on an annual basis from the start. In France and certain other countries, the quarterly accounts were developed much later than the annual accounts (in the mid-1970s for

II. This does not apply to the accounts published in the United States, which are annualised, and thus multiplied by 4 (see Box 1 "Annualisation and various growth indicators").

France, as compared with 1950 for the US and the UK). It is in fact only recently that the teams of INSEE accountants involved have been attached to the same department. This means that the user could think there were two separate sets of publications.

However, there is *strictly* no difference between the quarterly accounts and the annual accounts as regards the basic principles and the definitions of the variables. The difference is merely that the size of the flows shown in the quarterly accounts are roughly one quarter of those shown in the annual accounts (as is logical, given that one calendar quarter accounts for only three months out of 12). ▶ **II.** Conversely, the annual flows are equal (in theory, as we will see later) to the sum of the flows for the four quarters.

Box 1. **Annualisation and various growth indicators**

The most important use made of the national accounts is to forecast the following year in order to provide the macroeconomic framework for the government budget. The prime aim is to evaluate the volume growth in GDP for the following year, on an "annual average" basis. This expression signifies that one is trying to evaluate the variation between GDP in calendar year Y and GDP in year Y + 1, *i.e.* $(Y + 1)/Y$. The information given in the quarterly accounts generally shows quarterly changes, *i.e.*, $(Q + 1)/Q$. The further one moves into the year, the more information there is on recent quarters thanks to the quarterly accounts, and the closer one comes to the prime aim of forecasting annual average growth.

Certain national accountants (Canada, Japan, Mexico, United States) usually express quarterly figures "at annual level", meaning that quarterly levels are multiplied by four. They also express quarterly changes "at annualised rate", which amounts to raising them to the power of 4. The advantage of this method is to place the quarterly growth rate on a slope that uses the same measurement framework as for the annual data. This practice has not however been generalised to the other countries. This practice is indeed not without problems as it is based on the assumption that the observed changes for the quarter are going to continue, which is by no means certain. Thus some short-term analysts prefer to use "year-on-year changes" and/or "the statistical carryover" in order to give indications regarding the annual growth rate. Year-on-year changes consist of calculating the change for the current period (quarter, in this case) since the corresponding period of the previous year (Q/Q-4). The "statistical carryover" consists of calculating an annual average for the current calendar year on the assumption that the remaining quarters are at the same level as the last known quarter. The further one moves into the year, the closer the statistical carryover comes to the future annual average, the two becoming equal when the fourth quarter is known. Exercise 1 at the end of this chapter provides an opportunity to work with these notions. One of the indispensable conclusions to be drawn is that one should be careful to avoid the trap of comparing an American growth figure (raised to the power of 4) with a French or European figure that is not. To make valid comparisons, either one takes the fourth root of the American growth or one raises the European figure to the power of 4.

The aim of the quarterly accounts is to provide at the earliest possible moment reliable figures for the changes in the major macroeconomic aggregates. Thus, the quarterly accounts are simplified compared with the annual accounts and are presented slightly differently. In France, for example, quarterly accounts are calculated using a classification consisting of 41 items, and the accounts made available to the users are based on a 16-item classification. The detailed analyses of structural changes in the economy are left to the annual accounts, which are calculated for a 472-item classification and published for a 116-item classification. On the same lines, the detail of the transactions in the accounts for institutional sectors is not as great in the quarterly accounts as in the annual accounts. This enables INSEE to reduce the workload entailed by the more frequent calculation of quarterly accounts which are calculated three times for each quarter, as shown in the following table. This frequency of calculation is made possible by highly effective estimation procedures using rapidly available indicators (see "Sources and methods for the French quarterly accounts" and "Resources of national accounts departments").

Table 1. **France calendar for the publication of the accounts for quarter Q**
2006[*]

Q + 42 days	Q + 50 days	Q + 90 days
Preliminary estimate: GDP in volume only	First results: Revised GDP + goods and services accounts + certain elements of the income approach of GDP.	Detailed results: Revised GDP + revised goods and services accounts + fairly complete accounts for institutional sectors

* This calendar reflects the situation as of May 2006. It is not carved in stone: France has recently announced that it may suppress the Q + 42 and the Q + 50 publications to replace them by a new Q + 45 publication containing the same data as the current Q + 50 publication.

The "preliminary estimate" of the change in French GDP in volume in quarter Q is published 42 days[1] after the end of the quarter concerned. For the time being, no other figures are provided at this time, since INSEE considers that subsequent revisions would be too substantial. This GDP figure is then revised at Q + 50 days, at the time of the publication of the "first results", and is then accompanied by a complete set of goods and services accounts and certain elements regarding profits and the total wage bill. The next revision takes place at Q + 90 days in the form of "detailed results", this time including fairly complete accounts for institutional sectors. As a result, figures are published quarterly for the household saving ratio or the corporate profit ratio at Q + 90 days. A similar calendar applies for other countries (see Table 2). For completeness, mention should also be made of the existence in some countries of a monthly series of national accounts. In France, it is limited to "household expenditure on consumption of manufactured goods". This monthly national accounts series makes it possible to know, roughly 23 days after the end of the month, the change in consumption expenditure – limited to manufactured goods, admittedly. However, since changes in total consumption are closely linked to consumption of manufactured goods, this indicator is useful for the short-term analysts.

Despite the fact that the definitions of the variables are the same in the two sets of accounts, it turns out in practice that the sums of the four quarters from the quarterly accounts are not equal to the corresponding annual figures, because the French quarterly accounts are "working-day adjusted" (wda). To be more precise, the French quarterly national accounts are now calculated "wda-sa" meaning that they are adjusted both for the number of working days and for seasonal variations.[2] In statisticians' terminology and in this context, "wda" and "sa" are in opposition to the unadjusted figures. The working-day adjustment consists of calculating the quarterly accounts as if each quarter contained the same number of working days. This means that changes in GDP are not affected by differences in the numbers of working days in each quarter. The adjustment gives a better indication of the actual ongoing tendency in the economy and leads to smoother quarterly variations than shown in the unadjusted figures. Many countries make this adjustment (see Table 2).

The difficulty created in some countries (France, Italy and Germany) by the working-day adjustment is that the sum of the four quarters no longer equals *by definition* the unadjusted figures for the year because there are often differences in the number of working days between one year and the next, partly because of leap years, but it is not the most important factor. More important, for example, is the fact that public holidays fall on week-ends in some years, but on working days in other. The difference can be quite significant, as in the case of the year 2004 compared with 2003 (see Box 2). Does this not suggest that all national accounts, including annual accounts, should be calculated after adjustment for the number of working days? Economists are divided on this point because, while adjusted data is more useful to analyse the trend, some major economic aggregates are unadjusted. For example, the government budget that is voted by Parliament is unadjusted (*i.e.* is not working-day-adjusted). The best solution would be to have a choice between the two, as is given in the case of France where there are two sets of accounts: one (wda) consisting of the quarterly accounts and one (unadjusted) for the annual accounts. In order to obtain the annual accounts on a wda basis, one merely has to add up the four quarters from the quarterly accounts; to have the unadjusted annual figures, all that is needed is to take the figures in the annual accounts. In some other countries, such as the US, wda is conducted for quarters but the data are then benchmarked to the unadjusted annual figures, or the annual data are obtained by the sum of the quarters so that, at the end, there is no difference between the sum of the four quarters and the annual figure.

The other calendar adjustment of the quarterly accounts is the seasonal adjustment. This consists in eliminating, by means of complex statistical processes based on moving averages, the changes from one quarter to the next that are due simply to seasonal effects. For example, the output of transport services rises systematically and steeply before Christmas and the summer holidays. It is therefore better to eliminate the impact of this seasonal effect in order to know whether holidaymakers actually consumed more or less in

Box 2. Calendar effects: the years 2003 and 2004

In France, the years 2003 and 2004 were very special from the point of view of the calendar. The number of working days in 2003, at 252, was in fact slightly below the average of 253. The year 2004 was exceptional with 255 working days, a figure not seen since 1976. The impact of this greater number of working days on the annual change in GDP, everything else remaining equal, is estimated to have been 0.2/0.3 of a percentage point, which is by no means negligible. It is nevertheless smaller than the simple ratio of the numbers of working days: 255/252 = +1.2%. This is because INSEE's estimate of the impact of the number of working days attaches different weights to individual days of the week, especially for the months of July and August, and the "catching-up" that takes place between different months. The estimation method used is econometric. The unadjusted monthly figures are projected on variables representing the different types of days of the week (number of non-worked Mondays, non-worked Tuesdays, etc.) and the number of Sundays.

Table 2. Some features of quarterly national accounts for selected OECD countries

	First estimate (Q + 60 means published 60 days after end of quarter)	Second estimate	Third estimate	Working Day Adjustment (in italics countries for which the sum of four quarters do not equal the annual value)	Mean absolute revision of quarterly GDP growth[*] (in %)
Australia	Q + 60			Yes	0.36
Canada	Q + 60			Yes	0.24
France	Q + 42	Q + 50	Q + 90	*Yes*	0.29
Germany	Q + 44	Q + 54		*Yes*	0.36
Italy	Q + 44	Q + 70		*Yes*	0.20
Japan	Q + 48	Q + 73		Yes	0.69
Korea	Q + 26	Q + 80		Yes	0.97
United Kingdom	Q + 25	Q + 56	Q + 86	Yes	0.18
United States	Q + 30	Q + 60	Q + 90	Yes	0.33

[*] In terms of quarterly rates (*i.e.* Q/Q-1), absolute rates, first estimate *versus* three years after (see the "Revision Database" on the OECD website). This is different from what appears in the US tables of revision published for the accounts of the United States, in which all quarterly growth rates are systematically "annualised" (see Box 1 "Annualisation and various growth indicators").

the quarter in question than in the previous quarter. Unlike the working-day adjustment, things are so arranged that the sum of the quarterly seasonal adjustments for the year as a whole is zero. In other words, the sum of the quarterly seasonally adjusted figures is equal to the unadjusted figure for the year.

2. The annual national accounts

If all one needs are the major economic aggregates, one needs look no further than the series and publications of the quarterly accounts. However, if one wants detailed results, it is necessary to consult the series and publications of the annual national accounts. In particular, the very important general government account is still, for many OECD countries, available only on an annual basis, as are the financial accounts and the balance sheet accounts. However, there is a sustained effort by OECD countries to expand the number of tables compiled quarterly. It is therefore possible that in the coming years, general government accounts will be available quarterly for most OECD countries.

In France, like in all OECD countries, there are major dates for publications. The main publication for the annual accounts is the report entitled *The French Economy*, published in June and providing indispensable analysis of the recent economic evolution. This publication goes hand-in-hand with the publication on the INSEE website of a set of tables giving details for institutional sectors accounts, external flows of goods and services, gross fixed capital formation by products and institutional sectors, final consumption expenditure and population and employment.

The annual accounts are the backbone of the whole system of national accounts. They are based mainly on four sources: 1) the aggregation of company accounts (in France, INSEE receives and processes each year the accounts of more than 2 million corporations and unincorporated enterprises); 2) the complete accounts of all general government, consisting of central government and the attached agencies, local authorities and all the Social Security bodies (around 120 000 organisations in all in France); 3) the detailed accounts of the financial institutions that are supervised by the central bank (Banque de France) whose statistical directorate is, as in all countries, the main collaborator of the National Statistical Office for production of the national accounts; 4) the balance of payments (generally published by the central bank), which makes it possible to trace relations with the rest of the world.

Much of these data, however, are available only after a certain timelag, generating a specific calendar of compilation and publication. In what follows, Y will refer to the year for which new accounts are calculated. In France, each year, at the end of April in year Y + 1, new annual accounts are published containing new data for year Y (the so-called "provisional" accounts), for year Y – 1 (the so-called "semi-final" accounts) and for year Y – 2 (the so-called "final" accounts). The mechanism used for the annual accounts therefore implies two systematic revisions for each set of published accounts, revisions that obviously, by definition, have an impact on the quarterly accounts. For example, the annual GDP for year Y will be published in April Y + 1 as "provisional", in April Y + 2 as "semi-final" and in April Y + 3 as "final" (as we shall see later, the term "final" is in fact inappropriate). This sequencing is explained mainly by the delays in obtaining data from the principal source mentioned earlier, namely company accounts. Other countries may have some difference in the timing and terminology, but basically the system is similar to that of France.

THE NATIONAL ACCOUNTS MACHINERY:
COMPILATION AND REPORTING
3. The revisions to the national accounts
and their precision

11

In France, the "provisional" accounts are mainly the combination of the quarterly accounts for the goods and services accounts *plus* the complete accounts for the general government *plus* the financial accounts. At the time these provisional accounts are published, INSEE has not yet received any company accounts and has to wait until Q4 of year Y + 1 before receiving and processing a first substantial set of corporate accounts (for roughly 400 000 large firms), but still excluding the smallest firms. This information can thus only be processed to be published in April of the next year, on the occasion of the publication of the next year's provisional accounts. Finally, the totality of corporate accounts (for roughly 2 500 000 firms) is received and processed by INSEE only in Q4 of year Y + 2. Table 3 below recapitulates this sequence. In the end, it is necessary to wait two years and five months for national accounts that have "digested" the totality of the available statistical sources used for the national accounts for calendar year Y.

Table 3. **France: Sequencing of the calculation of the annual accounts for year Y**

April Y + 1	April Y + 2	April Y + 3
Provisional accounts	Semi-final accounts	Final accounts
Accounts at the F level (41 headings). Complete accounts for institutional sectors. *Source:* quarterly accounts, general government accounts.	Revised accounts at the G level (116 headings). Complete revised accounts for institutional sectors. *Source:* first version using directly corporate accounts, excluding the smallest firms. Complete revised version of the general government accounts.	Re-revised accounts at the G level. Complete revised accounts for institutional sectors. *Source:* version fully using the corporate accounts, including the smallest firms.

3. The revisions to the national accounts and their precision

As we have just seen for France (and the situation is similar in other countries), the complete sources for the national accounts are available only in Q4 of year Y + 2. If they had to wait as long as this for this information, short-term macroeconomic analysts would have no use for the national accounts. This explains the complex sequencing of successive quarterly and annual accounts, the aim being to provide the most reliable information possible as rapidly as possible. However, the price paid for this rapidity is the need to revise the initial figures. Some macroeconomists complain about revisions to the national accounts. However, it is not possible to "have one's cake" in the form of reliability and at the same time "eat it" in the form of rapidity. Nor should one be fooled: the countries that performed little or no revision were the Soviet bloc countries, where statisticians, for political reasons, were forbidden to make revisions. This did not mean

11

THE NATIONAL ACCOUNTS MACHINERY:
COMPILATION AND REPORTING
3. The revisions to the national accounts
   and their precision

that the national accounts were reliable – quite the contrary. On the other hand, major revisions are obviously not a good thing. The professionalism of national accountants is judged by their capacity to combine a high degree of reliability with satisfactory rapidity.

When does a figure for quarterly GDP growth become "final"? The somewhat surprising answer is "never". As an illustration, this is the sequence of events that in France covers the repeated revision of the quarterly GDP change: 1) first publication at Q *plus* 42 days; 2) first revision at the time of the "first results" at Q + 50 (the source of the revision being the availability of figures for the final month of the quarter); 3) second revision at the time of the "detailed results" at Q + 90 (source: availability of new indicators); 4) minor revisions due to changes in the seasonal adjustment coefficients[3] occur at the time of publication for the following quarters; 5) major revision in April in the following year due to benchmarking on the semi-final annual accounts; 6) significant revision in April in the following year due to the benchmarking on final annual accounts; 7) later still, possible minor revisions due to changes in the seasonal adjustment coefficients, etc.

Clearly, the most significant revisions are the first two, followed in April of the following year at the time of the benchmarking of the unadjusted quarterly accounts on the annual accounts. The other revisions are very small. Even so, the user of the national accounts, if he or she wants to be really up-to-date, must study each publication to find the whole new series and not be content with adding the latest figure to an already existing series. Today, thanks to computer processing and the Internet, downloading an entire series costs no more than downloading the last figure, so no one need complain about this state of affairs. French policy regarding revision is an extreme case. Some other countries make revisions less systematically.

Numerous studies have addressed the question of the scale and sign of the revisions. In France, it is thought that the average revision of the GDP growth rate in volume for a given quarter (*i.e.*, $Q/(Q-1)$) is 0.3% in absolute value. In other words, there is a 90% chance that the revision in the quarterly growth rate (after a few years have passed) is between + 0.6% and – 0.6% compared with the initial published figure. This range is comparable to that for the American quarterly accounts (see Table 2). Some other OECD countries make slightly larger revisions, on average. As regards the annual accounts, the following chart illustrates a sequence of revisions between the provisional accounts and the final accounts for France. On average, over this period the average revision amounted to 0.4% (in absolute value). As can be seen, there are no earth-shaking revisions, but on occasion the annual revision has amounted to as much as 1.0% (for example, in 1988, a year of strong recovery), which is quite significant. Some observers have seen signs that the initial figures in the national accounts are understated in years of recovery and overstated in years of recession, because the sources used in the first estimates exclude small businesses that are more affected by the business cycle than large businesses.

UNDERSTANDING NATIONAL ACCOUNTS – ISBN 92-64-02566-9 – © OECD 2006

THE NATIONAL ACCOUNTS MACHINERY:
COMPILATION AND REPORTING
3. The revisions to the national accounts
   and their precision

11

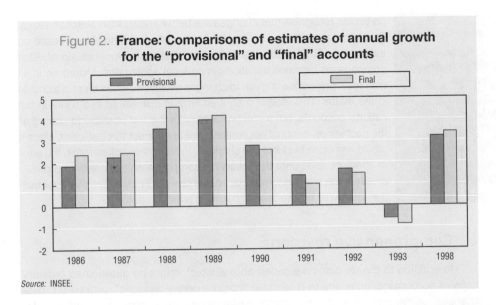

Figure 2. **France: Comparisons of estimates of annual growth for the "provisional" and "final" accounts**

Source: INSEE.

The various revisions to the GDP *growth rate* listed above show that the national accounts cannot claim to be absolutely precise. It would in fact be by no means wrong to conclude from the previous paragraphs that the initial estimates of the quarterly GDP growth rate for France should probably be presented in the form of a range of ±0.5% of the estimated figure (and even greater amplitude for the other detailed items in the accounts, especially GFCF). American quarterly accounts are indeed presented with an accompanying note presenting this type of range for the main aggregates. ▶ III.

It would be good to know the precision attached to the *level* of GDP. Unfortunately, there is no way of knowing this. While it is fully possible to calculate scientifically the precision of an extrapolation of a random sample survey to the total population, it is impossible to do so for the national accounts, whose sources are a blend of surveys and comprehensive databases that are then the subject of "arbitration". ▶ IV. vis-à-vis many other sources. Another consideration is that, as we saw in Chapter 4, the national accounts attempt to take into account the "underground economy", but the calculations to do this are inevitably tainted with substantial error. In the end, the "real" level of GDP could well differ from the published figure by several percentage points, although probably less than 5% in France. Just as there is no need to react to all the exaggerated accusations levelled at statisticians, it is equally necessary to recognise the limitations of the national accounts, and in

III. As explained in a previous footnote, US quarterly growth rates are systematically annualized in US publications (see Box 1 "Annualisation and various growth indicators"), so the range of deviation published in the US quarterly accounts may (wrongly) appear much larger than for France or other countries.

IV. "Arbitration" is a key word in the machinery of annual national accounts. In France, there are two ways of estimating GDP: the approach based on output and final uses and the income-based approach. It is therefore necessary to "arbitrate" (... see next page)

IV. (...) between the two resulting values. This is an operation that INSEE is trying to make increasingly scientific. Some countries, like the United States, do not perform arbitration, and there are therefore officially two GDPs and a statistical adjustment reconciling the two.

particular, recognise that changes are better known than absolute levels. Thus, as was explained in Chapter 3, international comparisons based on the levels (of GDP or other variables) are to be treated more cautiously than comparisons between variations in national aggregates. Moreover, in all countries, preference is given to changes over levels when there is a choice in the matter. This means that, if an error is discovered in a figure in the national accounts, but for technical reasons it is not possible to correct all the past series, national accountants will not correct this last point, since it would introduce bias into the changes. Instead, they will maintain the error in absolute level until the following comprehensive revision in order to preserve the changes. National accountants in France give this approach the somewhat bizarre title of "constant error computation".

4. Comprehensive revisions

In addition to the revisions described above, which might be qualified as ordinary, national accountants from time to time make "comprehensive revisions", also called "base changes" or "benchmark years", and these involve much more substantial overhauls of the system. In France, INSEE has recently decided to carry out base changes every five years. The last took place in 2005, and the next will be in 2010 (see Box 3 "France: Latest and future base changes".). A base change involves four distinct operations: 1) the absolute levels for the year known as the "base year" are re-estimated using statistical sources that are not available every year (population or economic census, housing surveys, etc.) and corrected for past errors; 2) changes of a definitional nature are introduced in conformity with the evolution of the international standards for national accounts; 3) the reference year for chained prices is modified; 4) all past data are re-estimated using past changes, corrected as needed for benchmarking on the new level of the base year. The latter operation, known as "retropolation" or "back-calculation", is quite costly in terms of resources.

A base change therefore leads to fairly generalised modification of all the series, often accompanied by changes in classifications. The macroeconomists using these series need a certain amount of time to update their databases and re-estimate their models. The principal difficulty from their point of view is that statistical offices do not always immediately provide the long time-series, because of the difficulty of "retropolation".

5. Other datasets related to the national accounts

For reasons of space, we can only describe in this manual the central national accounts framework. However, numerous other datasets gravitate around this framework and use broadly the same definitions as the national accounts, while at the same time adjusting them

---

Box 3. **France: Latest and future base changes**

In France, the latest base change (the so-called "base 2000") was introduced in May 2005. The main conceptual change was the allocation of imputed banking services (FISIM), which raised the level of GDP by roughly 1%. In addition to this "conceptual" rise, there were also modifications in absolute levels related to numerous upward or downward revisions affecting the base year, one of which was an upward revision in GFCF in the form of software. All the volume series are presented on the 2000 base year (instead of on the 1995 base in the preceding base). The next base change (base 2005) will take place in 2010 and will take into account the new international statistical classification (ISIC 4). It will probably not be before the base change in 2015 (base 2010) that the French accounts will apply the recommendations of the new SNA manual published in 2008. Significant changes should then be introduced, such as the recording of R&D and military hardware spending as GFCF.

---

for their own special purposes. They are known as "satellite accounts". Below is a listing of satellite accounts existing in France, including the agencies that compile them:

- Regional accounts, or GDP by region. Most OECD countries calculate regional accounts. In Europe, these accounts are used by the European Commission as the basis for the allocation of structural funds; in Canada, they are used to allocate VAT.

- Housing accounts – data published by the statistical service of the Ministry of Equipment and Housing.

- Health accounts – statistical service of the Health Ministry.

- Social welfare accounts – statistical service of the Health Ministry.

- National defence accounts – statistical service of the Defence Ministry.

- Education accounts – statistical service of the Education Ministry.

- Research accounts – statistical service of the Research Ministry.

- Environment accounts – IFEN (French Institute for the Environment).

These accounts are not necessarily available every year. In countries other than France, the range of satellite accounts differs from country to country. Most countries compile health, tourism and environment satellite accounts. Some researchers (such as in the US) publish a household satellite account, which includes an estimate for unpaid domestic services produced by household members.

Notes

1. This figure is an order of magnitude. The exact number of days depends on weekends and holidays. The same is true for the other publication dates.

2. In the methodology used for the French quarterly accounts (see "The sources and methods used for the French quarterly accounts"), it is the indicators that are adjusted, first for the number of working days and then for seasonal variations. The calibration (see a definition of this term later in the same box) is then applied to each type of indicator: unadjusted, sa, wda-sa. There are thus three sets of quarterly accounts: the unadjusted accounts; the seasonally adjusted accounts; and the wda-sa accounts. The quarterly calibration residuals are the same in the three cases. The wda-sa accounts are the ones appearing in the principal publication and subjected to comment. The unadjusted figures are available on request.

3. The "seasonal adjustment coefficients" are the coefficients applied to the unadjusted quarterly series to eliminate seasonal variations. In the methodology used for the French quarterly accounts, these coefficients are re-estimated every quarter, leading to slight revisions, even affecting quarters going back as far as the 1970s, although to an almost imperceptible degree.

UNDERSTANDING NATIONAL ACCOUNTS – ISBN 92-64-02566-9 – © OECD 2006

Key points

▶ The quarterly national accounts constitute the most important source of data for macroeconomists.

▶ Most OECD countries publish quarterly growth as the simple growth ratio based on Q/Q – 1. Some countries, however, "annualise" this figure. The OECD often uses annualised figures. Another indicator of growth is the year-on-year change which is the variation between the current quarter and the corresponding quarter of the previous year (Q/Q – 4).

▶ Most quarterly accounts are seasonally adjusted ("sa"); in addition, some are "working-day adjusted", or wda. In this case, the sum of the four quarters may not equal the corresponding annual account.

▶ The national accounts are the subject of regular revision. It is therefore necessary to use the whole of the newly published series and not be content with the latest published figure.

▶ In France, revisions to the growth rates in the national accounts average around 0.3% in absolute value for the quarterly accounts (Q/Q – 1) and 0.5% for the annual accounts (Y/Y – 1). The scale of revisions in other countries is slightly different.

Going further

Sources and methods used for the French quarterly accounts

In all countries, the full wealth of annual statistical data is not available on a quarterly basis. For example, there is no substantial quarterly database for company accounts, which are on an annual basis and often are one of the principal sources for the annual accounts. Instead, the quarterly accounts use monthly or quarterly "indicators" whose annual changes are similar to the change of the corresponding figures in the national accounts. For example, France's INSEE publishes monthly production indices, derived from small-scale surveys of a sample of firms. The quarterly accountants use the changes in this indicator to deduce movements in the figures for the quarterly accounts, basing themselves on the pre-existing structure of the annual accounts (*i.e.* the quarterly accounts are not themselves capable of providing levels, so they rely for this purpose on the annual accounts).

Many countries use indicators in a simple way: they simply use the change of the indicator to extrapolate the quarterly account. In France, and in some other OECD countries, a more sophisticated statistical method has been developed for using indicators to derive quarterly accounts. This is known as "benchmarking" or also "calibration/fitting" ("étalonnage/calage" in French). Calibration consists of estimating an econometric model that relates the annual value of the indicator to the annual series in the national accounts. Once the coefficients of this model have been estimated, the assumption is made that the same coefficients (divided by four) can be applied on a quarterly basis and this provides the basis for the calculation of the so-called "non-fitted" quarterly accounts. The annual sum of these quarterly accounts is not equal to the annual account, since there is no reason why the annual residuals estimated by the econometric method should be zero. Thus, there is an additional step to the calculation, known as "fitting", which consists of interpolating the sum of the annual residuals in a relatively "smooth" manner (one talks of "quarterly smoothing") in order to obtain a series of quarterly residuals which, combined with the non-fitted series, produce a quarterly so-called "fitted" series. These are equal by definition to the annual accounts series (ignoring at this stage the adjustment for the number of working days). Exercise 3 gives a simplified example of calibration/fitting. Because of the sophistication of the method used for the French quarterly accounts, some people consider that the quarterly accounts are more in the nature of an economic model. Fortunately, this is not true. If this were indeed the case, there would be confusion between statistical calculations and modelling. There are in fact no "behavioural" relationships in the calculation of the French quarterly accounts. The calibration/fitting relationship is purely statistical, linking two time series that are intended to measure roughly the same thing.

In France, the principal indicators for the quarterly accounts are as follows: for output, the industrial production indices and the sales indices derived from processing VAT declarations; for consumption, a variety of sources derived from panels of distributors (business surveys by the Banque de France) or from administrative data (for example, new vehicle registrations in the case of car consumption); for exports and imports, the sources are the same as for the annual accounts, and since customs figures are available monthly the calibration is of excellent quality; investment (GFCF) is estimated either from sales sources or from indicators of availability on the domestic market (output + imports – exports). In France, contrary to some other countries that have better surveys, there is no direct source for variations in inventories and they are estimated as a balancing item in the supply-use balance. The price indicators are the major price indices compiled by INSEE (consumer price indices or producer price indices), which are available either monthly or quarterly. In this case, too, the sources are the same as for the annual accounts and calibration is therefore almost perfect.

Values added for institutional sectors are obtained by difference between output and intermediate consumption. Wages and salaries in the market sector are estimated using statistics of hours worked combined with hourly wage rates. Recently, the French quarterly accountants have introduced a direct quarterly indicator of the wage bill paid by general government. Taxes, social contributions and social benefits are for the most part available on a quarterly basis. The gross operating surplus is obtained as the difference between resources and uses, and not from a direct survey of profits, as in some other countries. Relations with the rest of the world are obtained through the balance of payments, which is available monthly. For certain items, no quarterly indicator is available. In this case, quarterly interpolation within the annual series is carried out by an automatic method known as quarterly smoothing; therefore, the quarterly accounts do not provide any real information regarding the within-year pattern of the series.

The French system of quarterly national accounts covers all the input/output tables and institutional sector accounts (see Chapter 10), even if they are simplified compared to the annual accounts. The three approaches of GDP (expenditure, production, income) are thus present (even if they are not estimated independently from each other). Some other countries, such as the US, do not cover all approaches. For example, the production approach is not yet available quarterly in the US national accounts.

Box 4. **Resources of national accounts departments**

Good statistics are the result of a complex process which needs appropriate human resources. For example, INSEE, the French statistical office, employs 6 300 staff. National accounts departments constitute only a very small part of this: only 126 are directly employed to process the national accounts in France. In Japan, the staff for national accounts is even less: 47. This is explained by the fact that national accountants do not directly organize surveys and/or other basic statistics, which are resource-costly. They use statistical or administrative data that are already processed by other statistical units and transform these data into the definitions of the national accounts. Thus, in fact, the total cost for processing national accounts is much more than the cost of the staff directly devoted to its compilation. Still, when compared to the resources devoted to company accounts, those devoted to national accounts appear low. Some may consider that it is already sufficiently costly for statistics. Others consider that, in the context of the increasing importance of national accounts, in particular for the monitoring of public finance, the resources directly devoted to national accounts remain insufficient.

Exercises   *Answers at www.SourceOECD.org/understandingnationalaccounts*

Exercise 1: Quarterly *versus* annual results

Calculate the annual averages for years A and B of the series for quarterly GDP in volume as shown in the following table. Make a graph for the quarters, including points for the annual averages. Illustrate the difference between the change in the annual averages and the within-year economic situations.

AQ1	600.00
AQ2	420.00
AQ3	300.00
AQ4	150.00
BQ1	180.00
BQ2	250.00
BQ3	380.00
BQ4	450.00

Exercise 2: Annualisation, year-on-year changes, statistical carryover

The table below shows the quarterly series for French GDP in volume for the years 2001, 2002 and 2003. *Question 1:* calculate the annual GDP for the years 2001 and 2002. *Question 2:* show the quarterly absolute levels in 2001 "at annual level". *Question 3:* calculate the 2001 annual average on the basis of these figures and find the GDP for 2001. *Question 4:* calculate the annual average change between 2001 and 2002. *Question 5:* calculate the quarterly change between Q3 2003 and Q2 2003. *Question 6:* Express this change at "annualised rate". *Question 7:* calculate the year-on-year change for Q3 2003. *Question 8:* calculate the statistical carryover in Q3 2003. Comment on all these results.

Table 4. **GDP at constant 1995 prices**

	2001	2002	2003
Q1	345.75	348.61	350.91
Q2	345.78	350.94	349.68
Q3	347.22	351.70	350.98
Q4	346.22	350.73	

Exercise 3: Calibration/fitting: the French method for calculating the quarterly accounts

This exercise consists of breaking down the stages of the "calibration/fitting" method used for the French quarterly accounts and described in the section "The sources and methods used for the French quarterly accounts". Note that the statistical methods used in this exercise are ultra simplified compared with the methods used by INSEE or other countries that also use this type of methods, but the exercise at least makes it possible to understand the underlying principles.

The tables below show a series for the quarterly indicator (QI) and the corresponding annual item in the national accounts (AA). *Stage 1:* calculate annual averages AI for the indicator series. *Stage 2:* draw a graph showing the point cloud for the abscissa AI and the ordinate AA. Verify that the straight line regression equation AA = a*AI + b is an acceptable approximation. *Stage 3:* estimate, by the least squares method, the parameters a and b for the model AA = a*Ai + b. *Stage 4:* calculate the non fitted quarterly series (QA) by applying the same model to the quarterly absolute figure QA = (a/4).*QI + b/4 and calculate the annual residuals. *Stage 5:* deduce from this the quarterly residuals (by simply dividing by 4). *Stage 6:* calculate the calibrated/fitted QA series. This constitutes the final quarterly accounts series.

Table 5. Quarterly indicator QI (over five years)

	Y1	Y2	Y3	Y4	Y5
Q1	105.2	103.9	111.5	117.6	116.3
Q2	106.7	105.9	117.2	118.1	115.8
Q3	104.3	107.8	117.3	119.1	114.2
Q4	104.2	109.6	117.5	117.4	112.0

Table 6. Annual accounts series AA (over same five years)

Y1	Y2	Y3	Y4	Y5
6 658.1	6 813.2	7 435.4	7 455.9	7 302.4

Chapter **12**

THE NATIONAL INCOME
AND PRODUCT ACCOUNTS
OF THE UNITED STATES (NIPA)

Following several quarters of falling real gross domestic product (GDP) in 2000 and 2001, the US economy showed considerable strength. For example, from the fourth quarter of 2001 through the fourth quarter of 2005, growth in the US economy as measured by real GDP averaged 3.2% per quarter (at an annual rate). ▶ I. However, because real GDP increased only 1.7% in the last quarter of 2005, it has been questioned whether the expansion that began in 2002 will continue.

> I. Estimates presented in this chapter reflect the official GDP estimates available on April 1, 2006. For a definition of "annual rates", see Chapter 11.

In its forecast published in March 2006, the OECD confirmed that this marked economic slowdown in the US in the fourth quarter of 2005 primarily reflected the adverse effects of the late-summer and early autumn hurricanes rather than fading underlying strength. Job creation has remained robust, and business confidence is consistent with "above-par" growth. All this confirmed that as forecasted in the December 2005 *OECD Economic Outlook*, US real GDP growth was expected to remain around 3.5% per year for 2006 and 2007.

This December 2005 OECD forecast was slightly more optimistic than US forecasters in early 2006. In the US, the National Association for Business Economics (NABE) has regularly published projections of economic activity since 1965 based on projections from a survey of a panel of expert forecasters.[1] The survey, released on February 27, 2006, was the first NABE survey to provide forecasts for both 2006 and 2007. According to the survey results, real growth for 2006 was projected to be 3.3%, a slight slowdown from the 3.5% growth in 2005. For 2007, the panel projected another slight slowdown in real growth to 3.1%, slightly less than the OECD forecasts. Despite unexpectedly weak fourth-quarter 2005 growth, the NABE panel has forecast an optimistic assessment of growth in early 2006. The panel projects 4.5% growth in the first-quarter GDP of 2006 (the largest since the third quarter of 2003) and 4% growth in the first half of the year. For the second half of 2006, the panel forecasted that growth will slow to about 3% and thinks that there is only a 15% chance the expansion will end in 2006 and a 25% chance that it will end in 2007.

Thus, many forecasters – whether at OECD or in the United States – predicted in 2006 that growth in the US economy will remain strong. Forecasts are of course prone to error. Reading this manual after 2007, the reader will be in a good position to judge whether the forecasts were right. In any case, all these projections are primarily based on the GDP and related measures from the US national income and product accounts, or NIPAs, which are the US non-financial national accounts. NIPAs are used by the executive and the legislative branches of government to prepare budget estimates and projections, by the central bank (the Federal Reserve Board) to set interest and exchange rates, by international organisations, and by the private sector to track and develop financial and investment strategies.

1. Background

The Great Depression of the 1930s and the resulting growing role of government in the US economy made clear the need for comprehensive measures of national income and output, leading to the development of a set of national income accounts. To meet this need, the Department of Commerce commissioned Nobel laureate Simon Kuznets of the National Bureau of Economic Research (NBER) to develop a set of national economic accounts. Kuznets directed a small group of economists within the Commerce Department's Bureau of Foreign and Domestic Commerce. He coordinated the work of researchers at the NBER and his staff at the Department of Commerce. The first official continuing series on national income was prepared with assistance from the NBER and published in 1934. The first set of accounts was presented in a report to Congress in 1937 and in a research report, *National Income, 1929-35*, and by the late 1930s estimates were expanded to include income by state and a monthly income series.

To support the World War II efforts, it became necessary to expand the income measures to include product, or expenditure, estimates. By the mid-1940s, annual estimates of gross national product (GNP) had been developed and formed the basis for a set of income and product accounts, consisting of: a consolidated production account; sector income and outlay account; and a consolidated saving-investment account. When these three accounts became available, they were used for the analysis of wartime production goals and the development of anti-inflation policies. Wartime planning needs also contributed to the development of input-output accounts by Nobel laureate Wassily Leontief. The publication of *National Income, 1947 Edition* by the Office of Business Economics (OBE), created by the Commerce Department in 1945, resulted from a major effort to refine concepts, to expand the available data sources and to improve estimating techniques.

During the next three decades, interest in stimulating economic growth and in the sources of growth led to the development of official input-output tables, capital stock estimates, and more detailed and timely state and local personal income estimates. In the late 1960s and 1970s, concerns about inflation led the Bureau of Economic Analysis (BEA) to develop improved measures of prices and inflation-adjusted (real) output. In 1972, BEA was formed as the successor agency to OBE.

In the 1980s, BEA expanded the information on international trade in services in both the International Transactions Accounts and the NIPAs. To improve the measurement of real output, BEA worked with the IBM Corporation to develop quality adjusted price and output measures for computers. BEA also dealt with rising concerns about the underground economy's impact on US economic statistics by revamping how it adjusted tax-return information used to prepare the NIPAs, resulting in major upward revisions to several income components.

BEA began the 1990s by recognising GDP as the most appropriate measure of US output. In the mid-1990s, three major improvements were incorporated: BEA adopted a chain-type Fisher index formula for measuring changes in real GDP and prices; BEA reclassified government fixed investment from consumption to investment; and BEA introduced a methodology for calculating depreciation (based on empirical evidence on the prices of used equipment and structures in resale markets) that showed that depreciation for most types of assets approximates a geometric pattern. In 1999, BEA recognized investment in software, introduced a new methodology for estimating the real value of banking that better captures productivity growth in the industry, and identified capital transfers.

It should be noted that several of the changes made by BEA in the 1990s brought the NIPA measures of GDP, investment, and saving more closely in line with the 1993 System of National Accounts (SNA). In 2003, some of the improvements incorporated by BEA also helped bring the NIPA classifications of various transactions into conformity with the SNA classifications. These improvements included: the redefinition of national income; a more complete measure of implicit financial services that recognizes that both borrowers and depositors receive these services from banks; and the introduction of new measures into the NIPAs, including the operating surplus, income payments (or receipts) on assets, and net saving. In addition, the NIPA framework, as expressed in a series of summary accounts, was expanded from five to seven accounts, including the creation of two foreign transactions accounts – the foreign transactions current account and the foreign transactions capital account. BEA also made several changes to sector definitions to improve consistency with the SNA, as well as with BEA's input-output (IO) accounts, the Federal Reserve Board (FRB) flow of funds accounts, and the Bureau of Labor Statistics (BLS) productivity statistics. BEA made other improvements to the NIPAs in 2003. It recognized the implicit services provided by property and casualty insurance, introduced a new methodology for insured losses that reduced large swings in measured services, and began to present industry estimates on the basis of the new North American industry classification system (NAICS), adopted in 1997 by the United States, Canada and Mexico.

Although these changes to the NIPAs have increased the consistency of the NIPAs and SNA, a few differences remain. Some of these differences are likely to continue since they reflect the needs of the US users, the availability of reliable source data and the structure of the US economy. An overview of these differences is provided at the end of this chapter in section "Going a step further: Differences between the NIPAs and SNA". Many differences occur only in terminology and not in substance. For example, the NIPA name for household final consumption expenditures is personal consumption expenditures (PCE).

Most of the US economic accounts are prepared by BEA, a statistical agency located in the Department of Commerce. In addition to the NIPAs, BEA prepares estimates of the stock of fixed assets and the US international transactions accounts (ITAs), which provide US transactions and balances with the rest of the world and include current, capital and financial accounts, as well as the net US international investment position. The Federal Reserve Board (FRB) prepares the Flow of Funds Accounts (FFAs) that provide capital accounts, a financial account and balance sheets for selected sectors. Productivity estimates are prepared by the

BLS, a statistical agency located in the Department of Labor. Although both the FFAs and the productivity estimates are prepared separately from the NIPAs, there is close coordination between BEA and the other agencies.

BEA describes its mission as providing timely, relevant and accurate economic accounts data in an objective and cost-effective manner. It also works to promote a better understanding of the US economy in the publication of its accounts. The accounts and the supporting information are available either in its monthly magazine, the *Survey of Current Business* or on its website at *www.bea.gov*.

In producing its economic accounts, BEA reflects the mandates of the President and Congress as indicated in annual budget appropriations. In addition to the budget, BEA adheres to the provisions of the applicable legislation and policy directives. For example, these provisions specify the release procedures for certain key economic indicators and require the release of detailed information about the quality of the data published by all federal government agencies.

Although the NIPAs are BEA's main project, BEA has extended its estimates to cover a wide range of economic activities. In addition to the NIPAs, BEA now prepares national, regional, industry and international accounts, providing information on such key issues as economic growth, regional economic development, inter-industry relationships and the US position in the global economy.

To produce these programs, BEA collects data from other statistical agencies as well as from businesses. Most of these data come from over 400 surveys and other data collections sponsored by other federal agencies, that is, from statistical agencies, aggregate tax data, administrative and regulatory sources, and private trade sources. BEA also conducts its own surveys, mostly on direct investment and on international trade in services. To make sure that its programs are providing appropriate measures for a changing economy, BEA staff engages in research and consults with researchers in other government agencies and the FRB. BEA also participates in the activities of the privately sponsored Conference on Research in Income and Wealth (CRIW). For almost 70 years, the CRIW has sponsored conferences and workshops that deal with measurement issues primarily related to economic accounting. These activities bring together economists from government, academic, business and non-profit organisations to discuss problems of vital importance to BEA, the FRB and the BLS.

BEA obtains more direct input through a BEA Advisory Committee and through participation with the Census Bureau and BLS in the Federal Economic Statistics Advisory Committee. Both committees, which consist of economists and statisticians from academia and business, meet regularly to provide advice and recommendations on agency policy, including the advisability of following international guidelines.

2. NIPA Tables

The NIPAs consist of the NIPA summary accounts (see Table 1) and other NIPA tables. The summary accounts provide the conceptual framework for the NIPAs; the other nearly 300 regularly published NIPA tables provide monthly, quarterly and annual detailed estimates, including key measures not presented in the summary accounts. NIPA estimates are regularly published in the *Survey*; supplemental estimates, including additional detail, are made available on BEA's website.[2] As with most countries, the framework, frequency, timeliness, coverage and presentation of the US national accounts largely reflect the availability of reliable source data and the needs of data users.

Table 1. Summary national income and product accounts, 2004

Billions of US dollars, current prices

Line			Line		
	Account 1. Domestic income and product account				
1	Compensation of employees, paid	6 693.4	15	Personal consumption expenditures (3-3)	8 214.3
2	Wage and salary accruals	5 395.2	16	Durable goods	987.8
3	Disbursements (3-12 and 5-11)	5 395.2	17	Nondurable goods	2 368.3
4	Wage accruals less disbursements (4-9 and 6-11)	0.0	18	Services	4 858.2
5	Supplements to wages and salaries (3-14)	1 298.1	19	Gross private domestic investment	1 928.1
6	Taxes on production and imports (4-16)	852.8	20	Fixed investment (6-2)	1 872.6
7	Less: Subsidies (4-8)	43.5	21	Non residential	1 198.8
8	Net operating surplus	2 719.4	22	Structures	298.4
9	Private enterprises (2-19)	2 722.4	23	Equipment and software.	900.4
10	Current surplus of government enterprises (4-26)	−3.0	24	Residential	673.8
11	Consumption of fixed capital (6-13)	1 435.3	25	Change in private inventories (6-4)	55.4
			26	Net exports of goods and services	−624.0
12	Gross domestic income	11 657.5	27	Exports (5-1)	1 173.8
			28	Imports (5-9)	1 797.8
13	Statistical discrepancy (6-19)	76.8	29	Government consumption expenditures and gross investment (4-1 *plus* 6-3)	2 215.9
			30	Federal	827.6
			31	National defense	552.7
			32	Nondefense	274.9
			33	State and local	1 388.3
14	**Gross domestic product**	**11 734.3**	34	**Gross domestic product**	**11 734.3**
	Account 2. Private enterprise income account				
1	Income payments on assets	2 182.4	19	Net operating surplus, private enterprises (1-9)	2 722.4
2	Interest and miscellaneous payments (3-20 and 4-21)	2 057.8	20	Income receipts on assets	1 736.4
3	Dividend payments to the rest of the world (5-14) ..	68.4	21	Interest (3-20)	1 426.9
4	Reinvested earnings on foreign direct investment in the United States (5-15)	56.2	22	Dividend receipts from the rest of the world (5-6)	104.3
5	Business current transfer payments (net)	91.1	23	Reinvested earnings on US direct investment abroad (5-7)	205.2

Table 1. Summary national income and product accounts, 2004 (cont.)

Billions of US dollars, current prices

Line			Line		
6	To persons (net) (3-24)	33.0			
7	To government (net) (4-24)	51.5			
8	To the rest of the world (net) (5-19)	6.6			
9	Proprietors' income with inventory valuation and capital consumption adjustments (3-17)	889.6			
10	Rental income of persons with capital consumption adjustment (3-18)	134.2			
11	Corporate profits with inventory valuation and capital consumption adjustments	1 161.5			
12	Taxes on corporate income	271.1			
13	To government (4-17)	258.9			
14	To the rest of the world (5-19)	12.3			
15	Profits after tax with inventory valuation and capital consumption adjustments	890.3			
16	Net dividends (3-21 *plus* 4-22)	493.0			
17	Undistributed corporate profits with inventory valuation and capital consumption adjustments (6-10)	397.3			
18	Uses of private enterprise income	4 458.9	24	Sources of private enterprise income	4 458.9

Account 3. Personal income and outlay account

Line			Line		
1	Personal current taxes (4-15)	1 049.1	10	Compensation of employees, received	6 687.6
2	Personal outlays	8 512.5	11	Wage and salary disbursements	5 389.4
3	Personal consumption expenditures (1-15)	8 214.3	12	Domestic (1-3 less 5-11)	5 386.4
4	Personal interest payments (3-20)	186.7	13	Rest of the world (5-3)	3.0
5	Personal current transfer payments	111.5	14	Supplements to wages and salaries (1-5)	1 298.1
6	To government (4-25)	68.6	15	Employer contributions for employee pension and insurance funds	895.5
7	To the rest of the world (net) (5-17)	42.9	16	Employer contributions for government social insurance	402.7
8	Personal saving (6-9)	151.8	17	Proprietors' income with inventory valuation and capital consumption adjustments (2-9)	889.6
			18	Rental income of persons with capital consumption adjustment (2-10)	134.2
			19	Personal income receipts on assets	1 396.5
			20	Personal interest income (2-2 *plus* 3-4 *plus* 4-7 *plus* 5-5 *less* 2-21 *less* 4-21 *less* 5-13)	905.9
			21	Personal dividend income (2-16 *less* 4-22)	490.6
			22	Personal current transfer receipts	1 427.5
			23	Government social benefits (4-4)	1 394.5
			24	From business (net) (2-6)	33.0
			25	Less: Contributions for government social insurance (4-19)	822.2
9	Personal taxes, outlays, and saving	9 713.3	26	Personal income	9 713.3

Account 4. Government receipts and expenditures account

Line			Line		
1	Consumption expenditures (1-29)	1 843.4	14	Current tax receipts	2 169.9
2	Current transfer payments	1 423.4	15	Personal current taxes (3-1)	1 049.1
3	Government social benefits	1 397.5	16	Taxes on production and imports (1-6)	852.8

Table 1. Summary national income and product accounts, 2004 (cont.)

Billions of US dollars, current prices

Line			Line		
4	To persons (3-23)	1 394.5	17	Taxes on corporate income (2-13)	258.9
5	To the rest of the world (5-18)	3.0	18	Taxes from the rest of the world (5-18)	9.2
6	Other current transfer payments to the rest of the world (net) (5-18)	25.9	19	Contributions for government social insurance (3-25)	822.2
7	Interest payments (3-20)	310.3	20	Income receipts on assets	99.0
8	Subsidies (1-7)	43.5	21	Interest and miscellaneous receipts (2-2 and 3-20)	96.6
9	Less: Wage accruals less disbursements (1-4)	0.0	22	Dividends (3-21)	2.4
10	Net government saving (6-12)	−412.3	23	Current transfer receipts	120.1
11	Federal	−406.5	24	From business (net) (2-7)	51.5
12	State and local	−5.9	25	From persons (3-6)	68.6
			26	Current surplus of government enterprises (1-10)	−3.0
13	Government current expenditures and net saving	3 208.2	27	Government current receipts	3 208.2

Account 5. Foreign transactions current account					
1	Exports of goods and services (1-27)	1 173.8	9	Imports of goods and services (1-28)	1 797.8
2	Income receipts from the rest of the world	415.4	10	Income payments to the rest of the world	361.7
3	Wage and salary receipts (3-13)	3.0	11	Wage and salary payments (1-3)	8.8
4	Income receipts on assets	412.4	12	Income payments on assets	352.8
5	Interest (3-20)	102.9	13	Interest (3-20)	228.2
6	Dividends (2-22)	104.3	14	Dividends (2-3)	68.4
7	Reinvested earnings on US direct investment abroad (2-23)	205.2	15	Reinvested earnings on foreign direct investment in the United States (2-4)	56.2
			16	Current taxes and transfer payments to the rest of the world (net)	81.5
			17	From persons (net) (3-7)	42.9
			18	From government (net) (4-5 plus 4-6 less 4-18)	19.7
			19	From business (net) (2-8 plus 2-14)	18.9
			20	Balance on current account, national income and product accounts (7-1)	−651.7
8	Current receipts from the rest of the world	1 589.2	21	Current payments to the rest of the world and balance on current account	1 589.2

Account 6. Domestic capital account					
1	Gross domestic investment	2 300.6	8	Net saving	136.8
2	Private fixed investment (1-20)	1 872.6	9	Personal saving (3-8)	151.8
3	Government fixed investment (1-29)	372.5	10	Undistributed corporate profits with inventory valuation and capital consumption adjustments (2-17)	397.3
4	Change in private inventories (1-25)	55.4	11	Wage accruals less disbursements (private) (1-4)	0.0
5	Capital account transactions (net) (7-2)	1.6	12	Net government saving (4-10)	−412.3
6	Net lending or net borrowing (−), national income and product accounts (7-3)	−653.4	13	Plus: Consumption of fixed capital (1-11)	1 435.3
			14	Private	1 206.2

Table 1. **Summary national income and product accounts, 2004** *(cont.)*

Billions of US dollars, current prices

Line			Line		
			15	Government	229.1
			16	General government	192.0
			17	Government enterprises	37.2
			18	Equals: Gross saving	1 572.0
			19	Statistical discrepancy (1-13)	76.8
7	Gross investment, capital account transactions, and net lending	1 648.9	20	Gross saving and statistical discrepancy	1 648.9
			Account 7. Foreign transactions capital account		
			2	Capital account transactions (net) (6-5)	1.6
			3	Net lending or net borrowing (-), national income and product accounts (6-6)	−653.4
1	Balance on current account, national income and product accounts (5-20)	−651.7	4	Capital account transactions (net) and net lending, national income and product accounts	−651.7

The seven NIPA summary accounts presented above cover the transactions that are grouped in the SNA as the production account, the distribution and use of income accounts, and the capital accounts. Relative to the SNA (see Figure 1), the NIPA domestic income and product account (Summary account 1) provides estimates of GDP and is similar to the SNA production account for the total economy. NIPA Summary Account 1 also provides information about the income earned in the production of GDP; in the SNA, these items are included in the generation of income account. The NIPA personal income and outlay account (summary account 3) and the government current receipts and expenditures account (Summary Account 4), and part of the private enterprise income account (summary account 2) roughly correspond to the remaining SNA distribution and use of income accounts for the domestic sectors (summary account 2 actually corresponds most closely to the SNA entrepreneurial income account). The NIPA domestic capital account (summary account 6) corresponds to the SNA capital account for the total economy. Both the NIPAs and SNA include a current account and a capital account for the rest-of-the world sector (summary accounts 5 and 7). The major entries in the NIPA summary accounts are described below for each account.[3]

Account 1, the domestic income and product account, shows the consolidated production of all sectors of the economy as the sum of goods and services sold to final users on the right side and the income generated by that production on the left side. GDP, (1-34 ▶ **II.**) the featured measure of US output, is the market value of the goods and services produced by labor and property located in the United States. GDP is measured by the sum of goods and services produced in the

II. This means line 34 of Summary Account 1.

United States and sold to final users (type of expenditures approach). Gross domestic income (GDI) (1-12) is the costs incurred and the incomes earned in the production of GDP. Although,

Figure 1. **NIPA Summary Accounts**

Transactions	Domestic accounts			Rest of the world
	Economic sectors			
	Business	Government	Personal	
Production	Domestic income and product (Account 1)			Foreign transactions current account (Account 5)
Income and outlay	Private enterprise income (Account 2)	Government current receipts and expenditures (Account 4)	Personal income and outlay (Account 3)	
Saving and investment	Domestic capital account (Account 6)			Foreign transactions capital account (Account 7)

in theory, GDP should equal GDI, in practice they differ because their components are estimated using largely independent and less-than-perfect source data. In the US accounts, this difference, the "statistical discrepancy," is not allocated among various GDP or GDI components, but is recorded as an "income" component. The section "Going a step further: Statistical Discrepancies in the NIPAs", provides additional information.

Account 2, the private enterprise income account, provides additional information on the sources and uses of income by private enterprises, which account for most of the output in the US economy. This account shows sources of private enterprise income (2-24) on the right side of the account and uses of private enterprise income (2-18) on the left side. Private enterprises consist of private businesses, owner-occupied housing, and (for purposes of estimating monetary and imputed interest payments and imputed interest receipts) nonprofit institutions serving households. Government enterprises are not included in this account because complete estimates on sources and uses of government enterprise income are not currently available.

Accounts 3, 4 and 5 show the receipts and expenditures of the other major sectors of the US economy. Account 3 is the personal income and outlay account and covers the NIPA personal sector, which is made up of households and institutions. It shows "personal income" (3-26) on the right side and the disposition of this income in terms of personal taxes, outlays and saving on the left side. Account 4, the government receipts and expenditures account, shows government current receipts (4-27) on the right side and government current expenditures and net saving (4-13) on the left side. Account 5, the foreign transactions current account, shows current payments to the rest of the world and balance on current account (5-21) on the right side, and current receipts from the rest of the world and balance (5-8) on the left.

Account 6 is the domestic capital account and provides information on the saving and investment of the domestic sectors of the economy. Account 7 is the foreign transactions capital account and provides information on capital transactions with the rest of the world. Account 6 shows the gross saving and the statistical discrepancy (6-20) on the right side and gross domestic investment, capital account transactions and net lending (6-7) on the left side. Net lending or net borrowing (–), national income and product accounts (6-6) is equal to the balance on current account (5-20) less capital account transactions (6-5). Account 7 shows on the right side the sum of two entries from Account 6, capital transfer payments to the rest of the world (net) and net lending or net borrowing (–), national income and product accounts. The left side shows the balance on current account, national income and product accounts (7-1).

All of the NIPA tables, with the most recent estimates, are available on the BEA's website. There are about 100 tables with monthly or quarterly estimates. The remaining tables either show annual estimates of additional detail than shown quarterly, tables showing data on special topics, such as employment and hours worked, or tables showing comparisons of source data with NIPA aggregates. Several NIPA tables feature measures that have no counterparts in the seven NIPA summary accounts. Information about these measures, which also are shown in BEA's news releases, is provided in Box 1.

Box 1. **Featured Measures of NIPA Tables**

Gross domestic purchases is the market value of goods and services purchased by US residents, regardless of where those goods and services were produced. It is GDP *minus* net exports of goods and services; equivalently, it is the sum of PCE, gross private domestic investment and government consumption expenditures and gross investment. BEA uses gross domestic purchases for its featured measure of price change because it excludes prices paid by foreigners for US production and includes prices of imports. *Final sales to domestic purchasers* is gross domestic purchases *minus* the change in private inventories. Some analysts refer to this measure as **"domestic demand"** or **"final domestic demand"**. *Final sales of domestic product* is GDP *minus* change in private inventories; equivalently, it is the sum of PCE, private fixed domestic investment, government consumption expenditures and gross investment, and net exports of goods and services. *Gross national product* is the market value of the goods and services produced by labor and property supplied by US residents. In the SNA, this measure is called Gross national income (GNI). In the NIPAs, GNI and GNP differ by the statistical discrepancy. In the NIPAs, GNI is used to calculate a national saving rate. *Gross value added*, which in the NIPAs equals GDP measured using the expenditures approach, is shown in the NIPAs as the sum of the gross product of the business, household and institutions, and general government sectors. *Personal saving as a percentage of disposable personal income*, frequently referred to as **"the personal saving rate"**, is the ratio of personal saving to disposable personal income. *Gross saving as a percentage of gross national income*, sometimes referred to as **"the national saving rate"**, is calculated as the ratio of gross saving (the sum of gross private saving and gross government saving) to GNI.

3. Dissemination of NIPAs

Each month, BEA releases quarterly estimates of most NIPA tables and monthly estimates of personal income and outlays. (Although estimates of the NIPA summary accounts are prepared quarterly, they are usually released only annually.) The quarterly GDP estimates are released through a news release on the following schedule: "advance" estimates are released near the end of the first month after the end of the quarter; as more detailed and more comprehensive data become available, "preliminary" and "final" estimates are released near the end of the second and third months, respectively.[4] The three sets of quarterly GDP estimates – the advance, preliminary and final – are referred to by BEA as the "current" estimates.[5]

For the advance release, estimates of GNI, GDI, national income, corporate profits and interest payments and receipts are not prepared. Except for fourth-quarter estimates, the initial estimates for these series are released with the preliminary GDP estimates, and the revised estimates are released with the final GDP estimates. For the fourth quarter, these estimates are released only with the final GDP estimates. The monthly personal income and outlays estimates are released in another news release a day or so following the release of the quarterly estimates; the latest available month of data lags by one month.

When the quarterly GDP and monthly personal income and outlays estimates are released, estimates for preceding quarters or months are generally not revised except as follows. At the time of the release of the preliminary quarterly GDP estimate, revisions to the preceding quarter (and corresponding months) are made to private wages and salaries and related income components to reflect newly available comprehensive source data on wages and salaries. (See Section 5: "Compilation of quarterly gross domestic product".) Each July, an annual NIPA revision is usually carried out, and revisions are made to the months and quarters of the most recent calendar year and of the two preceding years. These revisions are timed to incorporate newly available major annual source data. Lastly, at about five-year intervals, comprehensive revisions are carried out. These revisions incorporate three major types of improvements: 1) definitional and classification changes that update the accounts to portray more accurately the evolving US economy; 2) statistical changes that update the accounts to reflect the introduction of new and improved methodologies and the incorporation of newly available and revised source data, such as new benchmark estimates for 1997 from the benchmark I-O accounts; and 3) presentational changes that update the NIPA tables to reflect definitional, classification, and statistical changes and to make the tables more informative. Because of the scope of these improvements, to the extent necessary and feasible, estimates are revised back to 1929.

The NIPA estimates are first published through the quarterly GDP and monthly personal income and outlays news releases. At 8:30 in the morning of each release date, a printed copy of the release is given to representatives of the media at BEA's main office in Washington, DC, and simultaneously posted on BEA's website. (The estimates in the GDP news releases cover about 30 NIPA tables; estimates in the personal income release cover the eight monthly NIPA tables.) For GDP, the release is accompanied by a "Technical Note", which provides information about BEA's assumptions for key missing source data and provides information about methodologies used to prepare the newly released estimates.

Later that same morning and in the following several days, additional information is posted on BEA's website. The posting usually starts with the 100 NIPA tables that will appear in the next issue of the *Survey*. This detail supplements the quarterly estimates included in the news release. In addition, a set of "Interactive NIPA tables" on BEA's website provide quarterly and annual estimates for all previous periods, as well as estimates for the NIPA tables showing monthly estimates. The next issues of the *Survey* also will include an analysis of the US economy as depicted by the newly released NIPA estimates. This analysis, "The Business Situation", also is posted on BEA's website prior to printing the *Survey*.

In addition, BEA posts to its website what it calls "supplemental estimates". These estimates include monthly and quarterly detail not included in the NIPA tables, additional information on BEA's assumptions for missing source data in the latest advance GDP estimates and SNA-related NIPA data. The additional (underlying) NIPA detail consists primarily of estimates used by BEA to prepare the monthly and quarterly NIPA estimates that BEA considers unreliable as individual series. The information on "Key source data and assumptions" for the first (advance) estimate of each quarter provides the key source data and assumptions used by BEA in preparing the quarterly estimates of GDP and its major expenditure components; it differs from the information provided in the "Technical Note" in that it provides information on all monthly source data. A table identifies each of these source data, indicates the assumptions for missing data, and notes the source data that are subject to revision by the source agency before the preliminary GDP estimate is released.

The information on SNA-related estimates consists of two entries. The first is "Estimates prepared by BEA for international comparisons based on the System of National Accounts". These estimates are SNA-based estimates prepared annually, usually several weeks after the release of revised annual data, which occurs in late July. The estimates are prepared in response to a questionnaire used by the OECD and are slightly different from the official NIPA estimates published by BEA; the OECD estimates are more comparable with those of other countries. The second set of SNA-related estimates appears as "Gross Domestic Product by final expenditure category (International Style)". These tables present quarterly NIPA final expenditure data in a format that is more consistent with accounts and presentations used by the OECD. The estimates show final consumption expenditures (government and personal consumption expenditures) and gross domestic investment (government gross investment and gross private domestic investment).

The remaining NIPA tables mostly provide annual estimates and usually are published each year in the August issue of the *Survey* at the time of an annual NIPA revision. At the time of a comprehensive revision, all NIPA tables are published in the *Survey*; the data shown in these tables usually is limited to the period since the last comprehensive revision.

4. Other NIPA-related programmes

The NIPA summary accounts and tables discussed here do not include estimates from other BEA programmes that provide source data used for the preparation of the NIPAs or that use NIPA estimates as benchmarks. The following discussion, summarised in Figure 2, covers the programmes that produce these estimates, which are the ITAs, the benchmark I-O accounts, fixed assets and the annual industry accounts programme. Detailed information on each of the programs is available on BEA's website.

International Transactions Accounts

The ITAs provide monthly estimates of international trade in goods and services (prepared jointly by BEA and the Census Bureau) and quarterly and annual estimates of the US international transactions accounts. The ITAs also are revised annually, with the revised estimates published in the July issue of the *Survey*. The balance on current account, which is measured as net receipts or payments on goods, services, income and unilateral current transfers, is the basis for all foreign transactions in the benchmark and annual I-O accounts as well as in the NIPAs. Annually, NIPA Table 4.3 reconciles differences between the two accounts. Quarterly, an abbreviated reconciliation is published in the *Survey* in Appendix A, under "Additional Information About the NIPA Estimates".

Benchmark Input-Output accounts

The SNA includes an integrated set of supply and use tables that are related to the goods and services account. BEA produces these tables as part of its industry accounts program and uses the benchmark tables to provide the goods and services estimates for the NIPAs. The benchmark I-O accounts provide standard "make" (supply) and "use" tables at market prices. The standard make and use tables, which are constructed before the redefinitions of selected secondary products, provide data on gross output and intermediate inputs that are consistent with the GDP-by-industry and annual I-O accounts. As discussed below, the benchmark I-O accounts also provide capital flow tables for use in the preparation of BEA's fixed assets estimates. Benchmark I-O accounts for 1997 were published in 2002; the 2002 benchmark will be released in 2007.

Fixed assets

BEA prepares annual estimates of the stocks of equipment and software and of structures owned by business and by government.[6] The estimates are presented at current-cost and as real estimates, expressed both as chain-type quantity indexes and chained dollars. Estimates also are provided for depreciation, the usual name for consumption of fixed capital (CFC), investment and historical-cost private net stocks and depreciation. And detailed estimates are provided for net stocks, depreciation, and investment by industry and by asset type. The estimates of CFC are derived using the perpetual inventory method, which

Figure 2. **Integration of US national accounts**

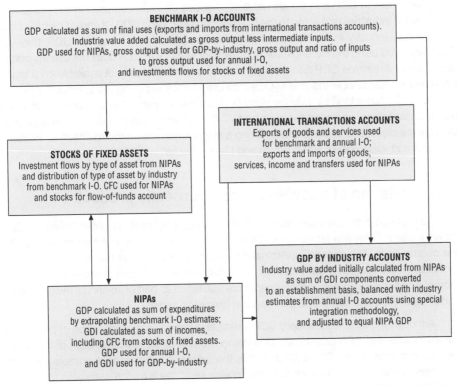

is based on investment flows and a geometric depreciation formula; the gross investment flows used for these calculations are the NIPAs. The industry distribution of investment by asset type is from the capital flow tables from the benchmark I-O accounts. The CFC estimates are used for the NIPA CFC component of GDI and to derive net investment in fixed assets. The CFC for private fixed assets also are used to derive the NIPA estimates of the capital consumption adjustment, which in turn are used to produce NIPA estimates of corporate profits and other types of business income. However, for general government fixed assets, BEA does not recognize catastrophic losses in NIPA CFC because including these losses, which are minor except during war times, would cause government output to increase.

Annual industry accounts

In 2004, BEA introduced integrated annual industry accounts, which consist of GDP-by-industry and annual I-O accounts. The integration provides detailed, consistent information on the structure of the US economy, including the annual contributions of private industries and government to GDP and the annual flow of goods and services used in the production processes of industries and going to the final uses that comprise GDP.[7] It should be noted that BEA's annual industry accounts do not provide an independently measured GDP; they use GDP measured using the expenditures approach, or NIPA GDP. BEA does not use the output approach to determine GDP because the source data needed are not available on a timely basis and are less reliable than the source data used for the expenditures approach. Also, the estimates of value added by industry published by BEA are calculated at market prices, and not at basic prices, as called for by the SNA. The different definitions of value added by industry are discussed in the section, "Going a step further: Alternative methods of valuation of output and value added: Basic Prices and Market Prices".

5. Compilation of quarterly gross domestic product

As reported in the previous section, BEA prepares a series of current estimates of GDP for each quarter. The first (advance) estimate is published at the end of the first month after the quarter ends. The second (preliminary) estimate is published at the end of the second month after the quarter ends. The third (final) estimate is published at the end of the third month. Additional estimates of each quarter are published as part of an annual revision (at the end of each July) or a comprehensive revision (every five years).

Although the advance quarterly GDP estimate is based on a combination of preliminary survey results and BEA projections of missing months of survey data, both of which are revised in subsequent GDP estimates, it is the advance estimate that attracts the most attention by users. This focus reflects the timeliness of the advance estimates (one of the most timely of OECD countries), the transparency of the processes used by BEA to prepare the estimates and their history of reliability. For example, a key to the transparency of the quarterly GDP estimates is the public availability of the source data and estimating procedures used by BEA to prepare these estimates. BEA provides this transparency with the following: 1) annual publication in the *Survey* of the source data and estimating methods for the major NIPA components; 2) public announcement, preferably in advance, of any changes of source data or estimating methods, including special adjustments; 3) publication of BEA's assumptions for missing source data for key indicator series at the time of the release of the advance estimate; and 4) publication of the underlying detail used to prepare the current quarterly GDP estimates.

As for the reliability of the advance and two other current quarterly GDP estimates, these estimates have a long history of reliability, defined as whether the GDP estimates present a consistent, general picture of the economy. This history, which is based on published studies of reliability, have found that the advance estimates have consistently indicated whether growth is positive or negative, whether growth is accelerating or decelerating, whether growth is high or low relative to the trend and where the economy is in relation to the business cycle.[8]

These studies show that the quarterly estimates correctly indicate the direction of change of real GDP 98% of the time, correctly indicate whether it is accelerating or decelerating 74% of the time, and correctly indicate whether real GDP growth is above, near or below trend growth more than 60% of the time. Other results of these studies are summarised in a special section of the advance quarterly GDP news release as shown in the section below, "Revisions to GDP".

Revisions to GDP

In the news release for the advance quarterly GDP estimates, BEA provides summary information on revisions by comparing successive estimates of current-dollar and real GDP. Based on data for 1983-2002, from the advance estimate to the preliminary estimate (one month later), the average revision to real GDP without regard to sign is 0.5 percentage point in terms of annual rate; from the advance estimate to the final estimate (two months later), it is 0.6 percentage point, and from the advance estimate to the latest estimate, it is 1.3 percentage points. The larger average revisions to the latest estimate reflect the fact that comprehensive revisions include major improvements to the NIPAs, such as the introduction of chain indexes, improved measurement of banking and the capitalisation of software.

The current quarterly GDP estimates are developed from summing individual estimates of the expenditure components of GDP. These individual quarterly estimates are prepared by the extrapolation of estimates of the previous quarter using, for example, direct indicators from monthly or quarterly surveys and indirect indicators, such as past trends. (Specific information on these source data is provided in the next section of this chapter.) The extrapolation procedure that is used is designed to prepare estimates based on the "best change method" from the previous quarterly estimates. Using this method, estimates for the most recent quarter are determined by calculating the change (usually in percentage terms) in the indicator series and multiplying that change with the published value for the previous quarter.[9] This calculation means that if the level of an indicator series has been revised, the revised "best level" is not reflected in the current estimate. Instead, best levels are not reflected until the time of an annual or comprehensive revision. Incorporating the source data on a best-change basis provides accurate measures of the change in the estimates for all periods, but it results in levels of the estimates that are not "best" and that are not fully consistent with the source data. In general, BEA incorporates source data on a best-change basis in order to preserve accurate estimates of growth and consistent time series.[10]

The process for all quarterly GDP estimates starts with a group of BEA specialists who prepare estimates for specific components.[11] This estimation process takes place over a two-week period set to coincide with the availability of key source data. The specialists work with the standard methodologies, obtain the source data and apply the appropriate estimating methodology that, depending on the quarterly estimate that is being prepared, may include developing assumptions for missing source data. In general, assumptions of missing source data are judgmental and are not based on projections using special statistical or econometric techniques. In addition, the assumptions are made about the seasonally adjusted values of the source data because BEA only prepares and publishes values that are not seasonally adjusted at the time of an annual revision. The specialists also review the source data for changes that would affect consistency, such as a new survey methodology, reliability (such as a high no response rate) or relevance for estimating the GDP component for a particular period, such as a natural disaster. Based on this review, the specialist determines if special adjustments are needed. For example, the wages and salaries in a given industry may exhibit a significant month-to-month drop because of a drop in average weekly hours, which are measured only for the middle week of the month. If this middle week is not representative of the entire month because severe weather occurred at the end of the month and forced many businesses to close, the specialist would recommend that an adjustment is needed. Another example where the specialist might make an adjustment also involves bad weather, such as hurricanes or tornadoes that cause major disruptions to retail businesses in a particular part of the country. If the sample underlying the survey of retail businesses used by BEA did not adequately represent that geographic area, the specialist might make a recommendation for an adjustment.

The estimates recommended by the specialists are then subject to a two-step review process. The first review is conducted by a special review team of senior economists who work with the specialists. This team reviews all of the recommended estimates to make sure that the assumptions for missing source data for all components have been made in a consistent manner, that adjustments have been made where needed, and that economic relationships between components, such as between inventory change and sales, are consistent with the state of economic activity depicted by the overall GDP estimate. Frequently, this review results in specialists revising their initial estimates. This review takes place over a three- to four-day period and ends two days before the publication of the GDP estimate. The team concludes its work by preparing a complete set of NIPA estimates for presentation for the second review step. This second review is conducted by BEA's senior staff the day before the estimates are published. They conduct a high-level review of the impact of assumptions for key source data on the major aggregates and compare the proposed GDP estimates to alternative measures of output, such as hours worked, industrial production, or private sector forecasts of GDP growth. They also review the reasonableness of the implications of the GDP estimate to the forthcoming quarterly estimates of labor productivity, which will be published the week after the publication of the GDP estimates. The senior staff review seldom results in changes to the estimates proposed by the review team, but the review does prepare them to respond to questions from users about the implications of the estimates.

Although the steps in the estimation process are the same for each of the three current GDP estimates, there are some important differences in the processes depending on the estimate. For the advance estimate, many of the monthly key source data series are available only for the first two months of the quarter, and the data for the first two months are subject to revision in subsequent months. As a result, the specialists and two groups that review the estimates focus on the assumptions for missing source data and, based on historical information, likely revisions to the available source data. For series for which there are data for all three months of the quarter, differences between the source data and the corresponding NIPA component are reviewed for anomalies. For example, such a review would be made of differences between the Consumer Price Index (CPI) and the PCE measures of price change; the known differences in these series are discussed in section "Going a step further: Differences between the Consumer Price Index and the Personal Consumption Expenditures Price Index". In addition, because there is no independent estimate of GDI, the implied estimates of corporate profits are reviewed partly through the use of available profits data from publicly held corporations.

For the preliminary estimates, more source data become available to replace the specialists' assumptions for missing data, and for the first three quarters of the year, direct estimates of corporate profits are available. Consequently, the review of the specialists estimates shifts from the assumptions for missing source data to the revisions from the incorporation of new and revised source data. The availability of direct estimates of corporate profits also shifts the focus of the review to the specialists' assumptions for missing source data for profits of certain industries. The most important difference between the review of the advance and the preliminary GDP estimates is that the availability of corporate profits provides an estimate of GDI and the statistical discrepancy. Because large changes in the statistical discrepancy indicate source data problems, when there are such changes, the review team in particular looks at the reliability of the NIPA expenditures and income components to determine if new adjustments are needed. For the final GDP estimate, there is even less missing source data and fewer assumptions to review. As previously noted, the direct measure of corporate profits and the statistical discrepancy become available for the first time so these estimates are reviewed for the first time in a manner similar to that used for the preliminary estimates for the other quarters. In addition, the specialists and review team look at past revisions to source data to determine any patterns of future revision that might warrant additional adjustments.

As in other OECD countries, one of the major purposes of BEA's release process is to insure the integrity of these estimates.[12] This process consists of steps to ensure that the estimates have been prepared without any interference or influence by persons outside of BEA and that the estimates to be published are not given to anyone not authorised to have them. In particular, considering the importance given in the financial markets, for example, to the advance estimate of the US quarterly GDP, pre-release access to confidential information by people trading in the bond and stock market would give these traders an unfair advantage and infringe on the proper functioning of these and related markets. To preclude any outside influence or interference, BEA has put into place the following restrictions: 1) strict adherence to the release of data according to an announced schedule; 2) access to data prior to release is limited to certain BEA staff and to authorized policy officials outside of BEA by policy officials; and 3) physical and computer security necessary to limit access to those with a need to know.

A key security feature of the BEA process is reflected in the conduct of the senior management review of the proposed GDP estimates. This meeting, known as the "lock-up" meeting, is conducted the day before release, has limited attendance, and is conducted in a physically secure location at BEA's headquarters. Once the attendees of these meetings have been provided the proposed estimates, they may not be in contact with anyone outside BEA and are allowed only limited and monitored access to BEA staff for the duration of the meeting. Meetings usually begin before noon and continue until the estimates are finalised and the news release and supporting materials are completed and delivered to the Council of Economic Advisors. This delivery usually is made in the late afternoon by a member of the review team.

There is no additional distribution of the news release or the estimates until the next morning. If requested by policy officials of the Department of Commerce, BEA will provide these officials with a briefing on the estimates an hour before release under the condition that these officials remain at the briefing with no contact with anyone else until release time. This briefing is held in a secure room that prevents contact with anyone outside the room until release time; the room is equipped with computers for the media to prepare their stories and telephone lines for representatives of the broadcast media to record their stories at release time.

6. Methodologies for preparing selected components of current-dollar and real quarterly GDP

BEA publishes detailed and summary methodologies – both the source data and the estimating methods – used to prepare GDP and other NIPA components. Detailed methodologies are published either as separate methodology papers or in articles in the *Survey* that introduce new methodologies. Because improvements to these methodologies are regularly incorporated as part of each annual and comprehensive revision, BEA publishes a separate article in the *Survey* that provides summary information on the methodologies for the components of GDP and GDI.[13]

The methodologies used for the calculation of the advance quarterly estimate is the last step of a process that begins with the incorporation of the most recent benchmark I-O account into a comprehensive revision. First, revised annual estimates are calculated by extrapolating forward the estimates of NIPA components for the newly incorporated I-O benchmark.[14] Second, quarterly estimates are calculated by interpolating these new annual estimates. Third, quarterly estimates up to the most recent period are calculated by extrapolating forward the last interpolated quarterly estimate. Finally, the advance quarterly estimate for the latest quarter is calculated by extrapolation. For annual revisions for years when new benchmark I-O accounts are not available, the calculation of revised annual and quarterly estimates follows the same sequence, but only covers the three years.

This section provides information on the methodologies used to prepare the selected components of the advance quarterly estimates of current-dollar and real GDP. In Section 2, three aspects of the NIPAs were noted: current-dollar GDP is measured using the expenditures approach; the income approach measures GDI, which differs from GDP by the statistical discrepancy; and estimates using the output approach, or value added by industry, which are not prepared quarterly, are controlled to GDP from the expenditures approach. Thus, the discussion of the methodologies used for GDP is limited to the components that are the elements of final demand (household final expenditures, government final consumption, GFCF, exports *minus* imports).

For both quarterly and annual real GDP, the methodologies focus on the calculation of the detailed expenditures components of real GDP. These component estimates of prices and quantities are aggregated to GDP and its major components, such as PCE, using an index aggregation formula. BEA uses a Fisher index formula that allows for the effects of changes in relative prices and in the composition of output over time. As a result, the resulting quantity or price changes are not affected by the substitution bias that is associated with changes in quantities and prices calculated using a fixed-weighted (Laspeyres) formula. Annual changes in quantities and prices are calculated that incorporate weights from two adjacent years. Quarterly changes in quantities and prices are calculated using a Fisher formula that incorporates weights from two adjacent quarters, and quarterly indexes are adjusted for consistency to the annual indexes before per cent changes are calculated.

The chained-dollar values for the detailed GDP components will not necessarily sum to the chained-dollar estimate of GDP (or to any intermediate aggregate) in a table, because the relative prices that are used as weights for any period other than the reference year differ from those of the reference year. A measure of the effect of such differences is provided by a "residual" line – the difference between the chained-dollar value of the main aggregate in the table and the sum of the most detailed components in the table. For periods close to the reference year, when the relative prices that are used as weights have usually not changed much, the residuals tend to be small, and the chained-dollar estimates can be used to approximate the contributions to growth and to aggregate the detailed estimates. For periods further from the reference year, the residuals tend to be larger, and the chained-dollar estimates are less useful for analyses of contributions to growth (see Chapter 2).

For the current-dollar NIPA estimates, the 13 components of final demand covered in this section have been selected as representative of the estimating methods used by BEA and of the availability of source data for the advance GDP estimate, which for most users is the most important. In its annual presentation of summary methodologies, BEA shows source data and estimating method for components grouped by estimation method for the complete NIPA calculation and revision process. The presentations cover about 50 groupings of GDP components and 40 groupings of GDI components. For the components of real GDP, each of the three methods is discussed and examples of each method are provided.

12
THE NATIONAL INCOME AND PRODUCT
ACCOUNTS OF THE UNITED STATES (NIPA)
6. Methodologies for preparing selected components
of current-dollar and real quarterly GDP

Time availability of source data

For each component of GDP, methodologies used by BEA depend on the availability, timeliness and revision schedule of source data. BEA uses a wide range of monthly, quarterly and annual source data, or indicator series, to extrapolate from benchmark-year estimates. These data come from statistical agencies, federal tax returns, federal government regulatory programs, and private trade sources, and they vary greatly in their publication and revision practices.

The timely availability of the source data determines their use in the calculation of the estimates. For most components, source data are not available for all the months of the quarter at the time of an advance GDP estimate, thus BEA calculates trend-based data for the missing source data, some of which are quarterly and some of which are monthly. For most components, these trend-based estimates are replaced by indicator series in successive revisions. For example, for an advance GDP estimate, about 45% of GDP is calculated using quarterly indicators or monthly indicators that are available for all three months of a quarter; 30% is calculated using two months of the indicator series and one month of trend-based data; and 25% is calculated using only trend-based data.[15] For the final quarterly estimate of GDP, which is published two months later, 78% of GDP is calculated from indicator series, only 1% from a combination of indicator series and trend-based data, and 21% from only trend-based data. Only a few new indicator series, such as the Census Bureau's quarterly services survey and monthly data on electricity consumption, become available for the subsequent quarterly GDP estimates.

Because the trend-based data are important to the reliability of the advance GDP estimates, BEA provides users with these data by component. The most important of these data are those that are replaced by source data-based indicator series in successive current GDP estimates. To allow users to assess the validity of these trend-based data, which are usually based on the judgment of the BEA specialists, BEA provides users with the "assumptions for missing source data", and publishes the most important of these assumptions at the time of the GDP news release.

Estimating methods

BEA selects the estimating method for a component depending on the availability and reliability of the source data and the extent to which these source data meet NIPA definitions. To calculate the current-dollar estimates, BEA converts these source data using either a set of direct adjustments or one of the following estimating methods: the commodity-flow method; the retail control method; the perpetual inventory method; or the fiscal year analysis method. The commodity-flow method starts with estimates of domestic output, adjusts the output for imports, exports and inventory change, and allocates the result to purchases by households, business and government. The complete commodity-flow method is used for most expenditure components of the benchmark I-O accounts; an abbreviated form of this method is used to prepare annual and quarterly NIPA estimates for components for which the necessary source data are available.[16] The retail control method uses retail store sales data, adjusted to reflect sales to households, to estimate annual and quarterly household purchases of specific products. The perpetual inventory method, which cumulates flows to derive stocks, is used to calculate estimates of the stock of fixed assets, which is used to estimate annual and quarterly estimates of CFC. The fiscal year analysis method is used to estimate annual estimates of consumption expenditures and gross investment by the federal government. The estimates of expenditures are calculated by a programme based on detailed outlays data from budget documents. BEA adjusts these budget outlays to NIPA definitions and allocates them to the appropriate NIPA component, such as consumption expenditures or transfer payments. The fiscal year analysis also provides a set of control totals for quarterly NIPA estimates.

For the estimates of real GDP, BEA uses three methods: deflation, quantity extrapolation and direct valuation. The most widely used method is the deflation method in which a quantity index is calculated by dividing the current-dollar index by an appropriate price index. In the quantity extrapolation method, quantity indexes are used to extrapolate from the base-year value of 100. In the direct valuation method, quantity indexes are calculated by multiplying the base-year price by actual quantity data for the index period. In all three methods, quantity indexes are converted into real or chained-dollar GDP by multiplying the index number by the base year current-dollar value.

Methodologies for current-dollar GDP estimates of selected components of final demand

Table 1 of the November 2005 *Survey* summary methodology article shows the methodologies for about 50 groups of GDP components, organized by types of estimating method. The components selected below illustrate the various combinations of estimating methods and source data used for the annual estimates, other than a benchmark year, and for the advance quarterly GDP estimates. The first 12 components are listed in sequence by the number of months of source data available for the advance estimate. For components 1-4, key source data are available for the advance estimate for all three months of the quarter. For components 5-10, key source data are available for only two months of the quarter. For components 11 and 12, the advance quarterly estimate is based primarily on trend-based data calculated by BEA. The last component, investment in software, illustrates the use of different source data for the quarterly and annual estimates.

1. *PCE for most durable and nondurable goods.* Both the annual and quarterly estimates of these PCE components are calculated using the retail control method. For all but the most recent years, annual estimates are based on estimates of retail store sales from the Census Bureau (CB) annual retail trade survey. For the most recent year, the annual estimate is based on the CB monthly survey of retail trade. For the advance

12 THE NATIONAL INCOME AND PRODUCT
ACCOUNTS OF THE UNITED STATES (NIPA)
6. Methodologies for preparing selected components
of current-dollar and real quarterly GDP

quarterly estimate, all three months of survey results are available and subject to further revision.

2. *PCE for gasoline and oil.* Both the annual and quarterly estimates of this component are calculated as the product of physical quantities purchased and the average retail price. Except for the most recent year, gallons consumed, information on how to allocate that total among consumers and other purchasers, and average retail price are available from federal agencies and trade sources. For the most recent year, only the gallons consumed and average retail price are available. For the advance quarterly estimate, all three months of gallons consumed and average retail price are available.

3. *New autos (both PCE and private fixed investment).* Both the annual and quarterly estimates for these components are calculated as the product of quantity purchased and an average price. Unit sales, information on allocating sales among consumers and other purchasers, and average list price, are available from trade sources; transportation charges, dealer discounts, and rebates from the BLS monthly survey of auto sales prices; and, for all but the most recent year, sales tax rates from the CB annual survey of retail trade. For the advance estimate, all three months of unit sales and price data and two months of data to allocate sales among consumers and other purchasers are available. The sales tax rate is from the most recent annual survey of retail trade.

4. *State and local government compensation of employees.* Annual estimates for wages and salaries are from BLS tabulations from the quarterly census of employment and wages (QCEW). For the other components of compensation, employer contributions for government social insurance are from federal agencies administering these programs; employer contributions for employee pension and insurance funds are from trade sources and CB annual surveys of state and local government retirement funds. For the advance estimate of wages and salaries, BEA combines three months of employment data from monthly BLS employment with quarterly earnings data from the BLS employment cost index. The monthly employment data are subject to further revision. For other components, BEA calculates trend-based estimates.

5. *Private, non-defense federal, and state and local government investment for most types of new structures.* Both annual and quarterly estimates are from monthly the CB surveys of the value of construction put in place. For advance quarterly estimates, two months of source data are available from the CB monthly construction survey and are subject to further revision.

6. *Private fixed investment in equipment except new autos, heavy trucks, and net purchases of used motor vehicles.* For the annual estimates for all but the most recent year, estimates are calculated using the abbreviated commodity-flow method using shipments of aircraft from the CB industrial report survey and shipments of all other equipment from annual CB survey of manufactures, all adjusted for exports and

imports from the CB foreign-trade data. For the most recent year and the advance quarterly estimate, except for light trucks, an abbreviated commodity flow method calculated from shipments from CB monthly survey of manufactures is used. For light trucks, physical quantity purchased times average retail price based on unit sales, information to allocate sales among consumers and other purchasers, and average list price, all from trade sources are available. For the advance estimate, two months of monthly shipments, exports and imports data are available and subject to further revision. Three months of sales and prices of light trucks are available, and two months of information to allocate sales among consumers and other purchasers are available.

7. *Exports and imports of goods and services.* This GDP component is estimated by BEA as part of the preparation of the ITAs. For both annual and quarterly estimates of goods, estimates are calculated using monthly CB foreign trade data, with adjustments by BEA for coverage and valuation to convert the data to a balance-of-payments and NIPA basis. For the advance estimate, two months of trade data are available and are subject to further revision. Annual estimates of services are calculated for government transactions based on reports by federal agencies for government transactions, and for most other services are based on annual and quarterly BEA surveys. For coverage and valuation adjustments for both goods and services, BEA calculates trend-based estimates for the advance quarterly estimates.

8. *Federal government consumption expenditures and gross investment for most types of spending.* For spending except for structures, software, CFC, and financial services furnished without payment by banks, other depository institutions and investment companies (FISIM), BEA uses the fiscal year analysis method. Within a control total established by this analysis, estimates of military wages are based on data from the *Budget of the United States* and estimates of civilian wages and benefits are based on data from federal agencies. Estimates of employer contributions for social insurance programs are from the Department of Treasury's monthly report on outlays and receipts and from other federal agencies. For the advance estimate, compensation estimates are based on three months of employment data from the Department of Defense (DOD) and BLS. Other components are based on the control totals from the fiscal year analysis and two months of data from the monthly Department of Treasury report and reports from other federal agencies. Estimates for structures are explained above in item 5 above; software and CFC are explained below.

9. *Federal and state and local government CFC.* Both annual and quarterly estimates are based on perpetual-inventory calculations at current cost, based on gross investment and on investment prices. For the advanced quarterly estimate, three months of investment prices and two months of gross investment are available.

10. *Service of non-farm dwellings – space rent for owner-occupied dwellings and rent for tenant-occupied dwellings.* For all but the most recent year, estimates are based on

12 THE NATIONAL INCOME AND PRODUCT
ACCOUNTS OF THE UNITED STATES (NIPA)
6. Methodologies for preparing selected components
of current-dollar and real quarterly GDP

data on housing stock and average annual rent from the CB biennial housing survey. Estimates for the most recent year are based on the number of housing units from the CB monthly survey and BLS CPI for rent. For the advance quarterly estimate, three months of the CPI is available and the number of units is estimated using trend-based data.

11. *State and local government consumption and investment except CFC, compensation, structures and software.* For all years except the two most recent years, final estimates are based on total expenditures from CB annual surveys of state and local governments. Estimates for the most recent two years and the advance quarterly estimate are trend-based data.

12. *PCE for physicians, dentists, medical laboratories, eye examinations and all other professional medical services, except home health care.* For all but the most recent year, expenses of nonprofit professional services and receipts for the other services adjusted for government consumption are from the CB service annual survey. Estimates for the most recent year are based primarily on trend-based data and current quarterly estimates are based solely on trend-based data.

13. *Private and government investment in software.* Investment in software is estimated in two parts: purchased software and own-account software. For years except for the most recent year, purchased software is calculated using the abbreviated commodity flow method based primarily on industry receipts from the CB service annual survey and CB foreign trade data. For the most recent year, industry receipts data are from the CB quarterly services survey. For the advance estimate, estimates are based on receipts published by publicly held corporations. For all years, annual estimates for own-account software are based on annual production costs derived from BLS employment data from the quarterly census of employment and wages (QCEW). The advance estimates of own-account software are based on quarterly BEA estimates of private fixed investment in computers and peripheral equipment and are subject to revision.

Methodologies for real GDP estimates

Unlike the source data used to calculate current-dollar GDP estimates, source data used to calculate real GDP for the advance estimate are based on source data for all three months of the quarter, are not subject to revision, and are not replaced by annual source data. Consequently, quarterly, annual and benchmark-year estimates are almost all calculated using the same source data and estimating method.

For the deflation method, which is most widely used, price indexes are primarily available from the BLS price index programmes – the CPI, PPI and international price indexes (IPP). Elements of the CPI and PPI are used not only for components of PCE and fixed investment, but also for components of government consumption and investment where more appropriate indexes are not available. Elements of the IPP are used for exports and imports of goods and services and for other components where explicit estimates of imports are used to calculate the corresponding current-dollar estimate. For components for which the BLS indexes do not provide complete coverage, such as investment in structures, BEA uses cost indexes from private trade sources or special quality adjusted price indexes prepared by the Census Bureau. For the expenditures of non-profit institutions, such as educational and religious and welfare, BEA uses its own input cost indexes or cost indexes from other sources. For national defense and related non-defense consumption and investment expenditures, BEA has developed an extensive set of specially designed price indexes.[17]

GDP components for which BEA uses the quantity extrapolation method include: FISIM; brokerage charges; most types of insurance; mining exploration shafts and wells; and compensation of employees of federal and of state and local government. Components for which BEA uses the direct valuation method include net purchases of used motor vehicles, inventory change for utilities, government CFC and some defense expenditures for goods and services.[18]

Notes

1. NABE is a professional association of more than 2 500 members who use economics in their work. Additional information about the results of this survey is available on the NABE website at *www.nabe.com*.

2. The monthly *Survey* is BEA's official journal of record. It is available for purchase by subscription and for no charge on BEA's website *www.bea.gov*. Official estimates are also made available through BEA news releases posted on the website.

3. For information on the individual lines of the summary accounts see "Preview of the 2003 Comprehensive Revision of the National Income and Product Accounts: New and Redesigned Tables" in the August 2003 *Survey*, and "Guide to the NIPAs" on BEA's website.

4. BEA and other statistical agencies that prepare selected economic indicators, including GDP and personal income and outlays, are required each September to publish the release dates for the next year.

5. The quarterly estimates of the FFAs are released by the FRB early in the third month after the end of the quarter. Annual revisions are usually released in September. Quarterly estimates of productivity are released by BLS a week after the advance and preliminary GDP estimates.

6. This programme also provides estimates of durable goods purchased by persons. Estimates for 1994-2004 were published in "Fixed Assets and Consumer Durable Goods" in the September 2005 issue of the *Survey of Current Business*; additional estimates were posted subsequently on BEA's website *www.bea.gov*.

7. For a description of the balancing program used to accomplish the integration, see "Preview of the Comprehensive Revision of the Annual Industry Accounts" in the March 2004 issue of the *Survey*.

12 THE NATIONAL INCOME AND PRODUCT
ACCOUNTS OF THE UNITED STATES (NIPA)
6. Methodologies for preparing selected components
of current-dollar and real quarterly GDP

8. For additional details on BEA's studies of reliability see "Gross Domestic Product Revisions and Source Data" in the February 2006 *Survey* and "Reliability of the NIPA Estimates of US Economic Activity" in the February 2005 *Survey*.

9. Some other countries, such as France, use econometric methods for estimating the best change of the quarterly entry (see Chapter 11),

10. For additional information, see "Incorporating Source Data on the Basis of 'Best Change'", in the August 2000 *Survey*.

11. For a description of the work of a specialist, see Seskin, Eugene, "The Business Economist at Work: Government Economists Working on the National Accounts", July 1993 *Business Economics*.

12. As required by *Statistical Policy Directive Number 3*, all release dates for key economic indicators, which include quarterly GDP and several other BEA reports, are set in the fall of the preceding year and made available to the public at that time. This advance publication schedule is designed to prevent policy makers from an early release of "good" news and from delaying the release of "bad" news.

13. The most recent summary appeared in "Updated summary methodologies" in the November 2005 *Survey*. Similar information for the estimates of real value added by industry appears in "Gross Domestic Product by industry, 1987-2000" in the November 2004 *Survey*.

14. Estimates for periods between benchmark I-O accounts are calculated by a similar interpolation process.

15. These percentages are from "GDP revisions and source data" in the February 2006 *Survey*.

16. For a description of the full method, see "Benchmark Input-Output Accounts of the United States, 1997," in the December 2002 *Survey*.

17. For additional information on these special indexes, see "MP-5, Government Transactions", on the BEA website.

18. Table 2 in the summary methodologies article in the November 2005 *Survey* provides a detailed list of the estimating methods and source data used to prepare real GDP.

Going further

Differences between the NIPA and SNA

For many reasons, the United States has not adopted all of the guidelines for national accounting set forth in the 1993 version of the SNA, although users should not overestimate the impact of these differences. Indeed, major aggregates such as GDP are calculated in accordance with most all SNA guidelines. In a recent Survey article, BEA described the main differences and reported on BEA's continuing efforts to modify the NIPAs to more closely conform to SNA guidelines. However, BEA also reported that it most likely will continue to differ from the SNA by retaining several important NIPA measures, such as personal income and corporate profits, and some of the sector and industry classification systems currently used for the NIPAs. These differences will most likely continue because they reflect not only the needs of the US user community, which includes government and private decision makers, but also the availability of source data. Nevertheless, the goal of improving NIPA consistency with the SNA remains part of BEA's mission of producing "accurate, relevant and timely statistics, of responding to customers and of meeting the challenges of a changing economy.[1]"

This section identifies differences between the NIPAs and the SNA 1993.[2] It reviews the differences that affect: 1) the level of total GDP and its expenditure components; 2) valuation; 3) definitions of the sectors; and 4) the presentation of the accounts. It does not discuss other differences between the NIPAs and the accounts of other countries, such as the use of quality adjusted price indexes (see Chapter 3).

There are very few differences between the NIPA and SNA definitions of GDP:

- Illegal production, such as prostitution or the cultivation or manufacture of illegal drugs is, in theory, included in the SNA but currently excluded from the NIPAs. In this, the NIPAs are in line with the practice of all OECD countries, which do not apply the SNA in this regard.

- Expenditures for military weapon systems are treated as investment in the NIPAs and as consumption in the SNA. Because of this treatment, NIPA GDP includes the CFC associated with investment in these systems. This difference, which remains small (about 0.6% of GDP), should disappear with the new SNA to be implemented around 2012. Indeed, the new SNA will adopt the US method.

- Artistic originals, such as movies, and sound recordings as well as cultivated assets, such as orchards and dairy cattle, are treated in the SNA as investment. In the NIPAs, they are currently treated as intermediate consumption. This difference is negligible in term of impact on GDP.

Another difference between the NIPAs and the SNA affects the components of GDP, but not total GDP. Inventories held by governments are included in change in inventories in the SNA, but as government consumption expenditures in the NIPAs. In the NIPAs, the inventory component covers only private inventories, primarily because the available source data on inventories held by federal, state and local governments is incomplete. Consequently, government purchases of goods are recorded in the NIPAs as consumption regardless of whether they are immediately used or are entered into inventories.

As noted elsewhere in this chapter, BEA prepares a special set of annual NIPA estimates for international organisations, such as the OECD, that are more consistent with the SNA. These estimates are included in the OECD's annual national accounts database. (However, there are no corresponding quarterly estimates, thus OECD data on the US differ whether using quarterly or annual sources.) For example, these BEA annual estimates follow the SNA treatment of military weapons systems and include the change in government inventories as a component of investment for most types of inventories. For most of the other differences, including those identified below, BEA lacks the source data to eliminate them.

Both the NIPAs and the SNA value total GDP at market prices. However, for the valuation of sector and industry output, the SNA recommends valuation at basic prices. (For additional information, see the section "Going a step further: Alternative methods of valuation of output and value added: basic prices and market prices".) For the NIPAs and for its I-O and the GDP-by-industry accounts, BEA uses market prices. Consequently, the NIPAs include taxes on products and exclude subsidies for calculating value added of industries; using the SNA, taxes on products are excluded and subsidies on products are included. This difference is quite important for users. It means that for the US national accounts, GDP is equal to the sum of the value-added of the different industries, while for other OECD countries it is equal to the sum of the value added *plus* total net taxes on products.

The SNA values change in inventories at market prices, whereas (with the exception of farm products) the NIPAs value them at cost of production. In general, this difference causes a temporary difference in NIPA and SNA GDP. This difference in valuation also affects the timing of the recording of the operating surplus: in the SNA, a profit is recorded when the product is produced; in the NIPAs, a profit or loss is recorded when the product is sold.

Unlike the SNA, the NIPAs have two groupings for the institutional sector. First, the NIPAs show three sectors for measuring the contribution of various institutions to production: business, households and institutions, and general government. The business sector is defined as including all private entities that are organised for profit, including unincorporated enterprises, and other units (such as government enterprises) that are primarily engaged in producing goods and services for sale at a price that is intended to cover the costs of production. Thus, the business sector in the NIPAs differs from the corporations sector of the SNA in that it includes unincorporated enterprises that are, in principle, classified in the SNA in the household sector. The business sector in the NIPAs also excludes nonprofit institutions serving households (NPISHs) that are primarily engaged in producing goods and services for sale at a price that is intended to cover the costs of production. This NIPA presentation has the advantage of providing a measure of the output of the whole of the market production, a measure used as the numerator in the calculation of labor productivity. Several other countries also compile such a grouping (see Chapter 7). The households and institutions sector consists of households and NPISHs. The general government sector consists of all government agencies other than those classified as government enterprises. In the NIPAs, all private NPISHs are classified in the household sector; in the SNA, NIPSHs that are primarily engaged in producing goods and services for sale at a price that is intended to cover the costs of production are classified either in the non-financial or the financial corporations sectors.

Second, for measuring income, outlays and saving in the NIPAs, the institutions are grouped into three other sectors: personal, government and corporate. The personal sector includes the income that is earned by, or transferred to, households and all NPISHs as well as net income of businesses that are owned by households, including owner-occupied housing. The personal sector is thus close to the combination of the SNA household and NPISH sector, since it includes the income of unincorporated enterprises. The NIPA government sector includes general government and government enterprises, while the SNA government sector excludes government enterprises. The NIPA corporate sector consists of businesses organised for profit that are legally organised as corporations and that are required to file corporate tax returns. It differs from the SNA corporation sector by government enterprises, non-profit institutions that produce goods or services for sale at a price that is intended to cover the costs of production, and unincorporated businesses that operate like a corporation.

Several of the differences between the NIPAs and the SNA described above result in differences in presentation between the two systems. It is important to understand that these are only differences in presentation that can easily be overcome by reorganising the different tables. BEA uses seven summary accounts to describe the NIPA framework. The section of this chapter "Presentation of NIPAs and related tables" includes a discussion of the major presentational differences between the organisation of these NIPA summary accounts and the SNA production, distribution and use of the income account, and capital accounts.

In particular, the presentation of GDP by type of expenditure in the NIPAs and the SNA slightly differ. The NIPAs show GDP as the sum of four main components: personal consumption expenditures; gross private domestic investment; net exports of goods and services; and government consumption expenditures and gross investment. The SNA shows a different grouping. The SNA presents GDP as the sum of: final consumption expenditures; gross capital formation (GCF); exports of goods and services, *minus* imports of goods and services. The SNA final consumption expenditures is the sum of these expenditures by households, NPISHs and government. As noted above, GCF is presented as consisting of three items: gross fixed capital formation; change in inventories; and acquisitions less disposals of non-financial, non-produced assets.

The NIPAs include also some differences in terminology such as "gross national product" which is the NIPA name for "gross national income" in the SNA, and also several aggregates that are not in the SNA, such as corporate profits, and personal income (Box 1 in the main text "Featured measures of NIPA tables" discusses the aggregates not found in the SNA). Similar measures of disposable income appear in both the NIPAs and the SNA. However, these measures – NIPA disposable personal income (DPI) and SNA household disposable income (HDI) – differ not only because this NIPA measure includes NPISHs but also in the way the two measures are calculated.[3] The NIPA DPI measure includes all sources of personal income, less contributions for social insurance and personal taxes and includes interest and other transfers paid by persons. HDI excludes these items. DPI includes pension fund contributions but does not include pension fund benefits, while HDI excludes pension fund contributions and includes pension fund benefits. Despite these differences in disposable incomes, the NIPA and SNA measures of saving are comparable. The NIPAs treat interest paid by persons and personal transfer payments as a type of consumption, and the SNA includes an adjustment for pensions (called "D8 Adjustment for net equity of households in pension funds") so that both systems' saving figure reflects households as owners of pension funds.

The NIPA and SNA classification systems used to present industries and types of products also differ. For example, the industry detail shown in the NIPAs is based on NAICS (North American industry classification system), the system used by Canada, Mexico and the United States; SNA presentations are based on the international standard industrial classification system.

Another difference in the presentation of the NIPAs and some other countries' presentations relates to the use of balancing items in the two systems. As noted in the section "Going a step further: Statistical discrepancies in the NIPAs", GDI (gross domestic income), which is the NIPA name for what is called the "income approach of GDP" in this book (the sum of incomes), does not equal GDP, which is calculated as the sum of expenditures, because the components are measured independently. The difference between GDP and GDI in the NIPAs is called the statistical discrepancy and is shown as a type of income. Not all other OECD countries incorporate such an entry either because one or more expenditure or income types are calculated as a residual, or because they allocate such discrepancies to other components. It is thus important to remember that in the United States, the term GDP is strictly associated with the "expenditure" approach.

Finally, it is very important to remind international users of national accounts that all quarterly changes in the NIPAs are presented at an annual rate. Many other OECD countries simply use quarterly rates.

Statistical discrepancies in the NIPA

In the NIPAs, the difference between gross domestic income (GDI), which is the sum of incomes earned in the production of gross domestic product (GDP), itself the sum of expenditures, is called the "statistical discrepancy". This is not the only statistical discrepancy in the national accounts. There is also the statistical discrepancy between the net lending/borrowing obtained from the non-financial accounts and the financial accounts. However, this section focuses on the statistical discrepancy between GDP and GDI. In theory, GDI should equal GDP, but in practice they differ because their components are estimated using largely independent and less-than-perfect source data. As shown in NIPA summary account 1 (see Table 1), the statistical discrepancy is recorded as a type of income. This placement reflects BEA's view that GDP is a more reliable measure of output than GDI and that it has not identified a satisfactory methodology for allocating the discrepancy among GDP or GDI components.[4] Both of these views are explained below.

In the mid-1990s, there was considerable public debate about the growth of the US economy because growth measured by real GDI had increased faster that growth measured by real GDP.[5] Some analysts maintain that the higher rate of growth of real GDI was more consistent with other economic indicators, such as the unemployment rate. Private economists and government policymakers were concerned about what appeared to be a consistent divergence because of the use of the GDP growth rate to forecast long-term growth and because of the implications of an understated GDP for other major NIPA measures, such as the trade balance, investment and saving. Since 2000, the debate has subsided because for 2001 to 2005 the increase in real GDP has been greater than the increase in real GDI; for 2005, the increases in the two measures was about the same.

BEA's view that GDP is more reliable than GDI is based on its analysis of the source data underlying the two aggregates. For the initial quarterly estimates, there are direct extrapolators for most major expenditure components. The GDP estimates are missing direct source data for several components of consumer spending for services, for residential improvements and for most state and local government spending. For GDI, direct source data are missing for most employer contributions to employee pension and insurance funds, and for most of the net operating surplus of private enterprises. In addition, past trends in these components indicate that it is more difficult to make reliable assumptions about the missing data for the components of GDI than for GDP.

The source data availability situation is similar for the annual estimates. For example, most of the annual source data used for estimating GDP is based on complete annual enumerations, such as federal government budget data, or they are regularly benchmarked to complete enumerations, such as the economic censuses and census of governments done every five years that are incorporated into the other expenditure components to reflect BEA's benchmark I-O accounts. For GDI, only the annual tabulations of wages and salaries from employment tax returns and federal government budget data are complete enumerations, and only farm proprietors' and rental income and state and local government budget data are regularly adjusted to complete enumerations. For most of the remaining components of GDI, the annual source data are tabulations of samples of income tax returns. BEA also views GDP to be more accurate than GDI because critical annual source data are available on a more timely basis.

Adjustments also are made to conform the accounting concepts underlying the source data to the accounting concepts underlying the NIPAs. The major NIPA accounting adjustment to the estimates of GDP is the "inventory valuation adjustment" (called in other chapters of this book "inventory appreciation"), which converts inventories valued at historical cost to replacement cost; however, errors in this adjustment do not significantly affect the difference between GDP and GDI, because a similar adjustment is also made to business incomes in GDI. For the estimates of GDI, there are many NIPA accounting adjustments. For example, since 1986, BEA has had to make estimates of corporate business-entertainment expenses. In the NIPAs, these purchases are treated as intermediate inputs; for 1986 and later years, they were not allowed to be fully reported as expenses for tax return reporting.

In 2001, BEA reported to its Advisory Committee on the possibility of eliminating the discrepancy by a balancing technique.[6] This study reported the following with regard on efforts in other countries:

Balancing national economic accounts to obtain a single, consistent estimate of major aggregates was first proposed by Richard Stone, David Champernowne and James Meade in 1942. Their method assumed the availability of estimates of the variances of GDP components. Currently, some form of balancing is carried out for GDP in the national accounts of the UK, Canada and Australia. Within BEA, balancing is carried out in the preparation of the annual industry accounts. However, because of the difficulty of estimating the reliability of the full set of GDP components, none of these countries has adopted the Stone-Champernowne-Meade method. Canada averages the product-side and income-side estimates. The UK reconciles its product- and income-side estimates at annual revisions with the aid of an annual input-output table, for which a large-scale expenditures survey of businesses provides statistical support. However, the reconciliation process is ultimately subjective and takes place in staff meetings. Recently, Australia has adopted the British approach to reconciling the national accounts.

In their study, the authors noted the following arguments in favor of balancing GDP and GDI: 1) a single set of consistent NIPA expenditure and income estimates; 2) more accurate GDP growth rates; 3) smaller revisions to GDP; 4) an increase in user confidence in the estimates; and 5) possible improvement in the accuracy of GDP and GDI components. Arguments presented against balancing GDP and GDI were: 1) introduction of nontransparent adjustments could result in a loss in user confidence; 2) carrying the adjustment to GDP at the deflation level would result in a major computational burden and the need for major modifications to the GDP estimation systems; and 3) balancing the quarterly estimates could result in large revisions because source data for several GDI components are not available for the advance estimates.

Since 2001, BEA has continued to work to reduce the size of the statistical discrepancy, but it is highly unlikely that it can be eliminated completely, largely because of sampling and non-response errors and coverage limitations in the underlying source data, as well as the need for BEA to make adjustments for NIPA definitions based on incomplete information. In addition, some users have expressed the need to continue to publish both measures so that they can draw their own conclusions as to the accuracy of the two estimates.

Alternative methods of valuation of output and value added – basic prices and market prices

The valuation of the output of goods and service for the total economy and for the calculation of value added by industry can be measured in different ways with regard to the treatment of taxes and subsidies on products. The SNA discusses two valuation methods – basic prices and market prices.[7] Valuation with basic prices, the method preferred by the SNA and used by the OECD to present national accounts data, defines output as excluding taxes on products and including subsidies on products. Valuation with market prices, the method used by the United States for its I-O and the GDP-by-industry accounts and NIPAs includes taxes on products (taxes on production and imports) and excludes subsidies on products.[8]

Because industry value added is calculated as a balancing item between output and intermediate consumption, the valuation of value added is the same as the valuation of output. When value added is valued at basic prices, the sum of industry value added is considered to be valued at factor costs and equals GDP less taxes and *plus* subsidies on products. When value added is valued at market prices, the sum of industry value added is valued at market prices and thus equals GDP.

The rationale for the SNA recommendation to use basic prices is expressed in paragraph 6.206, which states: "The basic price measures the amount retained by the producer and is, therefore, the price most relevant for the producer's decision making." As a result of the use of basic price valuation, output can be used to analyse the impact of changes in taxes on products on the demand for these products. In addition, the use of basic prices facilitates inter-country comparison because taxes vary significantly across countries. Market price valuation causes very significant additions to the output of trade industries, thus rendering international comparisons of industry statistics and resulting productivity calculations difficult to determine.

The use of the market price method rather than the basic price method to value output in the United States starts with the preparation of the benchmark I-O accounts.[9] In these accounts, output at market prices is defined to exclude trade margins and transportation costs, to include customs duties and federal, state and local government excise and general sales taxes collected by producers, and to exclude subsidies received by the producers. As explained earlier in this chapter, the benchmark I-O accounts provide the output and gross value added benchmarks used for the annual I-O and GDP-by-industry accounts and the benchmarks for final uses (expenditures) for the NIPAs (see Figure 2).

The United States uses market prices in the I-0 accounts primarily because market prices facilitate the presentation of the relationship between the production of products and their purchase by intermediate and final users which, as in the SNA, are recorded at market prices. For the 1997 benchmark I-O accounts, tables were published showing this relationship for the product detail underlying personal consumption expenditures and private fixed investment in equipment and software. As noted above, the use of market prices also enables the United States to prepare measures of industry gross value added that sum to GDP. This property provides analysts with additive measures of industry contributions to GDP, measures that have been used extensively to track the changes in the industry composition of the US economy, such as those accounted for by goods-producing and service-producing industries. The identity between the sum of industry value added and GDP also is important to users as it indicates a high degree of consistency between the various accounts prepared by BEA.

Recently, BEA has been conducting research on changing from market prices to basic prices for valuing its I-O accounts.[10] It will consider the advantages of industry value added series that sum to GDP at market prices and the conceptual difficulty of treating the collection of taxes by the business enterprises as their revenue item. It also will address the lack of international comparability in its published data. Based on the data provided to the OECD, in 2004 taxes less subsidies accounted for about 7% of the published US GDP. However, there is a significantly larger impact on trade industries, where much of the taxes are allocated. If the United States were to adopt the use of basic prices, value added in both wholesale and retail trade would be reduced by about 20%, thus reducing the share of GDP accounted for by service-producing industries.

Differences between the consumer price index and the personal consumption expenditures price index

The CPI, which is prepared by the BLS, is a measure of the change in prices paid by urban consumers for a fixed market basket of goods and services.[11] The CPI is the most widely used measure of US inflation. It is used to adjust income payments for workers covered by collective bargaining agreements that tie wage increases to changes in the CPI and to adjust payments under various federal government benefit programs. Since 1985, the CPI has been used to index for inflation the federal income tax structure. The CPI and components of the CPI also are used to adjust other economic series for changes in prices, to measure purchasing power or to convert series into quantity indexes.

The PCE price index, often referred to as the PCE deflator, is prepared by BEA as part of the NIPAs. This price index and the GDP deflator itself also are widely used as PCE accounts for two thirds of GDP, and the GDP price index is the most comprehensive measure of aggregate US inflation. PCE represents the goods and services purchased by US households and nonprofit institutions serving households as defined in the NIPAs. The PCE price index represents the prices used to estimate real PCE; these prices are primarily detailed CPI items but also include detailed items from the BLS Producer Price Index program (PPI) and prices for PCE components not covered by the CPI.[12] PCE price indexes are published monthly and quarterly and are subject to revisions on the same schedule as other NIPA components.

Over the years, differences between the PCE prices and CPI have attracted considerable attention. In the 1970s and early 1980s, the two measures differed substantially, until 1983 when BLS adopted the rental equivalency method of measuring expenditures for owner-occupied housing. In the past decade, the differences between the two indexes had largely reflected BEA's switch to the use of the Fisher index formula to take into account product substitution; the CPI has continued to use the Laspeyres formula for its official series. In February 2000, interest in the difference between the two measures increased greatly, when the Federal Reserve Board announced to the US Congress that it preferred to monitor the PCE index rather than the CPI. The differences between the two price indexes come essentially from three origins: the index formula used, the scope and prices.

Formula. BLS constructs the CPI as a fixed-weight average of prices for individual goods and services, based on a Laspeyres formula. Weights are updated once every 10 years. BEA constructs the PCE price index using a chain-weight Fisher Ideal formula that incorporates weights from two adjacent years. For example, the 2003-04 annual per cent change in PCE prices uses quantities for 2003 and 2004 as weights. Thus, the PCE price index allows for broad year-to-year changes in the basket of goods and services purchased by consumers. The PCE price generally shows less inflation than the CPI because it takes into account the fact that consumers tend to substitute lower priced goods for higher priced goods as relative prices change.

Scope. The CPI and PCE price indexes have different underlying concepts that result in differences in scope. PCE, following NIPA concepts, includes certain items consumers obtain without explicit charge, such as free financial services and employer-funded medical care and health insurance. Thus, PCE is broader in scope than the CPI. In total, about 25% of PCE is not reflected in the CPI.[13]

Weights. In part reflecting differences in scope, the expenditure weights assigned to specific items differ for some components of the CPI and PCE. One major source of difference is that the CPI reflects only household out-of-pocket spending. The CPI excludes, but PCE includes, third-party spending on behalf of households, such as payments of medical costs by insurance companies and by the government. As a result, medical care receives a much larger weight (about 14 percentage points) in the PCE. In addition, differences in source data on expenditures lead to other differences in the weights. For owner's equivalent rent, the weight in the CPI, which is based on survey data on what consumers think they can charge to rent their home, is far greater (about 19%) than the weight in PCE, which is based on actual rents paid for similar homes.

Determining the impact of each of these differences is a major research undertaking. However, it is likely that all the differences noted above contribute to some extent at one time or another. Over the past decade, when changes in the CPI averaged about 2.7%, the PCE price index averaged about 0.7 percentage point less. Comparing the PCE price index to the new experimental CPI chained index, which has been calculated by BLS beginning with 2000, indicates that the difference in index number formula was the major source of these differences for 2000 forward.

Notes

1. For additional information, see "The NIPAs and the System of National Accounts" in the December 2004 *Survey.*

2. The differences discussed in this section are based primarily on the December 2004 *Survey* article and on a June 2003 Statistics Canada research paper, "Measurement of Output, Value Added, and GDP in Canada and the United States," posted on the Statistics Canada website.

3. For additional information, see "Income and Outlays of Households and Nonprofit Institutions Servicing Households" in the April 2003 *Survey*.

4. For the NIPA table that shows gross value added by broad sector (Table 1.3.5), BEA eliminates the discrepancy by calculating value added for the business sector. For its response to the OECD for NIPA estimates on an SNA basis, BEA does not eliminate the discrepancy. For the GDP-by-industry accounts, which are based on the industry distribution of GDI, BEA allocates the discrepancy to industries so that the sum of industry value added equals GDP.

5. BEA estimates real GDI using the GDP deflator; the estimates are shown in NIPA Table 1.7.6.

6. See "Balancing the GDP Account", a paper presented by Christian Ehemann and Brent Moulton at the May 2001 meeting of the BEA Advisory Committee.

7. In fact, the SNA discusses the difference between basic prices and producer prices. Market prices differ from producer prices by the Value Added Tax (VAT). As there is no VAT in the United States, producer prices are equal to market prices.

8. The United States does provide the OECD with industry value added data valued at basic prices.

9. For additional information on the valuation methods, see "Benchmark Input-Output Accounts of the United States: 1997" in the December 2002 *Survey*.

10. See "Strategic Plan Report Card for FY 2005" on BEA's website.

11. Information about the CPI is from "CPI Frequently Asked Questions" on the BLS website at *www.bls.gov*. Information about the PCE price index is from "National Accounts" on the BEA website. For additional information on the differences in the two measures, see Fixler and Jaditz, "An Examination of the Differences Between the CPI and the PCE Deflator," December 1997, on the BLS website.

12. For information on the prices used to calculate real PCE, see "Updated Summary NIPA Methodologies" in the November 2005 *Survey*.

13. Coverage percentages are from a presentation by Brian Moyer of BEA at the NABE Washington Economic Policy Conference, March 14-15, 2006.

Chapter **13**

CHINA'S NATIONAL ACCOUNTS

1. Introduction

With more than 1.25 billion inhabitants, China's population dwarfs that of all other countries except India. According to the World Bank estimates shown in Figure 1 below, China is also an economic giant, with a GDP in 2004 second only to that of the United States. China's GDP is shown as more than one and a half times bigger than that of the next largest country – Japan – and its GDP is larger than those of Germany, the United Kingdom and France combined. Question: how reliable are the numbers for China in Figure 1?

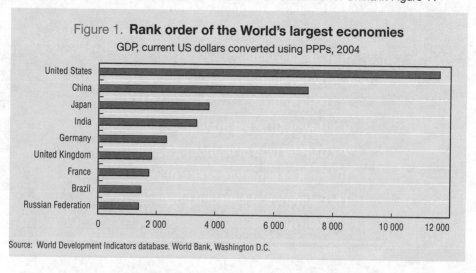

Figure 1. **Rank order of the World's largest economies**

GDP, current US dollars converted using PPPs, 2004

Source: World Development Indicators database. World Bank, Washington D.C.

In order to compare the levels of GDP between the countries shown in Figure 1, their GDPs in national currencies have been converted to US dollars using *Purchasing Power Parities (PPPs)*. For three countries – China, India and Brazil – the PPPs are World Bank estimates based on PPPs that were directly measured only several years ago. The China PPP is not even an official estimate and is based on an estimate made for 1995 by an independent Chinese researcher.[1] There are several indications that the PPP used for China in Figure 1 may be too low by a substantial margin – thereby exaggerating the size of China's GDP. It is probable, however, that in economic terms China is either number two or three in the world – either ahead of, or just behind, Japan.[2]

What about China's estimate of GDP in national currency? The reliability of both the level and growth rates of China's GDP have often been criticised in the European and

UNDERSTANDING NATIONAL ACCOUNTS – ISBN 92-64-02566-9 – © OECD 2006

American press and in academic literature. One of the most detailed criticisms was made by Professor Angus Maddison,[3] who concluded that both growth rates and GDP levels were being overstated. However, history does not seem to vindicate his assessment: China's GDP level was recently (December 2005) revised by 16.8% following the incorporation of new data on the service sector, and real GDP in the last decade has been revised by +0.5% per year (see Box 3).

The Chinese statisticians have reacted to criticism of their national accounts and related economic statistics in a way that does credit to them – by inviting advice and collaboration both from national statistical agencies (in the United States, Australia and Italy, for example), and from statisticians working in international organisations (such as the World Bank, the IMF and the OECD). This chapter draws on discussions between statisticians from the OECD and the Chinese National Bureau of Statistics (NBS) about the methods used to estimate the national accounts: how reliable are they and how might they be improved.[4]

The conclusion reached here is that China's national accounts are a reliable guide to the level and growth of GDP, even though the margins of error are certainly larger than for most developed countries.

2. Background

From 1952 to 1984, China's national accounts were compiled according to the *Material Product System (MPS)*. This system was developed by the Soviet Union to manage a planned economy in which the supply and use of resources were determined by multiyear plans. Up until the mid-1960s, China received technical assistance from Soviet statisticians in implementing the Material Product System and in designing the system of data collection on which it was based.

National accounts based on the United Nation's *System of National Accounts (SNA)* were first published on a regular basis in 1985, although these SNA estimates were essentially derived from the MPS accounts using an approximate conversion table developed by the United Nations Statistical Office. From 1985 to 1992, accounts were published according to both the MPS and the SNA, and in 1992 the SNA was adopted as the official accounting system for China. The MPS was abandoned, and since 1993 the national accounts have been compiled following SNA rules. Despite this, the statistical practices and habits learned during the MPS years still impinge to some extent on the way that Chinese statistics are compiled and presented (see Box 1).

China's national accounts cover mainland China. Therefore, they include the special economic zones within China but exclude the Special Administrative Regions of Hong Kong and Macao. Taipei Province of China, legally considered to be part of China, is also excluded.

Box 1. **Lingering effects of the MPS (Material Product System)**

Although the MPS has long been officially abandoned, old habits die hard and some features of the MPS, as well as the data collection system used to support it, remain. In particular:

The quarterly national accounts are compiled on a cumulative basis – *i.e.* January to March, then January to June, January to September, and finally January to December. Cumulative data collection – both monthly and quarterly – was the standard practice under central planning because the main concern of government officials was meeting the annual targets set by the central planners. At the end of each month or quarter, they needed to know how near they were to meeting the annual targets.

Under central planning, detailed information was collected from every farmer, every factory, every shop, every truck operator and indeed from every unit in which people were employed. Comprehensive reporting is unreliable because it is impossible in practice to monitor the quality of the reported data. It is particularly unreliable in China where information is collected by the lowest-level administrative agency relevant for the particular enquiry – typically villages, neighborhood committees and townships.

The data are then passed on to the next higher level where they are added up, and then on to next level, eventually ending up at the NBS or another agency of the central government. This long reporting chain allows many possibilities for inadvertent error. Since the early 1990s, the NBS has been progressively introducing sample surveys to collect data on important areas of the economy, notably in agriculture and industry. In particular, for most types of activities NBS has abandoned comprehensive reporting for enterprises below a certain size, and sample surveys have been introduced in their place. This has resulted in progressive improvement in the quality of the basic data underlying the Chinese national accounts, but there are still a few areas where comprehensive reporting continues to be used.

Central planning encourages dishonesty in statistical reporting. Local officials can expect to be rewarded when they report that planned output has been achieved or exceeded, but there are no thanks for missing a target. The sheer size of China limits the ability of the central authorities to monitor properly reporting at the local level. And although central planning has been effectively abandoned, overstatement of output and income remains a problem in the statistics reported by most of China's 30 Provinces.* In several recent years, the growth rate of China's GDP estimated by the National Bureau of Statistics has been lower than the growth rates of regional GDP estimated by almost all of the 30 provincial statistical offices. Statistically, this is almost impossible and the NBS is implicitly accusing most of the provincial statistical offices of overstating their GDP.

As its name implies, the Material Product System focused on the production of physical objects – agriculture, forestry, fishing, industry and construction – and only services directly linked to these goods-producing sectors were considered to be productive. Retail and wholesale trade and transport of goods were therefore included, but other services, such as financial, legal and business services, health, education, cultural and personal services, were not regarded as productive. Production and consumption of these services were defined as transfers and so did not contribute to national income.

3. Published national accounts

For *annual national accounts*, the following tables are published by China's National Bureau of Statistics:

- Gross domestic product at current market prices for 16 kinds of activities.

- For GDP at constant prices, only growth rates for the 16 kinds of activities are published. A fixed base year – now 2000 – is used.

- GDP by expenditure is compiled at current and constant prices, but the constant price estimates are not published. Only totals are shown for government consumption expenditure, gross fixed capital formation, changes in inventories, and exports less imports of goods and services. Household consumption expenditure is shown separately for *urban* and *rural* households.

- Income and outlay accounts are published for five institutional sectors: non-financial corporations sector; financial corporations sector; general government sector; household sector; and the rest of the world sector. Note that the sector "non-profit institutions serving households (NPISH)" is not recognised in China's national accounts. Political parties, religious organisations, trade unions, civil rights organisations and such that are allocated to the NPISH sector in most countries are considered to be part of the general government sector in China. (This seems to be a correct interpretation of the SNA since these organisations are largely funded and controlled by government.)

- The income components of GDP – compensation of employees, operating surplus and consumption of fixed capital – are published only in the input-output tables, which are generally produced every five years.

Quarterly national accounts are compiled in both current and constant 2000 prices, but only growth rates – referring to the change compared with the same period of the previous year – are published. Growth rates are shown separately for the three sectors – *primary, secondary* and *tertiary* (see below). As noted above, the quarterly accounts are on a cumulative basis rather than for discreet quarters (see Box 2). The cumulative quarterly accounts for January to December are considered preliminary estimates of the annual accounts.

Input-output tables according to the SNA were first published for 1987. The input-output tables are now compiled twice every five years. One is a detailed benchmark table, the other is a less-detailed updated table. In 1987, 1992, 1997 and 2002, benchmark tables based on special input-output surveys were compiled, while in 1990, 1995, 2000, the tables were updated in less detail. The input-output tables treat customs duties and "financial intermediation services indirectly measured" (or FISIM) differently from the GDP estimates. So the input-output tables are not fully consistent with the GDP estimates.

Box 2. "De-cumulating" China's quarterly national accounts

As noted, the quarterly national accounts are compiled on a cumulative basis and not for discrete quarters. Cumulative data can of course be "de-cumulated" by subtracting the previous quarter's results from the current quarter. NBS statisticians caution against doing this because errors and omissions detected in the course of the year are not assigned to their correct quarter but are all included in the latest cumulative estimates. As a result, de-cumulating may result in these corrections being assigned to the wrong quarter.

For some time, the OECD Statistics Directorate published de-cumulated quarterly national accounts for China in Main Economic Indicators (MEI). The editors of MEI believed that most of their readers are so unfamiliar with cumulative quarterly data that they will either regard them as unusable, or they will attempt to de-cumulate (incorrectly) the series themselves. However, publication of the de-cumulated quarters has now been discontinued for the reasons mentioned above.

---

4. Publication schedule

Annual national accounts.

The "preliminary" estimates for a given year are published 20 days after the end of the year. These are the quarterly estimates for January to December.

Revised estimates are published 9 months after the end of the year. These are estimates of annual GDP made independently from the quarterly estimates.

The final estimates are published 17 months after the end of the year.

The accounts for institutional sectors are published 24 months after the end of the year.

Quarterly national accounts

The first estimates of Quarterly GDP are published about 20 days after the end of the quarter.

The revised estimates are published about 45 days after the end of the quarter.

When the final annual estimates are published 17 months after the end of the year, the quarterly accounts are benchmarked to the annual figures and become final.

5. Classification

Types of activities

In tables and accounts showing GDP by type of economic activity, the NBS uses a classification based on the "historical sequence of economic development". Three kinds of production are distinguished – primary, secondary and tertiary. This designation is based on the theory that each sector will, in turn, dominate the economy as development proceeds. The full breakdown is:

Primary sector (consisting of agriculture, forestry and fishing).

Secondary sector broken down between *construction* on the one hand and *industry* on the other. Industry consists of mining and quarrying, manufacturing, gas, water and electricity production.

Tertiary sector, further broken down into:

- Services for agriculture, forestry and fishing.
- Geological prospecting and water conservancy.
- Transport.
- Post and telecommunications.
- Wholesale and retail trade and catering.
- Banking and insurance.
- Real estate.
- Social services.
- Health care, sports and social welfare.
- Education, culture and arts, radio, film and television.
- Scientific research and technological services.
- Government agencies, parties and social organisations.
- Other services.

What is striking about this classification is that there is only a two-part breakdown for the large secondary sector (construction, on the one hand, and all other secondary activities on the other), yet there is a much more detailed breakdown of the tertiary sector, which is considerably smaller. In 2004, the secondary and tertiary sectors accounted for 53% and 32% of GDP, respectively. The primary sector – 15% of GDP in 2004 – is also shown as a single total, although the components – agriculture, forestry and fishing – are very different kinds of activities.

According to NBS, the reason for these classifications is that data are collected for each enterprise as a whole. In the primary and secondary sectors, most large enterprises have many separate units that produce different kinds of products, and enterprises are assigned to the kind of activity that accounts for the greatest part of their gross output. For example, a single enterprise may extract mineral ore, refine it, produce several different kinds of metal products, construct its own buildings and generate its own electricity. Because the entire output and value added of the enterprise can be assigned to only one of these activities, the NBS consider it misleading to publish a more detailed breakdown for the primary and secondary sectors. This is less of a problem for the tertiary sector, since the vast majority of service enterprises produce only one kind of output.

Note, however, that the input-output tables provide a detailed breakdown of output and value added by kind of economic activity. The input-output tables are based on special surveys that collect detailed information on outputs and intermediate consumption for each production unit within the enterprise. The latest input-output table distinguishes 124 kinds of activities.

Table 1 shows the composition of GDP according to the primary, secondary, tertiary classification, from the beginning of the economic reforms in 1978 to 2004. The period averages in the bottom panel of the table show that the share of agriculture forestry and fishing has been halved over the period and that the tertiary sector has increased by around 50%. The secondary sector has been rather stable over the period although there has been a marked rise in construction activity.

Table 2 gives a more detailed breakdown of the tertiary sector. Posts and telecommunications, hotels and other tourism-related services have been growing rapidly. Within "other services", education, culture and arts, radio, film and television have all increased their shares of GDP.

6. Ownership

Chinese policy makers are much concerned with the trend and structure of economic ownership. In the past, the economy was completely dominated by state-owned and collective enterprises, but since the Reform and Opening Policy, which began in 1978, the structure of enterprise ownership has changed greatly.

Table 1. **Composition of gross domestic product**

Percentage of GDP, current prices

	Gross Domestic Product	Primary Sector	Secondary Sector			Tertiary Sector		
			Total	Industry	Construction	Total	Transport and com-munications	Wholesale and retail trade and catering
1978	100.0	27.9	47.9	44.1	3.8	24.2	4.7	7.3
1979	100.0	31.0	47.1	43.6	3.5	21.9	4.5	5.4
1980	100.0	29.9	48.2	43.9	4.3	21.9	4.5	4.7
1981	100.0	31.6	46.1	41.9	4.2	22.3	4.3	5.2
1982	100.0	33.1	44.8	40.6	4.1	22.1	4.4	3.7
1983	100.0	32.9	44.4	39.8	4.5	22.7	4.4	3.9
1984	100.0	31.8	43.1	38.7	4.4	25.1	4.5	5.7
1985	100.0	28.2	42.9	38.3	4.6	28.9	4.5	9.7
1986	100.0	26.9	43.7	38.6	5.1	29.4	4.6	9.2
1987	100.0	26.6	43.6	38.0	5.5	29.9	4.5	9.6
1988	100.0	25.5	43.8	38.4	5.4	30.7	4.4	10.8
1989	100.0	24.9	42.8	38.2	4.7	32.3	4.6	9.9
1990	100.0	26.9	41.3	36.7	4.6	31.8	6.1	7.6
1991	100.0	24.3	41.8	37.1	4.7	33.9	6.5	9.6
1992	100.0	21.5	43.5	38.2	5.3	35.0	6.2	10.2
1993	100.0	19.5	46.5	40.1	6.4	34.0	6.3	9.1
1994	100.0	19.7	46.4	40.3	6.2	33.9	6.0	9.0
1995	100.0	19.7	47.2	41.1	6.1	33.1	5.6	9.0
1996	100.0	19.5	47.6	41.4	6.2	33.0	5.7	9.0
1997	100.0	18.0	47.6	41.7	5.9	34.4	5.8	9.3
1998	100.0	17.3	46.2	40.3	5.9	36.5	6.1	9.6
1999	100.0	16.2	45.8	40.0	5.8	38.0	6.5	9.8
2000	100.0	14.8	45.9	40.4	5.6	39.3	7.4	9.7
2001	100.0	14.1	45.2	39.7	5.4	40.7	7.7	9.8
2002	100.0	13.5	44.8	39.4	5.4	41.7	7.8	9.9
2003	100.0	12.6	46.0	40.5	5.5	41.5	7.4	9.9
2004	100.0	13.1	46.2	40.8	5.4	40.7	7.6	9.5
1978-1980	100.0	29.7	47.7	43.9	3.9	22.6	4.6	5.7
1981-1985	100.0	31.2	44.0	39.6	4.4	24.8	4.5	6.1
1986-1990	100.0	26.1	42.9	37.9	5.0	31.0	4.9	9.3
1991-1995	100.0	20.4	45.8	39.8	5.9	33.8	6.0	9.2
1996-2000	100.0	17.0	46.5	40.7	5.8	36.5	6.4	9.5
2001-2004	100.0	13.3	45.6	40.2	5.4	41.1	7.6	9.8

Table 2. **Composition of value added of the tertiary sector**

Percentage of value added, current prices

	1997	1998	1999	2000	2001	2002
Transport, storage, post and telecommunication services	16.9	16.8	17.1	18.8	18.8	18.7
Wholesale and retail trade and catering services	26.9	26.3	25.8	24.7	24.2	23.8
Finance and insurance	13.3	12.0	11.2	10.5	9.8	9.2
Real estate	10.8	11.2	10.8	10.7	10.6	10.7
Other services	32.1	33.7	35.2	35.3	36.7	37.6
Total	100.0	100.0	100.0	100.0	100.0	100.0

In 1998, the NBS promulgated Regulations on the Statistical Classification of Economic Ownership. The economy is classified into public and non-public sectors with five sub-types of ownership:

- Public sector
  1. State-owned economy
  2. Collective economy
- Non-public sector
  3. Private economy
  4. Economy funded by entrepreneurs from Hong Kong, Macao and Taiwan
  5. Foreign-funded economy

The share of the public sector has been reduced greatly in recent years, and most of the growth in the Chinese economy now comes from the non-public sector, which now accounts for more than one third of China's GDP.

7. Data sources

At the present time, most of GDP is based on data collected under NBS supervision. The main areas where administrative reporting is still important are: transportation, finance, insurance, education, health, culture, radio and TV broadcasting, and film production. The following are the most important data sources developed by NBS and used for the national accounts:

Censuses of the Tertiary Sector, Industry and Agriculture conducted in 1992, 1995 and 1996, respectively.

NBS carries out an annual sample survey of crop production because of the evident weaknesses in the reporting of crop production under the comprehensive reporting system; the NBS survey is based on random sampling, with crop production measured on a sample of farms at harvest time.

The NBS has a quarterly survey of small, non-state-owned industrial enterprises. The number of these enterprises has been growing rapidly in recent years, and the NBS believed their output and value added were being seriously overstated by local officials.

Other important NBS surveys include a household labour force survey and income and expenditure surveys of rural and urban households.

An Economic Census covering the secondary and tertiary sectors was carried out in 2004/5 and resulted in substantial revisions to both the level and growth rates of China's GDP during the period 1993 to 2004 (see Box 3 "2005 Revisions to China's national accounts").

8. How is GDP estimated?

The most reliable estimate of China's GDP is obtained as the total value added of different kinds of activities. For agriculture and industry, value added is obtained by subtracting intermediate consumption from gross output; this is usually termed the *production approach*. For other activities, NBS uses what it describes as the *input approach* – value added is obtained by adding up compensation of employees, consumption of fixed capital and operating surplus.

9. GDP by type of economic activity

For *mining, manufacturing, construction, electricity, gas and water, trade, hotels and restaurants*, the standard procedure is to divide producers into two groups 1) larger enterprises required to report to NBS; and 2) a second group consisting of smaller enterprises. Different criteria are used to distinguish the two groups depending on the kind of activity. For example:

In mining, manufacturing and utilities, the first group consists of all state-owned enterprises *plus* other enterprises with annual sales of five million yuan or more.

Box 3. **2005 Revisions to China's national accounts**

The table below shows the revisions to China's GDP estimates published in 2005. These revisions were mainly based on the results of the 2004/5 Economic Census, which covered the secondary and tertiary sectors. The revisions to the level of GDP following the Economic Census have been dramatic – for 2004, more than 16% for GDP and nearly 50% for value added in services.

Table 3. **Percentage of GDP and its components, current prices**

| | GDP | Primary sector | Secondary sector | | | Tertiary sector |
			Total	Industry	Construction	
1993	2.02	0.07	0.15	0.31	−0.83	5.90
1994	3.08	0.15	0.33	0.63	−1.59	9.05
1995	3.96	0.23	0.49	0.94	−2.38	11.96
1996	4.85	0.30	0.66	1.26	−3.16	14.82
1997	6.06	0.38	0.86	1.57	−3.93	17.96
1998	7.73	0.45	1.00	1.89	−4.68	22.27
1999	9.27	0.53	1.17	2.21	−5.47	26.10
2000	10.89	0.60	1.38	2.53	−6.22	30.22
2001	12.68	0.67	1.56	2.85	−6.95	34.61
2002	14.42	0.76	1.73	3.17	−7.71	39.15
2003	15.70	0.83	1.90	3.49	−8.43	43.71
2004	16.80	0.91	2.10	3.81	−9.17	48.71

These revisions are a reminder of the large margins of error that surround GDP estimates for China – and indeed for GDP estimates in many other countries as well. Most OECD countries revise the level of their GDP on the occasion of so-called "benchmark" revisions, which, as in China, are often based on new data from comprehensive economic censuses. In most cases, these revisions increase the size of GDP by between 1% and 4%, but much larger revisions have also been recorded: Italy (around +15% in 1987), Greece (around +17% in 1996), Turkey (around +25% in 1995).

Table 4 shows the changes to the estimated real growth rates over the same period. For the primary and secondary sectors, NBS considered that although the levels in current prices should be revised – particularly for construction – there were no reasons to change estimates of real growth rates. (This implies, of course, some substantial revisions to the deflators used to deflate the current price estimates.) For the tertiary sector, on the other hand, the revisions to volume growth rates averaged about 1.5% per year, and for volume GDP the growth rates for the periods 1993-2004 have been revised upwards by 0.5% per year, on average.

Box 3. **2005 Revisions to China's national accounts** *(cont.)*

Note that most foreign observers have argued that the NBS has been exaggerating both the size and growth rate of China's economy. The 2004/05 Economic Census suggests the exact opposite: both the level and growth of GDP have been underestimated for at least the last decade.

Table 4. **Revisions in volume growth rates (compared to pre-December 2005 data)**

	1993	1994	1995	1996	1997	1998	1999	2000	2001	2001	2003	2004
Primary and secondary sectors	0.0	0.0	0.0	0.0	0.0	0.0	0.0	0.0	0.0	0.0	0.0	0.0
Tertiary sector	1.4	1.4	1.4	1.5	1.6	0.0	1.6	1.6	1.8	1.7	1.7	1.7
GDP	0.5	0.5	0.4	0.4	0.5	0.0	0.5	0.4	0.8	0.8	0.5	0.6

For construction there is a government grading scheme that classifies enterprises according to their technical capability, and all enterprises assigned a grade of any level are assigned to the first group.

For retail trade, the first group consists of enterprises with both 60 or more workers and those with annual sales of 50 000 yuan per year.

For hotels, all those rated as one-star or higher are in the first group.

For *crop production,* NBS uses the data from its own survey on yields per hectare multiplied by the estimated area for each crop. Total production of each crop is then valued at producers prices in local markets. Expenditures on seeds, fertilisers, water, etc., are deducted to obtain value added. For *animal husbandry, forestry and fishing*, data from the comprehensive reporting system are used to estimate gross output and value added.

For *insurance,* value added is estimated directly from obligatory financial reports made to the China's Insurance Supervision and Management Commission. For *banks,* data are from the Peoples' Bank of China and the China Banking Regulatory Commission (See Box 4 for more).

Real estate covers imputed rents of homeowner-occupiers and activities of enterprises engaged in the development and operation of real estate and the provision of housing services. No estimates are made for housing provided by enterprises and general government free of charge to employees, nor for the for-profit leasing of housing by urban and rural households. Provision of free or subsidised housing by government and state-owned enterprises is declining although still extensive; house-leasing for profit by households is growing in urban areas but is still insignificant.

> ## Box 4. **Informal banking in China**
>
> In China, informal banking (*hui*) is widespread and has a long tradition. Neighbourhood loan clubs are formed with members making regular payments into a fund from which interest-bearing loans are made to club members selected by seniority, consensus, competitive bidding or (sometimes) lottery. Interest rates are high and *hui* is illegal. In practice, many small and medium-sized enterprises are funded in this way, but the activities of these loan clubs are not covered in the national accounts.
>
> Note that omission of *hui* does not affect GDP. There is no compensation of employees because *hui* is self-policing, and there are no paid staff to assess the risks of loans or to enforce repayment; there is no operating surplus since all interest is paid back to the fund. *Hui* does generate FISIM (or "financial intermediation services indirectly measured" – see Chapter 4). But FISIM in this case is all consumed by the enterprise sector, and so it is an intermediate and not a final expenditure. However, although GDP is not affected, omission of the activities of loan clubs means that the financial tables of the national accounts provide an incomplete picture of how enterprises are funded in China.
>
> It is worth noting that *hui* is not confined to China. Informal banking activities are common in Chinese immigrant communities throughout the world but, as in China, they are not recorded in the national accounts for practical reasons.

Imputed rents of homeowner-occupiers are considered as equal to depreciation (calculated at historic costs). This is a simplified version of the "user cost" measure of dwelling services – simplified because the other component of user cost, namely the net operating surplus, is assumed to be zero.

Government services cover administrative and legislative agencies at all levels of government – central, provincial and local – as well as the military, the Chinese Communist Party and its offices at each level, all the peoples' parties and their offices at each level, trade unions, the Chinese Communist Youth League, the women's federations, cultural federations, religious organisations and various types of urban household commissions and village commissions.

The value added of government services is calculated by summing the components of value added using information contained in the *Annual Statistical Report on Labour* (compensation of employees), the *Annual Report on Fixed-Asset Investment* (consumption of fixed capital) and other sources, including information from the Ministry of Finance.

Other services consist of services for: agriculture, forestry, animal husbandry and fishing, geological prospecting and water conservancy management, social services, health, sports and social welfare, education, culture, radio, film and television, scientific research and technological services, and personal services.

To calculate the value added for other services, the income approach is used (as with government services), based on the same sources: the *Annual Statistical Report on Labour* (compensation of employees), the *Annual Report on Fixed-Asset Investment* (consumption of fixed capital) and other sources, including information from the Ministry of Finance.

10. Final expenditure share of GDP

Household consumption expenditure has three components: goods and services purchased by households, and goods and services received as income in kind; the imputed value of goods (mainly crops and livestock); and housing services produced and consumed by households.

The data sources are the NBS statistics on total retail sales of consumer goods, and household expenditure surveys carried out in urban and rural areas by the NBS. Separate estimates are shown for rural and urban household consumption expenditure.

Government consumption expenditure consists of:

Current expenditures within the "scope of the budget". The data are taken from the annual final accounts of government, compiled by the Ministry of Finance.

Extra-budgetary current expenditures. These expenditures are made by government units financed from levies similar to taxes but earmarked for the provision of specific services. The data on extra-budgetary expenditures are supplied by the Ministry of Finance.

Depreciation of fixed assets of government administrative units and non-profit public utility units. This is estimated by NBS at historic costs and not at current market prices as required in the SNA. In a normal situation, where prices of fixed assets are rising, depreciation at historic costs will be lower than depreciation at current prices. With even moderate rates of inflation, the difference between the two estimates can be large.

The gross output less operating income of urban household commissions and rural village commissions. These commissions provide most of their services, such as family planning advice and road cleaning on a non-market basis, but they may also operate market establishments, selling such items as steam bread, milling grain, etc.

For gross *fixed capital formation*, data are collected by NBS on all fixed-asset investments of 500 000 yuan or more made by state-owned units, collective units, joint enterprises, joint-stock companies and foreign-owned enterprises. Sample surveys are used to collect information on investments of more than 200 yuan made by rural enterprises and government agencies and above 50 yuan for rural. A number of additions are made to the above estimates, including the costs of mineral prospecting and transaction costs on sales of dwellings. *Changes in inventories* are calculated for: agriculture, forestry and fishing, industry, construction, transport and communications, wholesale and retail trade, catering, and other services. Only the estimates for industry, wholesale and retail trade, and catering are adjusted to remove holding gains and losses.

Net export of goods and services is the difference between exports of goods and services and imports of goods and services. Both exports and imports of goods and services are taken directly from the Chinese Balance of Payments Statistics.

11. Estimates at constant prices

To convert estimates from current to constant prices, NBS uses a number of price statistics the most important of which are:

- Consumer price index, compiled separately for rural and urban households.
- Index of ex-factory prices of industrial output.
- Price index of fixed-asset investment.
- Price indices of exports and imports of goods.
- Farm-gate prices of crops and livestock products.

The quality of some of these price statistics is acknowledged by NBS to be poor – the price index of fixed-asset investment and the price indices of exports and imports, in particular.

There are also problems with the constant price estimates for value added in manufacturing. In the past, the NBS together with other departments drew up a "catalogue" covering a large range of industrial products to each of which a base year price was assigned. Enterprises then reported the value of their output each period using these constant prices. However, the base year prices were not necessarily transaction prices, there was no systematic updating of the catalogue to include new products, and the catalogue products and prices were updated at only infrequent intervals (the 1990 catalogue was still being used in 2001). This method was changed in 2004, and now current-price industrial output and value added are deflated by a producer price index. Although this is an improvement over the previous method, it would be better to obtain constant-price value added via double-deflation (*i.e.* by deflating both gross output and intermediate consumption separately). Double deflation is the standard method used by most OECD countries for industrial value added.

For a few types of activity, value added at constant prices is obtained by extrapolating base year value added by a volume index. For example, indices of freight and passenger kilometres are used to obtain constant-price value added for transport. Also, the volume of post and telecommunications traffic is used to extrapolate base year value added for post and telecommunications. To derive constant-price indices, NBS generally makes less use of volume indices than OECD countries.

12. Conclusions

To compile national accounts for a country with the size and complexity of China is no easy task, and it is made more difficult because some of the basic data are collected through an administrative procedure that uses comprehensive reporting. This provides many opportunities for both genuine mistakes and for deliberate misreporting.

Box 5. **Where to find China's national accounts**

The NBS publication, *The China Statistical Yearbook,* is the main source for the annual national accounts estimates. There are a total of 25 tables including GDP by kind of activity, household consumption expenditure by province, accounts for institutional sectors (which NBS refers to as *flow of funds* tables) and technical coefficients from the latest input-output table. Metadata is also provided on the definitions and methodology and the *Yearbook* contains a CD-ROM version of the text and tables.

The NBS website, *www.stats.gov.cn/english*, gives the latest quarterly national accounts: levels in current prices are shown for value added in the primary, secondary and tertiary sectors, together with growth rates at constant prices. The website provides a link to the *Yearbook* tables and text for the annual national accounts.

The IMF website *http://dsbb.imf.org/Applications* (the Web page for the IMF *Special Data Dissemination Standards*) gives detailed descriptions of the sources and methods underlying the Chinese national accounts and also gives the latest quarterly and annual national accounts.

The OECD publishes national accounts for China – annual and quarterly estimates of GDP for the three main kinds of activity – in the monthly *Main Economic Indicators*. This is the only source for China's seasonally adjusted quarterly GDP. These data and methodological notes are also available in the OECD Statistics web page, *www.oecd.org/statsportal*. Also, the OECD has published the most detailed description available in English of China's national accounts methodology: *National Accounts for China; Sources and Methods*, OECD, Paris 2000. This was written by two senior NBS statisticians, Xu Xianchun and Ye Yanfei, with advice from OECD staff. You can browse it free of charge on the OECD online bookshop (*www.oecdbookshop.org*).

However, while it is clear that China's *provincial* GDP estimates are flawed by systematic overstatement, there is less evidence of deliberate misreporting when it comes to the *national* GDP figures published by the NBS. For most economic activities, NBS has set up its own surveys for national accounts purposes. Independent checks on other economic activities are also available to NBS from its household expenditure and labour force surveys, and from the periodic censuses of agriculture, industry and services carried out under direct NBS supervision.

NBS acknowledges a number of weaknesses in its estimates:

Service activities have been poorly covered in the past, but the 2004/05 Economic Census has provided a new benchmark, creating the framework for a new system for surveying (on a regular basis) service activities, which in the past were poorly monitored or simply ignored.

Constant price estimates are acknowledged to be unreliable by NBS. Price information on capital goods and on imports and exports is particularly weak. This said, there is no evidence of bias in the NBS estimates of real GDP levels or growth, and they are just as likely to be under- as over-stated.

Value added of housing services is underestimated because housing services provided by publicly owned dwellings are excluded, because the imputation for ownership of dwellings does not include an operating surplus, and because depreciation is based on historic book values for the dwellings rather than the (much higher) current market values.

In a recent article in the *Review of Income and Wealth*, Xu Xianchun, Director of the National Accounts Department at the NBS, concluded that China's GDP in current prices may be understated by about 1.5% per year during the period 1991 to 1997. This was mainly due to the underestimation of housing services and of welfare services provided by enterprises to their employees but also to the large subsidies designed to keep prices of essential goods low for households, which Xu argues should properly be considered as a type of government consumption expenditure. While these errors would raise GDP, they are partially offset by likely errors in overstatement of value added in livestock production and rural industry.[5]

The above are all weaknesses in the system used to derive Chinese national accounts estimates, and NBS is working to correct them. But these weaknesses do not in any sense undermine the validity of Chinese national accounts. These remain a reliable guide to the level and growth of GDP in the world's largest nation, even though the margins of error are certainly larger than for most developed countries.

Critics sometimes suggest that the national accountants in China change their results to match government forecasts, or to support (rather than reflect the impact of) government policies. Close professional contact with China's national accountants during more than a decade has convinced the authors that this does not happen. The authorities in Beijing have no interest in falsifying NBS statistics, and neither do the national accounts statisticians at NBS. As with all countries, China's national accounts are wrong in the sense that they are point estimates within a range of plausible figures, but they are not politically manipulated.

Notes

1. Ren Rouen, *China's Economic Performance in an International Perspective*, OECD Development Centre, Paris, 1997.

2. All the countries in Figure 1 are taking part in the 2005 International Comparison Project and more accurate PPPs for the benchmark year 2005 will be published in the first part of 2007. Regrettably, the PPP for China is expected to refer only to 11 cities and so will not be representative of the country as a whole. This means that there will continue to be much uncertainty about the relative size of the Chinese economy.

3. Angus Maddison, *China's Economic Performance in the Long Run*, OECD Development Centre, Paris, 1998.

4. Since 1996, the National Bureau of Statistics and the Statistics Directorate of the OECD have held annual seminars on practical and conceptual issues of national accounts. The proceedings of these seminars are published by NBS in the bilingual series *Paper Collection for NBS-OECD Workshops on National Accounts*.

5. See Xu Xianchun, "Study on Some Problems in Estimating China's Gross Domestic Product" in The Review of Income and Wealth, Series 48, Number 2, June 2002

Chapter 14

INDIA'S NATIONAL ACCOUNTS

1. Introduction

With a population of more than 1 billion, India is the second-largest country in the world, and because of a higher growth rate, its population is expected to surpass that of China in the near future. However, as Figure 1 in Chapter 13 shows, despite a comparable population, India's GDP is less than half that of China. The latest World Bank estimates rank India's GDP (based on Purchasing Power Parities, or PPP) in fourth position – between that of Japan and Germany.

Since Independence in 1947, Indian governments have generally pursued economic policies designed to provide economic stability, ensure adequate food supplies and limit income disparities. Currency controls made India an unattractive target for foreign investors, and while this provided stability – for example, India avoided an economic downturn following the Asian financial crisis of 1997 – it also meant that India had to forego the many growth-promoting advantages that accompany foreign direct investment.

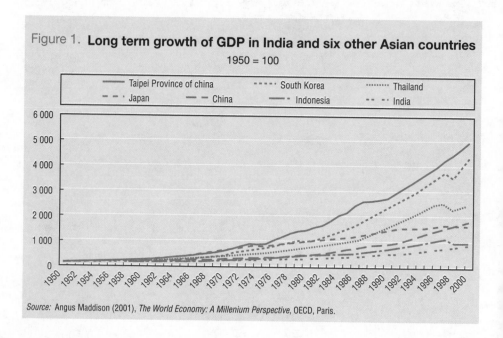

Figure 1. **Long term growth of GDP in India and six other Asian countries**
1950 = 100

Source: Angus Maddison (2001), *The World Economy: A Millenium Perspective*, OECD, Paris.

Figure 1 shows that India's long-term economic growth has been substantially less than that of other countries in Asia. Between 1950 and 2000, real growth of GDP in India averaged only 4.4% annually compared with growth of well over 6% in Taipei Province of China, South Korea, Thailand and China. Because of its high population growth rate, India's per capita GDP grew only 2.3% annually compared with more than 4% in China and more than 6% in Taipei Province of China.

India is now increasing its links with the outside world. With a large population of well educated, English-speaking and computer-literate young people, India is particularly well situated to exploit e-commerce and other information technology services. Since the mid-1990s, growth of GDP has averaged 6% annually, and the growth rate appears to be accelerating. If these higher rates of growth continue, India could begin to rival China as an economic giant.

In this chapter, we address the following questions: 1) how does India estimate its GDP; and 2) how reliable are the results?

2. Background

Indian statisticians helped develop the first UN *System of National Accounts* in 1953 and to revise it in 1968 and 1993. India has its own professional association devoted to national income measurement – the Indian Association for Research in National Income and Wealth – which brings together official statisticians from central and state statistical offices, academics, staff from research institutes, and data users from the business community. Also, the Indian statistical office hosts the Delhi Group, consisting of official statisticians from many countries working to improve measurement of the informal sector within the SNA framework.

Given this background, it is not surprising that India's national accounts have closely followed the recommendations of the successive versions of the SNA, although the lack of basic data has restricted their ability to implement the full system of accounts.

Since 1948, India's Central Statistical Organisation (CSO) has published estimates of the country's GDP by type of activity, but it was not until 1969 that the first estimates were made for capital formation and saving. Estimates of household consumption expenditure were released a few years after that, and estimates are now available for all the final expenditure components – household and government consumption, gross fixed capital formation, change in inventories and net exports.

The CSO is still working toward a full set of non-financial accounts for all sectors. These are available for the public sector, but the CSO has not yet compiled the income and outlay accounts for the household sector. This is a major gap in view of the importance of household enterprises in India.

Quarterly GDP estimates were first published for the quarter ending March 1999, with the estimates now carried back to 1996. The CSO now regularly publishes quarterly GDP estimates at both current and constant prices, showing value added according to type of economic activity. There are no quarterly estimates for the final expenditure component of GDP.

3. Some special features of India's national accounts

Public sector

The public sector plays an important role in the Indian economy, and the national accounts show separate accounts titled "public sector", which combine government, public financial and non-financial enterprises, and "departmental enterprises" (such as railways, irrigation, communication, forestry, public works departments and government printing works). The public sector generates nearly a quarter of the GDP, although the share is now declining.

Lakhs and crores

A *lakh* is a unit in the traditional number system used in India and Bangladesh, and it is equal to 100 000. A hundred lakhs make a *crore*. Indian statistics commonly use lakhs and crores to express large aggregates. Table 1 shows GDP estimates for India denominated in *crores* of rupees. One crore equals 10 million.

Accounting (or fiscal) year for national accounts

India is still predominantly an agricultural society with the majority of the population living in rural areas. The agricultural year runs from July, when the monsoon rains arrive, through June of the following year. The national accounts, and most other economic and financial statistics, follow a fiscal year that lies between the agricultural and calendar years. This fiscal year starts on 1st April and ends on 31st March of the following year.

4. How does the CSO estimate the national accounts?

Annual accounts

The most reliable estimates of India's GDP are those made from the production side – *i.e.* by summing the value added of different kinds of activities. Table 1 shows the standard format used in presenting these basic estimates of GDP. The last column in the table shows the rates of growth for the various kinds of activities from 1994 to 2004. Note the

Table 1. **Indian gross domestic product by economic activity**

Crore Rupees, 1993-94 prices.

	1993-4	1998-9	1999-0	2000-1	2001-2	2002-3	2003-4	Annual growth
Agriculture, forestry and fishing	241 967	286 094	286 983	286 666	304 666	283 393	310 611	2.7
Mining and quarrying	20 092	26 391	27 269	27 919	28 608	31 185	33 195	5.2
Manufacturing	125 493	184 578	191 925	206 189	213 681	227 642	243 400	6.9
Organised	81 873	120 116	124 514	134 324	140 517	150 412	161 115	7.1
Unorganised	43 620	64 462	67 411	71 865	73 164	77 230	82 285	6.6
Electricity, gas and water	18 984	26 988	28 401	29 632	30 715	31 659	32 827	5.6
Construction	40 593	54 389	58 740	62 651	65 161	69 911	74 819	6.3
Trade, hotels and restaurants	99 369	156 874	168 199	174 927	190 436	206 046	224 113	8.5
Trade	93 206	146 464	156 628	162 564	176 579	191 629	208 121	8.4
Hotels and restaurants	6 163	10 410	11 571	12 363	13 857	14 417	15 992	10.1
Transport, storage and communications	51 131	78 883	87 608	98 329	107 395	120 922	141 446	10.7
Transport and storage	41 711	57 821	61 910	65 748	68 686	72 684	80 076	6.8
Communications	9 420	21 062	25 698	32 581	38 709	48 238	61 370	20.7
Finance, real estate, business services	90 084	131 892	145 863	150 907	157 746	171 463	183 718	7.4
Banking and insurance	41 665	70 549	79 971	78 974	81 726	91 050	97 871	9.0
Real estate and business services	48 419	61 343	65 892	71 933	76 020	80 413	85 847	5.9
Community, social and personal services	93 632	136 658	153 379	161 372	169 537	176 141	186 419	7.2
Public administration and defence	43 636	62 209	70 432	72 073	73 965	75 230	79 482	6.3
Other community, social, personal services	49 996	74 449	82 947	89 299	95 572	100 911	106 937	7.9
Gross Domestic Product at factor cost	781 345	1 082 747	1 148 367	1 198 592	1 267 945	1 318 362	1 430 548	6.2

Source: Statement 10 in the Central Statistical Organizations's annual publication, *National Accounts Statistics.*

particularly rapid growth in communications, hotels and restaurants and trade. Growth in *organised* manufacturing, banking and insurance, and other community, social and personal services has also exceeded the overall growth rate.

In estimating GDP, a fundamental distinction is made between the *organised* and *unorganised* sectors of the economy.[1]

Basically, the *organised* sector consists of government administration, state-owned enterprises and other corporate enterprises. Thus, for example:

● In agriculture, the organised sector consists mainly of plantation crops – primarily tea, coffee and rubber.

- Organised forestry covers only production of timber and fuel-wood by the State Forestry Departments.

- In manufacturing, the distinction between organised and unorganised depends on whether the enterprise is registered under the 1948 Factories Act, the objectives of which were to ensure the safety, health and welfare of the workers employed in factories, and to prevent haphazard growth of factories. Enterprises are required to register under the Act (and thus count as organised) if they either have 10 employees and use electricity, or if they do not use electricity and have 20 or more employees.

- All electricity producers and suppliers are included, but only the suppliers of public gas and water (not the producers).

- Organised construction consists of federal and state construction departments and private corporate enterprises.

- The organised financial sector includes the commercial banks and insurance companies but excludes pawn-brokers and professional money lenders;

- Other services cover public health, education and sanitary services, TV and radio broadcasting and recognised educational institutions in the private sector.

The *unorganised* sector includes everything else and produces nearly 60% of GDP at the present time. Table 2 shows that the unorganized sector generates virtually all GDP in agriculture, forestry and fishing, and is larger than the organised sectors in construction, trade, hotels and restaurants, and transport and communications. Its contribution to manufacturing and other services is also substantial.

Table 2. **Share of the organised and unorganised sectors in India's economy**
2001-2002 (in %)

	Unorganised	Organised	Total
Agriculture, forestry and fishing	25.5	0.9	26.4
Mining and quarrying	0.2	1.8	2.0
Manufacturing	5.0	8.4	13.4
Electricity, gas and water supply	0.1	1.0	1.0
Construction	3.9	2.5	6.4
Trade, Hotel, restaurants	11.9	3.8	15.6
Transport and communications	3.9	2.8	6.7
Real estate, financial services and ownership of dwellings	5.4	7.6	13.0
Community, social and personal services	2.6	12.8	15.4
Total	58.5	41.5	100.0

Source: Ramesh Kolli and S. Hazra, Estimation of Informal Sector Contribution in the Net Domestic Product – Indian Experience, Eighth Meeting of the Expert Group on Informal Sector Statistics (Delhi Group), Nadi (Fiji Islands), 29-31 March, 2005.

For the organised sector, the main data sources for compiling the estimates are the budget documents of central and state governments, the annual accounts of public sector undertakings, the *Annual Survey of Industries,* as well as the results of company finance studies by the Reserve Bank of India. The workforce in the organised sector is estimated from the *Employment Review* published by the Directorate General of Employment and Training, Ministry of Labour.

With the exception of agriculture, forestry and fishing, estimates of value added in the *unorganised* sector are first prepared for a benchmark year. They are based on the number of workers in each economic activity together with estimates of value added per worker. Specifically:

- The data on unorganised employment for the benchmark year are taken from the Employment and Unemployment Survey, released every five years by the National Sample Survey Organisation (NSSO), as well as data from the decennial Population Census.

- The estimates of value added per worker for the benchmark year are compiled from the results of the follow-up Enterprise Surveys, carried out by the CSO and NSSO. These surveys use area frames provided by the Economic Census, conducted once in about seven years.

For other years, the benchmark estimates of GDP are extrapolated from various physical indicators and price indices. Clearly, the further the base year recedes into the past the less reliable the estimates become, and because of the large contribution of the *unorganised* sector, this significantly affects the overall reliability of the GDP estimates. Some of the physical indicators are also fairly crude and assume fixed ratios – for example between trade and commodity output – which may not be valid when the economy is undergoing structural change.

The estimates of value added in agriculture, forestry and fishing, for both the organised and unorganised sectors, are prepared using data from administrative sources, and they are based on the production approach. In the case of agriculture, production of crops is estimated from the total area devoted to each crop and the yield estimates. The value of output is estimated using the average prices in the primary marketing centers during the peak marketing period. Similarly, in the case of livestock products, output of milk, egg, wool, meat, etc., is estimated by the number of animals and the yield rates, and the value of output is derived using average farm-gate prices. Inputs of the agricultural sector are estimated using data from the Annual Cost of Cultivation Studies by the Ministry of Agriculture. Value added in respect to forestry and fishing is based on estimating ratios of inputs to outputs.

Final expenditure share of GDP

Estimates of household final consumption expenditure are obtained from a commodity flow table in which total supply (production plus imports) is allocated to intermediate or final uses. Total supply includes the value of farm products produced for consumption within the household. Household final consumption expenditure includes consumption expenditures of non-profit institutions serving households.

The annual estimates of government final consumption are compiled from budget documents of central and state governments.

Gross fixed capital formation is estimated by three different methods: as the sum of saving and net capital inflow from abroad; estimated purchases of capital assets; and capital outlays by user industries. Three independent – and different – estimates are thus generated. The first is considered to be the most accurate.

Estimates of changes in inventories are made separately for the public sector, the private corporate sector and the household sector. While estimates for the public and private corporate sectors are based on current data, those for the household sector use five-yearly benchmark surveys and assume steady net accumulation of inventories over the five-year period.

Acquisitions (*minus* disposals) of valuables are not currently accounted for in the national accounts due to lack of data (see Box 1).

Quarterly national accounts[2]

The CSO publishes quarterly GDP estimates, both at current and constant prices, for the following kinds of activities:

- agriculture, forestry and fishing;
- mining and quarrying;
- manufacturing;
- electricity, gas and water supply;
- trade, hotels, transport and communication;
- real estate, ownership of dwellings and business services; and
- other services.

The estimates are made by what is usually termed the *indicator approach*. The annual estimates for the previous year serve as the basis for the estimates, and the value added for each kind of activity is moved forward in line with various indicators. These include: quarterly agriculture production estimates; the monthly index of industrial production; monthly data on the production of cement, steel, commercial vehicles; cargo handled at

---

Box 1. **Household saving in India**

In India, gold plays an important role in household saving. As in many Asian countries, Indian women cherish gold jewellery, not only as a sign of wealth and proof of their husbands' devotion but also as an investment. Gold jewellery can easily be converted to cash at pawnbrokers or commercial banks, many of which have special counters for the purchase of gold ornaments. Prices are determined by weight without consideration of artistic merit. Much of this jewellery is bought by banks in Europe, where it is melted down to ingots before finding its way back to Asia to be converted into jewellery, thus restarting the cycle.

The *1993 SNA* came up with the notion of "valuables" in recognition of the fact that in countries like India acquisition and disposal of gold constitutes a significant form of household saving. But Indian statisticians have not devised a way of estimating inventories or net changes in the value of gold held by households and do not record valuables in the national accounts. However, this form of saving is important for people who do not have access to bank loans, such as farmers needing money for seeds or fertilisers or small-scale entrepreneurs wanting to purchase equipment or premises. The level and changes of true household saving, *i.e.* including gold, may be quite different from the published estimates.

A special feature of the CSO estimates of household saving is that they start from estimates of households' financial saving ("net lending" in SNA terminology). These are then adjusted by adding or subtracting capital transfers, capital accumulation and consumption of fixed capital to arrive at an estimate of household saving. This is an unusual way to proceed, since most countries prefer to estimate household saving by compiling a full set of income and outlay accounts, showing the progression from income earned from production through to disposable income and household saving. India's CSO cannot yet do this, which is why it must start from the side of financial saving.

---

major ports; bank credits and deposits; postal and telecommunication revenue; net premiums received on life and non-life insurance; and revenue expenditure of central government.

As each new set of annual estimates becomes available, the quarterly estimates are revised to be consistent with them.

As in most non-OECD countries, India does not seasonally adjust the quarterly accounts. Figure 2 shows that there is very marked seasonality in the quarterly series, and in the absence of a seasonal adjustment, users have to compare the current quarter with the same quarter in the previous year. In trying to detect the latest changes in the economy, users are effectively making use of only two quarterly observations, and is less efficient than using a seasonally adjusted series that makes use of several recent quarters. The seasonally adjusted series in Figure 2 is calculated by the OECD using the Census X-12 method and is published in the OECD's *Main Economic Indicators*.

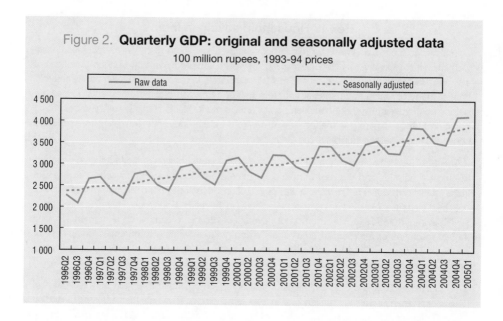

Figure 2. **Quarterly GDP: original and seasonally adjusted data**
100 million rupees, 1993-94 prices

Estimates at constant prices

For most kinds of economic activities, current price estimates are prepared first and then converted into constant prices. But for activities for which the estimates are first made using labour inputs, it is the other way round (constant prices are converted into current ones).

There is no unified approach for compiling the constant price estimates; for goods-producing activities double deflation is generally used, while for other activities either single deflation or extrapolation using a volume indictor is used.

5. Publication of national accounts

India releases its GDP estimates by economic activity every three months; the estimates for a given quarter are released at the end the next quarter.

Initial estimates of annual national income are released by the CSO, approximately two months before the end of the year, and they're known as "advance estimates" for national income. These cover the Gross National Product (GNP), Net National Product (NNP), Gross Domestic Product (GDP), Net Domestic Product (NDP), as well as per capita net national product at factor cost, and GDP by industry. Estimates are made at both current and constant prices (see Box 2).

UNDERSTANDING NATIONAL ACCOUNTS – ISBN 92-64-02566-9 – © OECD 2006

Box 2. **Advance estimates**

India's CSO is one of the few government statistical agencies to publish advance estimates of the main national accounts aggregates. These are released in January, or about two months before the close of the fiscal year used for national accounts, which runs from the beginning of April to the end of the following March. In most countries, forecasts of the annual output are published by private research institutes, or in some countries by finance ministries as part of the budget process.

The advance estimates give current and constant price estimates of Gross and Net National Income, Gross and Net Domestic Product and per capita National Income. The advance estimates use information on expected agricultural production – usually quite firm by that time – and data on production during the previous eight months for the mining, manufacturing, transport and banking sectors. Estimates for government are mainly based on the budget estimates. The advance estimates are subsequently revised four times – once when the "quick estimates" are released 10 months after the end of the financial year, and in the three following years. As Table 3 indicates, quite large revisions are often made to the advance estimates.

Table 3. **Real growth rates in GDP estimates**

	Advance estimates	Revised advance estimates	Quick estimates	First revision	Second revision	Third revision
1999-2000	5.9	6.4	6.4	6.1	6.1	6.1
2000-01	6.0	5.2	4.0	4.4	4.4	4.4
2001-02	5.4	5.4	5.6	5.8	5.8	
2002-03	4.4	4.3	4.0	4.0		
2003-04	8.1	8.2	8.5			
2004-05	6.9	6.9				

Advance estimates are released two months before the close of the year, on 7th February.
Revised advance estimates are released along with fourth-quarter estimates, three months after the close of the fiscal year.
Quick estimates are released 10 months after the close of the fiscal year, on 31st January.
Source: India's National Accounts Statistics (various publications and press notes).

The next estimate is referred to as the "quick estimate" and is released 10 months after the end of the fiscal year – *i.e.* in January. There are additional revisions in each of the three following years.

6. Where to find data on India's national accounts

The Central Statistical Organisation publishes full details of the national accounts in its annual publication, *National Accounts Statistics.* For long time series, see *National Accounts Statistics, Back Series 1950-51 to 1992-93* (CSO 1999). Recent national accounts can be accessed at *http://mospi.nic.in/mospi_nad_main.htm.* A convenient site for summary national accounts statistics is provided by the Reserve Bank of India – *www.rbi.org.in.*

The CSO last published methodological information in *National Accounts Statistics – Sources and Methods, 1989.* An exhaustive review of Indian national accounts by Uma Datta Roy Choudhury was published in 1995 (*National Income Accounting*, MacMillan India, New Delhi 1995). More recent methodological reports have been written by Ramesh Kolli of the CSO National Accounts Department and can be accessed via the Internet under his name.

There are several international sources for Indian national accounts statistics, including the OECD *http://stats.oecd.org/mei*, and the IMF *http://dsbb.imf.org/Applications/web/sddsnsdppage/.* Both websites contain methodological information as well as the latest statistics.

7. Conclusions

In her book, *National Income Accounting,*[3] Roy Choudhury summarises a long-standing debate within India on the reliability of the country's national accounts. She describes four approaches that have been used to assess the accuracy and reliability of the accounts:

Comparison of alternative estimates. In the national accounts, household consumption expenditure is estimated by the commodity-flow method in which the supply of goods and services is first estimated from statistics on imports and domestic production and is then allocated to its various uses – namely exports, intermediate consumption, net additions to inventories, government consumption and household consumption. But for many years, India has done a national sample survey of households (NSS), which provides data on expenditures and consumption of own produce that should be broadly comparable with the national accounts figures. Studies made in the 1970s[4] showed that the CSO figures used in the national accounts were generally 5% to 10% higher than the NSS figures, suggesting possible overestimation of household consumption and the possible under-estimation of other uses. ▶ I.

I. Many OECD countries record discrepancies of a similar size between the expenditures reported in household budget surveys and national accounts estimates of private final consumption expenditure. The difference is partly explained by under-reporting in household surveys of expenditure on tobacco, alcohol, gambling and other expenditures than members of the household wish to minimise or to conceal from other household members. In addition, the coverage of household surveys is usually more restricted than the household sector as defined in the national accounts.

Discrepancies in GDP estimates from the production and expenditure sides. Roy Choudhury shows that over a period of nearly 40 years the difference between GDP expenditure and GDP production has ranged from –2.6% to +1.4%. There is no evidence of bias (*i.e.* one estimate consistently exceeding the other), and the differences appear to be falling over time.

Revisions of estimates. Leaving aside the advance estimates, which are more like forecasts, she found that the revisions are usually upwards, but they are not large. And by the time the final revision has been made the difference is usually +1% or less. At first, this seems comforting, but it is really more a measure of the uncertainty surrounding the initial estimate rather than a measure of inherent reliability. The fact that later revisions are small may just mean that no better information subsequently became available to correct an estimate that was based on weak data in the first place.

Estimation procedures. For several parts of the accounts, only partial data are available, or complete data are available only for an earlier period. The national accountants then have to base their estimates on assumptions about relationships between some currently available statistic and their target statistic. Roy Choudhury cites several estimation procedures that she considers dubious, including the assumption that value added by household enterprises in trade and transport moves in line with the estimated total value of commodity output, and that rural household investment moves in line with the level of output in agriculture and related activities. Overall, Roy Choudhury finds that more than 60% of total GDP is based on current information that directly measures the target variable. This implies that a substantial portion of the accounts are still based on outdated statistics and assumptions that may be questionable.

This last point on the estimation procedures is particularly important. As noted above, nearly 60% of GDP generated is attributed to the *unorganised* sector, and these estimates are based on information that is only being updated at intervals of five years or more. This may have mattered less when GDP was growing slowly, but with the rapid growth recorded since the 1990s the assumptions of stable relationships between employment and value added that underlie the estimates are highly questionable.

Rapid structural changes also affect the reliability of the constant-price estimates. These use a fixed base year that is updated once every decade. The high growth rates now being recorded mean that the base year used will rapidly become out-of date; in general, the use of base year prices that are no longer representative exaggerates inflation.

An attempt to quantify error margins was made about 50 years ago by India's National Income Committee. Based on "expert guesses" of the likely margins of error for each kind of activity in the national accounts of 1948, the committee concluded that margins of error ranged from 10% in the *organised* sectors of mining, manufacturing, finance, rail transport, etc., to 20% in agriculture, and to more than 30% in *unorganised* manufacturing trade, transport and other services. The committee also concluded that assuming independence in the errors (so that some would cancel out), GDP was likely to have an overall error level of around plus or minus 10%. It is clear that data sources and estimation procedures have improved substantially since then, but it seems realistic to assume that at the present time error margins are at least 5% at the level of total GDP, with larger errors in economic activities in which unorganised producers are particularly important.

Notes

1. The CSO has presented a number of detailed papers describing the sources and methods of the Indian national accounts at meetings of the *Delhi Group on Informal Sector Statistics*. See in particular Ramesh Kolli and S Hazra, *Informal Sector Contribution in the Net Domestic Product – Indian Experience* and Ramesh Kolli *Measuring Non-Observed Economy – Practices Followed in Indian National Accounts Statistics.* These papers are available on the Delhi Group web-site: unstats.un.org/unsd/methods/citygroup/delhi.

2. For a full description of the sources and methods for India's quarterly accounts, see Ramesh Kolli, Data Sources used to Compile Quarterly GDP Estimates – Experience of India, OECD/ADB/ESCAP Workshop on Quarterly National Accounts, June 2002, Bangkok, *www.unescap.org/stat/meet/ qgdp/qgdp.asp.*

3. Uma Datta Roy Choudhury National Income Accounting, MacMillan India, 1995 (pp. 252-263).

4. Minhas *et al.*, Journal of Income and Wealth, July 1980.

There are three recent studies of the history of national accounts. The preface to the *1993 System of National Accounts* ("Perspectives on the 1993 SNA: Looking Back and Looking Ahead") describes the development of the 1953, 1968 and 1993 versions of the SNA. André Vanoli, the French expert in national accounts, gives what must surely be the definitive history of national accounts in *A History of National Accounts* (IOS press, 2005, ISBN: 1-59603-469-3). Angus Maddison, in the introduction of *The World Economy: Historical Statistics* (OECD, 2003), describes the very earliest attempts to measure national income. Maddison is the main source for the next section.

1. From the very beginnings...

Historically, wars and threats of war have provided the main impetus for the development of national accounts. They were seen as a quantitative framework for devising policies to mobilise a nation's resources to fight wars or to repair the subsequent damage. The first national accounts were developed in the 17th Century by William Petty. His *Verbum Sapienta* (1665) presented a set of national accounts for England and Wales designed for resource mobilisation during the second Anglo-Dutch war from 1664 to 1667. In 1694, Charles Davenant published a crude set of national accounts in *Essay upon Ways and Means of Supplying the War* (war of the League of Augsburg, 1668 to 1697), and this encouraged his friend Gregory King to produce a more detailed set of economic and demographic accounts in *Natural and Physical Observations and Conclusions on the State and Condition of England* (1696). In 1707, Sebastien le Prestre de Vauban published estimates of French national income in *La dîme royale*. Vauban's interest in the topic came from his experience in mobilising resources for the construction of military forts on the northern and eastern borders of France.

2. ... to the first modern accounts

Jumping across a few centuries to the modern era, the first official national income statistics were published in the United States (1934) by Simon Kuznets (Nobel Price 1971) and in the United Kingdom (1941) by Richard Stone (Nobel Prize 1984). The impetus was again to provide quantitative frameworks for war-time resource mobilisation and peacetime reconstruction.

In 1947, Richard Stone wrote a report, *Definition and measurement of the national income and related totals,* for the Sub-Committee on National Income Statistics of the League of Nations Committee of Statistical Experts. This was the first step toward an international accounting system. Stone was subsequently invited by the Organisation for European Economic Cooperation (later to become the OECD) to develop a system of national accounts that could be used by its member countries to monitor post-war reconstruction under the Marshall Plan. The Marshall Plan, named after a United States Secretary of State, was an extensive programme of financial aid from the US and Canada to the European countries that had been devastated by World War II. The result of Stone's work, *A Standardised System of National Accounts* published by the OEEC in 1952, can fairly be described as the first international system. The following year, the United Nations published a revised version of the OEEC system as *A System of National Accounts and Supporting Tables*. This is referred to below as the *1953 SNA*.

3. The 1953 SNA

The principal author of the *1953 SNA* – Richard Stone – noted that attempts to quantify the national economy had hitherto followed four separate paths:

- measuring the national income;

- constructing input-output tables;

- flow-of-funds analysis; and

- compiling balance sheets.

Stone saw the four approaches as being closely related and hoped that eventually they could be combined into a single system. The *1953 SNA*, however, confined itself to the first of these. Another limitation noted by the authors was that there were no tables at constant prices, and this was identified as another area for future development.

The *1953 SNA* consists of a simple set of six accounts: final expenditure on the GDP; national income; domestic capital formation; disposable income and net borrowing of households – and of government; and the external account. These accounts were supplemented by a set of standard tables that countries were to use in reporting national accounts statistics to the United Nations. In addition to establishing the basic accounting relationships – which have essentially remained in place to the present time – the *1953 SNA* was notable for having finally resolved a number of issues that were still under debate at that time. For example:

- Production was defined to include two important types of own-use production: subsistence farm production, and housing services produced by owner-occupiers. Other services produced for consumption within the household – cooking, cleaning and child rearing – were, however, excluded from the production boundary.

- No distinction was made between legal and illegal production. Provided goods or services were being traded between willing producers and willing buyers, the activities concerned were deemed to be productive. Despite this early recommendation, it is interesting to note that no large OECD country includes yet estimates of illegal production in the GDP.

- Governments were treated as producers, but because the services they produce are not sold, their output was to be measured as the total of the costs of production – compensation of employees, intermediate consumption and consumption of fixed capital. The same approach was to be used for non-profit institutions. However, this feature was not implemented in all countries immediately. For example, France included government production in its accounts only in 1976.

- Capital formation was defined as expenditure on physical objects – buildings, machinery, roads – that would provide productive services over a number of years. Other types of expenditure that could also be expected to produce a stream of future services but which had no *physical* embodiment, advertising and research and development, for example, were treated as current consumption. Expenditure on education, or investment in human capital as it is sometimes termed, was also excluded from capital formation "because human beings are not capital assets".

In the decade that followed publication of the *1953 SNA*, about 60 countries began to publish some kind of national accounts on a regular basis. Many OECD countries were able to complete all the supporting tables of the *1953 SNA*, but other countries published only estimates of GDP obtained by adding up the value added of different industries with a summary breakdown by final expenditure. Even these simple national accounts proved useful for monitoring economic developments and for fiscal and monetary policy. Equally important, the national accounts were increasingly used as a framework for organising other economic statistics, such as indices of industrial output, price statistics, retail sales and labour force data. The definitions and classifications of the *1953 SNA* were applied to these related areas.

4. The 1968 SNA

By the early 1960s, there was a consensus among national accountants that it was time to revise the *1953 SNA* to take into account developments in input-output tables (in France and the Netherlands, for example), in flow of funds statistics (in the United Kingdom) and in balance sheets (in the United States). In addition, most OECD countries had been developing accounts at constant prices and had also started publishing much greater detail than suggested in the 1953 system.

There had also been a shift in economic policymaking. Starting from using the national accounts to understand what had happened in the recent past and to forecast what could be expected in the near term, policymakers became increasingly drawn to the idea of actively planning the future course of the economy. Detailed five-year plans were being drawn up in India and Egypt, for example, while a looser form of "indicative planning" was being implemented by France and other western European countries. The new system was designed to support this growing interest in economic planning.

The *1953 SNA* was described in 46 pages, and the accounts were shown on 2 pages. The *1968 SNA* (titled *A System of National Accounts,* United Nations, 1968) required 250 pages and the accounts alone filled 12. In addition to greater detail in describing the various transactions and their sources and the extra detail in the accounts, the *1968 SNA* made a number of innovations (see Box 1). But it did not change the accounting identities, the size of the production boundary or the distinction between capital formation and current expenditure, all of which were inherited from the earlier system.

Box 1. **What was new in the *1968 SNA*?**

All entities participating in monetary transactions were assigned to **institutional sectors**. In the 1953 SNA, only households and government had been explicitly identified. In the 1968 System, corporations were split into financial and non-financial sectors, and non-profit institutions were identified as a separate sector.

The accounts for institutional sectors were expanded to include: a production account; an income and outlay account with saving as the balancing item; a capital finance account with net lending as the balancing item; and a financial account showing the acquisition of financial assets and incurrence of liabilities.

Distinction was made between **market** and **non-market producers**. The former (termed "industries") sold goods and services at a profit, while the latter (termed "other producers"), typically government and non-profit institutions, provided services and sometimes goods for free, or at nominal prices. A similar distinction was made between "commodities" (sold at a profit) and "other goods and services".

A full chapter was devoted to "The System as a Basis for Quantity and Price Comparisons" – *i.e.* national accounts at constant prices. Although it gave some practical guidance for national accountants and price statisticians, the discussion was mainly theoretical. One important contribution was to identify the limits to constant price measurement. Final expenditures can be converted to constant prices by deflating them with the relevant price indices. And value added can be expressed in constant prices by the ingenious method (apparently invented by the Irish statistical office) of deflating gross output and intermediate consumption by their own price indices and deriving constant price value added as the difference between them. Both of these statistics can be expressed in constant prices because the underlying flows can be decomposed into price and quantity components. Other entries in the accounts – compensation of employees, property income, taxes, operating surplus, etc. – cannot be broken down in this way. They can be expressed in constant purchasing power – how much of a fixed basket of goods can this year's salary buy compared to last year – but constant purchasing power is a different concept from constant prices.

The 1968 SNA was a major step toward integrating the four approaches to national economic measurement that Stone had identified in 1953. **Input-output** tables were integrated into the production accounts; the financial accounts included a **flow of funds** table showing both parties to transactions in various financial instruments; and the links were explained (partially) between the opening and closing **balance sheets** and the transactions recorded in the accounts during the year.

5. The 1993 SNA

The *1968 SNA* represented a major step forward in macroeconomic measurement, but no system could possibly remain relevant for all time. Economies evolve and international accounting systems must adapt to reflect new realities. The decision to revise the 1968 SNA was made in the early 1980s, largely as a result of discussions at the annual meetings organised by the OECD for national accountants from member countries, and at the biennial conferences of the International Association for Research in Income and Wealth. The archives of the meetings of the OECD are available on the website of the OECD.

The *1953 SNA* had been written by a committee of five and the *1968 SNA* by a group of about fifteen. For the 1993 SNA, it was decided to involve a much wider group of experts and more than 50 statisticians and economists were involved in the revision process. A wider group of international agencies also took part. The two earlier versions had been published by the United Nations alone, but the *1993 SNA* was a joint publication of the OECD, Eurostat, the World Bank, the International Monetary Fund and the United Nations. Other international agencies were also consulted, including the International Labour Office, United Nations regional commissions and the Commonwealth of Independent States.

While the revision was already under way, the internationalist aspirations of the *1993 SNA* received a further boost from the fall of the Berlin Wall. The Soviet bloc countries had previously used their own system of national accounts – the *Material Product System* (see Box 3) – but in the early 1990s, these countries announced that they would switch to the *SNA*. China, Mongolia and Vietnam followed suit. At the present time, only two countries have not formally adopted the *1993 SNA* as the basis for their official national accounts – Cuba and North Korea. The United States produces accounts that are conceptually consistent with the 1993 SNA but does not publish the same tables and groupings (See Chapter 12).

An important feature of the *1993 SNA* is that it is consistent with other international data systems, such as the OECD Guidelines on Foreign Direct Investment, the IMF's manuals on Balance of Payments and Government Finance Statistics. Clearly, this is a considerable advantage to both the users of these data and to national statistical offices. The *1993 SNA* is also much more explicit in dealing with issues that had been known to create difficulties for many countries, such as: insurance transactions; imputed bank-service charges (financial intermediation services, or "FISIM", as they are now termed); financial *versus* operating leasing; and the consumption of fixed capital. In addition, there are separate chapters on satellite accounts (a French invention) and on social accounting matrices, or "SAMs" (a Dutch invention). All this of course had a cost in terms of page inflation, and the *1993 SNA* has over 700 pages. Box 2 identifies the main innovations.

Box 2. **What was new in the *1993 SNA*?**

Balance sheets are fully incorporated into the system. Linking the opening and closing stocks of assets with the flow transactions during the year requires not only a revaluation account (as had been introduced in the 1968 SNA) but an additional account that records changes in the volume of assets. These may arise from new discoveries of mineral reserves, natural growth of cultivated forest and catastrophic losses due to earthquakes or tempests, depletion of oil reserves, and so on. The awkwardly named "Other Changes in the Volume of Assets Account" was introduced to record these events.

The four accounts for institutional sectors of the 1968 SNA were expanded to a total of sixteen. Much of the increase came from a fragmentation of the 1968 SNA accounts. The 1968 income and outlay accounts were split into six separate accounts in order to identify new balancing items that were thought relevant for economic analysis.

In the previous systems, government was shown as consuming its entire output. In the 1993 SNA, an important distinction is made between government services that are provided to households on an individual basis – health and education for example – and those that are provided on a collective basis to the community at large – security and defence, for example. While government pays for production of both collective and individual services, households can be regarded as the true consumers of the latter. A new concept, actual individual consumption of households, was introduced. This is the value of the individual services provided by government *plus* the goods and services that households buy with their own money.

Volume estimates are given much more consideration. Recent developments in price index theory are used to show that the best measures of price inflation are obtained by using chained Fischer indices, with chained Laspeyres indices as a second best.

The asset boundary was enlarged to include expenditures on software, mineral exploration and valuables. In earlier systems, software expenditure (generally insignificant before the 1970s) was treated as a current cost. But in the 1993 SNA, all software expenditures – off-the-shelf programmes, software written in-house and custom-designed software purchased from specialised companies – are treated as capital formation. Mining companies have usually treated exploration expenditures (money spent on looking for new deposits) as a capital outlay, and this same approach was adopted in the 1993 SNA. Note that the costs of exploration, whether anything is found or not, are treated as capital expenditures. Valuables are precious objects, such as paintings, antiques, jewellery and precious metals that are bought as "stores of value". In the earlier systems, most of these would have been included in household consumption expenditure.

---

6. The 1995 ESA

In the 1960s, the fledgling European Union realised that it needed harmonised national accounts statistics for its member states. The first such system was published in 1970 as the *European System of Accounts,* and a revised version came out in 1979. This was then replaced by the current *European System of Accounts 1995,* or *1995 ESA,* which is the European version of the *1993 SNA.*

The *1995 ESA* is 99% consistent with the *1993 SNA* and gives more precise guidelines on some border-line issues that were deliberately left open in the *1993 SNA.* For example, in the *1993 SNA* the distinction between "market" and "non-market" producers depends on whether they sell their output at "economically significant prices". In the *1995 ESA* a non-market producer is one whose output is sold at prices that cover less than 50% of the cost of production. All that has happened here is that the *1995 ESA* has defined an "economically significant price" as one that covers more than 50% of the production costs. These more precise guidelines are necessary because national accounts statistics are used by the European Commission to allocate regional development funds, calculate the contribution to the European budget, and more recently to monitor the sustainability of public finance (Maastricht criteria).

The administrative use of national accounts in Europe has at the same time boosted the harmonisation and use of these statistics, but it has also made their production more rigid. The *1995 ESA* is embedded in EU legislation so that international harmonisation of national accounts is a legal requirement for EU member states, as well as for countries that have applied for future membership. The *1993 SNA* was designed to have sufficient flexibility so that it could be applied by countries with very different economic systems and at various stages of economic development. The *1993 SNA* is therefore somewhat less effective than the *1995 ESA* in ensuring international comparability.

7. And the upcoming 2008 SNA?

The *1993 SNA* is more than 13 years old and plans for a revision are already well under way; the new edition is expected to come out in 2008, although it will probably not be implemented before 2012. Its official name is supposed to be "SNA 1993 Rev 1", but we will call it for simplification "2008 SNA". More than 50 changes to the *1993 SNA* are under review. While the formal decision has not been yet taken, the major changes will likely include:

Treating Research and development (R&D) as an asset. After decades of discussion, it will probably be decided to record R&D expenditures as GFCF (Gross Fixed Capital Formation) and not intermediate consumption, despite the difficulties associated with this change. One of the difficulties is that, in most countries, business accounting standards do not recommend the same (R&D is treated as intermediate consumption), so it will be difficult to obtain satisfactory data. This change will increase the level of GDP, but it will hardly affect the level of NDP.

Treating expenditure on large military weapons as assets. The new SNA will also record large military weapons – warships, ballistic missiles and tanks, etc. – as fixed capital assets. This will also raise the level of GDP, not because of the change in classification of these amounts from final expenditure to GFCF, but because a consumption of fixed capital will be recorded and will add to the measure of government consumption.

On government assets, including an estimated return on capital. As explained in Chapter 4, the *1993 SNA* was criticised for underestimating the cost of the government's use of capital because it did not add to capital consumption an estimated return on capital in order to reflect the full cost of "capital services". The SNA 2008 will probably recommend estimating a return on capital for government fixed assets, and this change will also increase the level of GDP.

Extending the measurement of pension liabilities. The *1993 SNA* only records pension liabilities for funded plans. The new SNA should extend this to all private employer pension plans, and possibly to some government schemes for their own employees and social security plans, albeit in "supplementary" accounts. This extension could have a major impact on the measurement of the government deficit, because unfunded retirement plans for government employees involve heavy liabilities in some countries.

Smoothing the measurement of insurance output. Currently, the gross output of insurance companies is essentially measured as the difference between premiums and claims. The terrorist attack of September 11 2001 highlighted a problem with this approach that has troubled national accountants in several countries – namely, the sharp fluctuations that can occur when claims are unexpectedly large in a given year. The suggestion is to deduct *expected* rather than *actual* claims in measuring output.

Including share options as part of compensation of employees. During the stock market bubble of the late 1990s, employees in many hi-tech companies accepted low salaries in return for the chance to buy their company's shares at bargain prices. The logic of the *1993 SNA* required share options to be treated as financial transactions, and so they are excluded from the compensation of employees. However, the employees receiving share options clearly regard them as part of their "compensation package". Thus, share options will be included in compensation of employees in the new SNA.

In conclusion, the SNA is a system of statistics that is being constantly updated, more and more widely used, and evolving in parallel with new economic developments. One interesting feature is that the measurement of GDP has systematically been modified under the different SNAs into a broader concept, thus extending progressively the production frontier. It is probable that this process will continue. For example, the concept of human capital, which is not incorporated into the SNA 2008, will become more and more relevant to OECD economies in the future. Its incorporation in the national accounts would once more enlarge the production boundary. But this will not happen soon…

Box 3. **The Material Product System**

Instead of the SNA, Communist bloc countries used the Material Product System (MPS). It was devised by Soviet Union economists and statisticians in the 1940s, and methodological manuals for the system were published in the mid-1960s.

Viewed purely as a system of accounts, the MPS differed from the SNA mainly because production and sale of many services were excluded from the production boundary. Services closely linked to goods production, notably transport and trade, were included in the Net Material Product, or NMP (which was the MPS aggregate nearest to GDP). But services provided to households, such as education, healthcare, restaurants, hotels and personal services, were excluded from NMP. They were treated as transfers to households, either from government or between households.

But there were two other important differences between MPS and SNA statistics, and these were often overlooked by researchers when they tried to compare levels of economic activity and growth between countries with centrally planned economies and those with market-oriented ones:

First, the prices used in the two systems were inherently different. In market economies, prices are assumed to equate marginal productivities in the production of goods and services with the marginal utilities of those who purchase them. In the centrally planned economies, on the other hand, the prices used for MPS statistics were determined by the central planners and not by the market. "Plan prices" generally valued capital goods relatively lower, and consumer goods relatively higher than in market economies, because the planners were seeking to divert resources from consumption to investment. In addition, plan prices were often only relevant for a small part of total sales with many goods changing hands at higher prices on unofficial markets. Thus, even when NMP is adjusted for the omission of services, the two different price bases make comparisons highly misleading.

Second, the MPS focused on measures in volume terms rather than in current prices. MPS volume statistics were described as being in "comparable prices". While this sounds similar to the "constant prices" used in the SNA, there was in fact an important difference. To get their volume measures, MPS statisticians deflated the current price figures using price indices that only took account of price changes for strictly identical goods.

In most centrally planned economies, producers were required to maintain a high degree of price stability. Consequently, they resorted to the artifice of making trivial changes to their products, allowing them to claim they were new models so they could be sold at higher prices. When the price statisticians found that the old model – a suitcase with a green handle, for example – had been replaced by a more expensive model whose only difference was that it now had a blue handle, they stopped tracking price changes of the old model and now followed the price movements of the new one. In reality, of course, there had been a price increase the moment the blue handles replaced the green ones, but because the two suitcases were considered to be different goods, the price hike was simply ignored and there was no increase in the comparable price index. Therefore, comparable price indices understated inflation and in doing so they exaggerated real growth. This was a contributing factor to the Western misconceptions about the true size and growth of the Soviet bloc countries.

Accounting identity
Ch. 10

An equality between national accounts variable which stands by definition.

For exemple, supply = use is an accounting identity.

Accrual accounting
Ch. 10

Accrual accounting records flows at the time economic value is created, transformed, exchanged, transferred or extinguished; this means that flows which imply a change of ownership are entered when ownership passes, services are recorded when provided, output is entered at the time products are created and intermediate consumption is recorded when materials and supplies are being used.

Actual consumption
Ch. 5

Actual individual consumption is measured by the total value of household final consumption expenditure, non-profit institutions serving households (NPISHs) final consumption expenditure and government expenditure on individual consumption goods and services.

Actual final consumption of households is the value of the consumption goods and services acquired by households, whether by purchase in general, or by transfer from government units or NPISHs, and used by them for the satisfaction of their needs and wants; it is derived from their final consumption expenditure by adding the value of social transfers in kind receivable.

Actual final consumption of general government is measured by the value of the collective (as opposed to individual) consumption services provided to the community, or large sections of the community, by general government; it is derived from their final consumption expenditure by subtracting the value of social transfers in kind payable.

There is no actual final consumption of non-profit institutions serving households (NPISHs) because, in practice, most of their services are individual in nature and so, for simplicity, all services provided by NPISHs are treated by convention as individual (as social transfers in kind).

Aggregate
Ch. 1

Data obtained by aggregation, as distinct from unit record data.

Apparent productivity
Ch. 4

Apparent labour productivity is defined as output or value added per person employed or per hour worked.

Balance sheet
Ch. 15

A balance sheet is a statement, drawn up at a particular point in time, of the values of assets owned and of liabilities outstanding. The balancing item is called net worth. In national accounts a balance sheet is drawn up for sectors, the total economy and the rest of the world. For a sector the balance sheet shows the value of all assets – produced, non-produced and financial – and liabilities and the sector's net worth. For the total economy the balance sheet provides as balancing item what is often referred to as national wealth: the sum of non-financial assets and net financial assets with respect to the rest of the world.

Basic price
Ch. 10

The basic price is the amount receivable by the producer from the purchaser for a unit of a good or service produced as output minus any tax payable, and plus any subsidy receivable, on that unit as a consequence of its production or sale; it excludes any transport charges invoiced separately by the producer.

Basic wage
Ch. 2

Wage rates measure the basic remuneration per time unit or unit of output.

Although the Resolutions of the 12th International Conference of Labour Statisticians (ICLS, 1973) does not contain a specific definition of "wages" as such, it recommends the compilation of wage rate statistics which should include basic wages, cost-of living allowances and other guaranteed and regularly paid allowances, but exclude overtime payments, bonuses and gratuities, family allowances and other social security payments made by employers. Ex gratia payments in kind, supplementary to normal wage rates, are also excluded.

Wage rate data should relate to an appropriate time period- hour, day, week or month.

Wage rates may be viewed from the perspective of a "price" of labour services.

Capital stock
Ch. 8

Gross capital stock is the value of all fixed assets still in use, at the actual or estimated current purchasers' prices for new assets of the same type, irrespective of the age of the assets.

Net capital stock is the sum of the written-down values of all the fixed assets still in use is described as the net capital stock; it can also be described as the difference between gross capital stock and consumption of fixed capital.

Changes in inventories
Ch. 1

Changes in inventories (including work-in-progress) consist of changes in: (a) stocks of outputs that are still held by the units that produced them prior to their being further processed, sold, delivered to other units or used in other ways; and (b) stocks of products acquired from other units that are intended to be used for intermediate consumption or for resale without further processing; they are measured by the value of the entries into inventories less the value of withdrawals and the value of any recurrent losses of goods held in inventories.

Collective consumption expenditure — Ch. 9

Goods and services that are consumed simultaneously by a group of consumers or by the community as a whole: for example, defence services provided by the state.

Compensation of employees — Ch. 1

Compensation of employees is the total remuneration, in cash or in kind, payable by an enterprise to an employee in return for work done by the latter during the accounting period.

Compensation of employees has two main components:

a) Wages and salaries payable in cash or in kind;

b) The value of the social contributions payable by employers: these may be actual social contributions payable by employers to Social Security schemes or to private funded social insurance schemes to secure social benefits for their employees; or imputed social contributions by employers providing unfunded social benefits.

Constant prices — Ch. 15

Constant prices are obtained by directly factoring changes over time in the values of flows or stocks of goods and services into two components reflecting changes in the prices of the goods and services concerned and changes in their volumes (i.e. changes in "constant price terms"); the term "at constant prices" commonly refers to series which use a fixed-base Laspeyres formula.

Consumption of fixed capital — Ch. 1

Consumption of fixed capital represents the reduction in the value of the fixed assets used in production during the accounting period resulting from physical deterioration, normal obsolescence or normal accidental damage.

Demand — Ch. 5

Final demand is the short term used by economists to qualify the sum of final consumption expenditures, investment expenditures and net exports.

Disposable income — Ch. 1

Disposable income is derived from the balance of primary incomes of an institutional unit or sector by adding all current transfers, except social transfers in kind, receivable by that unit or sector and subtracting all current transfers, except social transfers in kind, payable by that unit or sector; it is the balancing item in the Secondary Distribution of Income Account.

Domestic demand — Ch. 5

Final domestic demand is the short term used by economists to qualify the part of final demand that is domestic: final consumption expenditures + investment expenditures.

Economic territory — Ch. 5

The economic territory of a country consists of the geographic territory administered by a government within which persons, goods, and capital circulate freely.

It includes: (a) the airspace, territorial waters, and continental shelf lying in international waters over which the country enjoys exclusive rights or over which it has, or claims to have, jurisdiction in respect of the right to fish or to exploit fuels or minerals below the sea bed; (b) territorial enclaves in the rest of the world; and (c) any free zones, or bonded warehouses or factories operated by offshore enterprises under customs control (these form part of the economic territory of the country in which they are physically located).

Economically significant — Ch. 9

Prices are said to be economically significant when they have a significant influence on the amounts the producers are willing to supply and on the amounts purchasers wish to buy.

External demand — Ch. 5

External demand is the short term used by economists to qualify net exports.

Final consumption expenditure — Ch. 9

Government final consumption expenditure consists of expenditure, including imputed expenditure, incurred by general government on both individual consumption goods and services and collective consumption services.

Household final consumption expenditure consists of the expenditure, including imputed expenditure, incurred by resident households on individual consumption goods and services, including those sold at prices that are not economically significant.

Final consumption expenditure of non-profit institutions serving households (NPISHs) consists of the expenditure, including imputed expenditure, incurred by resident NPISHs on individual consumption goods and services.

Final uses Ch. 5

Short terminology used to qualify the sum of final consumption expenditures, gross capital formation and net exports.

Financial corporations Ch. 10

Financial corporations consist of all resident corporations or quasi-corporations principally engaged in financial intermediation or in auxiliary financial activities which are closely related to financial intermediation.

Financial intermediation Ch. 4

Financial intermediation is a productive activity in which an institutional unit incurs liabilities on its own account for the purpose of acquiring financial assets by engaging in financial transactions on the market; the role of financial intermediaries is to channel funds from lenders to borrowers by intermediating between them.

Financial intermediation services indirectly measured (FISIM) Ch. 4

Financial intermediation services indirectly measured (FISIM) is an indirect measure of the value of financial intermediation services provided but for which financial institutions do not charge explicitly.

Financial transaction Ch. 8

Financial transactions between institutional units and between institutional units and the rest of the world cover all transactions involving change of ownership of financial assets, including the creation and liquidation of financial claims.

Flow of funds table Ch. 15

Synonym for "financial accounts".

GDP deflator Ch. 1

GDP at current prices divided by GDP in volume.

GDP in volume Ch. 1

Gross Domestic Product (GDP) in volume often refers to GDP at constant prices which is obtained by expressing values in terms of a base period.

In theory, the price and quantity components of a value are identified and the price in the base period is substituted for that in the current period. Two main methods are adopted in practice.

The first, referred to as "quantity revaluation", is based on a methodology consistent with the above theory (i.e., by multiplying the current period quantity by the base period price).

The second, commonly referred to as "price deflation", involves dividing price indexes into the observed values to obtain the volume estimate. The price indexes used are built up from the prices of the major items contributing to each value.

General government Ch. 1, 9

The general government sector consists of the totality of institutional units which, in addition to fulfilling their political responsibilities and their role of economic regulation, produce principally non-market services (possibly goods) for individual or collective consumption and redistribute income and wealth.

Goods Ch. 4

Also called "merchandises". All products that are not services.

Goods and services accounts Ch. 10

The goods and services account shows for the economy as a whole and for groups of products, the total resources in terms of output and imports, and the uses of goods and services in terms of intermediate consumption, final consumption, gross capital formation and exports.

Gross capital formation Ch. 1

Gross capital formation is measured by the total value of the gross fixed capital formation, changes in inventories and acquisitions less disposals of valuables for a unit or sector.

Gross domestic product (GDP) Ch. 1

Gross domestic product is an aggregate measure of production equal to the sum of the gross values added of all resident institutional units engaged in production (plus any taxes, and minus any subsidies, on products not included in the value of their outputs). The sum of the final uses of goods and services (all uses except intermediate consumption) measured in purchasers' prices, less the value of imports of goods and services, or the sum of primary incomes distributed by resident producer units.

Gross fixed capital formation Ch. 1

Gross fixed capital formation is measured by the total value of a producer's acquisitions, less disposals, of fixed assets during the accounting period plus certain additions to the value of non-produced assets (such as subsoil assets or major improvements in the quantity, quality or productivity of land) realised by the productive activity of institutional units.

Gross national income (GNI) Ch. 1

Gross national income (GNI) is GDP less net taxes on production and imports, less compensation of employees and property income payable to the rest of the world plus the corresponding items receivable from the rest of the world (in other words, GDP less primary incomes payable to non- resident units plus primary incomes receivable from non-resident units).

An alternative approach to measuring GNI at market prices is as the aggregate value of the balances of gross primary incomes for all sectors; (note that gross national income is identical to gross national product (GNP) as previously used in national accounts generally).

Gross national product (GNP) Ch. 1
See Gross national income (GNI).

Household Ch. 1, 6
The concept of household is based on the arrangements made by persons, individually or in groups, for providing themselves with food or other essentials for living. A household may be either (a) a one-person household, that is to say, a person who makes provision for his or her own food or other essentials for living without combining with any other person to form part of a multi-person household or (b) a multi-person household, that is to say, a group of two or more persons living together who make common provision for food or other essentials for living. The persons in the group may pool their incomes and may, to a greater or lesser extent, have a common budget; they may be related or unrelated persons or constitute a combination of persons both related and unrelated.

A household may be located in a housing unit or in a set of collective living quarters such as a boarding house, a hotel or a camp, or may comprise the administrative personnel in an institution. The household may also be homeless.

Household final consumption expenditure Ch. 1
Household final consumption expenditure consists of the expenditure, including imputed expenditure, incurred by resident households on individual consumption goods and services, including those sold at prices that are not economically significant.

Household saving ratio Ch. 1
The household saving ratio is most often defined as net saving divided by the sum of net disposable income and the adjustment D8. A gross version exists: gross saving divided by the sum of gross disposable income and the adjustment D8.

Households' actual final consumption Ch. 9
Actual final consumption of households is the value of the consumption goods and services acquired by households, whether by purchase in general, or by transfer from government units or NPISHs, and used by them for the satisfaction of their needs and wants; it is derived from their final consumption expenditure by adding the value of social transfers in kind receivable.

Imputed expenditures Ch. 5
Some transactions which it is desirable to include in the accounts do not take place in money terms and so cannot be measured directly; in such cases a conventional value is imputed to the corresponding expenditure (the conventions used vary from case to case and are described in the SNA as necessary).

Individual consumption expenditure Ch. 9
Part of general government expenditure thant can be attributed to households plus all expenditure of NPISHs.

Input-output table Ch. 10, 13
An input-output table is a means of presenting a detailed analysis of the process of production and the use of goods and services (products) and the income generated in that production.; they can be either in the form of (a) supply and use tables or (b) symmetric input-output tables.

Institutional sector Ch. 9, 10
The SNA 93 states that Institutional units are grouped together to form institutional sectors, on the basis of their principal functions, behaviour, and objectives.

Institutional unit Ch. 9, 10
An institutional unit may be defined as an economic entity that is capable, in its own right, of owning assets, incurring liabilities and engaging in economic activities and in transactions with other entities.

Intermediate consumption Ch. 1
Intermediate consumption consists of the value of the goods and services consumed as inputs by a process of production, excluding fixed assets whose consumption is recorded as consumption of fixed capital; the goods or services may be either transformed or used up by the production process.

Market producers Ch. 15
Market producers are producers that sell most or all of their output at prices that are economically significant.

Market price Ch. 10
Market prices are the actual price agreed upon by the transactors. In the absence of market transactions, valuation is made according to costs incurred (non-market services produced by government) or by reference to market prices for analogous goods or services (services of owner-occupied dwellings).

Market sector Ch. 4
Also called "business sector". The sector comprising all enterprises selling their output at economically significant prices.

Mixed income Ch. 1
Mixed income is the surplus or deficit accruing from production by unincorporated enterprises owned by households; it implicitly contains an element of remuneration for work done by the owner, or other members of the household, that cannot be separately identified from the return to the owner as entrepreneur but it excludes the operating surplus coming from owner-occupied dwellings.

Net disposable income Ch. 8
Gross disposable income minus consumption of fixed capital.

Net domestic product (NDP) Ch. 1
Net domestic product (NDP) is obtained by deducting the consumption of fixed capital from gross domestic product.

Net exports Ch. 5
Difference between exports and imports of goods and services. Also referred to as net foreign balance, or balance of imports and exports.

Net lending/net borrowing Ch. 8
Net lending is the net amount a unit or a sector has available to finance, directly or indirectly, other units or other sectors.

It is the balancing item in the capital account and is defined as: (Net saving plus capital transfers receivable minus capital transfers payable) minus (the value of acquisitions less disposals of non-financial assets, less consumption of fixed capital).

Negative net lending may also be described as "net borrowing".

Net lending/net borrowing of general government Ch. 1, 9
See "Net lending/net borrowing".

Net value added Ch. 1
Net value added is the value of output less the values of both intermediate consumption and consumption of fixed capital.

Non-financial accounts Ch. 9
The complete sequence of national accounts excluding financial accounts and balance sheet.

Non-financial corporations Ch. 7
Non-financial corporations are corporations whose principal activity is the production of market goods or non-financial services.

Non-financial transaction Ch. 8
A transaction not included in the financial accounts of the system of national accounts.

Non-market producers Ch. 4, 15
Non-market producers are producers that provide most of their output to others free or at prices which are not economically significant.

Non-market sector Ch. 4
The sector comprising all non-market producers which are producers that provide most of their output to others free or at prices which are not economically significant.

Non-observed Ch. 3
The groups of activities most likely to be non-observed are those that are underground, illegal, informal sector, or undertaken by households for their own final use. Activities may also be missed because of deficiencies in the basic statistical data collection programme.

Non-profit institutions serving households (NPISHs) Ch. 5
Non-profit institutions serving households (NPISHs) consist of NPIs which are not predominantly financed and controlled by government or by corporations and which provide goods or services to households free or at prices that are not economically significant.

Operating surplus Ch. 1
The operating surplus measures the surplus or deficit accruing from production before taking account of any interest, rent or similar charges payable on financial or tangible non-produced assets borrowed or rented by the enterprise, or any interest, rent or similar receipts receivable on financial or tangible non-produced assets owned by the enterprise.

Note: for unincorporated enterprises owned by households, this component is called "mixed income".

Net operating surplus Ch. 6
Gross operating surplus minus consumption of fixed capital.

Output Ch. 4
Output consists of those goods or services that are produced within an establishment that become

available for use outside that establishment, plus any goods and services produced for own final use.

Output gap Ch. 4

An output gap refers to the difference between actual and potential gross domestic product (GDP) as a per cent of potential GDP.

Output of non-market services Ch. 9

Other non-market output consists of goods and individual or collective services produced by non-profit institutions serving households (NPISHs) or government that are supplied free, or at prices that are not economically significant, to other institutional units or the community as a whole.

Such output is one of three broad categories of output in the System of National Accounts (SNA), with the others being market output and output produced for own final use.

Potential GDP Ch. 4

Potential gross domestic product (GDP) is defined in the OECD's Economic Outlook publication as the level of output that an economy can produce at a constant inflation rate. Although an economy can temporarily produce more than its potential level of output, that comes at the cost of rising inflation. Potential output depends on the capital stock, the potential labour force (which depends on demographic factors and on participation rates), the non-accelerating inflation rate of unemployment (NAIRU), and the level of labour efficiency.

Production function Ch. 4

Production function is the maximum set of output(s) that can be produced with a given set of inputs. Use of a production function implies technical efficiency. Synonym for production frontier, the technically efficiency part of a feasible production set, the set of all input-output combinations that are feasible (but not necessarily efficient).

Purchase price Ch. 10

The purchaser's price is the amount paid by the purchaser, excluding any deductible VAT or similar deductible tax, in order to take delivery of a unit of a good or service at the time and place required by the purchaser; the purchaser's price of a good includes any transport charges paid separately by the purchaser to take delivery at the required time and place.

Purchasing power of household gross disposable income Ch. 2

Household gross disposable income deflated by an appropriate price index, in general the implicit deflator of household final expenditure.

Purchasing power parities Ch. 3

Purchasing power parities (PPPs) are the rates of currency conversion that equalise the purchasing power of different currencies by eliminating the differences in price levels between countries. In their simplest form, PPPs are simply price relatives which show the ratio of the prices in national currencies of the same good or service in different countries.

Residence Ch. 5

A unit is said to be resident in a country when its "center of economic" interest is situated in that country's economic territory.

Rest of the world Ch. 1

The rest of the world refers to all non-resident institutional units that enter into transactions with resident units, or have other economic links with resident units. Included are certain institutional units that may be physically located within the geographic boundary of a country, for example, foreign enclaves such as embassies, consulates or military bases, and also international organisations.

Saving Ch. 1, 6

Saving is disposable income less final consumption expenditure (or adjusted disposable income less actual final consumption), in both cases after taking account of an adjustment for pension funds; saving is an important aggregate which can be calculated for each institutional sector or for the whole economy.

Seasonal adjustment Ch. 11

Seasonal adjustment is a statistical technique to remove the effects of seasonal calendar influences operating on a series. Seasonal effects usually reflect the influence of the seasons themselves either directly or through production series related to them, or social conventions.

Other types of calendar variation occur as a result of influences such as number of days in the calendar period, the accounting or recording practices adopted or the incidence of moving holidays (such as Easter).

Services Ch. 4

Services are outputs produced to order and which cannot be traded separately from their production. Services are not separate entities over which ownership rights can be established. They cannot be traded separately from their production. Services are heterogeneous outputs produced to order and typically consist of changes in the conditions of the consuming units realized by the activities of producers at the demand of the consumers. By the time their production is completed they must have been provided to the consumers.

Social benefits in kind
Ch. 9

Social benefits in kind consist of (a) social security benefits, reimbursements, (b) other social security benefits in kind, (c) social assistance benefits in kind; in other words they are equal to social transfers in kind excluding transfers of individual non-market goods and services.

Social benefits other than social transfers in kind
Ch. 9

Social benefits other than social transfers in kind consist of all social benefits except social transfers in kind.

In other words, they consist of:

a) all social benefits in cash – both social insurance and social assistance benefits – provided by government units, including social security funds, and NPISHs; and

b) all social insurance benefits provided under private funded and unfunded social insurance schemes, whether in cash or in kind.

Supply and use balance
Ch. 2

Supply and use tables are in the form of matrices that record how supplies of different kinds of goods and services originate from domestic industries and imports and how those supplies are allocated between various intermediate or final uses, including exports.

Taxes net of subsidies
Ch. 1

Taxes minus subsidies.

Taxes on income and wealth
Ch. 9

Most current taxes on income, wealth, etc consist of taxes on the incomes of households or profits of corporations and taxes on wealth that are payable regularly every tax period (as distinct from capital taxes levied infrequently).

Taxes on production and imports
Ch. 9

Taxes on production and imports consist of taxes payable on goods and services when they are produced, delivered, sold, transferred or otherwise disposed of by their producers plus taxes and duties on imports that become payable when goods enter the economic territory by crossing the frontier or when

services are delivered to resident units by non-resident units; they also include other taxes on production, which consist mainly of taxes on the ownership or use of land, buildings or other assets used in production or on the labour employed, or compensation of employees paid.

Terms of trade indices
Ch. 5

Terms of trade is the ratio of export and import prices.

Underground
Ch. 3

Underground production consists of activities that are productive in an economic sense and quite legal (provided certain standards or regulations are complied with), but which are deliberately concealed from public authorities for the following reasons:

a) to avoid the payment of income, value added or other taxes;

b) to avoid payment of social security contributions;

c) to avoid meeting certain legal standards such as minimum wages, maximum hours, safety or health standards, etc;

d) to avoid complying with certain administrative procedures, such as completing statistical questionnaires or other administrative forms.

Value added
Ch. 1

Gross value added is the value of output less the value of intermediate consumption; it is a measure of the contribution to GDP made by an individual producer, industry or sector; gross value added is the source from which the primary incomes of the SNA are generated and is therefore carried forward into the primary distribution of income account.

Volume index
Ch. 2

A volume index is most commonly presented as a weighted average of the proportionate changes in the quantities of a specified set of goods or services between two periods of time; volume indices may also compare the relative levels of activity in different countries (e.g. those calculated using PPPs).

Working-day adjustment
Ch. 11

Working day or trading adjustments refer to the correction for differences in the number of working or trading days in a given month or quarter which differ from year to year which will impact upon the level of activity in that month or quarter for flow series or the sort / type of day for stock series.

In most countries working day adjustment and trading day adjustment are used as synonyms.

OECD PUBLICATIONS, 2, rue André-Pascal, 75775 PARIS CEDEX 16
PRINTED IN FRANCE
(30 2006 06 1P) ISBN 92-64-02566-9 – No. 55111 2006